Brief Contents

The Academic Writer

A BRIEF GUIDE

THIRD EDITION

LISA EDE

Oregon State University

Chapter 7, "Doing Research: Joining the Scholarly Conversation," with
ANNE-MARIE DEITERING
Oregon State University

BEDFORD/ST. MARTIN'S

Boston · New York

For Bedford/St. Martin's

Senior Developmental Editor: Jane Carter
Senior Production Editor: Harold Chester
Senior Production Supervisor: Steven Cestaro
Executive Marketing Manager: Molly Parke
Editorial Assistant: Leah Rang
Copy Editor: Mary Lou Wilshaw-Watts
Indexer: Melanie Belkin
Photo Researcher: Susan Doheny
Art Director: Lucy Krikorian
Text Design: Anne Carter
Cover Design: Donna Lee Dennison
Composition: Achorn International, Inc.
Printing and Binding: RRD-Harrisonburg

President, Bedford/St. Martin's: Denise B. Wydra
Editorial Director, English and Music: Karen S. Henry
Director of Development: Erica T. Appel
Director of Marketing: Karen R. Soeltz
Production Director: Susan W. Brown
Director of Rights and Permissions: Hilary Newman

Manufactured in the United States of America.

8 7 6 5 4 3
f e d c b a

For information, write: Bedford/St. Martin's, 75 Arlington Street, Boston, MA 02116
   (617-399-4000)

ISBN: 978-1-4576-3263-1

Acknowledgments

To my students
and
(of course)
to Gregory

Preface for Instructors

What does it mean to be an "academic writer" in today's world? What is the role of traditional print texts in a world that increasingly favors visual and multimedia presentations? How can students strengthen their conventional academic writing skills while also developing their ability to employ multimedia and other forms of communication? How can students think critically and effectively evaluate the abundance of sources to which they now have access? How can students make informed decisions about how and where to access texts, whether in print or on a variety of devices, including smartphones, at a time when computing is increasingly mobile? In a world of YouTube, Facebook, Twitter, and other social media, what role does and should traditional print communication play? Does writing really *matter* anymore?

Most of us are asking these same questions, as the ways in which all of us read, write, access, and create texts continue to evolve rapidly and in sometimes bewildering directions. In this new edition of *The Academic Writer*, I offer my (always provisional) answers to these questions and focus on the kinds of writing, reading, and research that students in college do *now*, using contemporary digital and online as well as traditional print technologies. At the same time, I have kept true to the goals that guided me in creating the first edition of the text:

- ***The Academic Writer* is a practical guide to the essentials of academic writing and research.** It does not try to be everything to everyone, and it does not try to convey everything students will need to know to succeed as writers in college and in life: Rather, in as clear and straightforward a fashion as I could manage, it shares key concepts and practical strategies for writing and research that have helped students I have worked with over the years become effective writers.

- **The text is flexible and open to multiple pedagogical approaches.** Depending on teachers' goals for the course and their preferred methods for teaching, the book can be used either on its own or with a collection of readings or a handbook. It reflects current research on the teaching of writing without insisting on a single theory or method, making it well suited for writing programs that use a common text but allow multiple curricular and/or thematic approaches.

- **The text respects students and speaks to them in a language they understand.** In recognition of both the financial and time pressures students face, I have tried to make *The Academic Writer* as brief, and hence as inexpensive, as possible. Every sentence has been framed with students in mind: I've included (and explained) key vocabulary students will need for composition and other courses, but I've avoided unnecessary jargon. Wherever possible, I've used examples from the media-rich lives students lead today and the real-world contexts that matter to them.

Thinking Rhetorically: A Foundational Concept for the Book

The longer and harder I thought about the new challenges and opportunities that contemporary writers face, the more I found myself wondering about the continued relevance of the **rhetorical tradition**. Could this ancient tradition have anything left to say to twenty-first-century students?

I concluded that it still has a *lot* to say. Some of the most important concepts in Western rhetoric were formulated in Greece during the fifth century B.C.E., a time when the Greeks were in the midst of a transition from an oral to an alphabetic/manuscript culture. This was also a time when principles of democracy were being developed. In Athens — an early limited democracy — citizens met in the Assembly to make civic and political decisions; they also served as jurors at trials. Those arguing for or against an issue or a person made public speeches in the Assembly. Because each case varied, rhetoricians needed to develop flexible, situation-oriented strategies designed to achieve specific purposes.

Modern rhetorical practices derive from these ancient necessities. A rhetorical approach to communication encourages writers to think in terms of *purpose* and *effect*. Rather than providing "rules" about how texts should be organized and developed, rhetoric encourages writers to draw on their commonsense understanding of communication — an understanding they have developed as speakers, listeners, writers, and readers — to make local, situated decisions about how they can best communicate their ideas. As the new Chapter 2, "Rethinking Reading: Reading on Page and Screen," indicates, a rhetorical approach can also help students make appropriate decisions about how best to access texts in any given situation.

In keeping with these principles, the rhetorical approach in *The Academic Writer* encourages writers to think — and act — like problem solvers. In its discussion of rhetoric and of the rhetorical situation, *The Academic Writer* shows students how best to respond to a particular writing challenge —

whether they are writing an essay exam, designing a Prezi presentation for work, writing an email to their teacher or supervisor, or conducting research. "Thinking Rhetorically" icons that appear throughout the book highlight the rhetorical advice, tips, and strategies that will help them do so efficiently and effectively.

Organization

PART I, "WRITING MATTERS: WRITING AND RHETORIC IN THE TWENTY-FIRST CENTURY," provides the foundation for the book. In addition to introducing the principles of rhetoric — with particular emphasis on the **rhetorical situation** — Part I focuses on another central concept: **writing as design**.

Increasingly, scholars of rhetoric and writing argue that the most productive way to envision the act of composing texts is to think of it as a kind of design process: Among other things, both activities are open-ended, creative, persuasive, and problem solving in nature. In fact, given the extent to which visual and multimedia elements are now routinely incorporated into composition classrooms and other writing spaces, the distinctions between what was traditionally conceived of as "design" and what was traditionally conceived of as "writing" are disappearing. *The Academic Writer* draws on this research, and it does so in a clear, user-friendly manner. This discussion creates bridges between students' self-sponsored writing on such social networks as Facebook and Pinterest (where they literally design self-representations) and the writing they undertake as college students. It also creates bridges between the diverse ways that students now consume texts — in print or on their smartphone, iPad, or computer — and the reading and writing they do as students.

PART II, "WRITING IN COLLEGE," focuses, as its title suggests, on the demands that contemporary students face. **Analysis**, **synthesis**, **argument**, and **research** are central to academic writing, and this section provides coverage of each of these topics, as well as a chapter on **writing in the disciplines**.

PART III, "PRACTICAL STRATEGIES FOR READING AND WRITING," provides concise, reference-friendly advice for students on **reading**, **analyzing visual texts**, **invention**, **planning**, **drafting**, **document design**, and **revision**.

Key Features

- **Every feature of the text, in every chapter, reinforces the book's primary aim: to help students learn to think rhetorically.** The text as a whole encourages transfer by emphasizing decision making over rules — in other words, as the old trope goes, it teaches students to fish, rather than presenting them with a fish. **Guidelines** and **Questions boxes** summarize key concepts, and **"Thinking Rhetorically" icons** flag passages where they are fully explained. **"For Exploration," "For Collaboration,"** and **"For Thought, Discussion, and Writing"** activities encourage students to apply and extend what they have learned.

■ **A wide range of model student essays** includes a multipart case study and eleven other samples of student writing, which serve both to instruct students and to inspire them.

■ **Thoughtful discussions of visuals and of writing as design** in Chapters 1, 10, and 13 suggest strategies for reading, writing, and designing multimodal texts.

■ **Strong coverage of reading, research, and writing in the disciplines** in Chapters 2, 5, 7, 8, and 9 emphasizes the importance of consuming and creating texts rhetorically and enables students to succeed as academic readers and writers.

■ **Guidelines and Questions boxes** present key processes in flowchart format, reinforcing the importance of decision making and active engagement in the processes of writing, thinking, and reading and helping students easily find what they need.

New to This Edition

A NEW CHAPTER 2 ON "RETHINKING READING: READING ON PAGE AND SCREEN," PLUS NEW SECTIONS ON READING IN EACH PART OF THE TEXT, addresses the challenges that today's students face as they read in a variety of media and on a variety of devices.

INCREASED COVERAGE OF SYNTHESIS IN CHAPTERS 5, 6, AND 7, including a new student essay demonstrating synthesis in action in Chapter 5.

EXPANDED DISCUSSION OF THE ESSENTIAL MOVES OF ACADEMIC WRITING IN CHAPTER 6, including highlighted passages from a student's paper, demonstrates these moves in action.

THOROUGHLY REVISED AND UPDATED ADVICE ON CONDUCTING ACADEMIC RESEARCH, written by Anne-Marie Deitering, Franklin A. McEdward Professor for Undergraduate Learning Initiatives at Oregon State University. This cutting-edge chapter helps students meet the challenges and take advantage of the opportunities of conducting research today.

NEW EXAMPLES OF PROFESSIONAL AND STUDENT WRITING, including the introductions to three professional essays on the same general topic by psychologist Jean Twenge, author of *Generation Me: Why Today's Young Americans Are More Confident, Assertive, Entitled — and More Miserable Than Ever Before,* allow students to see how one author successfully responds to three different rhetorical situations.

A NEW "STRATEGIES" CHAPTER ON ANALYZING VISUAL TEXTS, which had appeared as part of Chapter 4 in the second edition, has been moved to its own chapter in Part III to make it easier for instructors and students to find this material.

The Instructor's Edition of *The Academic Writer*

We have designed *The Academic Writer* to be as accessible as possible to all kinds of people teaching composition, including new graduate teaching assistants, busy adjuncts, experienced instructors, and writing-program administrators. To that end, we provide detailed *Instructor's Notes*, written by Lisa Ede and revised and expanded by Sara Jameson of Oregon State University. This material, bound together with the student text in a special Instructor's Edition (ISBN 978-1-4576-6589-9), includes correlations to the Council of Writing Program Administrators' Outcomes Statement, multiple course plans, practical tips for meeting common classroom challenges and for teaching key concepts, detailed advice for working with each chapter in the text, and nine sample student papers. These new *Instructor's Notes* are also available for download by authorized instructors at **bedfordstmartins.com /academicwriter/catalog**.

Acknowledgments

Before I wrote *The Academic Writer*, acknowledgments sometimes struck me as formulaic or conventional. Now I recognize that they are neither; rather, acknowledgments are simply inadequate to the task at hand. Coming at the end of a preface — and hence twice marginalized — acknowledgments can never adequately convey the complex web of interrelationships and collaborations that make a book like this possible. I hope that the people whose support and assistance I acknowledge here not only note my debt of gratitude but also recognize the sustaining role that they have played, and continue to play, in my life and in my work.

I would like to begin by thanking my colleagues in the School of Writing, Literature, and Film at Oregon State University who supported me while

I wrote and revised this text. I am indebted to my colleagues Chris Anderson, Vicki Tolar Burton, Anita Helle, Sara Jameson, and Ehren Pflugfelder for their friendship and their commitment to writing. I am especially grateful for Sara Jameson's and my multiple collaborations, which include the instructor's manual for *The Academic Writer* and our work together for OSU's writing program. I also wish to acknowledge the support and friendship of Ann Leen, Felicia Phillips, and Aurora Terhune — office staff extraordinaire.

I have dedicated this book to my students, and I hope that it in some way reflects what *they* have taught me over the years. I also owe a great debt of gratitude to another friend and teacher, Anne-Marie Deitering, who is at the cutting edge of all things involving digital literacies, writing, research, and undergraduate learning. I am deeply grateful for her work on the chapter on research for *The Academic Writer*.

I also wish to acknowledge the students whose writing appears in this text. Your writing inspires me, as it does the teachers and students who use this textbook.

For this edition, I particularly thank the five members of the editorial advisory board: Beth Buyserie, Washington State University; Deborah Brothers, Lincoln Land Community College; Janet Zepernick, Pittsburg State University; Brittany Stephenson, Salt Lake Community College; and Patricia Ericsson, Washington State University. This indispensable collection of scholars provided much useful feedback and thoughtful criticism on the revisions I made to this text, especially on the new chapter on reading in the digital age.

Others read this new chapter and provided helpful feedback. I would like to thank Matt Dodson and Chad Iwertz, students in our master's program, who read and responded to early drafts. Thanks as well to Christie Bogle at Salt Lake Community College. And special thanks to Nick Carbone, guru of all things involving new technologies and digital literacies for Bedford/St. Martin's, who generously read and responded to multiple drafts of this chapter, even though doing so is in no way part of his job description. Those on WCenter, the listserv for writing center faculty and staff, are well aware of Nick's intellectual and professional generosity. His involvement with my chapter is yet another example of his commitment to writing, teaching, and learning.

I would also like to thank the many dedicated teachers of composition I have worked and talked with over the years. By their example, comments, suggestions, and questions, they have taught me a great deal about the teaching of writing. A number of writing instructors took time from their teaching to look carefully at *The Academic Writer* as well as drafts of this edition. Their observations and suggestions enriched and improved this book. These reviewers include the following instructors: Amy Anderson, Sacramento State University; Andrea Ardans, Oregon State University; Alex Blazer, Georgia College and State University; Deborah Brothers, Lincoln Land Community College; Naomi Carrington, California State University–Northridge;

Peter Caster, University of South Carolina Upstate; Sara Coffman, University of Tennessee at Chattanooga; Emily Cope, University of Tennessee–Knoxville; Brock Dethier, Utah State University; Tracy Duckart, Humboldt State University; Lori Feyh, Missouri State University; Jeanne Guerin, Sierra College; Jordana Hall, Texas A&M University–Commerce; Hayley Haugen, Ohio University Southern; Jane Hoogestraat, Missouri State University; Lauren Ingraham, University of Tennessee at Chattanooga; Karen Jackson, North Carolina Central University; Sara Jameson, Oregon State University; Elizabeth Kubek, Benedictine University; Pam Fox Kuhlken, San Diego State University; Celena Kusch, University of South Carolina Upstate; Debra Lohe, Washington University in St. Louis; Shauna MacDonald, Missouri State University; Lisa Maruca, Wayne State University; Lee-Nickoson Massey, Bowling Green State University; Matthew Moberly, New Mexico State University; Janine Morris, University of Cincinnati; Barbara Pogue, Essex County College; Jennifer Richardson, SUNY Potsdam; Lori Rogers, Missouri State University; Cathy Rusco, Muskegon Community College; Jeff Tate, Northern Oklahoma College; Shevaun Watson, University of Wisconsin–Eau Claire; Patricia Webb, Arizona State University; and Brandi Westmoreland, Texas A&M University–Commerce.

Colleagues and students play an important role in nurturing any project, but so do those who form the intangible community of scholars that is one's most intimate disciplinary home. Here, it is harder to determine who to acknowledge; my debt to the composition theorists who have led the way or "grown up" with me is so great that I hesitate to list the names of specific individuals for fear of omitting someone deserving of credit. I must, however, acknowledge my friend and frequent coauthor Andrea Lunsford, who writes with me even when I write alone. Andrea generously allowed me to reprint material from *The St. Martin's Handbook*, Seventh Edition, in the appendix of this text, and for that I thank her as well.

I wish to thank the dedicated staff of Bedford/St. Martin's. Any textbook is an intensely collaborative effort, and I count myself particularly fortunate in having had Jane Carter as the senior editor on this project. From start to finish, I have valued Jane's expertise and insight, as well as her ability to keep the big picture always in view, while also carefully attending to local details, and to ask tough but essential questions. I am sure that *The Academic Writer* is a better book as a result. In addition, I want to thank senior project editor Harold Chester, whose patient attention to detail proved especially valuable; editorial assistant Leah Rang, who kept all of us organized and on track; and executive marketing manager Molly Parke, whose frequent reminders about the needs of instructors and students were always appreciated.

Finally, I want to (but cannot adequately) acknowledge the support of my husband, Gregory Pfarr, whose passionate commitment to his own creative endeavors, and our life together, sustains me.

Lisa Ede

You Get More Choices for *The Academic Writer*

Bedford/St. Martin's offers resources and format choices that help you and your students get even more out of the book and your course. To learn more about or order any of the following products, contact your Bedford/ St. Martin's sales representative, email sales support (sales_support@ bfwpub.com), or visit the Web site at **bedfordstmartins.com/academic writer/catalog**.

Let Students Choose Their Format

Bedford/St. Martin's offers a range of affordable formats, including the portable, downloadable *Bedford e-Book to Go for The Academic Writer* at about half the price of the print book. To order access cards for the *Bedford e-Book to Go* format, use ISBN 978-1-4576-6591-2. For details, visit **bedfordstmartins .com/academicwriter/catalog/formats** and click on the formats and packages tab.

Choose the Flexible *Bedford e-Portfolio*

Students can collect, select, and reflect on their coursework and personalize and share their e-Portfolio for any audience — instructors, peers, potential employers, or family and friends. Instructors can provide as much or as little structure as they see fit. Rubrics and learning outcomes can be aligned to student work, so instructors and programs can gather reliable and useful assessment data. Every *Bedford e-Portfolio* comes preloaded with *Portfolio Keeping* and *Portfolio Teaching*, by Nedra Reynolds and Elizabeth Davis. *Bedford e-Portfolio* can be purchased separately or packaged with the print book at a significant discount. An activation code is required. To order *e-Portfolio* with the print book, use ISBN 978-1-4576-7573-7. For details, visit **bedfordstmartins.com/eportfolio**.

Watch Peer Review Work

Eli Review lets instructors scaffold their assignments in a clearer, more effective way for students — making peer review more visible and teachable. Because teachers get real-time analytics about how well students have met criteria in a writing task *and* about how helpful peer comments have been, they can intervene in real time to teach how to give good feedback and how to shape writing to meet criteria. When students can instantly see which comments are endorsed by their teacher and how their feedback has been rated by their peers, they're motivated to give the best reviews, get the best ratings, think like writers, and revise with a plan. *Eli Review* can be purchased separately or packaged with the print book at a significant discount. An activation code is required. To order *Eli Review* with the print book, use ISBN 978-1-4576-7890-5. For details, visit **bedfordstmartins.com/eli**.

Select Value Packages

Add value to your text by packaging one of the following resources with *The Academic Writer*. To learn more about package options for any of the following products, contact your Bedford/St. Martin's sales representative or visit **bedfordstmartins.com/academicwriter/catalog**.

- **■ *LearningCurve for Readers and Writers*,** Bedford/St. Martin's adaptive quizzing program, quickly identifies what students already know and helps them practice what they don't yet understand. Gamelike quizzing motivates students to engage with their course, and reporting tools help teachers discern their students' needs. *LearningCurve for Readers and Writers* can be packaged with *The Academic Writer* at a significant discount. An activation code is required. To order *LearningCurve* packaged with the print book, use ISBN 978-1-4576-7892-9. For details, visit **bedfordstmartins.com/englishlearningcurve**.

- **■ VideoCentral** is a growing collection of videos for the writing class that captures real-world, academic, and student writers talking about how and why they write. Writer and teacher Peter Berkow interviewed hundreds of people — from Michael Moore to Cynthia Selfe — to produce over 140 brief videos about topics such as revising and getting feedback. VideoCentral can be packaged with *The Academic Writer* at a significant discount. An activation code is required. To order VideoCentral packaged with the print book, use ISBN 978-1-4576-7593-5.

- **■ i series.** This popular series presents multimedia tutorials in a flexible format — because there are things you can't do in a book.

  - ■ *ix visualizing composition 2.0* helps students put into practice key rhetorical and visual concepts. To order *ix visualizing composition* packaged with the print book, use ISBN 978-1-4576-7594-2.

  - ■ *i-claim: visualizing argument* offers a new way to see argument — with six multimedia tutorials, an illustrated glossary, and a wide array of multimedia arguments. To order *i-claim: visualizing argument* packaged with the print book, use ISBN 978-1-4576-7893-6.

- **■ *Portfolio Keeping*, Third Edition,** by Nedra Reynolds and Elizabeth Davis, provides all the information students need to use the portfolio method successfully in a writing course. *Portfolio Teaching*, a companion guide for instructors, provides the practical information instructors and writing-program administrators need to use the portfolio method successfully in a writing course. To order *Portfolio Keeping* packaged with the print book, use ISBN 978-1-4576-7573-7.

Try *Re:Writing 2* for Fun

bedfordstmartins.com/rewriting
What's the fun of teaching writing if you can't try something new? The best collection of free writing resources on the Web, *Re:Writing 2* gives you and your students even more ways to think, watch, practice, and learn about writing concepts. Listen to Nancy Sommers on using a teacher's comments to revise. Try a logic puzzle. Consult our resources for writing centers. All free for the fun of trying it. Visit **bedfordstmartins.com/rewriting**.

Instructor Resources

bedfordstmartins.com/academicwriter/catalog
You have a lot to do in your course. Bedford/St. Martin's wants to make it easy for you to find the support you need — and to get it quickly. In addition to the instructor's edition of the text (and the *Instructor's Notes* available for download from the URL above), instructors may also be interested in the following:

- **TeachingCentral** offers the entire list of Bedford/St. Martin's print and online professional resources in one place. You'll find landmark reference works, sourcebooks on pedagogical issues, award-winning collections, and practical advice for the classroom — all free for instructors.

- **Bits** collects creative ideas for teaching a range of composition topics in an easily searchable blog format. A community of teachers — leading scholars, authors, and editors — discuss revision, research, grammar and style, technology, peer review, and much more. Take, use, adapt, and pass the ideas around. Then, come back to the site to comment or share your own suggestion.

- **Bedford Coursepacks** for the most common course management systems — Blackboard, Angel, Desire2Learn, WebCT, Moodle, or Sakai — allow you to easily download digital materials from Bedford/St. Martin's for your course. To see what's available, visit **bedfordstmartins.com /coursepacks**.

Contents

PART III

Practical Strategies for Reading and Writing

Rethinking Writing: A Rhetorical Process for Composing Texts

What does it mean to be a writer in the twenty-first century? In a media-saturated world where visual images surround us, does writing still matter, and if so, how much? How has the increasing emphasis on the visual — and the availability of digital and online media — influenced how ordinary people communicate? One need only search Google to notice the power that images hold for many people. While revising this chapter, for instance, I typed *black labs* into Google's search box and promptly got over 39 million hits. Conducting the same search in Google Images, I got 116 million results. Clearly, black lab owners are using the Web to communicate how much they love their dogs.

As a medium, photographs are not new, and neither is sharing them. But now just about anyone with a computer and Internet access can establish a visually rich presence on the Web. On p. 2, for instance, is a screenshot from a site hosted by an organization that rescues Labrador retrievers. The text encourages viewers to adopt a dog, but it's the photographs that are designed to win viewers' hearts. On social-networking sites such as Facebook and Twitter, on video-sharing sites like YouTube, and on many blogs, images, video clips, and audio clips can be as important as the written text.

Written language has hardly lost its power, however. If anything, the power of the written word has probably grown with writers' increased ability to reach readers. In a developed country like the United States, individuals with access to computers and online technologies are writing more than ever before. On the same day that I searched Google for black labs, I also searched Amazon for the first book in Suzanne Collins's *Hunger Games* trilogy, and I found 9,169 customer reviews of this novel. Even outside of school, many students read and write virtually all the time, via texting, tweeting, blogging, posting on Facebook, and so on. Technology, of course, has engendered many changes in the kinds of texts produced, and the design, or look, of these texts has become increasingly important, with more and more written texts integrating video, photographs, music, and the spoken word.

Screenshot Using Photographs to Enhance Appeal

If you're an eighteen- to twenty-two-year-old student, you've grown up with the Web. You probably write online all the time, texting friends and posting Facebook updates for example. You may think that the writing you do for fun is irrelevant to the writing you do for your classes. It's not. *All* your experiences as a writer, reader, speaker, and listener will help you learn how to meet the demands of academic writing. But to communicate effectively, you will need to develop your rhetorical sensitivity—your ability to adjust your writing (and reading, speaking, and listening) to your purpose, your audience, and the genre and medium in which you're composing and presenting. As you well know, a text to a friend is very different from an essay for a history class. Learning how to recognize your rhetorical situation and to adjust your writing (and reading, speaking, and listening) appropriately will play a powerful role in helping you transfer what you already know about writing to an academic setting. This chapter (and this book) will help you gain that understanding.

Understanding the Impact of Communication Technologies on Writing

One helpful way to understand the impact of technology [o]... sider the history of the printed text. For centuries in W... only means of producing texts was to copy them by han... the Middle Ages. The limited number of manuscripts ... few people owned manuscripts and fewer still could rea[d]... hannes Gutenberg invented the printing press, which ... tiple copies of texts and therefore dramatically increase... the written word. The rise of printing tended, howeve... the role of visual elements because the technologies for... images were largely incompatible. In the 1800s, it again... print high-quality illustrated texts. Since that time, readers have come to expect increasingly sophisticated combinations of words and images.

Handwritten note:
- *Johannes Gutenberg invented the printing press.*
- *History of text produced by individuals writers differs from that of printed text.*
-

The history of texts produced by individual writers differs from that of printed texts. The invention of the typewriter in 1868 enabled writers to produce texts much more efficiently, and by using carbon paper, they could even make multiple copies. But typewriters were designed to produce only words. Writers could manipulate spacing and margins, and they could underline words and phrases, but that was about it.

The development of the personal computer, and of sophisticated software for writing, designing, and imaging, changed all of that. Today anyone with a computer and access to the Internet can compose texts that have most, if not all, of the features of professionally produced documents, including integrated visual and auditory elements. An art history student who's convinced that graffiti represents an important genre of contemporary art could use a computer to write a traditional essay to make this argument, but she could also create a video, develop a PowerPoint or Prezi presentation, or record a podcast to make her point. If this student has an ongoing interest in graffiti art, she might even host a blog on this subject.

|||||||||||||||||||||||||||||||||||||||||||||||||||||||||||||||||||||||||||||||||

FOR EXPLORATION
Take some time to think about—and list—all the kinds of writing that you do, from traditional print and handwritten texts such as essays, class notes, and "to do" lists to texts, tweets, Facebook posts, and blog comments.

Now turn your attention to the media you use to write.

■ In writing essays for your classes, do you first brainstorm and write rough drafts by hand and then revise at your computer; do you write entirely in a digital medium (on your computer, laptop, tablet, or smartphone); or do you switch back and forth, depending on the project and situation?

■ How many programs do you typically have open, and how often do you move back and forth from, say, email to Google or Facebook as you compose?

■ Does your smartphone play a role in your writing?

■ Do you ever incorporate images or graphics (yours or other people's) into your informal or formal writing? Are design elements and visual images more important to some kinds of writing that you do than to other kinds?

Take a few more minutes to reflect about what—and how—you write. What insights have you gained from this reflection?

|||||||||||||||||||||||||||||||||||||||||||||||||||||||||||||||||||||||||||||||||||

The ability to compose in diverse media and to integrate visual and textual elements represents an exciting opportunity for writers—but opportunity can also bring difficulties and dilemmas. Consider the art history student writing an essay on graffiti as art. If she followed the conventions of traditional academic writing, she would double-space her essay and choose a readable font that doesn't call attention to itself (like 12-point Times New Roman). If she's using headings, she might make them bold; she might also include some photographs. But in general her essay would look and read much like one written twenty, or even fifty, years ago.

Suppose, however, that her instructor required the class to prepare a presentation using software like PowerPoint or Prezi. The student would still need to communicate her ideas in a clear and understandable way, but she might manipulate fonts and spacing to give her presentation an urban and edgy feel. While she would hardly want to use an unusual font like the graffiti-style B𝘙𝘖𝘖𝘒𝘓𝘠𝘕 𝘒𝘐𝘋 throughout, she might employ it at strategic points for emphasis and to evoke the graffiti she's writing about (see p. 5). She might show visual examples of graffiti and choose and arrange her images in prominent or unusual ways to create the kind of "in your face" feel that characterizes much graffiti.

How can this student decide on the best way to convey her ideas and meet her professor's expectations? In this case, she can probably discuss the assignment with her teacher. But eventually, when she has a job in which she will be responsible for creating texts—from reports to Web sites and memos—she will need to learn how to respond effectively to a variety of writing situations and how to make effective *choices* as a writer in the context of the demands and opportunities that twenty-first-century writers face.

Settings for

→ Subways eliminated in late 1980s as most popular venue

→ Moved above ground to walls and buildings

→ Freight trains took art across continent

Fig. 3. New York subway graffiti. Edward Hausner. *The New York Times Agency Photos.* The New York Times, 18 Jan. 1973. Web. 15 Feb. 2010.

Tools for GRAFFITI

→ Paint cans using custom spray nozzles

→ Keith Haring's work with chalk

→ Markers and stickers

→ Cutouts and posters applied with glue

Fig. 5. Artist "Swoon" pastes a cutout on a wall in Brooklyn. Michael Kamber. *The New York Times Agency Photos.* The New York Times, 9 July 2004. Web. 15 Feb. 2010.

PowerPoint Slides from a Student Presentation

Writing and Rhetoric

One of the most powerful resources that students, and other writers, can draw upon is one of the oldest fields of study in Western culture: rhetoric. Rhetoric was formulated by such Greek and Roman rhetoricians as Isocrates (436–338 B.C.E.), Aristotle (384–322 B.C.E.), Cicero (106–43 B.C.E.), and Quintilian (35–96 C.E.). Originally developed to meet the needs of speakers, rhetoric came to be applied to written texts as well.

When you think rhetorically, you consider the art of using words and images to engage—and sometimes to persuade—others. Writers who think rhetorically apply their understanding of human communication in general, and of written texts in particular, to the decisions that will enable effective communication within a specific situation.

A rhetorical approach to writing encourages you to consider four key elements of your situation:

1. Your role as a *writer* who has (or must discover) something to communicate

2. One or more *readers* with whom you would like to communicate

3. The *text* you create to convey your ideas and attitudes, whether your text is comprised of words, images, or graphics, such as charts, graphs, and borders

4. A *medium* (print text, PowerPoint presentation, poster, brochure, report, video clip, blog, and so on)

The relationship among these elements is dynamic. Writers compose texts to express their meaning, but readers are equally active. Readers don't simply decipher the words on the page; they draw on their own experiences and expectations as they read. As a student, for instance, you read your economics textbook differently than you read the comics or a popular novel, and you read an online newspaper differently than you do the print variety. You also know that the more experience you have reading certain kinds of writing—textbooks in your major or the sports or financial pages of the newspaper, for example—the more you will get out of them. Rhetoric is a practical art that helps writers make effective choices by taking each of these four elements into consideration within specific rhetorical situations.

Let's return to the student who wants to write an essay on graffiti as art. To analyze her situation, she would first consider her own position as a writer. As a student in a class, how much freedom does she have? In academic writing, this question leads immediately to the second element of the rhetorical situation: the reader. In academic writing, the reader is primarily the teacher, so the student would want to consider the nature of her assignment—how open it is, what statement (if any) the teacher has provided about format, expectations, and so on. But the writer would also want to draw on her general understanding of writing in the humanities. Instructors in the humanities often favor a conservative approach to academic writing, so while this student might use headings and images in her research paper, her safest bet would be to focus primarily on the clear and logical development of the ideas in her essay.

This student would have considerably more flexibility in approaching her PowerPoint or Prezi presentation. The conventions for presentations are more open than those of traditional academic writing. Moreover, instructors and students alike expect individuals who compose presentations to take full advantage of the medium. Since this would be a presentation for a class, however, the student would still want to focus on the development and presentation of her ideas, and any visual and design elements would need to enhance and enrich the expression of those ideas.

In this example, the student's teacher has specified the media she should use: a print essay and a presentation using PowerPoint or Prezi. For this reason, constructing a blog or creating a video would be an inappropriate response to the assignment. In a different situation, employing one or both of these media might be not only appropriate but also effective. If this student were writing an honors thesis on graffiti as art, for instance, she might well create a blog to express and explore her ideas during the year that she works on this major project. At her thesis defense, she might share relevant blog posts and comments with her committee. She might also show film clips of interviews with graffiti artists. As this example indicates, a rhetorical approach to writing encourages you to think in practical, concrete ways about your situation as a writer, to think and act like a problem solver.

Composing—and Designing—Texts

When you think and act like a problem solver, you use skills that have much in common with those used in the contemporary profession of design. There are many kinds of design—from industrial design to fashion design—but writing is especially closely allied with graphic design, thanks in large part to the development of the Web and such software programs as Adobe InDesign and Adobe Photoshop. In fact, given ongoing developments in communication technologies, conventional distinctions between these two creative activities seem less and less relevant. While it is true that in the humanities the most traditional forms of academic writing emphasize words over images and other design elements, increasingly student writers—like all writers—are integrating the visual and verbal in texts.

In his influential book *How Designers Think*, Bryan Lawson lists the essential characteristics of design:

- Design problems are open-ended and cannot be fully specified.
- The design process is endless.
- There is no infallibly correct process of design; rather, design is a persuasive activity that involves subjective value judgments.
- The design process involves finding as well as solving problems.

These characteristics apply, Lawson argues, to all kinds of design, from product design to graphic design.

Like design, writing is a creative act that occurs within an open-ended system of opportunities and constraints, and the writing process, too, is potentially endless in the sense that there is no objective or absolute way to determine when a project is complete. Instead, writers and designers often call a halt to their process for subjective and pragmatic reasons: They judge the project to be ready and believe that their audience or clients will be pleased, *or* they run out of time or money. Indeed, the open-ended nature of writing and design is typical of activities that require creativity.

Precisely because writing and design are creative processes, there is no infallibly correct process that writers and designers can follow. Experience enables writers and designers to determine the strategies appropriate to the task, but each project requires them to consider anew their situation, purpose, medium, and audience. As they do so, designers and writers do not just solve problems; they find, or create, them. This may sound intimidating at first. "I don't want to find problems," you might think. "I want to solve them quickly and efficiently." Here's the rub: Often you can't do the latter until you do the former.

Let's say, for example, that you and your roommate are frustrated because your room is always a mess. You talk it over, and you realize that the problem is that you just don't have enough storage space, so rather than put clothes and other items away in already-overstuffed closets and chests, you leave them out everywhere.

To address this problem, you have to go beyond the general recognition that you need more storage space to pinpoint the problem more specifically. After reading a Web feature on organizing and redecorating dorm spaces (see p. 9), you realize that your real problem is that you've neglected to consider systematically all your storage options. Once you've identified the crux of your problem, you can address it—in this case, by taking advantage of unused space against the wall and at the top of your closet. So you take measurements and head to the local discount store to look for inexpensive storage

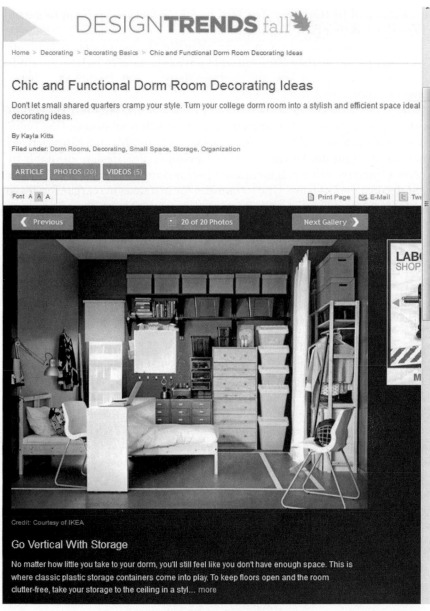

Design Advice for Organizing Dorm Space

units that will fit the space. You've solved your storage problem in part by correctly identifying, or creating, it.

In writing and in design, as in everyday life, the better you are at identifying your problem, the better you will be at addressing it. In fact, the ability to create complex and sophisticated problems is one feature that distinguishes experienced from inexperienced writers and designers. A professional interior designer, especially one whose work emphasizes working within the constraints of small spaces, might develop solutions to the roommates' dorm room problems more quickly, and possibly more innovatively, than the students do. Furthermore, as Lawson argues, design inevitably involves subjective value judgments and persuasion to convince clients to accept the designer's vision. One roommate, for instance, may argue for design purchases that reflect her commitment to sustainably produced products, while the other roommate may feel that the least expensive product that meets their needs is the best choice.

Both writing and design offer individuals the opportunity to make a difference in the world. Someone who redesigns wheelchairs, and in so doing improves their comfort and mobility, for instance, will improve the quality of life for all who rely on this mode of transportation. It's easy to think of writers who have made a difference in the world. Most environmentalists agree, for example, that Rachel Carson's 1962 *Silent Spring* played a key role in catalyzing the environmental movement. Yet there are other, less visible but still important examples of the power that writing can have to effect economic, social, political, and cultural change. Writing is one of the most important ways that students can become members of a disciplinary or professional community. For example, in order to be recognized as professional civil engineers, engineering students not only need to learn how to plan, design, construct, and maintain structures: They also must learn to write like civil engineers. Writing not only plays a key role in most careers but it also represents an important way that citizens express their views and advocate for causes (see the poster on p. 11). Think, for example, of the role that Twitter and blogs now play in politics and in public affairs. In these and other ways, writing provides an opportunity for ordinary people to shape the future of local, regional, and national communities.

||||||||||||||||||||||||||||||||||||||||||||||||||||||||||||||||||||||||||||||||||||

FOR EXPLORATION

Write for five to ten minutes in response to this question: What has this discussion of the connections between writing and design helped you better understand about written communication?

tap
water
is, on
average,
500 times
cheaper than
bottled water.*
**boycott the
bottle.**

*The Chartered Institution of Water and Environmental Management (CIWEM) - Policy about Bottled Drinking Water - November 2005

Poster Advocating for a Cause

FOR COLLABORATION

Bring your response to the preceding Exploration to class and meet with a group of peers. Appoint someone to record your discussion, and then take turns sharing your writing. Be prepared to share your discussion with the class.

|||||||||||||||||||||||||||||||||||||||||||||||||||||||||||||||||||||||||||||

Developing Rhetorical Sensitivity

Both graphic designers and writers understand that to create a successful project they must do all of the following:

- Draw on all their resources, learning from their experiences, exploring their own ideas, and challenging themselves to express those ideas as clearly and powerfully as possible

- Consider their audience—who they are, what they know and like, and what they feel and believe

- Assess the purpose and goals of the project—the meaning they wish to communicate and their reasons for composing

- Make use of all the tools available to them (such as word processing, image editing, and spreadsheet programs, as well as specialized programs), given the medium in which they are working

In all of these activities, experienced writers and designers practice *rhetorical sensitivity*.

Designers and writers practice rhetorical sensitivity when they explore the four elements of rhetoric—writer/designer, audience, text/project, medium—in the context of specific situations. The student writing about graffiti art, for example, drew on her rhetorical sensitivity in determining how best to respond to her assignment. She realized that as a student writing for a class she was constrained in significant ways and that her reader's (i.e., her teacher's) expectations were crucial to her decision making. She also knew that the textual conventions governing essays are more conservative than those governing presentations and that differences in media—print versus PowerPoint or Prezi—reinforce this distinction. As a result of her analysis, this student realized that she had more freedom to experiment with visual elements of design in her presentation than in her essay.

In order to respond to her assignment, this student consciously explored her rhetorical situation. Writers and designers are particularly likely to do this when they undertake an important assignment or work for a new client. At other times, this kind of analysis takes the form of rhetorical common sense. In your daily life, you already practice considerable rhetorical sensitivity. As you make decisions about how to interact with others, you naturally draw on your commonsense understanding of effective communication. If you are preparing for a job interview, everything you do before and during—what you wear, how you act, what you say—is in an effort to make the interview a success. Much of your attention will focus on how best to present yourself, given the company you are applying to: You would dress differently were you interviewing at your local fitness center rather than at Bank of America, for example. But you would probably also recognize the importance of being well prepared and of interacting effectively with your interviewer. Savvy applicants know that everything they do is an effort to persuade the interviewers to hire them.

NOTE FOR MULTILINGUAL WRITERS

It is more challenging to "read" a rhetorical situation when you are new to the context. You may find it helpful to consult your teacher or classmates, asking specific questions in order to understand the rhetorical situation for a particular assignment.

You also employ rhetorical sensitivity when you "read" contemporary culture. As a consumer, for instance, you're bombarded with advertisements urging you to buy various products or services. Wise consumers know that ads are designed to persuade, and they learn ways to read them with a critical eye (even as they appreciate, say, a television commercial's humor or a magazine ad's design).

thinking
rhetorically

You read other aspects of contemporary culture as well. Much of the time, you may do so for entertainment: While watching sports or other programs on television, for instance, your primary goal may be to relax and enjoy yourself. If you find the plot of a detective show implausible or the action of the Monday night football game too slow, you can easily click to a more interesting program.

At times, however, you may take a more critical, distanced perspective on various forms of popular culture. After arguing with a friend about whether the video game *Mortal Combat* advocates sexism and violence, you may read reviews of (and play) this game with a careful eye, ultimately making your own judgment. When you analyze a video game like *Mortal Combat*

thinking
rhetorically

to determine whether it advocates sexism and violence, you're analyzing its *rhetoric*.

Writers and designers who think rhetorically understand that writing and reading do not occur in a vacuum. The language you grow up speaking, the social and cul⋯ ⋯wor ds you inhabit, and the technologies available to you, among othe⋯ ⋯tors, all influence how you communicate. For example, wherever they co⋯ ⋯ from, most students find that the writing they do in college differs cons⋯derably from the language they use in their everyday lives. The language that feels comfortable and natural to you when you speak with your family and friends may differ considerably from that required in academic reading and writing assignments.

Like life, writing involves negotiation. When you prepare for a job interview, you must decide how much to modify your everyday way of dressing to meet the demands of the situation. Similarly, when you write—whether in college, at work, or for civic or other organizations—you must consider the expectations of others. At times it can be difficult to determine, let alone meet, these expectations. In your first weeks at a new job, for instance, you probably felt like the new kid on the block. Gradually, however, you became sensitive to your supervisor's and coworkers' expectations. Likewise, as a college student you may at times feel like a new writer on the block. Both *The Academic Writer* and your composition course will help you build on the rhetorical sensitivity that you already have so that you can use all the resources available to you to meet the demands of writing in the twenty-first century.

||||||||||||||||||||||||||||||||||||||||||||||||||||||||||||||||||||||||||||||

FOR EXPLORATION

Take a look at the billboards on the following pages. Both are advertising products offered by the Gap, a clothing company that has mainly focused on attracting young shoppers but that also tries to retain customers as they age.

After carefully examining the two billboards, respond in writing to these questions:

1. How do the designers of the billboards use words, images, and graphics to persuade? Do some of these elements seem more important than others? Why?

2. In what ways do the billboards reinforce Lawson's observation that design involves "subjective value judgments"? Do they, for instance, rely on culturally sanctioned stereotypes? If they do, how do these stereotypes reinforce the message?

thinking rhetorically

3. In what ways do these billboards demonstrate rhetorical sensitivity on the part of those who created them?

||||||||||||||||||||||||||||||||||||||||||||||||||||||||||||||||||||||||||||||

Advertisement for Gap Jeans

Advertisement for Gapstretch Pants

NOTE FOR MULTILINGUAL WRITERS

If you learned to write in a language other than English, you may sometimes feel frustrated when teachers ask you to stop speaking and writing in a way that feels natural to you and instead to adopt the conventions of academic writing in the United States. Many students who have grown up in the United States speaking English share this discomfort. Your goal as a writer should not be to abandon your first or home language but rather to become so fluent in the conventions of standard written English that you can write effectively in both languages and for both communities.

|||||||||||||||||||||||||||||||||||||||||||||||||||||||||||||||||||||||||||||||||||||

FOR THOUGHT, DISCUSSION, AND WRITING

1. Take a few moments to recall an incident in your daily life when you were called on to demonstrate *rhetorical sensitivity*. Write a paragraph describing this incident. Then write a paragraph or two stating your current understanding of the terms *rhetoric* and *rhetorical sensitivity*. Finally, write one or two questions that you still have about these terms.

2. Write an essay in which you describe and reflect on the many kinds of writing that you do and the role that visual and design elements play in your writing. After writing the essay, create a text that uses words, images, and (if you like) graphics to convey the ideas you discuss in your essay. You can use any mix of photographs, drawings, text, or other material that will help others understand your experience.

3. Interview two or three students in your current or prospective major to learn more about writing in this field. Ask these students the following questions:
    - What kinds of writing are students required to do in classes for this field?
    - How would they characterize the role of images and other graphic elements in this writing? What roles, if any, do multimedia play in their writing?
    - How is their writing evaluated by their professors?
    - What advice about writing would they give to other students taking classes in this discipline?

Your instructor may ask you to report the results of these interviews to the class. Your instructor may also ask you to write an essay summarizing and reflecting on the results of your interview.

|||||||||||||||||||||||||||||||||||||||||||||||||||||||||||||||||||||||||||||||||||||

Rethinking Reading:
Reading on Page and Screen

Writing and reading are interrelated activities, so it should come as no surprise that the question of what it means to be a reader in the twenty-first century is as complicated—and as full of opportunities and challenges—as what it means to be a writer. For centuries, the activity of reading has been primarily associated with texts printed on paper. Today, readers have a variety of options about how and where to read texts: on paper or on-screen, and if on-screen, on a PC or Mac, desktop or laptop, tablet or smartphone. This is not to suggest, of course, that all college students have equal access to communication technologies. A "digital divide" still exists in America, let alone in the wider world. For some, replacing a smartphone or tablet with the latest model is almost automatic; for others, cost represents a significant barrier to buying one at all. But the trend seems clear: As prices for tablets, smartphones, and other devices fall, their use among college students increases.

Today, many college students already read in a variety of media and on a variety of devices. If that is the case for you, you may not think that the medium or device matters much. What's the big deal? It's the message that's important, not the delivery system, right? Maybe not. How people read, what they remember, how they see information—even what reading is—can be radically altered when the medium or device changes. Imagine reading a detailed graphic in a print magazine. In that medium, the graphic appears across two pages and can be taken in all at once. Now imagine reading that graphic on a smartphone (even one with a large screen): You'd have to scroll up and down, left and right, and still you'd only be able to see the image piecemeal. Now consider seeing it on a tablet or laptop, on which the once-static graphic of the print magazine may now include animations and other digital enhancements.

Some educators and critics worry that individuals who read online texts are less likely to engage with the material with the same critical depth as individuals who read print texts. In his best-selling book *The Shallows: What the Internet Is Doing to Our Brains* (2011), Nicholas Carr makes just such an argument. In a study grounded partly in his personal experience and partly in brain research, Carr argues that a reliance on the Internet is reducing users' capacity for concentration and for sustained deep thought.

Others, such as Clay Shirky (author of *Cognitive Surplus: Creativity and Generosity in a Connected Age*, 2010), applaud the opportunities for collaboration and creativity afforded by the Web and praise the opening up of reading to multiple media, devices, and apps. They point out, as just one of many examples, the enhancements available to texts—including college textbooks—designed to be read on digital platforms: enhancements such as zoomable art, embedded videos and lectures, and tools for sharing reading notes with classmates.

At this point, the jury is still out: The research available on this topic is limited, and more data is needed before we can determine whether those in Carr's camp or those in Shirky's will be proved right. Still, most of us will be reading at least some texts online—academic research, for example, often begins with an online search for scholarly articles accessed through academic databases—so it is important to develop the rhetorical sensitivity needed to make informed decisions about how best to access and interact with them. This chapter will help you take advantage of the benefits seen by Shirky and also help you read texts—including digital texts—with the critical depth that Carr fears is being lost.

|||||||||||||||||||||||||||||||||||||||||||||||||||||||||||||||||||||||||||||||||||||||||||

FOR EXPLORATION

Write for five to ten minutes about your own experience of and response to the Internet:

■ How has access to the Internet enhanced your experience as a person, as a student, and as a worker?

■ What challenges, if any, has it posed for you?

■ Do you find yourself with concerns or reservations about your Internet use and the time you spend online? Explain why. Be prepared to share your thoughts with your classmates.

|||||||||||||||||||||||||||||||||||||||||||||||||||||||||||||||||||||||||||||||||||||||||||

As a student negotiating the multiple demands of school, work, family, and friends, you must make decisions about how and when to access texts. (By the way, texts can include visual and auditory elements. Political cartoons, advertisements, and podcasts are all examples of texts.) If you own a smartphone, you may find yourself taking advantage of its technology to read or review assigned material: It may not be the best device for the job, but if it's the device you have with you—right there in your pocket—it's better to read the material on it than not to read the material at all. In a situation like this, the most pressing question you face becomes how you can use your mobile device to read actively and critically, given the *type of text* you're reading (a novel for a literature class, an academic article for a sociology class, a geology textbook with integrated media) and *your purpose* (to ace a multiple-choice psychology test, to identify plant species on a biology quiz, to write a paper on the symbolism in *Moby-Dick*). A rhetorical approach to reading (and writing), as well as an understanding of the limits and opportunities afforded by various media (and by programs, or apps, developed for these media), can help you decide which medium or device makes the most sense for the kind of reading you need to do and can help you make the most of your reading experience.

thinking rhetorically

Awareness of your strengths and limitations as a writer is a good place to start. The more aware you are of the impact of your own experiences and preferences, particularly in terms of reading in print and on-screen, the more self-conscious you can be as a reader. The following quiz will help you reflect on these issues.

Quiz: Reading on Page or Screen

1. As a reader, not just of academic writing, but of all kinds of writing, how would you describe yourself?

a. I still prefer print when possible.
b. I prefer to read online and on my e-reader whenever possible.
c. I move back and forth from reading print to reading online and downloaded texts depending on my situation, purpose for reading, nature of the texts, and so forth.

How do you think these preferences affect your ability to engage with academic texts critically and in depth?

2. What factors thus far have influenced your experiences and preferences for reading on page and screen?

a. My age
b. My finances
c. My current work/life/school schedule
d. My knowledge of and experience with communication technologies
e. The expectations of my instructors

continued

f. The expectations of my employer

g. One or more additional factors (please specify)

How have these factors influenced your ability to benefit from contemporary electronic technologies?

3. **If you have a smartphone, how would you characterize how you use it?**

a. It's important in my daily life, but I use it mainly for communicating with others.

b. I use my smartphone for communicating but also for navigating, using the GPS feature.

c. I use my smartphone for communicating and navigating, but I also use it for entertainment and shopping.

d. I use my smartphone for all the above purposes, but I also use it for professional and academic purposes.

Smartphones are playing an important role in the ongoing shift to mobile computing. What do you see as the advantages and disadvantages of your current use of a smartphone? If you don't have a smartphone, is it by choice or out of financial necessity?

4. **What are the most important questions you have about your current practices as a reader?**

————

————

————

5. **What are the most important goals that you would like to set for yourself as a reader in general and, especially, as a student reader of academic texts?**

————

————

————

Understanding the Impact of Communication Technologies on Reading

To understand the impact that communication technologies have had on the reading experience, consider the history of reading. You might be surprised to learn, for instance, that until the ninth century people who could read and write—a small minority of the population—read texts out loud, rather than silently. (We take silent reading for granted—but this practice was actually developed by monks living in monasteries.) Since the printing press had

Before the printing press, books were painstakingly copied by hand in monasteries and then sold to support the monastic community. Silence was generally enforced in the scriptorium, the room set aside for the production of texts.

yet to be invented—Gutenberg invented the printing press around 1440—people read texts that were copied and illustrated by hand. (For an amusing take on the difficulties of adjusting to the new "technology" of the printed book, watch the video *Medieval Help Desk*, which at the time I was writing this chapter was available on YouTube. Be sure to click on the original Norwegian version with English subtitles and not the later—and less successful—adaptations of this video.)

Changes in communication te_____ conse-quences. The printing press reduce_____apers, ballads, novels) dramatically, oper_____ pub-lics of the middle and lower classes _____etween the "expert" author and the "ordina_____ to the Internet, reading today is much m_____on be-tween author and reader is shifting _____ their *authority* by publishing reviews of b_____m and other sites. They can respond dire_____hether those articles appear in their local n_____or on a friend's blog—and their comments may themselves elicit further responses. Many writers today are bypassing traditional publishing venues and self-publishing their work. And messages sent via Twitter, Facebook, and other social-media sites can have substantial and even revolutionary conse-quences, as has been demonstrated by their use during the Arab Spring of 2011 and other popular uprisings. In these and many other instances, read-ing leads to writing, which leads again to reading. As social commentators have noted, increasingly we are immersed in a participatory, interactive culture.

As Chapter 1 notes, and as this discussion of reading confirms, we are experiencing a major transition in what it means to be a reader and a writer. This massive shift brings challenges as well as opportunities. Individu-als writing today need, for instance, to be scrupulous about where they get information and how they use and cite it. A less ethically grounded but still important challenge is keeping up with the constantly changing landscape of communication technologies. Today, mobile reading devices abound, and so do programs and apps designed to improve the mobile reading ex-perience. If you do an Internet search of *digital annotation and notetak-ing tools* you will get a huge array of results—from Evernote and Zotero to GoodReader, iAnnotate, and MyStickies. And other developments are in the pipeline. Currently, Google is developing an eyeglass-mounted device that allows users to take and share photos, participate in video chats, and access the Internet. In the future, will we search the Web via a computer mounted inside the frame of a special pair of digitally enhanced glasses?

Even if you're not yet Google-eyed, communication devices, and the technologies that power them, are changing fast. How they will change is

Sergei Brin, one of Google's founders, wearing a prototype of Google Glass

unclear. In the 2012 report "10 Ways Your Phone Is Changing the World," for instance, *Time* magazine noted that "[a] typical smartphone has more computing power than *Apollo 11* when it landed a man on the moon."* Would a futurist in 1969 ever have predicted this?

||||||||||||||||||||||||||||||||||||||||||||||||||||||||||||||||||||||||||||||||||||||||||||||||

FOR EXPLORATION

Take some time to think about all the reading you do during a typical week. Include reading for school and work, but also include reading newspapers, magazines, fiction, comics or manga, blogs, wikis, Web sites, reviews on shopping sites, social-media posts, and so forth.

■ What percent of this reading is done using an electronic device? What percent of your reading is in print?

Time, August 27, 2012, 32.

■ For the different types of reading you do, how do you decide which platform to use (such as print publication, computer, e-reader, tablet, or smartphone)?

■ How does the platform you use affect your reading experience?

After responding to these questions, take a few moments to reflect on what you have learned about yourself as a reader. Compare this response with your response to the Exploration activity on page 3.

|||||||||||||||||||||||||||||||||||||||||||||||||||||||||||||||||||||||||||||||||||||||||||||||||||

Reading and Rhetoric

thinking rhetorically

As a student today, you face a dizzying array of choices about how to access and interact with the texts you read for school, work, and fun. A rhetorical approach to reading and writing can help you effectively negotiate these choices. Rhetoric emphasizes the importance of attending to the specifics of your situation as a reader and writer. (Turn back to Chapter 1, or page forward to Chapter 4, to learn more about rhetorical situations.) Rather than making once-and-for-all judgments about whether it's better to read an academic text in print or on your desktop, laptop, tablet, e-reading device, or smartphone, a rhetorical approach to communication emphasizes the importance of drawing on the rhetorical sensitivity you have already developed as a writer, reader, speaker, and listener to make effective choices in specific situations. A rhetorical approach to reading also emphasizes the importance of attending to ethical issues, such as your responsibility to evaluate the reliability of material you find on the Web and to read critically. (For more on evaluating sources for reliability, for example, see Chapter 7, "Doing Research"; for more on reading critically, see Chapter 9, "Strategies for Reading.")

Chapter 1 identified the four key elements of the rhetorical situation. Let's reconsider them from the reader's point of view:

■ Your role as a *reader*, with a variety of reasons or purposes for reading, such as to gather information, assess an argument, or synthesize information from a variety of sources and generate a new text of your own

■ One or more *writers* who have something to communicate

■ The *text* you read to gather information, analyze and critique an argument, share your ideas and experiences, and so forth

■ The *medium* — a text printed on *paper*, an e-book read on a *mobile reading device*, an online magazine accessed on a *tablet*, a Facebook post read on your *smartphone* — that makes this communication possible

Let's consider each of these elements in turn while also considering the demands — and the opportunities — that contemporary readers encounter.

READER.   It's common to think of writing as active and reading as passive, but reading is also an active process in which readers construct meaning — and do so more or less effectively. Readers come to a text with varying degrees of interest in and knowledge of a subject as well as their own motivations for reading. As a student reading academic texts, you need to read strategically: Do you need to absorb names and dates (as for a history quiz) or synthesize information from a number of sources to get a sense of an academic research topic? What practical constraints are you facing, such as competing deadlines or pragmatic and logistical issues, such as the need to do laundry and grocery shop while studying for a big test? Each of these purposes (and many others) will influence your approach to a text.

As a student, what should you take into consideration when you are deciding how to access and interact with an academic text that is required reading for a class? At the most general level, you would do well to remember that, whatever their discipline your instructors share a strong commitment to a deep engagement with texts (whether scientific or humanistic) and to critical reading and writing, so your ability to interact with a text — whether in print or online — is key. Even if your instructors are as addicted to their tablets, e-readers, and smartphones as you are, they may take it for granted that (unless they have chosen to use an e-textbook) you will buy and use print textbooks (or download and print materials from your course management site). However, instructors are increasingly aware that you have options in terms of how you access texts, and some may indicate which option they require or prefer you to choose. Here, for instance, is a statement included on a syllabus for a creative writing course whose instructor clearly recognizes that students might access texts in multiple ways:

> Texts/Resources and Policies: All weekly readings (both published work and student work) are posted to Blackboard. Please either print these essays <u>as I have uploaded them</u> for class or have a full-screen format (tablet or laptop, *NOT A PHONE SCREEN*) to refer to in class. Please make sure your e-device is fully charged.

As a student in college today, you need to take responsibility for the choices you make when you access academic texts. When in doubt, ask your instructors what their preferences are.

WRITER.   Just as the reader has a purpose for reading, the writer has some reason for writing. That reason may be to convey information, to persuade readers to accept a position or take action, to entertain, or some combination of reasons. Today, writing and reading are increasingly interconnected, mutually reinforcing activities. You may read an article in your favorite blog and post a response — and then check the blog later to read responses to your and others' comments. Perhaps your response will draw readers' attention, and you will discover that people who you never expected to be interested in your thoughts are reading and responding to your ideas. Or perhaps you are checking a Wikipedia entry on a topic you know well and you recognize an inaccuracy. Suddenly the act of reading becomes a call to write and correct that inaccuracy. Even if you are unlikely to post to a blog or edit a Wikipedia entry, you probably take advantage of the many opportunities for communication and interaction that social media such as Facebook, Twitter, and Tumblr offer. Social media are changing what it means to be a writer and a reader today — bringing new opportunities, but also new challenges, for communicators.

One of the challenges that contemporary writers increasingly face is composing texts that can be accessed and viewed on multiple devices and multiple platforms, which in the case of the Internet primarily means functioning on both Android and iOS systems. Web designers involved in what is often characterized as the responsive Web design movement are attempting to address this challenge. Those who compose and design Web sites also need to be fully compliant with standards of accessibility set by the Americans with Disabilities Act (ADA). Such standards require, for instance, that every image have a text equivalent so that a Web user with a vision disability can have an alternative way of understanding what the image is.

Although those writing and designing for the Web must think about how their texts will (or will not) be able to be shared across media and platforms and how they can be accessed by people of varying abilities, these issues are not currently urgent for most college students, at least not in their academic writing. Most often, your instructors will specify the medium you should use when you communicate, whether you are writing a traditional print essay, creating a PowerPoint or Prezi presentation, or contributing to a class wiki, blog, or Twitter feed. If you are engaged in an activist- or a community-oriented project, however, you may need to consider questions of media if you want to reach multiple audiences. For example, if your campus sustainability group were to develop a Web site, how could they ensure that it is easily and effectively accessible by smartphone and by people with visual impairments? Increasingly writers in various professions will need to consider issues like these as well.

TEXT.   The kind, or genre, of text you are reading (and the reason you are reading it) is crucially important when determining how best to access and interact with texts. For example, if you're reading an op-ed, which is a relatively short, nontechnical genre, using a smartphone makes sense. If you decide that you might quote from the op-ed and take notes, you might want to read it on a device with a keyboard that makes note taking easier.

Complexity is another concern: Reading a text-only page-turner on your dedicated e-reader with a small screen may be fine. But reading a novel by J. K. Rowling or Stephen King is a very different experience from that of reading a scholarly book or article that puts forward a complex argument, a graphic novel that depends on the relationship between image and text for its meaning, or a novel like *War and Peace* that depicts complex relationships and events and is peopled by characters with multiple names and nicknames.

Reading many different sources for a research project—whether for a first-year writing class or for an advanced class in your major—can certainly start on a smartphone. But given the need to take careful notes and to keep research materials organized, you'll find yourself quickly shifting to reading on a device—perhaps a laptop—that gives you tools for taking and organizing notes, marking excerpts for citation, writing drafts, and doing the other tasks inherent in the research process. For some digital sources, you may want to print a copy. And in many disciplines consulting print books is essential. (For more on the research process, see Chapter 7.)

MEDIUM. The medium is the mechanism of delivery. The medium may be print (such as a print book, magazine, or newspaper) or electronic (as is the case with texts accessed via your laptop or tablet, a podcast listened to on your smartphone, and so forth). The medium of delivery the reader or writer chooses is a crucial factor affecting the reader's interaction with the text, as well as the kinds of texts a writer can produce. Often, several different media are combined in one reading experience—books with words and video; images with audio. With digital technologies, in fact, it is more unusual to have only one medium than to have a mix of media.

Sometimes you have no choice in terms of the medium you will use: The text you need to read or view exists in a single format, such as a print book that has not been digitized or a YouTube video for which printing is not possible. At other times, you can choose your medium—a book in electronic or print format, a newspaper you read online or pick up at a newsstand. Choosing the most appropriate medium for accessing a text depends on all three of the factors—reader/writer/text—discussed above. (Remember: The elements of the rhetorical situation are fluid and interact with each other.) You may also want to consider the following:

Price Both downloadable and Web-based e-books are generally cheaper than books printed on paper (and many classics are available free electronically), and they can be accessed by downloading them to your device or via the Internet. But some e-books are available only by subscription, and they may become inaccessible or require repurchase after the subscription period of a semester, a year, or longer. (In effect, you are renting the text.) So consider whether you would like to keep the book for a semester only, throughout college, or for the long term. Interestingly, when surveyed, many students say they still prefer print textbooks over e-books; you might find yourself in that camp.

Complexity The more intensively a person needs to read—the more challenging and complex the reading, the greater the importance of the relationship between text and image or sound—the greater the effect the medium can have. Some readers find, for instance, that they can more easily grasp the "big picture" of an argument and engage it deeply and critically when they read a print text, rather than a digital one; they may learn better when they annotate a text by hand, or they may find it easier to focus when not tempted to surf the Web or respond to a friend's latest text message. Others prefer to read a text on a device that allows them to look up the meaning of a word by clicking on it, zoom in on detailed images, watch a video of a process, or access a dictionary or other texts that can aid understanding.

Your preferred mode of interacting with texts One of the advantages of print texts is that there are an endless number of ways that readers can interact with them. Look at three students' annotations of the same text and they may look quite different but be equally effective in terms of engagement and critical thinking. Increasingly, electronic or downloaded texts offer similar opportunities for interaction. Many devices make it possible for readers to highlight, bookmark, search, tag, and add notes. The program Scrible (www.scrible.com), for instance, allows readers to highlight and annotate Web pages, add sticky-note responses and reminders, categorize annotations with legends (a feature that might be useful when studying for an exam), share online texts via email, save texts to an online account, and organize and search saved texts. This is just one of hundreds of programs designed to increase the productivity of online reading and research, and new programs are being developed all the time. Clearly, programs for note taking, sharing annotations, making citations, and other tools for engaged reading can help you to read critically and deeply. The key is choosing a program that works for you, learning its strengths and limitations (and depending on the complexity of the program there can be a steep learning curve), and gaining enough experience so that the benefits become real for you.

Just as composing preferences vary—see Chapter 3, "Academic Writing: Committing to the Process," for more information on this topic—so too can reading preferences. One reader may love using iAnnotate to mark online texts, while another may find this app cumbersome and prefer to annotate important texts by hand. Over time, as new programs are developed and your experiences change, your preferences as a reader may alter.

NOTE FOR MULTILINGUAL WRITERS

If you are a multilingual writer, you may especially appreciate some of the features of e-books, such as the inclusion of definitions, pronunciation guides, audio options that allow readers to hear the text while reading, and enhanced visuals. Features such as these can definitely enhance your experience as a reader and as a student.

Analyzing Your Experiences and Preferences as a Reader

This chapter encourages you to analyze your experiences and preferences as a reader — and also to recognize that, like writing, reading is best understood as a rhetorical activity. Though you may not think about it consciously, as you move throughout your day you naturally adapt your reading to your rhetorical situation. If you are reading a magazine or an online comic series to relax, you may read casually. If you are reading to prepare for a test or to write an essay in response, you may read more actively and critically, with pencil (or keyboard) at the ready. The more difficult, complex, and important the reading, the more essential it is that you have a well-developed repertoire of critical reading skills. The strategies suggested in Chapter 9 can help you strengthen these skills.

Reading Rhetorically in a Time of Transition

thinking
rhetorically

As a student in college today you are living in a time of transition in terms of communication technologies. At the moment, e-books are changing the reading habits of many individuals, especially those reading for entertainment and personal enrichment, but there is little evidence that the rise of e-books will lead to the demise of print books. In a report released in April 2012 by the Pew Internet and American Life Project, researchers noted that while "[t]he prevalence of e-book reading is markedly growing . . . printed books still dominate the world of book readers." In a survey conducted in December 2011, Pew Internet researchers "found that 72 percent of American adults had read a printed book . . . in the previous year, compared with the 17 percent of adults who had read an e-book." Bowker, a company that tracks information for book publishers, booksellers, and libraries, pub-

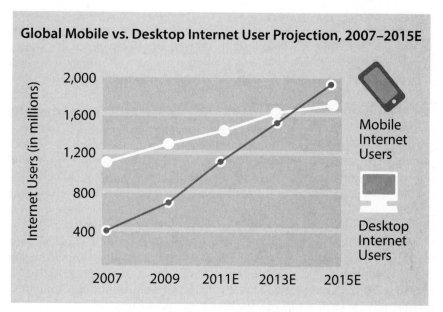

Global Mobile vs. Desktop Internet User Projection, 2007–2015E

Mobile Internet Users

Desktop Internet Users

Growth of Mobile Internet Use (2007–2015)

lished a report indicating that "traditional print book output grew 6 percent in 2011, from 328,259 titles in 2010 to a projected 347,178 in 2011." Much of this growth is attributed to the self-publishing market.

Magazines and newspapers are faring less well. According to articles in the *New York Times*, newsstand sales of print magazines fell by almost 10 percent in 2012, and the weekday readership of print newspapers was down by 9 percent in 2010 compared to 2009. And while the readership of digital newspapers has grown a bit, many more people read articles online without paying to subscribe.

One aspect of our changing communication landscape does seem clear: Increasingly readers and writers are communicating on mobile devices. A chart showing the predicted growth of mobile Internet use versus desktop Internet use is reproduced above.

thinking rhetorically

As a student, you have choices about how you access and interact with texts. This chapter emphasizes the helpfulness of taking a rhetorical perspective on negotiating these choices. In this regard, attending to your rhetorical situation as a student is paramount. While technologies of communication have changed and will continue to change, one thing has remained consistent: the desire of college teachers for their students to become engaged, critical readers. Chapter 9, "Strategies for Reading," presents concrete strategies you can use to strengthen your critical reading skills, whether reading in print or online. Chapter 7, "Doing Research: Joining the Scholarly Conversation," also presents important information and skills about conducting effective research, a process that today most often begins online.

What else can you do to maximize the productivity of the reading that you do online? Pay attention to programs and apps—such as Zotero or Mendeley—that can make your life as an online reader, writer, and researcher easier. If your instructor assigns an e-book as a textbook, be sure to take full advantage of its features, such as embedded interactive video, 3-D capability, hot links to glossary definitions, and so forth. Remember that research strongly suggests that people often read quite differently online than when they read texts printed on paper. People who read on-screen often do so erratically and selectively—skimming and scanning rather than reading intensively and critically. If you are reading important academic texts on your tablet, reading device, or smartphone, you may need to resist these behaviors consciously, reminding yourself that, whatever the discipline, your college instructors place a premium on engaged, critical reading.

You should also think about the specifics of your situation, as this chapter emphasizes. When reading an academic text for the first time, you may want to read in print or on a large screen so that you can focus on, annotate, and critically engage with the text. When reviewing for a test just before taking it, you might want the convenience of studying on your smartphone, especially if you are in the midst of a long commute to campus.

thinking rhetorically

Reading rhetorically means considering all aspects of your rhetorical situation—reader, writer, text, medium—to make effective choices as a twenty-first-century reader.

||||||||||||||||||||||||||||||||||||||||||||||||||||||||||||||||||||||||||||||||||||||

FOR THOUGHT, DISCUSSION, AND WRITING

1. For at least one full day keep track of all the reading that you do. Be sure to include both informal and formal material, from reading grocery lists—either handwritten or composed on a smartphone—to reading class assignments. Do you see any patterns in terms of preferences and habitual practices? Take a few minutes to write about what you have learned as a result of this inventory and reflection. Be prepared to share this writing with your classmates.

2. Write an essay in which you reflect on the challenges and opportunities you face as a reader—and college student—in the twenty-first century. What strengths do you bring to the process of reading today? How might you improve your abilities as a contemporary student reading both in print and on-screen?

3. Interview either a professional in your intended major or (if that's not practical) an advanced student in your major. Ask that person about the reading he or she does for professional or academic work and about the other kinds of reading he or she does for different purposes and for relaxation. What devices are used? What patterns emerge in his or her reading practices? What does he or she see as challenges and opportunities in the present moment? What advice would the interviewee give to a student just entering this area of study?

Academic Writing: Committing to the Process

Many people think that those who write well possess a magical or mysterious power. According to this view, people are either born with the ability to write well or not, and those who write well find writing easy: They just sit down, and the words and ideas begin to flow. Interestingly, people often feel the same way about those who work with images and graphics. They believe that designers and artists have a gift that enables them to create vivid and compelling designs, paintings, or other aesthetic objects.

In fact, most successful writers, designers, and artists study their craft for many years. What some would call "talent" or "a gift" might more aptly be characterized as interest, motivation, and commitment. Successful writers and designers know that their skills take time to mature. They also know that to develop their skills they must look for opportunities to practice them. As they practice, they reflect on the strengths and limitations not only of the products they produce but also of the processes they use to create them. This reflection, in turn, allows them to develop strategies to cope with the complexities of writing and design, and thus to experience the satisfaction of a job well done.

As a student, you probably know from experience that your writing is most successful when you give yourself ample time to develop your thoughts, draft, and revise. If you're like most students, though, you don't always act on this knowledge. This chapter will help you gain insight into your own preferences as a writer, enabling you to commit to a writing process that works for you—and that results in successful academic writing.

||||||||||||||||||||||||||||||||||||||||||||||||||||||||||||||||||||||||||||||||||||||

FOR EXPLORATION

Take some time to reflect on your own assumptions about writing and your experiences as a writer. Set aside at least half an hour, and respond in writing to the following questions. As you do so, be sure to reflect on both your academic and your personal writing and reading experiences.

1. What are your earliest memories of learning to read and write?

2. How were reading and writing viewed by your family and friends when you were growing up?

3. What role did reading play in your development as a writer? What kinds of texts were you drawn to—traditional print texts; visual texts, such as comics and graphic novels; a mix; or some other kind(s)?

4. Can you recall particular experiences in school or on the job that influenced your current attitude toward writing?

5. If you were to describe your history as a writer, what stages or periods in your development would you identify? Write a sentence or two briefly characterizing each stage or period.

6. What images come to mind when you hear the term *writer*? What images come to mind when you think of yourself as a writer?

7. Draw up a list of metaphors, such as "As a writer, I'm a turtle—slow and steady" or "As a writer, I'm a racehorse—fast out of the gate but never sure if I've got the stamina to finish." Write two or three sentences that use images or metaphors to characterize your sense of yourself as a writer.

8. What kinds of writing do you enjoy or dislike? What kinds of writing do you do outside of school? Do you regularly tweet or text? Do you keep a personal journal or blog? Do you write poetry? In answering this question, include any print or multimedia texts that you regularly create simply because you enjoy doing so.

9. What role have multimedia texts (such as Web sites, hypertext documents, or video games) played in your reading and writing experiences? What role do images and graphics play in your writing—both in and out of school?

10. What do you enjoy most—at least—about the writing process?

11. What goals would you like to set for yourself as a writer?

FOR EXPLORATION

Using the notes, responses, and reflections generated by the previous Exploration, write a letter to your classmates and teacher in which you describe who you are as a writer today and how you got to be that way. Alternatively, create a text that uses words and, if you like, images and graphics to describe who you are as a writer today. You could hand-draw your text or create it on the computer; you could also make a collage.

For her response to this assignment, student Mirlandra Ebert created a collage, which is shown on p. 36. (To read Mirlandra's analysis of her rhetorical situation, turn to pp. 57–58.)

FOR COLLABORATION

Bring enough copies of the letter or visual text you created in response to the previous Exploration to share with members of your group. After you

Mirlandra Ebert's Collage, "Who I Am as a Writer"

have all read one another's texts, work together to answer the following questions. Choose one person to record the group's answers so that you can share the results of your discussion with the rest of the class.

1. To what extent are your attitudes toward writing and experiences as writers similar? List three to five statements with which all group members can agree.

2. What factors account for the differences in your attitudes toward writing and experiences as writers? List two or three factors that you agree account for these differences.

3. What common goals can you set for yourselves as writers? List at least three goals you can agree on.

Managing the Writing Process

Successful writers know that they must develop and commit to a writing process that enables them to succeed as students. But how do writers actually manage the writing process? Notice how differently the following students describe their process.

> My writing starts with contemplation. I let the topic I have chosen sink into my mind for a while. During this time my mind is a swirl of images, words, and ideas. Sometimes I draw clusters or diagrams that show how my ideas relate; sometimes I make lists. Whatever works works. But this period of letting my ideas develop is essential to my writing. Gradually my ideas take shape — and at a certain point I just know whether I have the right topic or approach or not. If I think I don't, I force myself to start over. If I do, then I make a plan for my essay. I can't really write without at least a skeleton plan that I can refer to: It stresses me out not to know where I'm headed. Before I get very far into my draft I try to stop and ask myself whether I should write something that is straight text — a regular academic essay — or whether this is a project that needs visuals or graphics. By the time I'm done with my plan, I usually have a pretty clear idea of where I'm going. Next I write a draft, possibly several drafts, before I do a final revision. — **Sara Steinman**

> Maybe it's just my personality, but when I get an assignment I have to leap right into it. It's hard to describe what I write at the beginning. It's part brainstorming, part planning, part drafting, part letting off steam. I just have to write to see what I think! I make notes to myself. What's the best evidence for this argument? Would a graph strengthen my point? What do I really think about this topic? I do most of this early writing

by hand because I need to be able to use arrows to connect ideas, circle important points, draw pictures. At this point, no one but me could understand what I've written. I take a break if I can, and then I sit down and reread everything I've written (it can be a lot). That's when I move to the computer. Even at this point I still basically write without doing a lot of conscious planning—I'm going on intuition. The time comes when I've got to change gears and become my own harshest critic. That's when I do a kind of planning in reverse. I might outline my draft, for instance, and see if the outline makes sense. It takes a lot of time and work for me to get to the point where my ideas have really jelled, and even then I've often got several drafts ahead of me. —**Eduardo Alvarez**

As a writer, I am first a thinker and then a doer. I've always had to think my ideas out in detail before I begin drafting. Even though for me this is essentially a mental process, it still involves words and images. I can't really describe it—I just keep thinking things through. It's always felt like a waste of time to me to sit down to write without having a clear idea of what I want to say. Since I have two children, I also don't have a lot of time to focus solely on my writing, so I try out different ideas while folding laundry, driving the kids to day care, after they're in bed. I'm a new media major, so part of my mental planning always involves thinking about media. If the assignment specifies the medium, then I always think how to make the best possible use of it. If it doesn't, then I run through all my options. Eventually I have a pretty clear sense of what I want to say and what medium will best convey it. Sometimes I make a plan before I get to work, especially if it's a long or complicated project. But sometimes I just begin writing. With some projects, my first draft is strong enough that I just have to edit it. Of course, that's not always the case. —**Wei Liao**

thinking rhetorically On the surface, these students' writing processes seem to have little in common. Actually, however, all involve the same three activities: planning, drafting, and revising. These activities don't necessarily occur in any set order. Wei Liao plans in her head and postpones making a written plan until after she has generated a rough draft, whereas Sara Steinman plans extensively before she writes her first word. To be successful, however, all these writers must sooner or later think rhetorically and make choices about their own situation as writers, their readers, their text, and the medium. Then they must try out these choices in their heads, on paper, or at the computer; evaluate the effects of these choices; and make appropriate changes in their drafts. Rather than being a magical or mysterious activity, writing is a process of planning, drafting, and revising.

Identifying Composing Styles

When designers and writers take their own composing processes seriously, they attempt to build on their strengths and recognize their limitations. They understand that they must vary their approach to writing depending on the task or situation. A student who prefers to spend a lot of time developing written or mental plans for an essay simply doesn't have that luxury when writing an in-class essay exam. For this reason, it's more accurate to refer to *writing processes* rather than *the writing process*. As a writer and designer, you must be pragmatic: You decide how to approach a project based on such factors as the nature and importance of the task, the schedule, the nature and demands of the medium, the experience you have with a particular kind of writing, and so on. Most experienced writers and designers do, however, have a preferred way of managing the composing process.

HEAVY PLANNERS.   Like Wei Liao, heavy planners generally plan their writing so carefully in their heads that their first drafts are often more like other writers' second or third drafts. As a consequence, they revise less intensively and less frequently than other students. Many of these students have disciplined themselves so that they can think about their writing in all sorts of places—on the subway, at work, in the garden pulling weeds, or in the car driving to and from school.

Some heavy planners write in this way because they prefer to; others develop this strategy out of necessity. Wei Liao, for instance, says that she simply has to do a great deal of her writing in her head because she's a mother as well as a student, and at home she often has to steal spare moments to work on her writing. As a result, she's learned to use every opportunity to think about her writing while she drives, cooks, or relaxes with her family.

HEAVY REVISERS.   Like Eduardo Alvarez, heavy revisers use the act of writing itself to find out what they want to say. When faced with a writing task, they prefer to sit down at a desk or computer and just begin writing.

Heavy revisers often state that writing their ideas out in a sustained spurt of activity reassures them that they have something to say and helps them avoid frustration. These students may not seem to plan because they begin drafting so early. Actually, however, their planning occurs as they draft and especially as they revise. Heavy revisers spend a great deal of time revising their initial drafts. To do so effectively, they must be able to read their work critically and, often, discard substantial portions of first drafts. For one example of heavy revision in action, see the accompanying photo of President Obama holding a heavily revised text of one of his speeches.

As you've probably realized, in both of these styles of composing, one of the components of the writing process is apparently abbreviated. Heavy planners don't seem to revise as extensively as other writers. Actually,

President Barack Obama and Speechwriter John Farreau Edit a Speech on Health Care, Sept. 9, 2009.

however, they plan (and, in effect, revise) so thoroughly early in the process that they often don't need to revise as intensively later. Similarly, heavy revisers may not seem to plan; in fact, though, once they write their rough drafts, they plan and revise simultaneously and, often, extensively.

SEQUENTIAL COMPOSERS.   A third general style of composing is exemplified by Sara Steinman. These writers might best be called sequential composers because they devote roughly equivalent amounts of time to planning, drafting, and revising. Rather than trying out their ideas and planning their writing mentally, as heavy planners do, sequential composers typically rely on written notes and plans to give shape and force to their ideas. And unlike heavy revisers, sequential composers need to have greater control over form and subject matter as they draft.

Sequential composers' habit of allotting time for planning, drafting, and revising helps them deal with the inevitable anxieties of writing. Like heavy revisers, sequential composers need the reassurance of seeing their ideas written down: Generating a volume of notes and plans gives them the confidence to begin drafting. Sequential composers may not revise as extensively as heavy revisers, for they generally draft more slowly, reviewing their writing as they proceed. But revision is nevertheless an important part of their composing process. Like most writers, sequential composers need a break from drafting to be able to critique their own words and ideas.

Composing Styles: Advantages and Disadvantages

COMPOSING STYLE	ADVANTAGES	DISADVANTAGES
Heavy planners	■ The writer spends less time drafting and revising.	■ The writer may lose her or his train of thought if unexpected interruptions occur. ■ The writer may miss out on fruitful explorations that result from reviewing notes, plans, or drafts. ■ The writer may face substantial difficulties if sentences and paragraphs look less coherent and polished on paper than they did in the writer's head.
Heavy revisers	■ The writer generates words and ideas quickly and voluminously. ■ The writer remains open to new options because of the frequency with which she or he rereads notes and drafts.	■ The writer may experience an emotional roller coaster as ideas develop (or fail to develop) through writing. ■ The writer must have the ability to critique her or his own writing ruthlessly. ■ The writer's work may suffer if he or she fails to allow adequate time for rewriting or, if necessary, for starting over.
Sequential composers	■ The writer has more control over the writing process because so much time is spent planning, drafting, and revising. ■ Writers are unlikely to mistake a quickly generated collection of ideas or a brainstormed plan for adequate preparation.	■ The writer may become too rigidly dependent on a highly structured writing process. ■ The writer may waste valuable time developing detailed plans when he or she is actually ready to begin drafting.

There is one other common way of managing the writing process, though it might best be described as management by avoidance — procrastination. All writers occasionally procrastinate, but if you habitually put off writing a first draft until you have time only for a final draft (and this at 3 A.M. on the day your essay is due), your chances of success are minimal. Though you may have invented good reasons for putting off writing ("I write better under pressure"; "I can't write until I have all my easier assignments done first"), procrastination makes it difficult for you to manage the writing process in an efficient and effective manner.

Is procrastination always harmful? Might it not sometimes reflect a period of necessary incubation, of unconscious but still productive planning? Here's what Holly Hardin — a thoughtful student writer — discovered when she reflected about her experiences as a writer.

> For me, sometimes procrastination isn't really procrastination (or so I tell myself). Sometimes what I label procrastination is really planning. The trouble is that I don't always know when it's one or the other.
>
> How do I procrastinate? Let me count the ways. I procrastinate by doing good works (helping overtime at my job, cleaning house, aiding and abetting a variety of causes). I procrastinate by absorbing myself in a purely selfish activity (reading paperbacks, watching TV, going to movies). I procrastinate by visiting with friends, talking on the telephone, prolonging chance encounters. I procrastinate by eating and drinking (ice cream, coffee, cookies — all detrimental). Finally, I procrastinate by convincing myself that this time of day is not when I write well. I'd be much better off, I sometimes conclude, taking a nap. So I do.
>
> Part of my difficulty is that I can see a certain validity in most of my reasons for procrastinating. There are some times of day when my thoughts flow better. I have forced myself to write papers in the past when I just didn't feel ready. Not only were the papers difficult to write, they were poorly written, inarticulate papers. Even after several rewrites, they were merely marginal. I would much rather write when I am at my mental best.
>
> I need to balance writing with other activities. The trouble is — just how to achieve the perfect balance!

Holly's realistic appraisal of the role that procrastination plays in her writing process should help her distinguish between useful incubation and unhelpful procrastination. Unlike students who tell themselves that they should never procrastinate — and then do so anyway, feeling guilty every moment — Holly knows that she has to consider a variety of factors before she decides to invite a friend over, bake a batch of chocolate chip cookies, or take a much-needed nap.

NOTE FOR MULTILINGUAL WRITERS

If your first or home language is not English, you may be familiar with different approaches to the composing process of planning, drafting, and revising. Educational systems throughout the world have different approaches to writing and to the teaching of writing. In thinking about your writing process as a student in college, reflect on how your previous experiences as a writer enhance or interfere with your efforts to compose in standard written English. (Different approaches to revision may be especially relevant.) You may want to discuss the results of your reflection with your teacher or a tutor in the writing center.

Analyzing Your Composing Process

The poet William Stafford once commented that "a writer is not so much someone who has something to say as he is someone who has found a process that will bring about new things he would not have thought if he had not started to say them." Stafford's remarks emphasize the importance of developing a workable writing process—a repertoire of strategies that you can draw on in a variety of situations.

thinking rhetorically

FOR COLLABORATION

Meet with classmates to discuss your responses to the quiz on pp. 44–45. Begin by having each person state two important things he or she learned as a result of completing the quiz. (Appoint a recorder to write down each person's statements.) Once all members of your group have spoken, ask the recorder to read their statements aloud. Were any statements repeated by more than one member of the group? Working as a group, formulate two conclusions about the writing process that you would like to share with the class. (Avoid vague and general assertions, such as "Writing is difficult.") Be prepared to discuss your conclusions with your classmates.

Writing is a *process*, and stopping to think about your own composing process can prove illuminating. One of my students, for example, formulated an analogy that helped us all think fruitfully about how the writing process works. "Writing," he said, "is actually a lot like sports." Writing—like sports? Let's see what this comparison reveals about the writing process.

Quiz: Analyzing Your Composing Process

You can use the following questions to analyze your composing process. Your teacher may ask you to respond to some or all of these questions in writing.

1. **What is your general attitude toward writing?**
   a. love it   b. hate it   c. somewhere in between
   How do you think this attitude affects your writing?

2. **Which of the composing styles described in this chapter best describes the way you compose?**
   a. heavy planner   b. heavy reviser   c. sequential composer   d. procrastinator
   If none seems to fit you, how do you compose?

3. **How do you know when you are ready to begin writing?**
   a. I have a "start-up" method or ritual.
   b. I just feel ready.
   c. It's the night before the assignment is due.
   If you have a "start-up" method, what is it? If you don't have a ritual, do you think establishing one would help?

4. **How long do you typically work on your writing at any one time?**
   a. less than an hour   b. from one to two hours   c. more than two hours
   Do you think you spend about the right amount of time at a given stretch, or do you think you should generally do more (or less)? Why?

5. **Are you more likely to write an essay**
   a. in a single sitting?   b. over a number of days (or weeks)?
   Have you had success doing it this way? How do you think adjusting your approach would affect the essays you end up writing?

6. **Do you have any writing habits and rituals?**
   a. yes   b. no
   If you answered "yes," what are they? Which are productive, and which interfere with your writing process? If you answered "no," can you think of any habits you would like to develop?

7. **How often do you import visuals and graphics into texts you are composing?**

   a. sometimes   b. never   c. always

   If you do use visuals and graphics, do you enjoy doing so? Find it a challenge? Take it for granted? How have your instructors received your efforts?

8. **What planning and revising strategies do you use?**

   a.   specific strategies (e.g., outlining, listing, etc.)
   b.   general strategies (e.g., "I think out a plan, and I reread what I've written.")
   c.   no strategies I'm aware of

   How do you know when you have spent enough time planning and revising?

9. **If your first or home language is not English, how does knowing two or more languages influence your writing process?**

   a. a great deal   b. somewhat   c. not at all

   If you do have a second language, reflect on how it affects your writing in English (or why you think it doesn't). Also consider: What language do you typically think in? In what language do you freewrite, brainstorm, or make notes?

10. **What role do exchanges with others (conversations, responses from peers or tutors) play in your writing?**

    a. an important role   b. an occasional role   c. no role

    Would you like to make more use of exchanges like these? Why or why not?

11. **How do you procrastinate? (Be honest! All writers procrastinate occasionally.)**

    a. I procrastinate very little.
    b. I start later than I should, but I get the job done.
    c. I don't start until it's too late to do a good job.

    Do you need to change your habits in this respect? If you do need to change them, how will you do so?

12. **Thinking in general about the writing you do, what do you find most rewarding and satisfying about writing? Most difficult and frustrating? Why?**

WRITING AND SPORTS ARE BOTH PERFORMANCE SKILLS   You may know who won every Wimbledon since 1980, but if you don't actually play tennis, you're not a tennis player—just somebody who knows a lot about tennis. Similarly, you can know a lot about writing, but to demonstrate (and improve) your skills, you must *write*.

WRITING AND SPORTS BOTH REQUIRE INDIVIDUALS TO MASTER COMPLEX SKILLS AND TO PERFORM THESE SKILLS IN AN ALMOST INFINITE NUMBER OF SITUATIONS.   Athletes must learn specific skills, plays, or maneuvers, but they can never execute them routinely or thoughtlessly. Writers must be similarly resourceful and flexible. You can learn the principles of effective essay organization, for instance, and you may write a number of essays that are well organized. Nevertheless, each time you sit down to write a new essay, you have to consider your options and make new choices. This is a primary reason that smart writers don't rely on formulas or rules but instead use rhetorical sensitivity to analyze and respond to each situation.

thinking rhetorically

EXPERIENCED ATHLETES AND WRITERS KNOW THAT A POSITIVE ATTITUDE IS ESSENTIAL.   Some athletes psych themselves up before a game or competition, often using music, meditation, or other personal routines. But any serious athlete knows that's only part of what having a positive attitude means. It also means running five miles when you're already tired at three or doing twelve repetitions during weight training when you're exhausted and no one else would know if you did only eight. A positive attitude is equally important in writing. If you approach a writing task with a negative attitude ("I never was good at writing"), you create obstacles for yourself. Having a positive, open attitude is essential in mastering tennis, skiing—and writing.

TO MAINTAIN A HIGH LEVEL OF SKILL, BOTH ATHLETES AND WRITERS NEED FREQUENT PRACTICE AND EFFECTIVE COACHING.   "In sports," a coach once said, "you're either getting better or getting worse." Without practice—which for a writer means both reading and writing—your writing skills will slip (as will your confidence). Likewise, coaching is essential in writing because it's hard to distance yourself from your own work. Coaches—your writing instructor, a tutor (or writing assistant) at a writing center, or a fellow student—can help you gain a fresh perspective on your writing and make useful suggestions about revision as well.

EXPERIENCED ATHLETES AND WRITERS CONTINUOUSLY SET NEW GOALS FOR THEMSELVES.   Athletes continuously set new challenges for themselves and analyze their performance. They know that coaches can help but that *they* are ultimately the ones performing. Experienced writers know this too, so they look for opportunities to practice their writing. And they don't measure their success simply by a grade. They see their writing always as work in progress. Successful athletes, like successful writers, know that they must *commit* to a process that will enable them to perform at the highest possible level.

> For a case study of student Daniel Stiepleman's process of interacting with a text, exploring ideas, and developing an essay for a first-year writing class, see "Composing an Academic Argument: A Case Study of One Student's Writing Process" (Chapter 6, pp. 152–68).

Writing Communities

Finding a Community

For many people, one big difference between writing and sports is that athletes often belong to teams. Writers, they think, work in lonely isolation. In fact, this romanticized image of the writer struggling alone until inspiration strikes is both inaccurate and unhelpful. If you take a careful look at the day-to-day writing that people do, you quickly recognize that many people in business, industry, academia, and other professions work as part of one or more teams to produce written texts. In many cases, these individuals' ability to work effectively with others is key to a successful career. Those who write for school, community-based projects, or even for personal enrichment also often turn to others for ideas and advice.

Even when writers do a good deal of their composing alone, they often find it helpful to talk with others before and while writing. A group of neighbors writing a petition to their city council requesting that a speed bump be installed on their street might well ask one person to compose the petition. In order to do a good job, the writer would have to talk extensively with her neighbors to generate the strongest ideas possible. She would probably also present drafts of the petition for her neighbors' review and approval.

Most writers alternate between periods of independent activity, composing alone at a computer or desk, and periods of social interaction—meeting with friends, colleagues, or team members for information, advice, or responses to drafts. They may also correspond with others in their field, or they may get in touch with people doing similar work through reading, research, or online technologies. These relationships will help them learn new ideas, improve their skills, and share their interest and enthusiasm.

Sometimes these relationships are formal and relatively permanent. Many poets and fiction writers, for instance, meet regularly to discuss work in progress. Perhaps more commonly, writers' networks are informal and shifting, though no less vital. A new manager in a corporation, for instance, may find one or two people with sound judgment and good writing skills to review important letters and reports. Similarly, students working on a major project for a class may meet informally but regularly to compare notes and provide mutual support.

Online technologies and the Web have increased the opportunity for writers to work collaboratively. Using online spaces, from course Web sites to blogs and public writing communities such as Writing.com ("for writers and readers of all interests and skill levels"), writers everywhere are sharing their writing and getting responses to works in progress.

Working Collaboratively

Because you're in the same class and share the same assignments and concerns, you and your classmates constitute a natural community of writers. Whether your instructor makes it a requirement or not, you should explore the possibility of forming a peer group or joining one that already exists. In order to work effectively, however, you and your peers need to develop or strengthen the skills that will contribute to effective group work.

As you prepare to work collaboratively, remember that people have different styles of learning and interacting. Some of these differences represent individual preferences: Some students work out their ideas as they talk, for instance, while others prefer to think through their ideas before speaking. Other differences are primarily cultural and thus reflect deeply embedded social practices and preferences. Effective groups are pragmatic and task oriented, but they balance a commitment to getting the job done with patience and flexibility. They value diversity and find ways to ensure that *all* members can comfortably participate in and benefit from group activities.

Effective groups also take care to articulate group goals and monitor group processes. Sometimes this monitoring is intuitive and informal. But sometimes a more formal process is helpful. If you're part of a group that meets regularly, you might begin meetings by having each person state one way in which the group is working well and one way in which it could be improved. If a problem such as a dominating or nonparticipating member is raised, deal with it immediately. The time spent responding to these comments and suggestions will ensure that your group is working effectively.

Group activities such as peer response and collaborative troubleshooting can help improve your writing ability and prepare you for on-the-job teamwork. Remember, though, that groups are a bit like friendships or marriages. They develop and change, and they require care and attention. You have to be committed to keeping the group going, be alert to signs of potential trouble, and be willing to talk problems out.

Students juggling coursework, jobs, families, and other activities can sometimes find it difficult to get together or to take the time to read and respond to one another's writing. Getting together with classmates to share your writing is well worth the effort it takes. If it proves impossible, however,

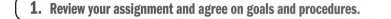

Guidelines for Group Work

1. Review your assignment and agree on goals and procedures.

> *Doing a brief activity in class?* Limit yourselves to a few minutes to set goals.

> *Doing an extended project with meetings outside of class?* Take ten to fifteen minutes to set goals.

2. Assign roles, but be flexible.
Effective group members are willing to assume multiple roles as needed.

- *Group leaders* assign tasks, set priorities, and take responsibility for progress.

- *Consensus builders* facilitate communication and mediate conflicts.

- *Task masters* try to keep everyone focused and productive.

3. Encourage productive conflict.
Capitalize on the diverse perspectives and strategies that people bring to a problem.

- *Encourage the discussion of new ideas.*

- *Consider alternative approaches to your subject.*

- *Don't be afraid to disagree.* Just be sure that the discussion remains friendly and focused on the task at hand.

you may have one important alternative: a campus writing center. Many colleges and universities have established writing centers as places where you can go to talk with others about your writing, get help with specific writing problems, or find answers to questions you may have. If your campus does have a writing center, take advantage of the opportunity to get an informed response to your work.

|||||||||||||||||||||||||||||||||||||||||||||||||||||||||||||||||||||||||||||||||||||

FOR COLLABORATION

Meet with your group to discuss how you can most effectively work together. Begin by exchanging names, phone numbers, and email addresses, and take time just to get to know each other. You might also see if your group can formulate some friendly rules to guide group activities. (You might all agree, for instance, to notify at least one member if you can't make a meeting.) Be sure to write these rules down and consult them as you work together. Try to anticipate problems, such as coordinating schedules, and discuss how to resolve them.

FOR EXPLORATION

If your campus has a writing center, make an appointment to interview a tutor (sometimes also called a writing assistant or peer consultant) about the services the center provides. You may also want to ask the tutor about his or her own experiences as a writer. Your instructor may ask you to present the results of your interview orally or to write a summary of your discussion.

FOR THOUGHT, DISCUSSION, AND WRITING

1. Now that you have read this chapter, make a list of several goals you'd like to accomplish in your composition class this term. What would you most like to learn or improve? What would you like to change about your writing process? Then write a paragraph or two discussing how you plan to achieve these goals.

2. You can learn a great deal about your own composing process by observing yourself as you write. To do so, follow these steps:

    ■ Choose an upcoming writing project to study. Before beginning this project, reflect on its demands. How much time do you expect to spend working on this project, and how do you anticipate allocating your time? What challenges does this project hold for you? What strengths and resources do you bring to this project?

    ■ As you work on the project, use a process log to keep track of how you spend your time. Include a record in this log of when you started and ended each work session, as well as a description of your activities and notes commenting on your process. What went well? What surprised you? What gave you problems? What might you do differently next time?

■ After you have completed the project, draw on your prewriting analysis and process log to write a case study of this project. As you do so, consider questions such as these: To what extent was your prewriting analysis of your project accurate? How did you actually allocate your time when working on this project? What strategies did you rely on most heavily? What went well with your writing? What was difficult? Conclude by reflecting about what you have learned from this case study about yourself as a writer.

3. All writers procrastinate occasionally—some just procrastinate more effectively than others. After brainstorming or freewriting about your favorite ways of procrastinating, write a humorous or serious essay on procrastination.

4. The Exploration activities on pp. 34 and 35 encouraged you to reflect on your assumptions about writing and your experiences as a writer. Drawing on these activities and on the rest of the chapter, write an essay in which you reflect on this subject. You may choose to write about pivotal incidents in your experiences as a writer, using particular occasions to support the general statements you make about your experiences.

| | | | | | | | | | | | | | | | | | | | | | | | | | | | | | | | | | | | | | | | | | | | | | | | | | | | | | | | | | | | | | | | | | | | | | | | | | | | | | | | | | | | | | | | | | |

Analyzing Rhetorical Situations

Whenever you write—whether you're word processing an essay or designing a brochure for a student organization—you are writing in the context of a specific rhetorical situation involving you as the writer, who you're writing for, what you're writing, and the medium you're using to share what you have written. Each rhetorical situation comes with unique opportunities and demands: A management trainee writing a memo to her supervisor, for example, faces different challenges than an investigative journalist working on a story for the *New York Times* or a student writing an essay for a history class. Successful writers know that they need to exhibit rhetorical sensitivity—an understanding of the relationships among writer, reader, text, and medium—to help them make decisions as they write and revise.

In this chapter of *The Academic Writer*, you will learn how to ask questions about your rhetorical situation—questions that will enable you to determine the most fruitful way of approaching your topic and of responding to the needs and expectations of your readers. You will also learn how to recognize the textual conventions that characterize different communities of language users. This kind of rhetorically sensitive reading is particularly helpful when you are learning new forms of writing—which is the case, for example, when you enter college or begin a new job.

Learning to Analyze Your Rhetorical Situation

thinking
rhetorically

Rhetoric involves four key elements: writer, reader, text, and medium. When you think about these elements and pose questions about the options available to you as a writer, you are analyzing your rhetorical situation.

The process of analyzing your rhetorical situation challenges you to look both within and without. Your intended meaning—what you want to communicate—is certainly important, as is your purpose for writing. But unless you're writing solely for yourself in a journal or notebook, you can't ignore

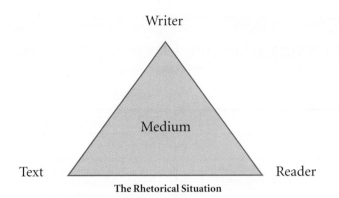

The Rhetorical Situation

your readers or your situation. You also need to consider which medium will best convey your ideas. Both at school and on the job, sometimes your medium will be predetermined; at other times, however, you will have options. Analyzing your rhetorical situation helps you respond creatively as a writer and yet keeps you aware of limits on your freedom.

In your daily life, you regularly analyze your rhetorical situation when you communicate with others — though you most often do this unconsciously and intuitively. Imagine, for instance, that you've been meaning to contact a close friend. Should you call, email, text, send a handwritten note, or contact him some other way? The answer depends on your situation. If you just want to let your friend know that you're thinking of him, you might choose text or

NOTE FOR MULTILINGUAL WRITERS

This chapter's approach to rhetoric and rhetorical sensitivity is grounded in the Western rhetorical tradition. Other traditions hold different values and assumptions about communication. For example, if part of your education took place in a non-Western culture, you may have learned an approach to communication that values maintaining communal harmony as much as (or more than) individual self-expression, which is highly valued in Western cultures. For some raised in non-Western cultures, English as it is written in school, business, and everyday contexts may seem abrupt and even rude. As a writer learning to communicate in different languages and communities, you need to understand the assumptions held by writers who are grounded in the Western rhetorical tradition — but you do not need to abandon your own culture's values. Your writing (and your thinking) will be enriched when you learn how to draw on *all* the rhetorical sensitivity that you have gained as a speaker, listener, writer, and reader.

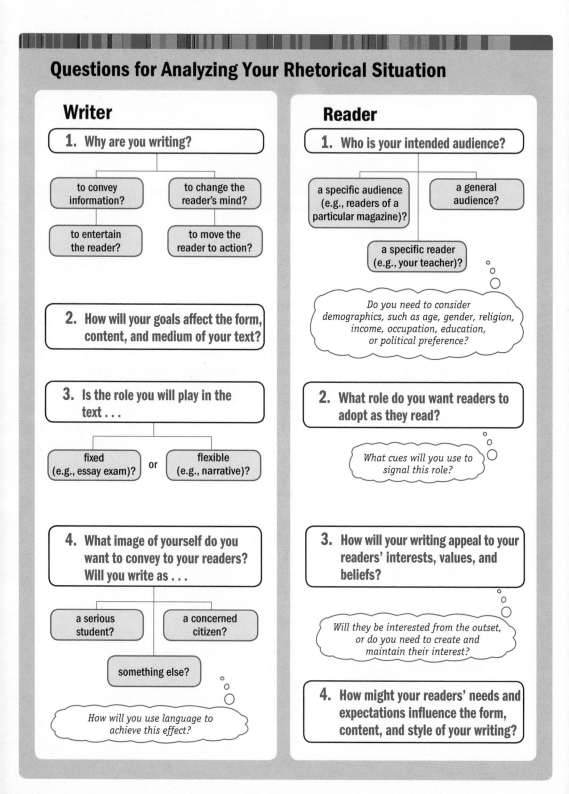

Questions for Analyzing Your Rhetorical Situation

Writer

1. **Why are you writing?**
   - to convey information?
   - to entertain the reader?
   - to change the reader's mind?
   - to move the reader to action?

2. **How will your goals affect the form, content, and medium of your text?**

3. **Is the role you will play in the text . . .**
   - fixed (e.g., essay exam)? **or** flexible (e.g., narrative)?

4. **What image of yourself do you want to convey to your readers? Will you write as . . .**
   - a serious student?
   - a concerned citizen?
   - something else?

   How will you use language to achieve this effect?

Reader

1. **Who is your intended audience?**
   - a specific audience (e.g., readers of a particular magazine)?
   - a general audience?
   - a specific reader (e.g., your teacher)?

   Do you need to consider demographics, such as age, gender, religion, income, occupation, education, or political preference?

2. **What role do you want readers to adopt as they read?**

   What cues will you use to signal this role?

3. **How will your writing appeal to your readers' interests, values, and beliefs?**

   Will they be interested from the outset, or do you need to create and maintain their interest?

4. **How might your readers' needs and expectations influence the form, content, and style of your writing?**

Questions for Analyzing Your Rhetorical Situation

Text

1. How much freedom do you have in deciding on form and content?

Are you responding to an *assignment*?

If so, does it dictate form and/or content?

What *genre* are you writing in? Are its styles and conventions . . .

rigidly defined (as in lab reports)? **or** flexible (as in a narrative or profile)?

Does your subject require certain kinds of evidence or exploration of certain issues?

2. Would it help you to look at examples of this kind of writing written by other people?

If so, where can you find the best examples of such writing?

Medium

1. How much freedom do you have in deciding what medium to use?

Are you responding to an *assignment*?

If so, does it limit your choice of media?

Do you face *practical constraints*—such as time, expertise, and expense—that might affect your choice of medium?

Does the *kind* of text you're writing make some media more appropriate than others?

2. What expectations might your audience have in terms of media?

Might some media be more *accessible* to your audience than others?

Might your audience be more *comfortable* with some media than with others?

email because their ease and informality suit this purpose well. If your friend maintains a Facebook page, you might visit his wall, read some posts to see what he's been up to, and then leave a greeting. But what if you're writing because you've just learned of a death in your friend's family? The seriousness of this situation and its personal nature might prompt you to send a card with a handwritten note instead.

Using Your Rhetorical Analysis to Guide Your Writing

Effective writers draw on their rhetorical sensitivity to determine the most effective ways to communicate with readers. Often, writers do this without thinking: The student deciding how best to get in touch with a friend didn't consciously run through a mental checklist but rather drew on his intuitive understanding of his situation. However, when you face the challenge of new and more difficult kinds of writing, as you do in college, it helps to analyze your rhetorical situation consciously.

||||||||||||||||||||||||||||||||||||||||||||||||||||||||||||||||||||||||||||||||||||

FOR EXPLORATION

Imagine that you need to compose the following texts:

- An application for an internship in your major
- A flyer for a march you are organizing to protest a tuition increase
- A response to a film that you viewed in class, posted to an online discussion board
- A substantial research-based essay for a class you are taking
- A status update for your Facebook page

Spend a few minutes thinking about how you would approach these different writing situations, and write a brief description of each, using the following questions:

- What is your role as writer? Your purpose for writing?
- What image of yourself do you wish to present? How will you create this image?
- How will your readers influence your writing?
- How will the medium you use affect your communication?
- What role, if any, should images, graphics, and multimedia play?

||||||||||||||||||||||||||||||||||||||||||||||||||||||||||||||||||||||||||||||||||||

Setting Preliminary Goals

Before beginning a major writing project, you may find it helpful to write a brief analysis of your rhetorical situation, or you may simply review these questions mentally. Doing so can help you determine your preliminary intentions or goals as a writer. (Your intentions will often shift as you write. That's fine. As you write, you'll naturally revise your understanding of your rhetorical situation.) Despite its tentativeness, however, your analysis of your situation will give you a sense of direction and purpose.

In Chapter 3, you saw Mirlandra Ebert's response to the Exploration activity on p. 35. Rather than writing a letter about her experience as a writer, Mirlandra created a collage (see p. 36). Here is the analysis of her rhetorical situation that Mirlandra composed before creating her visually rich text.

Mirlandra Ebert's Analysis

Writer: The poster I will create is about who I am as a writer. There are many experiences that have shaped me and that will continue to shape me, but I don't have to cover all of them. I just need to decide which are the most important and focus on them. I need content that's understandable, but I don't just want to say "I am _____." I don't think I know what goes in the blank. As a person, sometimes I feel like I reinvent myself every day, almost as if I see myself from a different angle and then I interpret myself differently. I feel the same way as a writer. This poster assignment is an opportunity to express that aspect of my life. The most important role I see for myself as a writer here is to have a voice in this piece. It should be a contradictory, busy, and chaotic voice (busy in the sense of visually rich and active), but still convey strength and fluidity.

thinking rhetorically

Reader: My intended audience is my professor and my classmates. I want to create a text that everybody in my class can connect with in some way. Most of our class is just out of high school, but there are also nontraditional students who may engage differently with my work. I also need to be aware of gender issues. I need to think about how some aspects of my project, such as the flowered background, will come across. Although my audience is diverse, I think I can hold their interest because there will be so much going on in my poster.

Text: In terms of my text, I have a lot of freedom in this assignment as long as I stay focused on the main topic. The only conventions I need to address are issues of size and readability. I want to be careful to reflect my busy and varied "writing self" but in a way that's not too cluttered to make sense. I don't have to be logical, as I have to be in an essay, so I've got lots of flexibility here. I know I want to express what I've learned from teachers and then engage many smaller ideas about who I am as a writer that have to do with other parts of my life. Before I started on this project, I looked at other posters that students had created.

This was helpful, but I want to express my own ideas in my own way. Many examples I looked at used only words and images. I want to move beyond that and include physical objects that represent me.

Medium: In terms of medium, I'm working with the advantages and limitations of posterboard and collage. If I can attach something to posterboard, then it's OK. My audience may expect a basic 2-D poster with pictures and graphics, but I don't think it will create confusion or discomfort if I include other objects. So far I intend to attach a pen I like to write notes with, sticky notes of all sizes, some push pins, my favorite outlining paper, and a hair tie because I'm always messing with my hair when I write. I think these personal objects will make for a more interesting medium.

thinking
rhetorically

Here is another analysis of a rhetorical situation, this one by student Alia Sands, whose essay appears on pp. 61–64. Alia analyzed her situation as a writer by using the questions provided on pp. 54–55. She begins with some general reflections about her assignment.

Alia Sands's Analysis

I am writing an essay for my first-year writing class. The assignment asked us to read an essay by Richard Rodriguez titled "Aria." This essay is included in Rodriguez's literacy narrative *Hunger of Memory*. The assignment asked us to respond personally to Rodriguez's text but also to engage with and synthesize his assertions about bilingual education.

Writer: I am writing a personal narrative regarding my experiences as a half-Hispanic, half-Caucasian middle-school student in Marshalltown, Iowa. This narrative will respond to Richard Rodriguez's chapter "Aria" from *Hunger of Memory*. I hope that by using my own experience I can show how special programs for bilingual students, however well-intentioned, raise complicated questions and may have multiple (and unintended) consequences. My purpose in writing this piece is to engage with Rodriguez's text while also conveying my own story. As I am not an expert on bilingual education, my goal is to situate my experience in its particular context, demonstrating the effect Marshalltown's separation of Hispanic students from the general school population had on my sense of identity.

The image I wish to present of myself is of particular concern to me. I am not the child of immigrants. Unlike Rodriguez, I have not felt that I had to choose between a public and private language in order to succeed in school and work. I wish to portray my experiences as unique to myself and decidedly *not* indicative of all or even most Hispanic students, as many have struggled in ways I have not.

I will use language that is academic while appropriate to a general audience who may not be familiar with issues faced by Hispanic students in public schools in the United States. I do not wish to convey anger or bitterness for what I feel was an error on the part of the school, but I do wish to use language that emphasizes the gravity of the situation and how important I feel it is for schools to recognize how much is denied to students and how their sense of identity is affected when they are not included in mainstream instruction.

Reader: I am assuming that my readers are my instructor as well as my fellow students at Oregon State University. I assume that they are from diverse backgrounds; some of them may have had experiences similar to my own and some of them may be unfamiliar with issues of bilingual education or the feeling of not having a public language or identity. As issues pertaining to race and education are often sensitive ones, I'm hoping to communicate in a way that acknowledges differences in opinion while still taking a clear stance based upon my own experience and my understanding of Rodriguez's text. I am trying not to be reductive when it comes to complicated situations. I don't want to imply that I know what kind of education will be beneficial to everyone. I do hope to show how my experiences overlap with the ideas discussed by Rodriguez and how those experiences have led me to conclusions about what can happen when students are excluded, rather than included, in the use of public language.

Text: I only have a few pages to do the following: summarize Rodriguez's text; convey a meaningful story about my own experiences; and discuss the connections between the two. The length of the paper, then, will be a significant constraint. I will have to carefully edit my narrative, deciding on the most essential details to include, and also figure out what elements (examples, quotes, ideas) of Rodriguez's text I need to discuss. I will not be using multimedia or images, so I must engage my readers through my prose — I'll have to write clearly and succinctly because I have so little space, but I'll also need to use vivid language that will bring my experiences and other examples to life. (For example, I will be mentioning a movie, *Stand and Deliver*, which I was required to watch repeatedly in middle school. I will need to summarize its plot in order to convey its significance, but I'll also want to give readers a clear sense of what watching it felt like — the impression it made on me when I saw it for the first, second, third, etc., time.)

Medium: I currently am not choosing to include any images, graphics, or multimedia in my essay. If I were writing a research paper on this topic, I would probably include graphics or images that would help readers better understand the information I am presenting. As most of my paper will respond to and synthesize Rodriguez's work, I do not feel that images or graphs are necessary to help readers better understand my own experiences or those of Rodriguez.

Here is Alia's essay. As you read it, keep her analysis of her rhetorical situation clearly in mind. In what ways did her analysis inform the essay that she wrote?

Alia Sands
Professor Rhoads
Writing 121
May 1, 2013

A Separate Education

Bilingual education and support for nonnative English speakers in classrooms are widely debated topics in academia today. While some argue that students benefit from learning in their native languages, others, like writer Richard Rodriguez, argue that bilingual education deprives students of a shared public identity, which is critical to their full participation in civic life. In middle school, as a half-Hispanic student who only spoke English, I was surprised to find myself in a special class for Hispanic students. My experience in the class brought Rodriguez's misgivings about the effects of separate education vividly to life: Being excluded from mainstream instruction even for a few class periods a week caused me to reevaluate my identity and question whether or not I was actually a member of the broader community.

In the chapter "Aria" from *Hunger of Memory: The Education of Richard Rodriguez*, Richard Rodriguez discusses his own experience of second-language acquisition. Rodriguez, who describes himself as "socially disadvantaged—the son of working-class parents, both Mexican immigrants" (10), did not receive bilingual instruction and was actively discouraged by the nuns running his school from speaking Spanish at home. Though at first Rodriguez was reluctant to embrace English as his primary language because he could not believe "that English was [his] to use" (18), he grew increasingly comfortable with it. His experience learning English led him to believe that the common practice of separating students from mainstream classroom instruction and from that public language "dangerously . . . romanticize[s] public separateness and . . . trivialize[s] the dilemma of the socially disadvantaged" (27).

My story is different from Rodriguez's. My sister Hannah and I grew up in Marshalltown, Iowa, the children of a Hispanic mother and an Anglo father, both college-educated. In school, I remember at some point checking off a box identifying myself as "Hispanic." In sixth grade, I received a small slip of paper instructing me to go to a basement classroom after lunch rather than to math class. When I arrived at the classroom, my older sister, Hannah, and about ten other students—all of whom were Hispanic—were already there.

There was a large Hispanic population in Marshalltown; many recent immigrants were employed in farming as well as in a local meat-packing plant. While there weren't many Hispanic students in my middle school, there were enough for the district to feel it necessary to send an instructor who said she would help us "integrate" more fully into the general school population. We were "at risk," she said. She promised to help us to learn English and to value our home culture while also becoming meaningful parts of American culture.

Unfortunately, our instructor did not speak Spanish and assumed that none of us spoke English. In fact, more than three-fourths of the students in the class were bilingual, and those who weren't bilingual only spoke English. None of them spoke *only* Spanish. My older sister and I had never spoken Spanish; many of the other students were from Mexico and had only recently come to the United States, but they had improved their English throughout the school year attending regular classes and spoke enough English to understand what was said in classrooms. It was clear we were all being singled out based solely upon ethnicity. We had no idea that we were "at risk" until the instructor told us we were.

Statistics showed, she said, that most of us would not go to college. Many of us would drop out of school. She told us she sympathized with how uncomfortable we must be in class, not understanding English. Her first act as instructor was to go around the room pointing to objects and saying their names, drawing out the vowels slowly. Oooverhead projeeectoor. Blaaackboard. Liiight. She stopped in front of me and held up a pencil. My blank expression must have confirmed her suspicions about our substandard English skills, so she said "pencil" over and over again until I replied,

Sands 3

"Uh, pencil?" hoping she would go away. One of the boys across the room laughed loudly and said something in Spanish.

When our instructor moved to the next student to teach "notebook," I leaned over to a girl sitting at my table.

"What did he say?" I asked, pointing to the boy across the table.

"He said that stupid woman can't tell you don't speak Spanish."

He was right—but that was not the only thing she didn't seem to understand. We spent the next few weeks watching the movie *Stand and Deliver* over and over. *Stand and Deliver* is the story of how Jaime Escalante began teaching a remedial math class in East Los Angeles and developed a program that led his students to take and pass the AP calculus exam. Our teacher would beam happily after showing us the movie and would tell us that this movie was proof that we didn't need to cheat to excel. She told us we could stay in school, not join gangs, and not get pregnant. The implication, of course, was that because we were Hispanic, we were somehow more likely than others to cheat, to join gangs, and to have unprotected sex. The teacher, and the school, attempted to "empower" us by using stereotypical and racist assumptions about our knowledge of English and our abilities.

In "Aria," Rodriguez argues that his mastery of English represented a social change, not just a linguistic one: It made him a successful student and participant in the larger community (32). Rodriguez emphasizes the "public gain" that comes with language acquisition, advising that people be wary of those who "scorn assimilation" and discount the consequences of not having access to the public language of power and the public community (27). These consequences had most likely been considered at some point by the students in the Hispanic class I was a part of; the fact that the native Spanish speakers were all bilingual indicated their awareness of the importance of speaking English in order to function in and become part of the Marshalltown community. The instructor, however, continued to emphasize our difference from the larger community.

Unlike Rodriguez, before that class I had always had a sense of myself as part of the public community. I assumed I would go to college: If my family could not afford to send me, I would get scholarships and jobs to fund my education. I assumed that being a native speaker of English guaranteed me a place in the public community. Being put in the basement caused me to question these assumptions. I learned what I imagine other students in the classroom may have already known—that even if you were bilingual or spoke English perfectly, there was no guarantee that you would be considered part of the public community.

Richard Rodriguez describes how becoming part of public society is a process with both benefits and costs. He asserts that "while one suffers a diminished sense of *private* individuality by becoming assimilated into public society, such assimilation makes possible the achievement of *public* individuality" (26). This process of developing a public identity is not always a simple one, especially when it involves changes in language or in relationships. As my experience and Rodriguez's demonstrate, schools play an active role in shaping students' sense of themselves as individuals. With increasingly diverse student bodies like the one in my middle school, educators face the difficult question of how best to educate students from a variety of backgrounds, while at the same time helping all students become members of a broader public community.

I don't think my middle school had the answer. I don't, either, and I'm not sure there is a one-size-fits-all solution. What I am sure about is this: Educators in every community need to honestly evaluate what they're doing now, and then, working with students and their parents, find ways to help students realize their full potential, both as individuals *and* as members of the larger society.

Work Cited

Rodriguez, Richard. "Aria." *Hunger of Memory: The Education of Richard Rodriguez*. New York: Bantam, 1982. 9–41. Print.

Note: In an actual MLA-style paper, Works Cited entries start on a new page.

|||||||||||||||||||||||||||||||||||||||||||||||||||||||||||||||||||||||||||||||||||||||||

FOR EXPLORATION

To what extent does Alia Sands's essay achieve the goals she established for herself in her analysis of her rhetorical situation? Reread Alia's analysis, and then reread her essay. Keeping her analysis in mind, list three or four reasons that you believe Alia does or does not achieve her goals, and then find at least one passage in the essay that illustrates each of these statements. Finally, identify at least one way that Alia might strengthen her essay were she to revise it.

|||||||||||||||||||||||||||||||||||||||||||||||||||||||||||||||||||||||||||||||||||||||||

Using Aristotle's Three Appeals

Analyzing your rhetorical situation can provide information that will enable you to make crucial strategic, structural, and stylistic decisions about your writing. In considering how to use this information, you may find it helpful to employ what Aristotle (384–322 B.C.E.) characterized as the three appeals. According to Aristotle, when speakers and writers communicate with others, they draw on these three general appeals:

Logos, the appeal to reason

Pathos, the appeal to emotion, values, and beliefs

Ethos, the appeal to the credibility of the speaker or writer

As a writer, you appeal to logos when you focus on the logical presentation of your subject by providing evidence and examples in support of your ideas. You appeal to pathos when you use the resources of language to engage your readers emotionally with your subject or appeal to their values, beliefs, or needs. And you appeal to ethos when you create an image of yourself, a persona, that encourages readers to accept or act on your ideas.

These appeals correspond to three of the four basic elements of rhetoric (writer, reader, and text). In appealing to ethos, you focus on the writer's character as implied in the text; in appealing to pathos, on the interaction of writer and reader; and in appealing to logos, on the logical statements about the subject made in your particular text. In some instances, you may rely predominantly on one of these appeals. A student writing a technical report, for instance, will typically emphasize scientific or technical evidence (logos), not emotional or personal appeals. More often, however, you'll draw on all three appeals in order to create a fully persuasive document. A journalist writing a column on child abuse might open with several examples designed to gain her readers' attention and to convince them of the importance of this issue (pathos). Although she may rely primarily on information about the

thinking
rhetorically

negative consequences of child abuse (logos), she will undoubtedly also endeavor to create an image of herself as a caring, serious person (ethos), one whose analysis of a subject like child abuse should be trusted.

This journalist might also use images to help convey her point. One or more photographs of physically abused children would certainly appeal to pathos. To call attention to the large number of children who are physically abused (and thus bolster the logos of her argument), she might present important statistics in a chart or graph. She might also include photographs of well-known advocates for child protection to represent the trustworthiness of her report's insights (and contribute to ethos). In so doing, the journalist is combining words, images, and graphics to maximum effect.

In the following example, Brandon Barrett, a chemistry major at Oregon State University, uses Aristotle's three appeals to determine how best to approach an essay assignment for a first-year writing class that asks him to explain what his major is and why he chose it.

In presenting the assignment, Barrett's teacher informed students that their two- to three-page essays should include "information about your major that is new to your readers; in other words, it should not simply repeat the OSU catalog. Rather, it should be your unique perspective, written in clear, descriptive language." The teacher concluded with this advice: "Have fun with this assignment. Consider your audience (it should be this class unless you specify a different audience). And remember Aristotle's three appeals. How will your essay employ the appeals of logos, pathos, and ethos? As you write, keep these two questions in mind: What is your purpose? What do you hope to achieve with your audience?" Brandon's essay is preceded by his analysis of his rhetorical situation and of his essay's appeals to logos, pathos, and ethos.

Brandon Barrett's Analysis

thinking rhetorically

I'm writing this essay to explain how I made the most important decision in my life to date: what to major in while in college. I want to explain this not only to my audience but to myself as well, for bold decisions frequently need to be revisited in light of new evidence. There are those for whom the choice of major isn't much of a choice at all. For them, it's a *vocation*, in the strict *Webster's* definition of the word: a summons, a calling.

I'm not one of those people, and for me the decision was fraught with anxiety. Do I still believe that I made the right choice? Yes, I do, and I want my essay not only to reflect how serious I feel this issue to be but also to convey the confidence that I finally achieved.

Writer: I'm writing this as a student in a first-year writing class, so while the assignment gives me a lot of flexibility and room for creativity, I need to remember that finally this is an academic essay.

Reader: My primary reader is my teacher in the sense that she's the one who will grade my essay, but she has specified that I should consider the other students in the class as my audience. This tells me that I need to find ways to make the essay interesting to them and to find common ground with them.

Text: This assignment calls for me to write an academic essay. This assignment is different, though, from writing an essay in my history class or a lab report in my chemistry class. Since this is based on my personal experience, I have more freedom than I would in these other classes. One of the most challenging aspects of this essay is its limited page length. It would actually be easier to write a longer essay on why I chose chemistry as my major.

Medium: Our assignment is to write an academic essay. While I could potentially import graphics into my text, I should only do so if it will enrich the content of the essay.

After analyzing his rhetorical situation, Brandon decided to use Aristotle's three appeals to continue and extend his analysis.

Logos: This essay is about my own opinions and experiences and therefore contains no statistics and hard facts. What it should contain, though, are legitimate reasons for choosing the major I did. My choice should be shown as following a set of believable driving forces.

Pathos: Since my audience is composed of college students, I'll want to appeal to their own experiences regarding their choice of major and the sometimes conflicting emotions that accompany such a decision. Specifically, I want to focus on the confidence and relief that come when you've finally made up your mind. My audience will be able to relate to these feelings, and it will make the essay more relevant and real to them.

Ethos: The inherent danger in writing an essay about my desire to be a chemistry major is that I may be instantly labeled as boring or a grind. I want to dispel this image as quickly as possible, and humor is always a good way to counter such stereotypes. On the other hand, this is a serious subject, and the infusion of too much humor will portray me as somebody who hasn't given this too much thought. I want to strike a balance between being earnest and being human. I also need to write as clearly and confidently as I can manage. If I seem insincere or uncertain, then my audience may question the honesty of my essay.

Brandon Barrett
Professor Auston
Writing 101
Jan. 20, 2013

The All-Purpose Answer

When I was a small child, I would ask my parents, as children are apt to do, questions concerning the important things in my life. "Why is the sky blue?" "Why do my Cocoa Puffs turn the milk in my cereal bowl brown?" If I asked my father questions such as these, he always provided detailed technical answers that left me solemnly nodding my head in complete confusion. But if I asked my mother, she would simply shrug her shoulders and reply, "Something to do with chemistry, I guess." Needless to say, I grew up with a healthy respect for the apparently boundless powers of chemistry. Its responsibilities seemed staggeringly wide-ranging, and I figured that if there was a God he was probably not an omnipotent deity but actually the Original Chemist.

In my early years, I regarded chemistry as nothing less than magic at work. So what is chemistry, if not magic — or a parent's response to a curious child's persistent questions? Chemistry is the study of the elements, how those elements combine, how they interact with one another, and how all this affects Joe Average down the street. Chemists, then, study not magic but microscopic bits of matter all busily doing their thing.

When all those bits of matter can be coerced into doing something that humans find useful or interesting — like giving off massive quantities of energy, providing lighting for our homes, or making Uncle Henry smell a little better — then the chemists who produced the desired effect can pat themselves on the back and maybe even feel just a little bit like God.

Chemists solve problems, whether the problem is a need for a new medicine or a stronger plastic bowl to pour our Wheaties into. They develop new materials and study existing ones through a variety of techniques that have been refined over the decades. Chemists also struggle to keep the powers of chemistry in check by finding ways to reduce pollution that can

Barrett 2

be a by-product of chemical processes, to curb the dangers of nuclear waste, and to recycle used materials.

Chemistry is a dynamic field, constantly experiencing new discoveries and applications—heady stuff, to be sure, but heady stuff with a purpose.

Chemistry isn't a static, sleepy field of dusty textbooks, nor does it—forgive me, geologists—revolve around issues of questionable importance, such as deviations in the slope of rock strata. Those who know little about chemistry sometimes view it as dull, but I am proud to say that I plan to earn my B.S. in chemistry. And from there, who knows? That's part of the beauty of chemistry. After graduating from college, I could do any number of things, from research to medical school. The study of chemistry is useful in its own right, but it is also great preparation for advanced study in other fields since it encourages the development of logical thought and reasoning. In one sense, logical thought (not to mention research and medical school) may seem a giant step away from a child's idle questions. But as chemistry demonstrates, perhaps those questions weren't so childish after all.

|||||||||||||||||||||||||||||||||||||||||||||||||||||||||||||||||||||||||||||||||||||||||||

FOR EXPLORATION

Where can you see evidence of Brandon's attention to Aristotle's three appeals? Write one or two paragraphs responding to this question. Be sure to include examples in your analysis.

|||||||||||||||||||||||||||||||||||||||||||||||||||||||||||||||||||||||||||||||||||||||||||

Analyzing Textual Conventions

When you analyze your rhetorical situation, you ask commonsense questions about your writing purpose and situation. As you do so, you draw on your previous experiences as a writer, reader, speaker, and listener to make judgments about the text's purpose, subject matter, and form. For familiar kinds of texts, these judgments occur almost automatically. No one had to teach

thinking
rhetorically

you, for instance, that a letter applying for a job should be written differently than a quick text asking a friend to meet up for pizza: Your social and cultural understanding of job hunting would cause you to write a formal letter. You make similar judgments as a reader. When you decide to read an academic assignment in print or on your desktop computer rather than on your smartphone, your decision is the result of an implicit rhetorical judgment you're making about the nature and complexity of this text.

When faced with less familiar kinds of texts, you may have to work harder to make judgments about purpose, subject matter, and form. I recently received an email from a former student, Monica Molina, who now works at a community health center, where one of her responsibilities is to write grant proposals. In her email, she commented:

> It took quite a while before I could feel comfortable even thinking about trying to write my first grant proposal. Most of the ones at our center run 50 to 100 pages and seem so intimidating—full of strange subheadings, technical language, complicated explanations. I had to force myself to calm down and get into them. First I read some recent proposals, trying to figure out how they worked. Luckily, my boss is friendly and supportive, so she sat down with me and talked about her experiences writing proposals. We looked at some proposals together, and she told me about how proposals are reviewed by agencies. Now we're working together on my first proposal. I'm still nervous, but I'm beginning to feel more comfortable.

Like Monica, those entering new professions often must learn new forms of writing. Similarly, students entering a new discipline will often have to work hard to master unfamiliar language or writing styles. Chapter 8, "Writing in the Disciplines: Making Choices as You Write," will help you as you write your way across the curriculum.

Indeed, writers who wish to participate in any new community must strive to understand its reading and writing practices—to learn how to enter its conversation, as the rhetorician Kenneth Burke might say. The forms of writing practiced in different communities reflect important shared assumptions. These shared assumptions—sometimes referred to as *textual conventions*—represent agreements between writers and readers about how to construct and interpret texts. As such, they are an important component of any rhetorical situation.

The term *textual convention* may be new to you, but you can understand it easily if you think about other uses of the word *convention*. For example, social conventions are behaviors that reflect implicit agreement among the members of a community or culture about how to act in particular situations. At one time in the United States, for example, it was acceptable for persons who chewed tobacco to spit tobacco juice into spittoons in restaurants and hotel lobbies. (In fact, the use of spittoons was at one time considered re-fined, compared to the frequently employed alternative of spitting directly on the ground, indoors or out.) This particular social convention has changed over time and is no longer acceptable.

If social conventions represent agreements among individuals about how to act, textual conventions represent similar agreements about how to write and read texts. Just as we often take our own social conventions for granted, so too do we take for granted those textual conventions most famil-iar to us as readers and writers. Even though many of us write more texts and emails than letters, we still know that the most appropriate way to begin a letter is with the salutation "Dear. . . ."

thinking
rhetorically

Textual conventions are dynamic, changing over time as the assump-tions, values, and practices of writers and readers change. Consider some of the textual conventions of email and other online writing. If you're writing your parents an email, you may not start it with "Dear Mom and Dad." In-stead, you might begin with something like "Hi there—" or just jump into your message with no greeting. (Note: While leaving out an email salutation is considered acceptable in less formal contexts—possibly because the name of the recipient is built into email systems—rhetorically savvy writers of email know that when they're writing a work- or school-related email to a superior or teacher, they should include both a salutation and a clear state-ment of their subject.) If you're texting a friend, you might use abbreviations, such as RU for "are you," because it's easier to enter on your phone.

Emoticons—symbols such as :-) to indicate happiness, :-(to indicate sadness, or :-O to indicate shock or surprise—provide another example of changing textual conventions. These symbols were developed by online writ-ers as a kind of shorthand for the kind of emotion conveyed by voice, gesture, and facial expression in face-to-face communication. Not all who use email use emoticons, and those who do use them know they're more appropriate in some situations than in others. But as a textual convention, emoticons clearly respond to the needs of online writers and readers.

When you think about the kind of writing that you are being asked to do, you are thinking in part about the textual conventions that may limit your options as a writer in a specific situation. Textual conventions bring con-straints, but they also increase the likelihood that readers will respond ap-propriately to your ideas.

The relationship between textual conventions and medium can be criti-cal. Students organizing a protest against increased tuition, for example, would probably not try to get the word out by writing an essay on the sub-ject. In order to get as many students as possible to participate in the pro-test, they would more likely put together an inexpensive, attention-getting flyer and post it around campus, while also sending tweets using a newly created hashtag. After the protest march, they might draft a letter to the edi-tor to summarize the speakers' most important points; they might set up a

Facebook group or blog to post announcements and to encourage student participation; they might even post a manifesto with many of the characteristic features of an analytical essay.

Some textual conventions are specific. Lab reports, for example, usually include the following elements: title page, abstract, introduction, experimental design and methods, results, discussion, and references. Someone writing a lab report can deviate from this textual convention but in doing so runs the risk of confusing or irritating readers.

Other textual conventions are more general. Consider, for instance, the conventions of an effective academic essay:

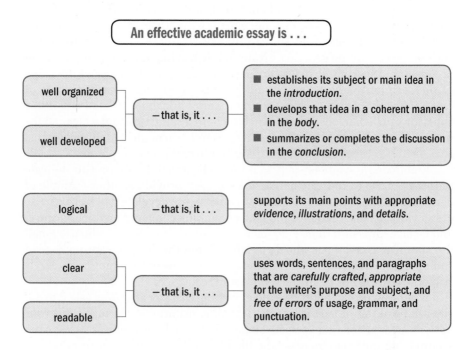

In writing an academic essay, you usually have more freedom in deciding how to apply the conventions than you do, say, when writing a lab report. For example, an introduction is called for, but its specific form is not prescribed: How you begin depends largely on who your audience is, why you're writing, the disciplinary context in which you're writing, your chosen medium, and other factors. As a result, deciding how to introduce your material can be challenging (though, with practice and effort, it *can* be mastered).

Observing a Professional Writer at Work: Comparing and Contrasting Textual Conventions

One way to strengthen your own writing skills is to observe successful writers in action. Let's look at three texts by psychologist Jean M. Twenge to see how one writer tackles the problem of creating an effective and appropriate selection. Each text is based on Twenge's research on differences between earlier and current generations in the United States, a subject she investigated in her 2006 book, *Generation Me: Why Today's Young Americans Are More Confident, Assertive, Entitled — and More Miserable Than Ever Before.* Twenge's research is based on data from 1.3 million young people born between 1982 and 1999—a group sometimes characterized as the millennial generation and called "Generation Me" by Twenge. Her book *Generation Me* is addressed to a general audience, but she has also published a good deal of academic research on this same topic. In addition to her book publications, she has published over seventy scholarly articles in such journals as *American Psychologist*, *Journal of Personality*, and the *Journal of Personality and Social Psychology*. Twenge also writes for such publications as *Time*, *Newsweek*, the *New York Times*, *USA Today*, and the *Washington Post.*

The first selection is an excerpt from the introduction to Twenge's *Generation Me* (pp. 74–75), a book written, as noted earlier, for a general audience. The second, "Generation Me on Trial" (pp. 76–77), was published in the March 18, 2012, issue of the *Chronicle of Higher Education*, a weekly newspaper read by faculty, staff, and administrators at community colleges, colleges, and universities. This commentary reflects on the events that led to the suicide of Tyler Clementi, a student at Rutgers University. (Clementi committed suicide on September 22, 2010; on March 16, 2012, his roommate, Dharun Ravi, was found guilty on charges related to Clementi's suicide. Twenge's column was published two days later.) The third, an excerpt from an article titled "Generational Differences in Young Adults' Life Goals, Concern for Others, and Civic Orientation, 1966–2009" (pp. 78–79), was co-authored with W. Keith Campbell and Elise C. Freeman and published in the November 2012 issue of the *Journal of Personality and Social Psychology*, a scholarly journal for psychologists.

Few academics attempt to reach such diverse audiences, and Twenge has clearly been successful in doing so. (Her research has been featured on *Today, NBC Nightly News, Fox and Friends, Dateline NBC,* and National Public Radio, for instance.) As a student writing in college, you won't write for such a broad range of audiences, but you will be writing for professors in a variety of disciplines, some of which can vary significantly in terms of textual conventions. Think, for instance, about the difference between writing a book review for your political science class and writing a lab report for your chemistry class. You can learn a good deal about what it means to be a rhetorically sensitive and an intellectually agile writer by studying these three Twenge selections.

Introduction

Linda was born in 1952 in a small town in the Midwest. After she graduated from high school in 1970, she moved to the city and enrolled in secretarial school. It was a great time to be young: Free Love was in, and everybody smoked, drank, and had a good time. Linda and her friends joined a feminist consciousness-raising group, danced at the discos, and explored their inner lives at est seminars and through meditation. The new pursuit of self-fulfillment led Tom Wolfe to label the 1970s the "Me Decade," and by extension the young people of the time the "Me Generation."

Compared to today's young people, they were posers.

Linda's Baby Boomer generation grew up in the 1950s and early 1960s, taught by stern, gray-suit-wearing teachers and raised by parents who didn't take any lip and thought that *Father Knows Best*. Most of the Boomers were well into adolescence or adulthood by the time the focus on the self became trendy in the 1970s. And when Linda and her friends sought self-knowledge, they took the ironic step of doing so en masse— for all their railing against conformity, Boomers did just about everything in groups, from protests to seminars to yoga. Their youthful exploration also covered a very brief period: the average first-time bride in the early 1970s had not yet celebrated her 21st birthday.

Today's under-35 young people are the real Me Generation, or, as I call them, Generation Me. Born after self-focus entered the cultural mainstream, this generation has never known a world that put duty before self. Linda's youngest child, Jessica, was born in 1985. When Jessica was a toddler, Whitney Houston's No. 1 hit song declared that "The Greatest Love of All" was loving yourself. Jessica's elementary school teachers believed that their most important job was helping Jessica feel good about herself. Jessica scribbled in a coloring book called *We Are All Special*, got a sticker

1

Generation Me

2   Introduction

on her worksheet just for filling it out, and did a sixth-grade project called "All About Me." When she wondered how to act on her first date, her mother told her, "Just be yourself." Eventually, Jessica got her lower lip pierced and obtained a large tattoo on her lower back because, she said, she wanted to express herself. She dreams of being a model or a singer. She does not expect to marry until she is in her late twenties, and neither she nor her older sisters have any children yet. "You have to love yourself before you can love someone else," she says. This is a generation unapologetically focused on the individual, a true Generation Me.

If you're wondering what all of this means for the future, you are not alone. Reflecting on her role as a parent of this new generation, *San Francisco Chronicle* columnist Joan Ryan wrote: "We're told we will produce a generation of coddled, center-of-the-universe adults who will expect the world to be as delighted with them as we are. And even as we laugh at the knock-knock jokes and exclaim over the refrigerator drawings, we secretly fear the same thing."

Everyone belongs to a generation. Some people embrace it like a warm, familiar blanket, while others prefer not to be lumped in with their age mates. Yet like it or not, when you were born dictates the culture you will experience. This includes the highs and lows of pop culture, as well as world events, social trends, economic realities, behavioral norms, and ways of seeing the world. The society that molds you when you are young stays with you the rest of your life.

Today's young people are experiencing that society right now, and they speak the language of the self as their native tongue. The individual has always come first, and feeling good about yourself has always been a primary virtue. Generation Me's expectations are highly optimistic: they expect to go to college, to make lots of money, and perhaps even to be famous. Yet this generation enters a world in which college admissions are increasingly competitive, good jobs are hard to find and harder to keep, and basic necessities like housing and health care have skyrocketed in price. This is a time of soaring expectations and crushing realities. Joan Chiaramonte, head of the Roper Youth Report, says that for young people "the gap between what they have and what they want has never been greater." If you would like to start an argument, claim that young people…

Generation Me on Trial

AP Images

Dharun Ravi, shown waiting during a break in his trial last week, was convicted on Friday of invasion of privacy and hate crimes for using a Webcam to spy on his roommate.

Enlarge Image

By Jean M. Twenge

"I dare you to chat me between the hours of 9:30 and midnight. Yes, it's happening again," the Rutgers University student Dharun Ravi wrote on his Twitter account in September 2010. "It" was Tyler Clementi, Mr. Ravi's roommate, having a sexual encounter with another man—while Mr. Ravi and his friends watched on a Webcam. The next day, Mr. Clementi committed suicide. On March 16, Mr. Ravi was found guilty on charges related to the incident and faces up to 10 years in prison.

This was an explosive case, and the actions of one college freshman cannot be used to characterize an entire generation. Yet the incident echoes several distressing trends rippling through American culture—trends that often appear first among young adults who have never known a culture without reality TV and Facebook. Three seem the most relevant:

- An empathy deficit. In a study of more than 14,000 college students, Sara H. Konrath and her colleagues found that millennials (usually thought of as born between 1982 and 1999) scored considerably lower on a measure of empathy than previous generations. I call this group Generation Me, and my colleagues and I recently found a similar, though smaller, decline in empathy among high-school students on survey items such as "Maybe some minority groups do get unfair treatment, but that's no business of mine.

  Empathy was clearly lacking in the Rutgers incident. One of Mr. Ravi's tweets gleefully announced, "Roommate asked for the room until midnight. I went into molly's room and turned on my webcam. I saw him making out with a dude. Yay." Not "yay" as in, "I'm happy my roommate is getting some," but, "Yay, what a great opportunity to laugh at someone else's expense." Mr. Ravi is not alone; his voyeuristic joy is similar to the pleasure we get watching rich, attractive people fighting on a reality TV show. No matter how embarrassing, it's all on display for our amusement. In Ms. Konrath's study, the empathy decline was especially steep after 2000—right around the advent of reality TV.

- A decline in taking responsibility. Since 1960, young Americans have become increasingly likely to say their lives are controlled by outside forces rather than their own efforts. Narcissism, a personality trait linked to blaming others for problems, has also increased among college students. Mr. Ravi's attorneys argued he was not guilty because he was young and immature; the attorneys of George Huguely V, convicted of beating his girlfriend to death at the University of Virginia, said he was drunk.

  These are extreme examples. Yet many university faculty and staff grapple almost daily with students who blame everyone but themselves when they do poorly or just don't bother to show up. The new twist, rarely seen until recently, is the parents who make excuses for the students. When we think we're fantastic, it must be someone else's fault when bad stuff happens—even when we did the bad stuff ourselves.

- More belief in equality for all. A third trend seems to contradict the incident at Rutgers—the growing acceptance of homosexuality, especially among the young. A recent Gallup poll, for example, showed 70 percent of Americans ages 18 to 34 now support gay marriage—nearly twice as many as among those over age 55.

However, a lack of prejudice is not the same as true empathy. Anyone who decides to broadcast someone else's sexual encounter, as Mr. Ravi did, is obviously not empathizing very well. Given the stigma and discomfort homosexuality still stirs among many people, telecasting a young gay man's sexual encounter is particularly callous. Mr. Ravi's actions reflect a common theme in many Generation Me mistakes: He seemed clueless that his actions would hurt someone more severely because that person belonged to a minority group. Mr. Ravi didn't seem to realize that Mr. Clementi's homosexuality made him more vulnerable. Treating people as equal, usually such a good thing, becomes harmful when individuals lose the ability to take someone else's perspective. "Tolerance" is not enough.

At the trial, students testified they had never heard Mr. Ravi say anything bad about gays. Mr. Ravi even wrote to Mr. Clementi, "I've known you were gay and I have no problem with it." Apparently Mr. Ravi didn't hate gays. He just thought watching them make out was funny.

RELATED CONTENT

Jury Convicts Rutgers U. Roommate in Webcam-Spying Case

How to Protect Your Students From Cyberbullying

A similar theme appeared in a February 2010 incident at the University of California at San Diego, when a fraternity sponsored a "Compton Cookout," where partygoers were asked to dress as pimps and "ghetto chicks." Many of the university's black students did not find that amusing, especially during Black History Month.

But to the fraternity brothers, it was just another theme party and just other costumes. Everybody's equal, right? It didn't seem to occur to them that making fun of a historically underprivileged group might cause offense, particularly on a campus where barely 2 percent of the students are black—and thus might feel isolated already. Like the case of Mr. Ravi and Mr. Clementi, it was cluelessness born of the combination of low empathy and the belief that we are all equal.

So should cluelessness and lack of empathy be prosecuted as a crime? Mr. Ravi's attorneys said he was simply an immature young man who played a prank. Although the decline in empathy is a worrying trend, and Mr. Clementi's death a true tragedy, it can still be debated whether cluelessness is a crime. The debate is likely to continue, but for now, the verdicts in New Jersey and Virginia are a reminder—to young people and to society as a whole—that cruelty has consequences.

Tolerance and equality are among Generation Me's greatest strengths, and should continue to be celebrated. But sometimes equality is not enough. For true peace and compassion, we need a healthy dose of empathy. It's not enough to realize that someone else is equal—we have to think about what it's really like to be him or her. That, perhaps more than anything else, is the lesson we must teach Generation Me—and ourselves.

Jean M. Twenge is a professor of psychology at San Diego State University, and author of Generation Me: Why Today's Young Americans Are More Confident, Assertive, Entitled—and More Miserable Than Ever Before (Free Press, 2006) and co-author, with W. Keith Campbell, of The Narcissism Epidemic: Living in the Age of Entitlement (Free Press, 2009).

PERSONALITY PROCESSES AND INDIVIDUAL DIFFERENCES

Generational Differences in Young Adults' Life Goals, Concern for Others, and Civic Orientation, 1966–2009

Jean M. Twenge
San Diego State University

W. Keith Campbell
University of Georgia

Elise C. Freeman
San Diego State University

Three studies examined generational differences in life goals, concern for others, and civic orientation among American high school seniors (Monitoring the Future; $N = 463{,}753$, 1976–2008) and entering college students (The American Freshman; $N = 8.7$ million, 1966–2009). Compared to Baby Boomers (born 1946–1961) at the same age, GenX'ers (born 1962–1981) and Millennials (born after 1982) considered goals related to extrinsic values (money, image, fame) more important and those related to intrinsic values (self-acceptance, affiliation, community) less important. Concern for others (e.g., empathy for outgroups, charity donations, the importance of having a job worthwhile to society) declined slightly. Community service rose but was also increasingly required for high school graduation over the same time period. Civic orientation (e.g., interest in social problems, political participation, trust in government, taking action to help the environment and save energy) declined an average of $d = -.34$, with about half the decline occurring between GenX and the Millennials. Some of the largest declines appeared in taking action to help the environment. In most cases, Millennials slowed, though did not reverse, trends toward reduced community feeling begun by GenX. The results generally support the "Generation Me" view of generational differences rather than the "Generation We" or no change views.

Keywords: birth cohort, generations, intrinsic and extrinsic values, civic orientation, concern for others

"People born between 1982 and 2000 are the most civic-minded since the generation of the 1930s and 1940s," say Morley Winograd and Michael Hais, co-authors of *Millennial Makeover: MySpace, YouTube, and the Future of American Politics.* . . . "Other generations were reared to be more individualistic," Hais says. "This civic generation has a willingness to put aside some of their own personal advancement to improve society.'"—*USA Today,* 2009

College students today show less empathy toward others compared with college students in decades before. With different demands at work—hours answering and writing e-mail—people have less time to care about others.—*USA Today,* 2010

American society has undergone significant changes during the past few decades. Opportunities for women and minorities have expanded, and beliefs in equality for all have become more common (e.g., Koenig, Eagly, Mitchell, & Ristikari, 2011; Thornton & Young-DeMarco, 2001). On the other hand, societal cohesiveness is on the decline, with more Americans saying they have no one to confide in (McPherson, Smith-Lovin, & Brashears, 2006) and more having children outside of marriage (U.S. Bureau of the Census, 2011).

How have recent generations been shaped by these trends? At base, generational differences are cultural differences: As cultures change, their youngest members are socialized with new and different values. Children growing up in the 1950s were exposed to a fundamentally different culture than children growing up in the 1990s, for example. Thus birth cohorts—commonly referred to as generations—are shaped by the larger sociocultural environment of different time periods (e.g., Gentile, Campbell, & Twenge, 1989; Twenge, 2006), just as residents of different cultures are shaped by regional variations in culture (e.g., Markus & Kitayama, 1991).

Many previous studies have examined generational differences in personality traits and positive self-views (e.g., André et al., 2010; Gentile, Twenge, & Campbell, 2010; Stewart & Bernhardt, 2010; Twenge, Campbell, & Gentile, 2011). Fewer studies, however, have examined generational trends in values, life goals, and young people's relationships to their communities. For example, have young people's life goals changed to become more or less community focused? How concerned are they for others? How much do they wish to be involved in collective or civic action? These questions about community feeling are important, as they address crucial elements of social capital and group relations (e.g., Putnam, 2000). As the epigraph quotes illustrate, there is a great deal of interest in—and disagreement

This article was published Online First March 5, 2012.

Jean M. Twenge and Elise C. Freeman, Department of Psychology, San Diego State University; W. Keith Campbell, Department of Psychology, University of Georgia.

Correspondence concerning this article should be addressed to Jean M. Twenge, Department of Psychology, San Diego State University, 5500 Campanile Drive, San Diego, CA 92182-4611. E-mail: jtwenge@mail.sdsu.edu

Journal of Personality and Social Psychology, 2012, Vol. 102, No. 5, 1045–1062
© 2012 American Psychological Association 0022-3514/12/$12.00   DOI: 10.1037/a0027408

about—whether or not today's young people are higher or lower in community feeling. Community feeling is also a key element of what Kasser and colleagues (e.g., Grouzet et al., 2005; Kasser & Ryan, 1993, 1996) label intrinsic values, those important to inherent psychological needs that contribute to actualization and growth such as self-acceptance, affiliation, and community. These are on the opposite end of the same dimension as extrinsic values, those contingent on external feedback such as money, fame, and image. The current study seeks to expand the literature on generational differences by assessing changes in community feeling and the contrasting extrinsic values.

The literature on generational differences is limited in other ways as well. Most analyses have gathered data from other studies using cross-temporal meta-analysis instead of analyzing responses from large national surveys (e.g., Konrath, O'Brien, & Hsing, 2011; Malahy, Rubinlicht, & Kaiser, 2009; Twenge & Foster, 2010). Cross-temporal meta-analysis has the benefit of examining changes in well-established psychological measures but lacks the stratified, nationally representative sampling of large national surveys. However, these national surveys have limitations of their own. For example, the meaning of some items in large national surveys is unclear. Although most items are straightforward or behavioral—for example, civic orientation items about political participation, or concern for others items about community service or charity donations—others, especially those asking about life goals, are more ambiguous. For example, when a respondent agrees that being a "community leader" is an important life goal, does that reflect the value of community (an intrinsic value) or of wanting to be a leader (an extrinsic value)? Several observers (e.g., Greenberg & Weber, 2008; Pry or, Hurtado, Saenz, Santos, & Korn, 2007) have assumed it reflects community feeling, but this has never been confirmed by validating this item—or any other from these surveys—against psychometrically valid measures such as the Aspirations Index, the most established measure of life goals (Grouzet et al., 2005).

In the present study, we attempt to address these issues by (a) examining changes in community feeling across as many survey items as possible in (b) two very large national databases and (c) validating relevant items against existing measures, particularly those measuring community feeling and the larger dimension of intrinsic–extrinsic values. Before describing our research in detail, however, we discuss past research and commentary on generational changes in community feeling.

Opposing Views on Generational Changes in Community Feeling

Kasser and Ryan (1996) defined community feeling as helpfulness and wanting to "improve the world through activism or generativity" (p. 281). As the epigraph quotes show, the level of community feeling among today's young adults is in dispute. The arguments fall into three basic camps: the "Generation We" view, the "Generation Me" view, and the no change view.

In the "Generation We" view, Americans born in the 1980s and 1990s, often called GenY or Millennials, are more community oriented, caring, activist, civically involved, and interested in environmental causes than previous generations were (Arnett, 2010; Greenberg & Weber, 2008; Rampell, 2011; Howe & Strauss, 2000; Winograd & Hais, 2008, 2011). Winograd and Hais (2011) wrote, "About every eight decades, a new, positive, accomplished, and group-oriented 'civic generation' emerges . . . The Millennial

Generation (born 1982–2003) is America's newest civic generation." Greenberg and Weber (2008) stated that *"Generation We is noncynical and civic-minded.* They believe in the value of political engagement and are convinced that government can be a powerful force for good. . . . By comparison with past generations, *Generation We is highly politically engaged"* (pp. 30, 32; emphasis in original). Epstein and Howes (2006) advised managers that Millennials are "socially conscious" and that "volunteerism and giving back to society play an important role in their lives" (p. 25). The view that Millennials are unusually inclined toward helping others is so widely held that many companies have instituted recruiting programs for young workers involving volunteer service and helping the environment (e.g., Alsop, 2008; Epstein & Howes, 2006; Hasek, 2008; Lancaster & Stillman, 2010; Needleman, 2008).

The contrasting "Generation Me" view sees Millennials as reflecting an increasingly extrinsic and materialistic culture that values money, image, and fame over concern for others and intrinsic meaning (e.g., Gordinier, 2009; Mallan, 2009; Myers, 2000; Smith, Christoffersen, Davidson, & Herzog, 2011; Twenge, 2006). A few studies have found empirical support for this idea. American college students' scores on a measure of empathy for others declined between 1979 and 2009 (Konrath et al., 2011). Malahy et al. (2009) found an increase over the generations in the belief in a just world, or the idea that people get what they deserve and thus are responsible for their misfortunes. They concluded that more recent students less likely to take the perspective of others in need and "less concerned with and less emotionally burdened by others' suffering and disadvantage" (p. 378). Narcissistic personality traits, which correlate with less empathy and concern for others, increased over the generations among college students in four datasets (Stewart & Bernhardt, 2010; Twenge & Foster, 2010).

A third view posits that generational differences do not exist, especially in representative samples, and that any perception of generational change is an illusion caused by older people's shifting frame of reference or a mistaking of developmental changes for generational changes (Trzesniewski & Donnellan, 2010). These authors analyzed a selected portion of items in the Monitoring the Future database of high school students and concluded that few meaningful generational differences existed (Trzesniewski and Donnellan, 2010; cf. Twenge & Campbell, 2010). Trzesniewski and Donnellan contended that young people in the 2000s are remarkably similar to those in the 1970s. They argued that previous studies finding generational differences were unreliable because they were not based on nationally representative samples.

The Current Research

Our primary goal in the present research was to assess generational changes in community feeling. To address the limitations of past research, we took several empirical steps. First, given previous concerns about sampling (Trzesniewski & Donnellan, 2010), we turned to two large, nationally representative samples of American young people collected over time: the Monitoring the Future (MtF) study of high school seniors conducted since 1976 ($N = 0.5$ million) and the American Freshman (AF) survey of entering college students conducted since 1966 ($N = 8.7$ million). Both include a large number of items on life goals, concern for others, and civic orientation.

Second, although much recent discussion has focused on the current generation of young people, we examine changes going back to

|||||||||||||||||||||||||||||||||||||||||||||||||||||||||||||||||||||||||||||||||||||||

FOR EXPLORATION

Read the Twenge selections (pp. 74–79) carefully, and write three paragraphs characterizing their approaches—one paragraph for each selection. (Be sure to read the abstract and the footnote on the first page of the article from the *Journal of Personality and Social Psychology*, which provides important cues about Twenge's rhetorical situation and the interests and expectations of her scholarly readers.) Here are some questions for you to keep in mind as you read.

- How would you describe Twenge's tone in each selection?
- What kinds of examples are used in each selection, and what function do they serve?
- What relationship is established in each selection between writer and reader, and what cues signal this relationship?
- What assumptions does Twenge make in each selection about what readers already know?
- How would you describe the persona, or image of the writer, in each selection?

|||||||||||||||||||||||||||||||||||||||||||||||||||||||||||||||||||||||||||||||||||||||

By glancing at the first pages of Twenge's three texts, you'll notice some important clues about the publications they appear in and about Twenge's expectations about their readers. For example, the first two pages of the introduction to Twenge's *Generation Me* begin with a story about Linda, who "was born in 1952 in a small town in the Midwest." Even though the title of Twenge's book makes it clear that she will be generalizing about an entire generation, Twenge begins with a specific story, as if to say to readers that, although the author is a psychologist and is drawing on empirical research, this book will be relevant to them in their personal lives. Twenge is clearly aware that the market is flooded with books about a diverse range of topics—from how to survive a divorce to how to succeed in business. She knows that her introduction needs to invite readers into the story that she will tell in her book—and her introduction does just that. Twenge's introduction does not include any illustrations, but whether potential readers have looked at her book in a brick-and-mortar bookstore or on Amazon.com or some other online site, most of them will have already viewed its intentionally provocative cover.

In the remainder of the introduction to her book, Twenge describes how she became interested in the topic of generational differences and birth cohort studies. She informs readers about her own education as a psychologist and about the research that led to *Generation Me*. The story of her own

"Twenge does a huge, decidedly un-GenX amount of research and replaces [hunches] with actual data. . . . [L]ucid and entertaining . . . bold . . . refreshing."
—Chris Colin, author of *What Really Happened to the Class of '93*

Generation Me

Why Today's Young Americans Are More Confident, Assertive, Entitled— and More Miserable Than Ever Before

Jean M. Twenge, Ph.D.

Cover of Jean M. Twenge's *Generation Me* (2007)

engagement with her topic complements and enriches the story of Linda that begins the introduction. Twenge ends her introduction by referring to the years of library research and empirical data collection that are the foundation of her book and concludes with this simple but compelling statement: "This book tells that story" (15).

Now consider Twenge's second text, an article titled "Generation Me on Trial" that was published in the *Chronicle of Higher Education*. This article is somewhat more visually dense than the introduction to Twenge's *Generation Me*, though it does have some white space and a photo of Dharun Ravi at the top of the page.

thinking rhetorically

Subscribers to the weekly *Chronicle of Higher Education* represent a more specialized readership than that of the trade book *Generation Me*. They either work in or are interested in higher education. Still, the diversity within this readership—which includes faculty across the disciplines, administrators, and staff in various offices on campus—means many readers skim the *Chronicle* to determine what to read. Given that Dharun Ravi's conviction was a major news story, the publication of Twenge's column was quite timely and designed to gain the attention of readers.

In her *Chronicle* essay, Twenge seldom refers directly to the research on which her discussion is based. She assumes that readers will make a connection between the title of her book, *Generation Me*, and the title of her article, "Generation Me on Trial." She also assumes that readers will draw on the biographical information at the end of her piece, including her position as a professor of psychology at San Diego State University, to assess her authority to write about her topic. Twenge thus keeps the focus on her three main points: that Generation Me has "an empathy deficit," that it has seen a "decline in taking responsibility," and that it has "more belief in equality for all." Whereas in the first pages of the introduction to *Generation Me* Twenge focuses on creating a story that will draw readers in and make them care about her research, in her *Chronicle* article Twenge draws conclusions—including her final one: "For true peace and compassion, we need a healthy dose of empathy. It's not enough to realize that someone else is equal—we have to think about what it's really like to be him or her. That, perhaps more than anything else, is the lesson we must teach Generation Me—and ourselves."

Twenge's final text, "Generational Differences in Young Adults' Life Goals, Concern for Others, and Civic Orientation, 1966–2009," appears in the *Journal of Personality and Social Psychology*, a specialized publication that has the most cramped and least inviting first page. Twenge's article is co-authored with two other scholars, a common practice in the social sciences, where the nature and scope of research projects often require collaboration. Twenge, however, is the first author and the corresponding author (see the note at the bottom of the page), which indicates to colleagues reading the article that her contributions to the research have been particularly important.

Rather than using an attention-getting title, Twenge and her coauthors straightforwardly describe the focus of their research project. The article begins with an abstract and keywords designed to help readers decide whether they want to read the entire article.

Although the article begins with two attention-getting epigraphs, it quickly focuses on the most important research questions the authors wish to address. Twenge and her coauthors are careful to distinguish the research reported in this article from previous studies of generational differences. They assess some of the limitations of earlier studies, argue for the value of their own approach, contrast opposing views on generational changes, and establish their primary research goal.

Twenge and her coauthors' essay in the *Journal of Personality and Social Psychology* is seventeen densely argued pages long. In subsequent sections, the authors argue for the value of their methodology and examine three studies they undertook on generational differences in life goals. Their essay includes several tables that summarize and evaluate data, as well as graphs and other figures that help readers grasp the significance of their research. Clearly, the authors assume that scholars who choose to read their article will want the opportunity not only to understand and evaluate the authors' conclusions but also to critique their methodology. Twenge and her coauthors conclude their article by considering contradictory data from other sources, the strengths and limitations of their own studies, and their own conclusions, which remain tentative. As the authors note in their final sentence, how the attitudes and behaviors that they discuss in their article "will shape the young generation and the country as more Millennials enter adult life remains to be seen" (1060).

Unlike in her commentary in the *Chronicle of Higher Education*, where Twenge reports some of the most important results of her research on generational differences, in the article in the *Journal of Personality and Social Psychology* Twenge and her coauthors take pains to make every step of their research process visible and available for other scholars to critique. Such critique might include efforts to replicate the studies described in the article. Clearly, Twenge expects much more of the readers of this scholarly article than she does of the readers of her commentary in the *Chronicle* or her trade publication, *Generation Me.* She assumes that readers will be familiar with the many references she and her coauthors cite or will at least appreciate their inclusion. She also assumes that readers will have considerable prior knowledge of her topic and will care deeply about it—assumptions she cannot make about readers of her book or *Chronicle* commentary.

Twenge also understands that readers of the *Journal of Personality and Social Psychology* bring specific expectations to their reading of the journal. Like readers of the *Chronicle of Higher Education,* subscribers to the *Journal of Personality and Social Psychology* don't have time to read every article, but they don't make their reading choices based on inviting titles, illustrations, or opening anecdotes. Instead, they skim the table of contents, noting articles that affect their own research or have broad significance for their field. The abstract in Twenge and her coauthors' article matters very much to these readers; they can review it to determine not only *if* but also *how* they will read the article. Some will read only the abstract, others will skim the major points, and others will read the entire article with great care, returning to it as they conduct their own research.

Although the excerpts of Twenge's three texts are grounded in the same research project, they differ dramatically in structure, tone, language, and approach to readers. Textual conventions play an important role in these differences. As shared agreements about the construction and interpretation of texts, textual conventions enable readers and writers to communicate successfully in different rhetorical situations.

|||||||||||||||||||||||||||||||||||||||||||||||||||||||||||||||||||||||||||||||||||||||||||||||||||||

FOR EXPLORATION

Take five to ten minutes to freewrite about your experience of reading the introductions to Twenge's three texts, as well as the subsequent analysis of them. What has this experience helped you better understand about the role that textual conventions—and rhetorical sensitivity—play in writing? If this experience has raised questions for you as a writer, be sure to note them as well. Be prepared to share your response to this Exploration with your classmates.

|||||||||||||||||||||||||||||||||||||||||||||||||||||||||||||||||||||||||||||||||||||||||||||||||||||

NOTE FOR MULTILINGUAL WRITERS

The conventions of academic writing vary from culture to culture. If you were educated in another country or language, you may have written successful academic texts that followed textual conventions that differ from those you have to follow now. Conventions that can differ in various cultures include the rhetorical strategies that introduce essay topics, the presence and placement of thesis statements, the kinds of information that qualify as objective evidence in argumentation, the use (or absence) of explicit transitions, and the use (or absence) of first-person pronouns.

Given these and other potential differences, you may find it helpful to compare the conventions of academic writing in North America with those of your home culture.

Using Textual Conventions

You already know enough about rhetoric and the rhetorical situation to realize that there can be no one-size-fits-all approach to every academic writing situation.

thinking rhetorically

What can you do when you are unfamiliar with the textual conventions of a particular discipline or of academic writing in general? A rhetorical approach suggests that one solution is to read examples of the kind of writing you wish to do. As she wrote, Jean M. Twenge, whose selections you read earlier in this chapter, undoubtedly drew on her experience as a reader of the publications in which her work would later appear. Discussing these models with an insider—your teacher, perhaps, or an advanced student in the field—can help you understand why these conventions work for such readers and writers. Forming a study group or meeting with a tutor can also increase your rhetorical sensitivity to your teachers' expectations and the conventions of academic writing.

Finally, a rhetorical approach to communication encourages you to think strategically about writing—whether personal, professional, or academic—and to respond creatively to the challenges of each situation. As a writer, you have much to consider: your own goals as a writer, the nature of your subject and writing task, the expectations of your readers, the textual conventions your particular situation requires or allows, the medium in which to express your ideas. The rhetorical sensitivity that you have already developed can help you respond appropriately to these and other concerns. But you can also draw on other resources—on textual examples and on discussions with teachers, tutors, and other students. As a writer, you are not alone. By reaching out to other writers, in person or by reading their work, you can become a fully participating member of the academic community.

|||||||||||||||||||||||||||||||||||||||||||||||||||||||||||||||||||||||||||||||||||

FOR THOUGHT, DISCUSSION, AND WRITING

1. From a newspaper or a magazine, choose an essay, an editorial, or a column that you think succeeds in its purpose. Now turn back to the Questions for Analyzing Your Rhetorical Situation on pp. 54–55, and answer the questions as if you were the writer of the text you have chosen. To answer the questions, look for evidence of the writer's intentions in the writing itself. (To determine what image or persona the writer wanted to portray, for instance, look at the kind of language the writer uses. Is it formal or conversational? Full of interesting images and vivid details or serious examples and statistics?) Answer each of the questions suggested by the guidelines. Then write a paragraph or more reflecting on what you have learned from this analysis.

2. Alia Sands and Brandon Barrett did a good job in anticipating their readers' expectations and interests. In writing their essays, they focused not just on content (what they wanted to say) but also on strategy (how they might convey their ideas to their readers). Not all interactions between writer and reader are as successful. You may have read textbooks that seemed more concerned with the subject matter than with readers' needs and expectations. Or you may have received direct-mail advertising or other business communications that irritated or offended you. Find an example of writing that in your view fails to anticipate the expectations and needs of the reader, and write one or two paragraphs explaining your reasons. Your teacher may ask you to share your example and written explanation with your classmates.

3. Analyze the ways in which one or more of the following print advertisements (pp. 86–89) draw on Aristotle's three appeals: logos, pathos, and ethos.

|||||||||||||||||||||||||||||||||||||||||||||||||||||||||||||||||||||||||||||||||||

Public Service Ad: "Dating Abuse Affects 1 in 3 Young People"

Public Service Ad: "We Know Where You're Coming From."

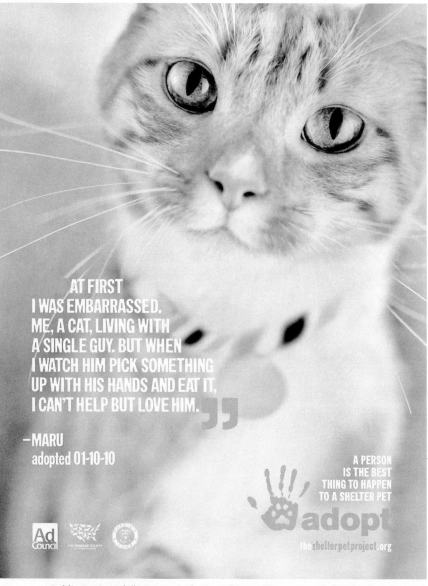

Public Service Ad: "A Person Is the Best Thing to Happen to a Shelter Pet."

When the Supreme Court handed down its historic decision on global warming, it wasn't just a bunch of lawyers who won.

When the Supreme Court delivered the landmark ruling that gave the EPA the power to fight global warming, it was just one in a long line of court victories that Earthjustice has helped win across the country. From Alaska to California to West Virginia, good lawyers are making the difference. And Earthjustice is putting more lawyers on the ground where they are needed most. With your help, we will continue to win. **Visit www.earthjustice.org or call (800) 584-6460.**

EARTHJUSTICE
Because the earth needs a good lawyer

Public Service Ad: "When the Supreme Court handed down its historic decision on global warming, it wasn't just the lawyers who won."

Analyzing and Synthesizing Texts

thinking rhetorically

A rhetorical approach to writing looks at the various contexts in which you write. Even if you are writing alone at your computer, you are writing in the context of a specific rhetorical situation. By analyzing that situation, you can identify your purpose and goals as a writer, develop an appropriate persona or voice, and respond to the expectations of your readers. You also can understand and implement the appropriate textual conventions for courses across the curriculum.

Understanding the Centrality of Reading to Academic Writing

One of the most important ways of recognizing and understanding the textual conventions appropriate to various disciplines is through reading. You already recognize that reading is central to academic writing. After all, as a student you are almost always writing in response to one or more texts. But you may not have realized that reading can help you understand how the methodologies that different disciplines are grounded in are reflected in their textual conventions.

For a full discussion of this topic, see Chapter 8, "Writing in the Disciplines: Making Choices as You Write." That chapter looks carefully at the histories, goals, and mission of the humanities, the natural and applied sciences, the social sciences, and business, and it demonstrates how these are reflected in various disciplines' textual conventions. Whatever kind of text you are reading—from a chapter in your sociology textbook to a poem in your literature class to a research report for psychology—the ability to read critically and to engage your reading at multiple levels is essential. Chapter 9, "Strategies for Reading," provides strategies you can use as you read your way across the disciplines, and Chapter 2, "Rethinking Reading: Reading on Page and Screen," shows how you can draw on your rhetorical sensitivity to make informed decisions about accessing and interacting with texts.

In this chapter, you will learn how to master two skills essential to all reading. These skills are analysis and synthesis. When you *analyze*, you determine how a text, an object, or a body of data is structured or organized; you also often assess its effectiveness or validity. Synthesis is a counterpart to analysis. When you *synthesize*, you explore connections and contradictions between two or more texts, objects, or bodies of data. Often, you also bring your own experience to bear on the subject under consideration, indicating where you agree and where you disagree with those whose words and thoughts you are exploring.

Considering Analysis and Synthesis in the Context of the Academic Community

Gaining an understanding of context is particularly important when you enter a new community of writers and readers. Accordingly, as you enter the academic community, you need to develop an insider's understanding of the conventions that characterize academic writing. Some of these conventions apply across the disciplines; for example, a successful academic argument must reflect an open, unbiased intellectual engagement with the subject, whether that subject is a Renaissance painting or the Federal Reserve System. Moreover, whatever your subject, the logic behind your conclusions and the evidence for them play a key role in any academic argument.

Most college instructors believe that *all* academic writing involves argument. But the model of argument they have in mind isn't about winning or losing a debate; it involves using evidence and reasoning to discover a version of truth about a particular subject. I use the words *a version* here to emphasize that in academic writing what constitutes the "truth" is always open to further discussion. A political scientist or an economist who makes a convincing argument about federal policy on harvesting timber in national forests knows that others will add to, challenge, or refine that argument. In fact, having others respond to an argument is a sign that the writing has successfully raised questions that others consider important. In this sense, the scholarly work of the academy is a conversation, rather than a debate.

Understanding Your Audience

Because your instructors are the primary readers of your college writing, you need to understand their values and their goals for you and other students. They all share a commitment to the ideal of education as inquiry. Whether they teach in business, liberal arts, agriculture, engineering, or other fields, your instructors want to foster your ability to think, write, and speak well.

When they read your papers and exams, they're looking for evidence of both your knowledge of a subject and your ability to think and write clearly and effectively.

But your instructors will not necessarily bring identical expectations to your writing. Methods of inquiry and research questions vary from discipline to discipline, and textual conventions reflect these differences. Despite such disciplinary differences, college instructors generally agree that educated, thoughtful, and knowledgeable college students share certain characteristics. They believe, for instance, that perhaps the worst intellectual error is oversimplifying. They want their students to go beyond simplistic analysis and arguments to achieve deeper and more complex understandings. Thus a historian might urge students to recognize that more was at stake in the American Civil War than freeing the slaves, and an engineer might encourage students to realize that the most obvious way to resolve a design problem isn't necessarily the best way.

Most college instructors want students to be able to do more than memorize or summarize information. Indeed, they strive to develop students' abilities to analyze, apply, question, evaluate, and synthesize information. What do instructors look for in students' writing? Most broadly, they want evidence of learning and a real commitment to and engagement with the subject. And they want you to adhere to academic standards of clear thinking and effective communication. More specifically, most instructors hope to find the following characteristics in student writing:

- A limited but significant topic
- A meaningful context for discussion of the topic
- A sustained and full development of ideas, given the limitations of the topic, time alloted, and length assigned
- A clear pattern of organization
- Fair and effective use of sources (both print and online)
- Adequate detail and evidence as support for generalizations
- Appropriate, concise language
- Conventional grammar, punctuation, and usage

The essay on pages 94–95, written by student Hope Leman for a class on politics and the media, meets these criteria. The essay was a response to the following assignment for a take-home midterm exam:

Journalists often suggest that they simply mirror reality. Some political scientists argue, however, that rather than mirroring reality journalists make judgments that subtly but significantly shape their resulting news reports. In so doing, scholars argue, journalists function more like flashlights than like mirrors. Write an essay in which you contrast the "mirror" and "flashlight" models of the role of journalists in American society.

Successful essays will not only compare these two models but will also provide examples supporting their claims.

Since Hope was writing a take-home midterm essay, she didn't have time to do a formal written analysis of her rhetorical situation. Still, her essay demonstrates considerable rhetorical sensitivity. Hope understands, for instance, that given her situation she should emphasize content rather than employ a dramatic or highly personal style. Hope's essay is, above all, clearly written. Even though it has moments of quiet humor (as when she comments on funhouses at the end of paragraph 2), the focus is on articulating the reasons why the "flashlight" model of media theory is the most valid and helpful for political scientists. Hope knows that her teacher will be reading a stack of midterms under time pressure, so she makes sure that her own writing is carefully organized and to the point.

thinking
rhetorically

Hope Leman
Professor Roberts
Political Science 101
April 20, 2013

The Role of Journalists in American Society: A Comparison
of the "Mirror" and "Flashlight" Models

The "mirror" model of media theory holds that through their writing and news broadcasts journalists are an objective source of information for the public. This model assumes that journalists are free of bias and can be relied on to provide accurate information about the true state of affairs in the world. Advocates of the "flashlight" model disagree, believing that a journalist is like a person in a dark room holding a flashlight. The light from the flashlight falls briefly on various objects in the room, revealing part—but not all—of the room at any one time. This model assumes that journalists cannot possibly provide an objective view of reality but, at best, can convey only a partial understanding of a situation or an event.

In this essay, I will argue that the "flashlight" model provides a more accurate and complex understanding of the role of journalists in America than the "mirror" model does. This model recognizes, for instance, that journalists are shaped by their personal backgrounds and experiences and by the pressures, mores, and customs of their profession. It also recognizes that journalists are under commercial pressure to sell their stories. Newspapers and commercial networks are run on a for-profit basis. Thus reporters have to "sell" their stories to readers. The easiest way to do that is to fit a given news event into a "story" framework. Human beings generally relate well to easily digestible stories, as opposed to more complex analyses, which require more thought and concentration. Reporters assigned to cover a given situation are likely to ask "What is the story?" and then to force events into that framework. Reality is seldom as neat as a story, however, with neat

Leman 2

compartments of "Once upon a time . . . ," "and then . . . ," and "The End." But the story framework dominates news coverage of events; thus the media cannot function as a mirror since mirrors reflect rather than distort reality (except in funhouses).

The "mirror" model also fails to acknowledge that journalists make choices, including decisions about what stories to cover. These choices can be based on personal preference, but usually they are determined by editors, who respond to publishers, who, in turn, are eager to sell their product to the widest possible audiences. Most people prefer not to read about seemingly insoluble social problems like poverty or homelessness. As a result, journalists often choose not to cover social issues unless they fit a particular "story" format.

In addition to deciding what to cover, journalists must determine the tone they will take in their reporting. If the "mirror" model of media theory were accurate, journalists wouldn't make implicit or explicit judgments in their reporting. But they do. They are only human, after all, and they will inevitably be influenced by their admiration or dislike for a person about whom they are writing or by their belief about the significance of an event.

From start to finish, journalists must make a series of choices. They first make choices about what to cover; then they make choices about whether their tone will be positive or negative, which facts to include or omit, what adjectives to use, and so on. Mirrors do not make choices — but a person holding a flashlight does. The latter can decide where to let the light drop, how long to leave it on that spot, and when to shift the light to something else. Journalists make these kinds of choices every day. Consequently, the "flashlight" model provides the more accurate understanding of the role that journalists play in American society, for the "mirror" model fails to take into account the many factors shaping even the simplest news story.

||||||||||||||||||||||||||||||||||||||||||||||||||||||||||||||||||||||||||||||||||||||

FOR COLLABORATION

Working with a group of classmates, respond to these questions about Hope Leman's essay. Appoint a recorder to write down the results of your discussion, which your instructor may ask you to present to the class.

1. Hope begins her essay not by attempting to interest readers in her subject but by defining the "mirror" and "flashlight" models of media theory. Why might this be an effective way to begin her essay?

2. Writers need to have a working thesis, or controlling purpose, when they write. ✱ Sometimes they signal this purpose by articulating an explicit thesis statement. Sometimes only subtle cues are necessary. (Students writing a personal essay might not want, for instance, to state their controlling purpose explicitly at the start of their essay but rather let readers discover it as they read.) In her essay, Hope includes an explicit thesis statement. Identify this statement, and then discuss the reasons that it is necessary in her particular situation.

3. Academic writing is sometimes viewed as dull and lifeless—as, well, *academic*. Yet even in this essay written under time pressure, Hope's writing is not stuffy, dull, or pompous. Examine her essay to identify passages where a personal voice contributes to the overall effectiveness of her essay. How does Hope blend this personal voice with the objective and distanced approach of her essay?

||||||||||||||||||||||||||||||||||||||||||||||||||||||||||||||||||||||||||||||||||||||

Understanding How Analysis Works

As a student, you must respond to a wide range of writing assignments. For an American literature class, you may have to analyze the significance of the whiteness of the whale in *Moby-Dick*, whereas a business management class may require a collaboratively written case study; you may need to write a lab report for a chemistry class and critique a qualitative research report for sociology. Although these assignments vary considerably, they all require and depend on your analysis.

As noted earlier, analysis involves separating something into parts and determining how these parts function to create the whole. When you analyze, you examine a text, an object, or a body of data to understand how it is structured or organized and to assess its effectiveness or validity. Most academic writing, thinking, and reading involve analysis. Literature students analyze how a play is structured or how a poem achieves its effect; economics students analyze the major causes of inflation; biology students analyze the enzymatic reactions that comprise the Krebs cycle; and art history students analyze how line, color, and texture come together in a painting.

· · · · · · · · · · ✱   See also Chapter 12, pp. 307–8.

As these examples indicate, analysis is not a single skill but a group of related skills. An art history student might explore how a painting by Michelangelo achieves its effect, for instance, by comparing it with a similar work by Raphael. A biology student might discuss future acid-rain damage to forests in Canada and the United States by first defining *acid rain* and then using cause-and-effect reasoning to predict worsening conditions. A student in economics might estimate the likelihood of severe inflation in the coming year by categorizing or classifying the major causes of previous inflationary periods and then evaluating the likelihood that such factors will influence the current economic situation.

Different disciplines emphasize different analytic skills. (For more on what's required in different disciplines, see Chapter 8.) But regardless of your major, you need to understand and practice these crucial academic skills. You will do so most successfully if you establish a purpose and develop an appropriate framework or method for your analysis.

Establishing a Purpose for Your Analysis

Your instructors will often ask you to analyze a fairly limited subject, problem, or process: Lily Briscoe's role in Virginia Woolf's *To the Lighthouse*, feminists' criticisms of Freud's psychoanalytical theories, Mendel's third law of genetics. Such limited tasks are necessary because of the complexity of the material, but the larger purpose of your analysis is to better understand your topic's role within a larger context—for example, a literary work that you are analyzing or a political or philosophical theory. When you analyze a limited topic, you're like a person holding a flashlight in the dark: The beam of light that you project is narrow and focused, but it illuminates a much larger area.

> thinking
> rhetorically

Even though the purpose of your analysis is to understand the larger subject, you still need to establish a more specific purpose for your analysis. Imagine, for instance, that your Shakespeare instructor has asked you to write an essay on the fool in *King Lear*. You might establish one of several purposes for your analysis:

- To explain how the fool contributes to the development of a major theme in *King Lear*

- To discuss the effectiveness or plausibility of Shakespeare's characterization of the fool

- To define the role the fool plays in the plot

- To agree or disagree with a particular critical perspective on the fool's role and significance

Establishing a specific purpose helps you define how your analysis should proceed. It enables you to determine the important issues to address or the questions to answer.

There are no one-size-fits-all procedures for establishing a purpose for your analysis. Sometimes your purpose will develop naturally as a result of reading, reflection, and discussion with others. In other instances, it may help to draw on the invention strategies described in Chapter 11; these strategies help you explore your subject and discover questions to guide your analysis. Since writing and thinking are dynamically interwoven processes, you may at times need to *write* your way into an understanding of your purpose by composing a rough draft and seeing, in effect, what you think about your topic.

Developing an Appropriate Method for Your Analysis

Once you have a purpose, how do you actually analyze something? The answer depends on the subject, process, or problem being analyzed. In general, however, you should consider the methods of inquiry characteristic of the discipline in which you're writing. While students studying *To the Lighthouse* or Mendel's third law may use the same fundamental analytic *processes* — for example, definition, causal analysis, classification, and comparison — the relative weight they give to these different processes and the way they shape and present their final analyses may well differ.

The questions on p. 99 can help you develop an appropriate method for your analysis. If, after considering these questions and reflecting on your experiences in a class, you continue to have difficulty settling on an appropriate method, meet with your instructor to get help. You might ask him or her to recommend student essays or professional articles that clearly model the analytical methods used in the field.

(thinking rhetorically)

Understanding the Relationship between Analysis and Argument

All academic writing has an argumentative edge, and sometimes that edge is obvious. If a student writes a political science essay arguing that the government should follow a particular environmental policy, that student is explicitly arguing that the government should do something. Essays that discuss whether something should or should not be done are easily recognizable as arguments — probably because they follow the debate format that many associate with argumentation.

But writers can express judgments — can present good reasons for their beliefs and actions — without explicitly endorsing a course of action. For example, a music theory student analyzing the score of a Beethoven sonata

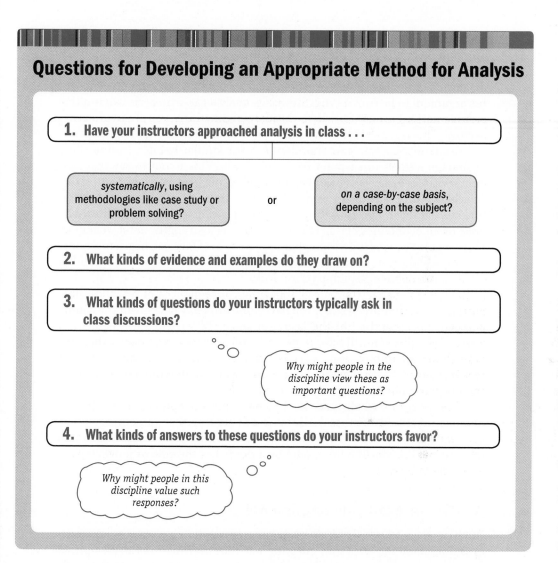

Questions for Developing an Appropriate Method for Analysis

1. Have your instructors approached analysis in class . . .

systematically, using methodologies like case study or problem solving?

or

on a case-by-case basis, depending on the subject?

2. What kinds of evidence and examples do they draw on?

3. What kinds of questions do your instructors typically ask in class discussions?

Why might people in the discipline view these as important questions?

4. What kinds of answers to these questions do your instructors favor?

Why might people in this discipline value such responses?

may argue that the second movement of the particular sonata is more daring or innovative than music historians have acknowledged. To do so, she must convince her reader, in this case her teacher, that she has a sophisticated understanding of the structure of the sonata. Analysis will play a particularly central role in this student's writing: By identifying specific features of the score and positing relationships among these features, she will demonstrate her understanding of Beethoven's use of the sonata form.

As this example demonstrates, analysis and argument are interdependent. Argumentation depends on analysis, for through analysis writers

thinking
rhetorically

clarify the logic of their thinking and provide evidence for their judgments. The student arguing that the government should follow a particular environmental policy, for example, would have to analyze the potential benefits and disadvantages of that policy and demonstrate that it's workable in order for his argument to be convincing. Similarly, analysis always carries an implicit argumentative burden, for when you analyze something, you are in effect asserting "This is how I believe X works" or "This is what I believe X means."

Academic analysis and argument call for similar habits of mind. Both encourage writers to suspend personal biases. This is not to say that academic writers are expected to be absolutely objective. Your gut feeling that "workfare" programs may not provide single parents with adequate support for their children may cause you to investigate this topic for a political science or an economics class. This gut feeling is a strength, not a weakness, for it enables you to find a topic that interests you. Once you begin to explore your topic, however, you need to engage it dispassionately. You need, in other words, to be open to changing your mind.

If you do change your mind about the consequences of workfare programs, the reading and writing you have done probably have given you a more detailed understanding of the issues at stake. To write a successful essay about this topic, you will have to describe these issues and analyze their relationships and implications, developing logical connections that make your reasoning explicit. In these and other ways, you will demonstrate to readers that you have indeed understood your subject.

The essay by Hope Leman that begins on p. 94 is a good example of academic analysis. In this essay, Hope is not arguing that something should or should not be done. Rather, she is attempting to understand whether the "mirror" or "flashlight" model best describes the role of journalists in American society.

Analyzing Academic Arguments

Analysis plays a key role in all academic writing. It helps readers and writers understand the texts they encounter as they move across the disciplines and recognize, examine, and formulate arguments about them. In the world of academia, written works, visual works, and even events or behaviors can be considered "texts" susceptible to analysis. While written texts are still most fundamental to academic study, the ability to analyze texts that depend heavily on images and graphics—whether they are television ads, multimedia presentations, or Web sites—has become increasingly important in our media-saturated culture. For advice on analyzing visuals, see the discussion in Chapter 10, as well as pp. 152–68 of Chapter 6, for a case study of student Daniel Stiepleman's analysis of a public-service ad for the National Center for Family Literacy.

The analysis of any complex text will feel less intimidating if you address three basic questions:

thinking rhetorically

- What question is at issue?

- What position does the author take?

- Do the author's reasons justify your acceptance of his or her argument?

Determining the Question at Issue

When you determine the question at issue, you get to the heart of any argument and distinguish major claims from minor elements of support. You can then identify the author's position and evaluate whether he or she has provided good reasons for you to agree with this position.

thinking rhetorically

Greek and Roman rhetoricians developed a method called *stasis theory* for determining the questions at issue in any argument. Stasis theory encourages readers to identify the major point on which a particular controversy rests. This method presents six basic questions at issue in argumentative writing.*

Stasis Questions

QUESTIONS OF FACT arise from the reader's need to know
"Does _____ exist?"

QUESTIONS OF DEFINITION arise from the reader's need to know
"What is it?"

QUESTIONS OF INTERPRETATION arise from the reader's need to know
"What does it mean?"

QUESTIONS OF VALUE arise from the reader's need to know
"Is it good?"

QUESTIONS OF CONSEQUENCE arise from the reader's need to know
"Will _____ cause _____ to happen?"

QUESTIONS OF POLICY arise from the reader's need to know
"What should be done about it?"

---

*In this discussion of stasis theory, I employ the categories presented in John Gage, *The Shape of Reason: Argumentative Writing in College*, 3rd ed. (Needham Heights, MA: Allyn and Bacon, 1991), 40.

As you determine the kinds of issues addressed in a particular argument, you will draw on your rhetorical sensitivity. You do this naturally in your everyday life. Imagine that a friend has urged you to drive with her to a concert in a city an hour away. You'd like to attend the concert, but it's on a midweek work night. Depending on your situation, the primary question at issue may be one of *value*. If you value the concert enough, then you can justify the time, expense, and late-night bedtime involved in attending the concert. On the other hand, the primary question at issue for you may be one of *consequence*: This would be the case if you couldn't justify time away from study, work, and family, especially on a weeknight.

Here is an argument by Amitai Etzioni about the advantages and disadvantages of traditional privacy protections in North America. Etzioni is a professor at George Washington University and former senior adviser to the White House. He has written over a dozen books, including *The Limits of Privacy*, from which this excerpt is taken. As you read his analysis, consider which of the six stasis questions—fact, definition, interpretation, value, consequence, or policy—are most clearly at stake in his argument.

Less Privacy Is Good for Us (and You)

AMITAI ETZIONI

Despite the fact that privacy is not so much as mentioned in the Constitution and that it was only shoehorned in some thirty-four years ago, it is viewed by most Americans as a profound, inalienable right.

The media is loaded with horror stories about the ways privacy is not so much nibbled away as it is stripped away by bosses who read your e-mail, neighbors who listen in on your cell phones, and E-Z passes that allow tollbooth operators to keep track of your movements. A typical headline decries the "End of Privacy" (Richard A. Spinello, in an issue of *America*, a Catholic weekly) or "The Death of Privacy" (Joshua Quittner, in *Time*).

It is time to pay attention to the other half of the equation that defines a good society: concerns for public health and safety that entail some rather justifiable diminution of privacy.

Take the HIV testing of infants. New medical data — for instance, evidence recently published by the prestigious *New England Journal of Medicine* — show that a significant proportion of children born to mothers who have HIV can ward off this horrible disease but only on two conditions: that their mothers not breastfeed them and that they immediately be given AZT. For this to happen, mothers must be informed that they have HIV. An estimated two-thirds of infected mothers are unaware. However, various civil libertarians and some gay activists vehemently oppose such disclosure on the grounds that when infants are tested for HIV, in effect one finds out if the mother is a carrier, and thus her privacy is violated. While New York State in 1996, after a very acrimonious debate, enacted a law that requires infant testing and disclosure of the findings to the mother, most other states have so far avoided dealing with this issue.

Congress passed the buck by asking the Institute of Medicine (IOM) to conduct a study of the matter. The IOM committee, dominated by politically correct people, just reported its recommendations. It suggested that all pregnant women be asked to consent to HIV testing as part of routine prenatal care. There is little wrong with such a recommendation other than it does not deal with many of the mothers who are drug addicts or otherwise live at society's margins. Many of these women do not show up for prenatal care, and they are particularly prone to HIV, according to a study published in the American Health Association's *Journal of School Health*. To save the lives of their children, they must be tested at delivery and treated even if this entails a violation of mothers' privacy.

Recently a suggestion to use driver's licenses to curb illegal immigration has sent the Coalition for Constitutional Liberties, a large group of libertarians, civil libertarians, and privacy advocates, into higher orbit than John Glenn ever traversed. The coalition wrote:

> This plan pushed us to the brink of tyranny, where citizens will not be allowed to travel, open bank accounts, obtain health care, get a job, or purchase firearms without first presenting the proper government papers.
>
> The authorizing section of the law . . . is reminiscent of the totalitarian dictates by Politburo members in the former Soviet Union, not the Congress of the United States of America.

Meanwhile, Wells Fargo is introducing a new device that allows a person to cash checks at its ATM machines because the machines recognize faces. Rapidly coming is a whole new industry of so-called biometrics that uses natural features such as voice, hand design, and eye pattern to recognize a person with the same extremely high reliability provided by the new DNA tests.

It's true that as biometrics catches on, it will practically strip Americans of anonymity, an important part of privacy. In the near future, a person who acquired a poor reputation in one part of the country will find it much more difficult to move to another part, change his name, and gain a whole fresh start. Biometrics see right through such assumed identities. One may hope that future communities will become more tolerant of such people, especially if they openly acknowledge the mistakes of their past and truly seek to lead a more prosocial life. But they will no longer be able to hide their pasts.

Above all, while biometrics clearly undermines privacy, the social benefits it promises are very substantial. Specifically, each year at least half a million criminals become fugitives, avoiding trial, incarceration, or serving their full sentences, often committing additional crimes while on the lam. People who fraudulently file for multiple income tax refunds using fake identities and multiple Social Security numbers cost the nation between $1 billion and $5 billion per year. Numerous divorced parents escape their financial obligations to their children by avoiding detection when they move or change jobs. (The sums owed to children are variously estimated as running between $18 billion to $23 billion a year.) Professional and amateur criminals, employing fraudulent identification documentation to make phony credit card purchases, cost credit card companies and retail businesses an indeterminate number of billions of dollars each year. The United States loses an estimated $18 billion a year to benefit fraud committed by illegal aliens using false IDs. A 1998 General Accounting Office report estimates identity fraud to cost $10 billion annually in entitlement programs alone.

People hired to work in child care centers, kindergartens, and schools cannot be effectively screened to keep out child abusers and sex offenders, largely because when background checks are conducted, convicted criminals escape detection by using false identification and aliases. Biometrics would sharply curtail all these crimes, although far from wipe them out single-handedly.

The courts have recognized that privacy must be weighed against considerations of public interest but have tended to privilege privacy and make claims for public health or safety clear several high hurdles. In recent years these barriers have been somewhat lowered as courts have become more concerned with public safety and health. Given that these often are matters of state law and that neither legislatures nor courts act in unison, the details are complex and far from all pointing in one direction. But, by and large, courts have allowed mandatory drug testing of those who directly have the lives of others in their hands, including pilots, train engineers, drivers of school buses, and air traffic controllers, even though such testing violates their privacy. In case after case, the courts have disregarded objections to such tests by civil libertarians who argue that such tests constitute "suspicionless" searches, grossly violate privacy, and—as the ACLU puts it—"condition Americans to a police state."

All this points to a need to recast privacy in our civic culture, public policies, and legal doctrines. We should cease to treat it as an unmitigated good, a sacred right (the way Warren and Brandeis referred to in their famous article and many since) or one that courts automatically privilege.

Instead, privacy should rely squarely on the Fourth Amendment, the only one that has a balance built right into its text. It recognizes both searches that wantonly violate privacy ("unreasonable" ones) and those that enhance the common good to such an extent that they are justified, even if they intrude into one's privacy. Moreover, it provides a mechanism to sort out which searches are in the public interest and which violate privacy without sufficient cause, by introducing the concept of warrants issued by a "neutral magistrate" presented with "probable cause." Warrants also limit the invasion of privacy "by specification of the person to be seized, the place to be searched, and the evidence to be sought." The Fourth may have become the Constitutional Foundation of privacy a long time ago if it was not for the fact that *Roe v. Wade* is construed as a privacy right, and touching it provokes fierce opposition. The good news, though, is that even the advocates of choice in this area are now looking to base their position on some other legal grounds, especially the Fourteenth Amendment.

We might be ready to treat privacy for what it is: one very important right but not one that trumps most other considerations, especially of public safety and health.

||||||||||||||||||||||||||||||||||||||||||||||||||||||||||||||||||||||||||||||||||||||||||

FOR COLLABORATION

After you have read Etzioni's argument, list the two most significant stasis questions (see p. 101) at stake in his argument. Find at least one passage that you believe relates to each question. Then meet with a group of classmates and share your responses to this assignment. (Appoint a timekeeper to ensure that all members of your group have a chance to share their responses.) To what extent did you agree or disagree with other group members on the stasis questions at stake in Etzioni's analysis? As a group, choose the two questions that best apply to Etzioni's argument, and agree on two or three reasons why each question is central to his argument. Be prepared to share the results of your discussion with your class.

||||||||||||||||||||||||||||||||||||||||||||||||||||||||||||||||||||||||||||||||||||||||||

Identifying an Author's Position on a Question

You may find it helpful to identify an author's position in two stages: *First, read the text carefully to determine the main question that the author has presented.* If you review the first three paragraphs of Etzioni's argument beginning on p. 102, for instance, you'll note that he observes in paragraph 1 that privacy "is viewed by most Americans as a profound, inalienable right" and goes on to argue in paragraph 3 that "[i]t is time to pay attention to the other half of the equation that defines a good society: concerns for public health and safety that entail some rather justifiable diminution of privacy." The remainder of the excerpt clarifies and supports his position on this issue.

After you have identified the author's position, you can read his or her argument critically. Reading critically doesn't mean simply looking for logical flaws, poor evidence, and so on. Rather, critical readers shift stances as they read to develop a complex understanding of the issues at hand.

The Questions for Critical Reading and Analysis on pp. 107–8 can help you become a more active and critical reader who reads both with and against the grain of an author's argument.

|||||||||||||||||||||||||||||||||||||||||||||||||||||||||||||||||||||||||||||||||||||||||||

FOR EXPLORATION

Reread the excerpt from Amitai Etzioni's *The Limits of Privacy* (pp. 102–5). After doing so, respond to each of the Questions for Critical Reading and Analysis on pp. 107–8. What did this guided rereading of Etzioni's text help you better understand about it?

FOR COLLABORATION

After you have analyzed Etzioni's argument with the help of the Questions for Critical Reading and Analysis, meet with a group of classmates to share your results. Appoint a timekeeper so that all group members have an opportunity to share their results. To what extent did other group members agree in their responses to the Questions for Critical Reading and Analysis? To what extent did they disagree? What did you learn as a result of this experience? Be prepared to share your responses with the rest of the class.

|||||||||||||||||||||||||||||||||||||||||||||||||||||||||||||||||||||||||||||||||||||||||||

Using Aristotle's Three Appeals

As the Questions for Critical Reading and Analysis on pp. 107–8 suggest, you may agree with a writer's position on a subject but nevertheless question the support that he or she provides. One of the hallmarks of a critical reader, in fact, is the ability to maintain a critical distance from an argument, even when you have strong feelings for or against the author's position. Aristotle's three appeals, introduced on p. 65 in Chapter 4, can help you evaluate the strength and limitation of academic arguments.

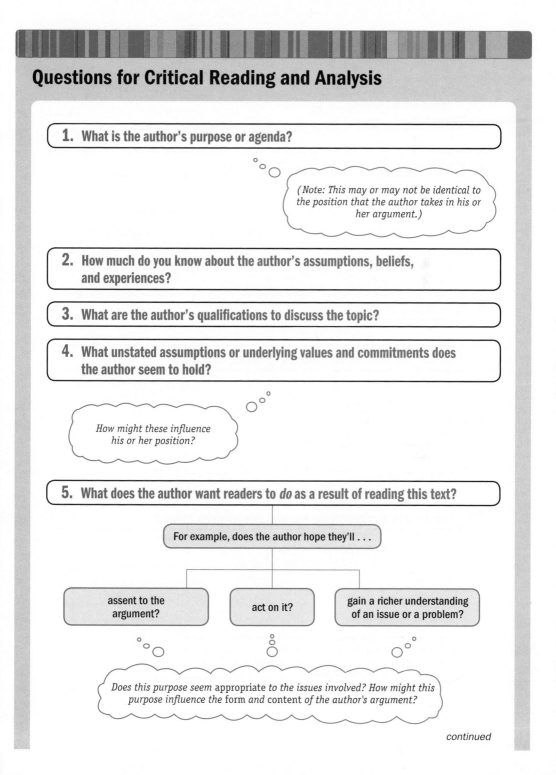

Questions for Critical Reading and Analysis

1. What is the author's purpose or agenda?

(Note: This may or may not be identical to the position that the author takes in his or her argument.)

2. How much do you know about the author's assumptions, beliefs, and experiences?

3. What are the author's qualifications to discuss the topic?

4. What unstated assumptions or underlying values and commitments does the author seem to hold?

How might these influence his or her position?

5. What does the author want readers to *do* as a result of reading this text?

For example, does the author hope they'll . . .

assent to the argument?

act on it?

gain a richer understanding of an issue or a problem?

Does this purpose seem appropriate to the issues involved? How might this purpose influence the form and content of the author's argument?

continued

6. **What reasons does the author offer in support of his or her ideas?**

(Are they good reasons?)

7. **What kinds of sources does the author rely on?**

How current and reliable are they? Are any perspectives left out?

8. **What objections might be raised to this argument?**

9. **Does this argument include images, graphics, or media?**

If so, how do they appeal to readers or listeners? Does their appeal seem appropriate or questionable?

10. **How open to persuasion are you with this particular topic?**

How willing are you to listen to another point of view?

If you agree with the author, can you maintain a critical distance so that you can examine the claims and support that the writer provides?

In his *Rhetoric*, Aristotle determined that speakers and writers draw on three general appeals when they attempt to persuade others:

- *Logos,* the appeal to reason

- *Pathos,* the appeal to emotion, values, and beliefs

- *Ethos,* the appeal to the credibility of the speaker or writer

One way to analyze an argument is to determine which type of appeal the author draws on most heavily and his or her effectiveness in using it. When you consider appeals to logos, ask yourself if the author has articulated clear and reasonable major claims and supported them with appropriate evidence. Appeals to pathos raise different issues: Here you identify the strategies that the author has employed to appeal to readers' values and interests. Finally, appeals to ethos encourage you to consider the author's credibility and trustworthiness as demonstrated in his or her argument.

Appeals to logos are often considered especially trustworthy by North American readers, particularly in academic contexts. Logical appeals include firsthand evidence—drawn from observations, interviews, surveys and questionnaires, experiments, and personal experience—and secondhand evidence—drawn from print and online sources. Critical readers do not automatically assume that support drawn from logical appeals is valid. After all, not all sources are equally valid, and facts can be out-of-date or taken out of context. (For a discussion of how to evaluate print and online sources, see pp. 198–206.)

Critical readers look at all three of Aristotle's appeals in context. Appeals to pathos—to readers' emotions, values, and beliefs—can certainly be manipulative and inappropriate. We've all seen ads that seem to promise one thing (youth, beauty, fitness) to sell another. Nevertheless, emotional appeals play key roles in many kinds of arguments, including academic arguments. A student writing about humanitarian issues growing out of the conflict in Syria might begin her essay by describing the loss of life, order, and basic material necessities that have resulted from the conflict. In so doing, she would be appealing to readers' emotions and emphasizing the importance of her topic. The same is true for appeals to ethos. While we might be skeptical when we see an ad in which a movie star or sports hero praises a product, this doesn't mean that all appeals to ethos are suspect.

In this regard, let's return to the excerpt from Etzioni's *The Limits of Privacy* (pp. 102–5). The biographical information that accompanies this excerpt provides information about Etzioni's experience and qualifications that can help readers determine whether Etzioni is an authority on issues of privacy. Critical readers will keep this knowledge in mind as they read his argument, but they'll also consider the credibility with which he makes his case. Does he use examples that are fair and reasonable? Does he develop a balanced, thoughtful argument? Does he seem to have society's best interest at heart, or is he pushing an agenda of his own personal assumptions and beliefs? By asking questions such as these, readers can determine whether they should trust Etzioni's credibility as a thinker and writer. In short, critical readers respect relevant experiences and qualifications that authors bring to various issues, but they focus primarily on what the author does and says in the text that they are currently reading.

||||||||||||||||||||||||||||||||||||||||||||||||||||||||||||||||||||||||||||||||||||||

FOR EXPLORATION

Drawing on your understanding of Aristotle's three appeals, analyze the excerpt from Etzioni's *The Limits of Privacy* (pp. 102–5). What appeals does he draw on most heavily? How effective is he in using these appeals? (Be sure to comment on each of the three appeals.)

FOR COLLABORATION

Meet with a group of classmates to share your responses to the previous Exploration. Appoint both a timekeeper and a recorder to summarize your group's responses. Begin by addressing this question: To what extent did members of your group agree about Etzioni's effectiveness in his use of Aristotle's three appeals?

After responding, develop a group position on Etzioni's use of Aristotle's three appeals. To do so, first agree on a statement that conveys your group's sense of how Etzioni employed each appeal. Then find one or two examples from his text that support your analysis. Be prepared to share the results of your discussion with the class.

||||||||||||||||||||||||||||||||||||||||||||||||||||||||||||||||||||||||||||||||||||||

Recognizing Fallacies

When you analyze an argument, you should be aware of *fallacies* that may be at work. Fallacies are faults in an argument's structure that may call into question the argument's evidence or conclusions. Some fallacies are easy to recognize. If someone told you that Bono's position on the AIDS pandemic in Africa is ridiculous because he's just a celebrity, you would probably recognize that this assertion is illogical and unfair. Such a statement is an example of an *ad hominem* fallacy, in which an attack on someone's character or actions masquerades as a critique of his or her position. This fallacy, like all fallacies, tends to shut down, rather than encourage, communication.

To determine whether an argument is grounded in a fallacy, you need to consider it in the context of its specific rhetorical situation, including the place and time in which the argument was or is being made. Sometimes judgments about a person's character or actions are relevant to an argument, for instance. In other words, just because a writer or speaker grounds part of an argument in such a judgment doesn't mean that he or she is committing an *ad hominem* fallacy.

Since the time of Aristotle, rhetoricians have developed diverse ways of naming, describing, and categorizing various fallacies. Often the fallacies are categorized according to Aristotle's three major appeals of argument—ethical appeals (appeals to ethos), emotional appeals (appeals to pathos), and logical appeals (appeals to logos).

The following guidelines list some of the most significant fallacies that appear in arguments. As you read the brief descriptions, remember that the point of studying fallacies is not to discredit the ideas of others, but rather to thoughtfully evaluate the arguments of others and to develop fair, well-reasoned arguments of your own.

Guidelines for Identifying Fallacies

Ethical Fallacies

Writers who employ ethical fallacies attempt to discredit their opponents. Examples of ethical fallacies include the following:

AN AD HOMINEM attack is an unfair assault on a person's character or actions. one that diverts attention from the issue at hand.

"Any American who opposes the war on terror is unpatriotic."

(A person's position on this topic does not indicate his or her patriotism.)

GUILT BY ASSOCIATION is an effort to damage a person's credibility by associating him or her with an unpopular or discredited activity or person.

"Hip-hop is bad because some hip-hop musicians have been involved in criminal activities."

(The behavior of hip-hop musicians is separate from the music they create.)

Emotional Fallacies

Emotional appeals can play a valid and important role in argumentation, but when these appeals are overblown or unfair, they distract readers from attending to the point that is being argued. Examples of emotional fallacies include the following:

A BANDWAGON APPEAL argues that readers should support a person, an activity, a product, or a movement because it is popular. This appeal is particularly common in advertising:

"Frosty Puffs™ is the best-selling cereal in America!"

A SLIPPERY SLOPE fallacy occurs when writers exaggerate the consequences of an event or action, usually with an intent to frighten readers into agreeing with their conclusion.

"If we ban *Beloved* from our school library, the next thing you know, we'll be burning books!"

Logical Fallacies

Logical fallacies are arguments in which the claims, warrants, or evidence are invalid, insufficient, or disconnected. Examples of logical fallacies include the following:

BEGGING THE QUESTION involves stating a claim that depends on circular reasoning for justification.

"Abortion is murder because it involves the intentional killing of an unborn human being."

(This is tantamount to saying, "Abortion is murder because it is murder." This fallacy often detracts attention from the real issues at hand, for the question of whether a fetus should be considered a human being is complex.)

A HASTY GENERALIZATION is drawn from insufficient evidence.

"Last week I attended a poetry reading supported by the National Endowment for the Arts, and several of the speakers used profanity. Maybe the people who want to stop government funding for the NEA are right."

(One performance doesn't constitute a large enough sample for such a generalization.)

A NON SEQUITUR is an argument that attempts to connect two or more logically unrelated ideas.

"I hate it when people smoke in restaurants; there ought to be a law against cigarettes."

(Eliminating smoking in restaurants and the negative effects of secondhand smoke do not require the elimination of legal tobacco sales.)

A RED HERRING is an argument that misleads or distracts opponents from the original issue.

"How can you expect me to worry about global warming when we're on the brink of war?"

(Whether or not we're on the brink of war is irrelevant to whether global warming is a problem.)

A STRAW MAN fallacy occurs when a misrepresentation, an exaggeration, or a distortion of a position is attacked.

"My opponent argues that drugs should be legalized without taking into consideration the epidemic that selling heroin in every drugstore would cause."

(Arguing in favor of legalizing drugs does not mean that all drugs would be available over the counter.)

|||||||||||||||||||||||||||||||||||||||||||||||||||||||||||||||||||||||||||||||||||||||||||||||||

FOR EXPLORATION

Locate three of the fallacies described above in such popular media as political Web sites, the editorial pages of your favorite newspaper, or in advertisements in print or online. Identify the fallacy and explain how it functions in its particular context.

|||||||||||||||||||||||||||||||||||||||||||||||||||||||||||||||||||||||||||||||||||||||||||||||||

Putting Theory into Practice I: Academic Analysis in Action

Readers engage in academic analysis not to criticize or dissect another's argument but rather to understand that argument as fully as possible. When you analyze an academic argument, you attempt to go beyond your immediate response — which often takes the form of binary-driven observations ("I agree/don't agree, like/don't like, am interested/not interested in X") — to achieve a fuller, more complex understanding of it.

Here is an example of a successful analysis of an academic argument. This essay by Stevon Roberts, a student at Oregon State University, analyzes the excerpt from Etzioni's *The Limits of Privacy* presented earlier in this chapter (pp. 102–5).

Stevon Roberts
Dr. Mallon
Composition 101
Oct. 10, 2013

The Price of Public Safety

As a former senior adviser to the White House and author of *The Limits of Privacy*, Amitai Etzioni is a formidable advocate for revision of one of America's most cherished luxuries: protection of personal privacy. In "Less Privacy Is Good for Us (and You)," an argument excerpted from the above volume, Etzioni urges Americans to look critically at traditional expectations for personal privacy and to be prepared to sacrifice those expectations for increased public health and safety. Although the volume was published before the terrorist attacks on September 11, 2001, the events of that day give an increased sense of urgency to Etzioni's message and consequently might make Americans more receptive to protocols that afford protection from public risks in general.

Etzioni opens his argument by discussing recent HIV testing procedures in hospitals that may infringe on the rights of pregnant women. He then shifts gears and takes a brief look at public outrage from the Coalition for Constitutional Liberties regarding driver's license availability. Next, he gives us a crash course in "biometrics," a controversial new technology that could save billions of dollars lost to fraud every year. Finally, Etzioni addresses our fears (and those of other civil libertarians) that these and other procedures that are designed to increase our public health and safety will not be implemented justly and ethically. Etzioni admits, however, that a growing number of people and interest groups are not convinced that old laws—such as the Fourth Amendment, which protects the United States from becoming a military state—can protect us from new technology. We are left to wonder: Is Etzioni justified in making his unconventional claims despite such well-founded opposition?

After some brief media references, Etzioni's first substantial argument involves a real-world privacy dilemma facing pregnant women as well as

Identifies the argument and suggests its author is credible

Identifies Etzioni's position

Contrasts rhetorical situations of writing the piece and reading it

Summarizes Etzioni's argument fairly and introduces main question: Is Etzioni's argument legitimate?

Roberts 2

various health and legal groups. Specifically, he focuses on HIV testing of newborns. This is an excellent place to start because the reactions of these groups help shed light on our current attitudes toward privacy. Etzioni refers to the *New England Journal of Medicine*, which published evidence suggesting that infants born to HIV-infected women could ward off the disease with early diagnosis and treatment with AZT. In order for the infants to be treated, they must be tested. This becomes a privacy issue because testing infants for HIV also reveals whether "the mother is a carrier, and thus her privacy is violated" (103).

Notes major evidence Etzioni provides to support his claim

As Etzioni acknowledges, arguments in favor of required HIV testing of infants have met strong—and even "vehement"—opposition from civil libertarians, as well as from some gay activists. Indeed, the question of whether to test infants for HIV has been so contentious that most states, as well as the federal government, have avoided taking it on. In this regard, Etzioni chastises Congress for "pass[ing] the buck by asking the Institute of Medicine (IOM) to conduct a study of the matter" (103). This effectively illustrates Congress's lack of willingness to become involved. IOM's solution suggests that all pregnant women should consent to HIV testing as part of their routine prenatal care. However, Etzioni feels this would leave out many women who "are drug addicts or otherwise live at society's margins" (103). Such women, he argues, "do not show up for prenatal care, and they are particularly prone to HIV, according to a study published in the American Health Association's *Journal of School Health*" (103). A succinct sentence sums up his solution: "To save the lives of their children, they [infants] must be tested at delivery and treated even if this entails a violation of mothers' privacy" (103).

Establishes own ethos by signaling he's providing balanced assessment of Etzioni's argument

This is a well-documented and compelling argument. Other parts of Etzioni's text, however, are not so well rounded. Instead of taking seriously the arguments forwarded by civil libertarians and others who raise concerns about privacy, Etzioni focuses on the media, which he believes tell "horror stories" about "The Death of Privacy" (102). When he does address the views of other groups, he represents their concerns by an inflammatory statement

Roberts 3

from the Coalition for Constitutional Liberties, which accuses those in favor of the plan of pushing the country "to the brink of tyranny" (103).

    With this brief (and wholly unsuccessful) transition, Etzioni moves from the Coalition's alarmist complaints to Wells Fargo's introduction of "a new device that allows a person to cash checks at its ATM machines because the machines recognize faces" (103). These machines rely upon a new technology called biometrics, which, Etzioni explains, can use "natural features such as voice, hand design, and eye pattern to recognize a person with the same extremely high reliability provided by the new DNA tests" (103). Etzioni acknowledges that biometrics is a controversial technology, and he concedes that "it will practically strip Americans of anonymity, an important part of privacy" (104). With this new technology, people would find it difficult to change their names, move to another part of the country, and gain a fresh start in life. His solution is a hope that "future communities will become more tolerant of such people, especially if they openly acknowledge the mistakes of their past and truly seek to lead a more prosocial life" (104).

    To his credit, Etzioni is quick to follow up the drawbacks of biometrics with compelling statistics about the potential benefits. He says, "Above all, while biometrics clearly undermines privacy, the social benefits it promises are very substantial" (104). He refers to the $1 billion to $5 billion lost annually to tax fraud, $18 billion to $23 billion annually in lost child support, and $18 billion a year lost to fraud committed by illegal aliens with false IDs. In addition to the potential economic benefits, he says sex offenders who use false IDs would be more effectively screened and would less easily find work at child-care centers or schools (104).

    Etzioni's presentation of biometrics is, ironically, both calculated and lacking in logic. His predominantly economic appeal doesn't mention the cost associated with Wells Fargo's new face-recognizing ATM machines. Because he makes no attempt, even hypothetically, to weigh the cost of biometrics implementation against the savings from fraud protection or other liabilities, readers are left to assume that the overall results are beneficial, when that might not, in fact, be the case. For example, although

Side annotations:

Asserts first criticism of Etzioni's argument: Etzioni's representation of opposing viewpoints is not balanced

Balances criticism of Etzioni's argument with praise

Presents another major criticism of Etzioni's use of evidence

Roberts 4

he discusses credit card fraud, there is no mention of Internet credit card fraud. Biometrics countermeasures to combat this threat are likely to manifest as computer hardware add-ons, putting an unfair financial burden on lower-level consumers while taking the liability away from the credit card companies. It seems reasonable that while calculating the potential benefits, Etzioni should also calculate potential losses or system limitations, as he does when admitting that biometrics would not single-handedly wipe out abusers from child-care centers.

Raises questions about Etzioni's appeals to pathos and points out that Etzioni does not anticipate potential limitation to argument

Additionally, the author's appeals to pathos lack substance. In fact, his only olive branch to the human condition is a concession that biometrics may make it difficult for criminals seeking a new life. His solution to this problem is a touchy-feely dream in which everyone magically becomes more tolerant of criminals that repent and sin no more. Further, he makes no mention at all of persons seeking new lives for reasons other than legal trouble, such as women who have fled abusive husbands.

Etzioni concludes his argument by considering court trends in balancing the need to protect personal privacy with concerns about public health and safety. Etzioni observes that courts have tended to "privilege privacy and make claims for public health or safety clear several high hurdles" (104). More recently, however, the courts are lowering these barriers with growing concern for public interest. For example, the courts have mandated drug testing for those who "directly have the lives of others in their hands, including pilots, train engineers, drivers of school buses, and air traffic controllers, even though such testing violates their privacy" (104). Etzioni reports that the ACLU feels these new laws "condition Americans to a police state" (104).

"All this," according to Etzioni, "points to a need to recast privacy in our civic culture, public policies, and legal doctrines. We should cease to treat it as an unmitigated good, a sacred right (the way Warren and Brandeis referred to in their famous article and many [other legal theorists have] since) or one that courts automatically privilege" (105). He feels that we should instead rely on the Fourth Amendment, which has built into its text

Roberts 5

safeguards that balance privacy and public security. His interpretation of the document's reference to "unreasonable" search protocols recognizes the difference between searches that "wantonly violate privacy" and those that "enhance the common good to such an extent that they are justified, even if they intrude into one's privacy" (105). Additionally, the amendment addresses sufficient cause by introducing warrants "issued by a 'neutral magistrate' presented with 'probable cause'" (105). Etzioni apparently believes interpretation of this document will be uniform from one court to the next. This assumption is problematic at best.

Challenges one of Etzioni's key assumptions

The author leaves us with a new vision of privacy as a "very important right but not one that trumps most other considerations, especially of public safety and health" (105). With this parting thought, the author packages a difficult and complex concept into a pill that is not terribly difficult to swallow. By the same token, however, his oversimplification may leave some readers feeling like something is missing.

Indeed, something is missing—the rest of Etzioni's book, from which this excerpt originates. Readers of this argument can only hope that Etzioni deals carefully and respectfully with the arguments of civil libertarians in other parts of his work, for he certainly does not do so here. His tendency to use only the most inflammatory statements from his opponents suggests he has no interest in fully addressing their respective concerns.

Adds to own ethos by acknowledging limitations of his perspective, as a reader not of the book but of the excerpt

All things considered, Etzioni begins his essay with a clear purpose and a logical, tangible starting point. Through the inclusion of several diverse public-interest groups, health organizations, courts, and governmental bodies, he initially appears to address all aspects of the moral dilemma. This is especially true in the obvious benefit to newborns with HIV who are diagnosed early. But in this excerpt, he distracts readers from the true opposition by focusing primarily on the media, while turning the Coalition for Constitutional Liberties and the ACLU into radical doomsayers that jeopardize public welfare. He marginalizes their concerns, argues for increased biometrics applications on the chance that billions of dollars might potentially be protected from fraud, and opposes legislation that would

Closes with careful summary of major points examining Etzioni's argument

Roberts 6

protect potential victims because society potentially could be more forgiving. Consequently, his venture into the hypothetical realm leaves opponents (and critical readers) unsatisfied.

Work Cited

Etzioni, Amitai. "Less Privacy Is Good for Us (and You)." *The Academic Writer: A Brief Guide*. Ed. Lisa Ede. 3rd ed. Boston: Bedford, 2014. 102–5. Print.

Note: In an actual MLA-style paper, works-cited entries start on a new page.

| | | | | | | | | | | | | | | | | | | | | | | | | | | | | | | | | | | | | | | | | | | | | | | | | | | | | | | | | | | | | | | | | | | | | | | | | | | | | | | | | | | |

FOR EXPLORATION

Now that you have read Etzioni's argument several times and have also read Stevon Roberts's analysis of it, reread Stevon's essay to determine its strengths and limitations. Identify two or three passages from the essay that struck you as particularly significant and helpful, and write several sentences of explanation for each passage. Next, identify one or more ways this essay might be even more successful.

FOR COLLABORATION

Bring your response to the previous Exploration to class to share with a group of peers. Appoint a timekeeper and a recorder. After all group members have shared their responses, answer these questions: (1) To what extent did other members of your group agree in their evaluation of Stevon Roberts's analysis? To what extent did they disagree? (2) Now that you have heard everyone's responses, what two or three passages does your group feel best demonstrate Stevon's analytical skills? (3) How might Stevon's essay be further strengthened? Be prepared to share the results of your discussion with the class.

| | | | | | | | | | | | | | | | | | | | | | | | | | | | | | | | | | | | | | | | | | | | | | | | | | | | | | | | | | | | | | | | | | | | | | | | | | | | | | | | | | | |

Understanding How Synthesis Works

Analysis often is connected with and leads to synthesis. When you analyze something, you examine it critically to understand how it is structured and how the parts work together to create the overall meaning. When you synthesize something, you draw on ideas or information from sources, as well as from your own experience, to create meaning of your own.

In much academic writing, synthesis is an important counterpart to analysis, for it enables you to make connections and identify contradictions within a text or group of texts that you have analyzed. Synthesis is an essential part of the research process. For a good example of synthesis, take a look at Alletta Brenner's essay in Chapter 7 (pp. 220–31). There Alletta synthesizes a variety of sources as part of her exploration of the role that human trafficking plays in the American garment-manufacturing industry.

In a research project you typically draw on multiple sources; Alletta Brenner cites almost twenty. Sometimes, however, an instructor will ask you to engage a limited number of texts. Your writing instructor might ask you, for instance, to read and respond to two or more articles on the same or a related topic, with the goal of analyzing and synthesizing these texts while also articulating your own views.

You might think of this kind of synthesis essay as a chronicle of your intellectual journey as you explore a topic and readings related to that topic. This is not to say that your essay should be a narrative; in most cases it is more likely to be an academic argument. But readers of your essay should be able to see that you have interacted at a serious level with the texts to which you are responding and that you have done so to promote your own independent analysis. It should be clear, in other words, that as a result of reading and reflecting on these texts you have gained new insights and perspectives.

Synthesis requires both the ability to analyze and to summarize, and this book contains a number of resources that you might want to review before undertaking a synthesis assignment. (For more on writing effective summaries, see pp. 215–16 in Chapter 7 and pp. 277–79 in Chapter 9; Chapter 9 also provides a number of strategies for strong reading on pp. 267–69.) But it is equally important that you develop your own views on your topic. This may feel difficult at first: How can you challenge the arguments of published authors when you are just a college student? The best way to work your way through this initial hesitation is to immerse yourself deeply in the texts you are engaging.

As you begin your synthesis, focus on developing an understanding of the authors' positions, the reasons and evidence they use to support these positions, the contexts in which they are writing, and any motivating factors, such as their goals, interests, and priorities. Creating a chart in which you can record this information may help you keep track of what you are learning.

The Questions for Critical Reading and Analysis that appear on pp. 107–8 of this chapter will help you consider key aspects of the authors' rhetorical situation, such as each author's purpose or agenda and the values and beliefs that motivate him or her. The questions also encourage you to consider the reasons and evidence the authors provide, the objections that might be raised in response to the authors' positions, their use of evidence, and so

thinking rhetorically

Questions for Synthesizing Texts

1. What are the authors' positions on the topic? Where do they clearly disagree? Where do they agree? What reasons and evidence do they offer? Are there areas of overlap?

2. How do the authors contextualize or frame their discussion of their topic?

3. What do you value about each author's text? What do you question or resist?

4. Having read these texts, how have they helped you consider the topic in new ways? If you cannot identify ways (however minor) in which you have revised your initial position, how can you be sure that you read these texts with an open mind?

5. If you were able to meet each author face-to-face, what are the three most important questions that you would ask him or her? How might these questions and the authors' hypothetical responses help you formulate your own position on the topic?

6. Having read these two essays, what is your position on the topic? How have your previous experiences and current values influenced your position?

forth. The Questions for Synthesizing Texts above can help you synthesize the sources and develop your own approach to the issue.

Putting Theory into Practice II: Academic Synthesis in Action

Synthesis assignments represent an exciting opportunity for students to enter into conversation with others—whether they are nonprofessionals expressing their ideas or professional journalists, politicians, or scholars.

Throughout your college career, and later at work, you will regularly be asked to synthesize ideas and texts. Your psychology teacher may ask you to read two articles taking different positions on whether it is possible to become addicted to social media, such as Facebook and Twitter, and to articulate your own views on this topic. Your business teacher may ask you to study two bids for a hypothetical project and to write a response that includes an evaluation of each bid and a recommendation. Once you graduate and join a company, you may find yourself writing an evaluation of two bids that are anything but hypothetical. In each of these cases, you must carefully and respectfully analyze the texts before you, and you must articulate your own position.

Here is an example of a successful essay analyzing and synthesizing two texts. This essay by Amy Edwards, a student at Oregon State University, was written in response to the following assignment:

> Choose two readings in our anthology that address the same general topic and write an essay that analyzes and synthesizes these two texts. Be sure to analyze these texts carefully, paying attention to their arguments, evidence, and rhetorical situations. But recognize that your goal in writing this essay is not just to respond to the two texts but also to advance your own views on this topic.

Edwards 1

Amy Edwards
Professor Jones
WR 121
March 5, 2013

Digital and Online Technologies: Friend or Foe?

Most people today believe that developments in communication technologies
such as the Internet and social media have consequences, but are these
consequences positive or negative—or mixed? Two writers who ponder this
question are Nicholas Carr and Sherry Turkle. In his 2008 *Atlantic* magazine
article, "Is Google Making Us Stupid?" Carr worries that as technology
improves and the information available from a simple Web search becomes
more and more pervasive, the human brain will adapt to take in a wealth of
information but will lose the propensity for the kind of deep reading and
analysis necessary for true understanding. Turkle, in her 2004 essay "How
Computers Change the Way We Think," published in the *Chronicle of
Higher Education*, similarly argues that new technologies have an impact
on how we think and, indeed, who we are. Both articles encouraged me to
reflect on the role of new technologies in my own life as a person and as a
student. As a result, I now see new digital and online technologies as neither
unilaterally beneficial nor harmful but instead as both shaped by and shaping
our culture. What is most important is that together as a culture we need to
consider questions such as these.

Nicholas Carr is a noted nonfiction writer, journalist, and 2011 Pulitzer
Prize finalist, while Sherry Turkle is a psychologist and professor in the
Program in Science, Technology, and Society at the Massachusetts Institute
of Technology, so perhaps it is not surprising that Turkle's approach is
somewhat more nuanced than Carr's. While Carr refers to research on the
brain, his most compelling arguments derive from his personal experience.
According to Carr, over the past few years he has noticed a change in his
thinking. He notes:

Margin annotations:

Identifies basic question she will address and provides information about authors whose essays she will synthesize and their positions

Articulates own view and presents thesis statement

Provides background about Carr and summarizes his argument

Edwards 2

> What the Net seems to be doing is chipping away my capacity for
> concentration and contemplation. My mind now expects to take
> in information the way the Net distributes it: in a swiftly moving
> stream of particles. Once I was a scuba diver in the sea of words.
> Now I zip along the surface like a guy on a Jet Ski. (2)

Carr's theory is that the brain is an infinitely malleable organ, and the
technologies that we use shape it so that the brain takes on the qualities of
those technologies. For example, he claims:

> The process of adapting to new intellectual technologies is
> reflected in the changing metaphors we use to explain ourselves
> to ourselves. When the mechanical clock arrived, people began
> thinking of their brains as operating "like clockwork." Today, in
> the age of software, we have come to think of them as operating
> "like computers." (4)

In her essay, Turkle agrees that "the tools we use to think change the
ways in which we think" (1). Like Carr, Turkle notes particularly the way
that our increasing reliance on digital and online technologies encourages
people to see the human brain as a computer. Turkle draws on her personal
experience, but she also refers to ongoing research on technology that she
first undertook in the 1980s, at the dawn of the computer and Internet age.
Her goal then was, as she notes in her article, to "study not only what the
computer was doing *for* us, but what it was doing *to* us, including how it was
changing the way we see ourselves, our sense of human identity" (1), and
she has continued to do so ever since.

Turkle touches on a number of issues in her article, from privacy to
online role-playing to the consequences of such programs as PowerPoint.
Unlike Carr, however, Turkle generally refrains from deterministic
predictions and does not attempt to argue whether contemporary digital
and online technologies are intrinsically positive or negative. Instead,

Provides background about Turkle and summarizes her argument

Differentiates between Carr's and Turkle's positions; Continues this analysis in next paragraph, looking for areas of agreement and disagreement, as well as differences in their approaches to topic

Edwards 3

she encourages readers to consider these changes in terms of ongoing interactions between culture and technology, arguing that "information technology is identity technology" (4). In fact, in reflecting on PowerPoint, Turkle asserts that this program "cannot be blamed for lower intellectual standards. Misuse of the former is as much a symptom as a cause of the latter. Indeed, the culture in which our children are raised is increasingly a culture of presentation, a corporate culture in which appearance is often more important than reality" (2).

While Turkle and Carr agree in principle that the Internet is affecting the way that we think and process information, their purposes in writing their essays differ substantially. Both essays are cautionary, designed to encourage scholars and nonscholars alike to consider the impact of the Internet and social media on our lives. However, while Carr focuses primarily on the ways in which Google is making us "stupid," Turkle ranges more broadly. Her final point emphasizes the need for all in our contemporary culture to reflect on their use of new technologies.

> When I first began studying the computer culture, a small breed of highly trained technologists thought of themselves as "computer people." That is no longer the case. If we take the computer as a carrier of a way of knowing, a way of seeing the world and our place in it, we are all computer people now. (4)

Rather than alarming readers, Turkle encourages them to consider their own uses of technology.

My immediate reaction to both essays was one of quiet skepticism. I am quite a bit younger than these two authors, and I have a different perspective about the computer and the Internet, which have always been a part of my life. My first response to Carr was to be defensive: Of course Google isn't making me stupid! But I also wanted to resist Turkle, since I am used to taking the technologies I use day in and day out for granted. That being said, as I read Carr's and Turkle's articles, I began to understand the validity and

Moves from synthesizing Carr's and Turkle's views to reflecting on her experience and its implications for her inquiry

Edwards 4

the timeliness of their concerns. When I was in high school, research often meant reading entire books, even if some of them only had a few sections that I would be able to quote in my papers. By the time I was in college, I did almost all my initial research online. I would still find books and read them, but I would also scan articles from journals and databases, and I began to use the indexes in those books to jump to the chapters or paragraphs that concerned my topic, often never reading the rest of the book. This was faster and more efficient, but perhaps in doing so, just as Carr predicts, I learned to skim over the surface of my topic and ignore or omit deeper connections and more complex readings.

Turkle's essay encouraged me to take a deeper look at my own use of contemporary technologies. When I did so, I quickly realized that my use of these technologies is varied and hard to summarize easily. When I was in high school, I participated frequently in fanfiction sites and enjoyed fantasy role-playing games. But this did not diminish my love of reading or deep analysis. After all, I became an English major! As a student, I couldn't manage without my computer and cell phone, but I am not someone who is constantly online. In fact, my friends sometimes complain because I don't answer their texts or emails as quickly as they would like. And I am not a fan of social-media sites like Facebook. I am often conflicted about my use of digital and online technologies, and Carr's and Turkle's articles have helped me better understand why this is the case. Digital and online technologies have shaped my life, but I also decide how I will use these technologies. And I know that I will be constantly making similar decisions as I move through college and beyond. Turkle makes one point in particular with which I agree wholeheartedly: "Never has our world been more complex, hybridized, and global. Never have we so needed to have many contradictory thoughts and feelings at the same time. Our tools must help us accomplish that, not fight against us" (4).

Before I read Nicholas Carr's and Sherry Turkle's essays, I had not thought deeply about my own use of technology or how Internet and online technologies might be influencing our culture. Having placed these two

Continues to integrate ideas from Carr and Turkle with her own experience and thoughts on topic

Reaffirms position stated in introduction to essay

Edwards 5

Concludes with thought-provoking observation that invites readers to continue scholarly conversation on topic

essays in conversation, I now have a better sense of the questions that I should be asking myself and others as we continue to face the challenges of our contemporary moment and of future moments. Are digital and online technologies friend or foe? Of course the answer is more complicated than that, but the question—as both Carr and Turkle suggest—is well worth asking.

Works Cited

Carr, Nicholas. "Is Google Making Us Stupid?" *Atlantic Monthly Group.* July 2008: n. pag. Web. 26 Feb. 2013.

Turkle, Sherry. "How Computers Change the Way We Think." *Chronicle of Higher Education* 50.21 (2004): n. pag. Web. 26 Feb. 2013.

||||||||||||||||||||||||||||||||||||||||||||||||||||||||||||||||||||||||||||||||||||||

FOR THOUGHT, DISCUSSION, AND WRITING

1. Interview an instructor who teaches a class you are taking this term or a class in your major area of study. Ask this person to describe his or her understanding of the goals of undergraduate education and the role that your particular class or field of study plays in achieving these goals. Discuss the special analytic skills required to succeed in this course or field. Ask this person what advice he or she would give to someone, like you, who is taking a class in this field or planning to major in it. Be prepared to report the results of this interview to the class. Your instructor may also ask you to write an essay summarizing and commenting on the results of your interview.

2. Find an editorial or opinion column that interests you in a newspaper or general news magazine, such as *Newsweek* or *Time.*

    ■ Using stasis theory as described on p. 101, determine the most important questions at issue in this editorial or column. Then use the Questions for Critical Reading and Analysis on pp. 107–8 to analyze the text you have chosen. Write a brief summary of what these activities have helped you understand about your reading. If your analysis has raised questions for you as a reader, articulate them as well.

■ Use Aristotle's three appeals (pp. 106–10) to further analyze the text you have chosen. After doing so, reread the summary you wrote earlier. What has this additional analysis helped you better understand about your reading?

Your teacher may ask you to write an essay analyzing the editorial or opinion column you have chosen.

3. Go to the editorial, opinion, and letter-to-the-editor pages of your favorite print or online newspaper. Find at least three examples of fallacies, as discussed in this chapter. Bring these examples to class and be prepared to share them with your classmates.

Making and Supporting Claims

As Chapter 5 emphasizes, analysis, synthesis, and argument are linked in powerful ways. To write an effective argument, you must analyze both your own ideas and those of others. But academic argument requires more than strong analytical skills. A successful academic argument also requires careful, well-supported reasoning that synthesizes or responds to ideas in sources and anticipates your readers' interests and concerns.

Understanding—and Designing—Academic Arguments

The first step in writing a successful academic argument is to understand the ways in which academic arguments are similar to and different from other kinds of arguments. Viewed from one perspective, all language use is argumentative. If you say to a friend, "You *have* to hear Mumford & Sons' new CD!" you're making an implicit argument that it's important (in order to be in the know, for sheer pleasure, or some other reason) to listen to that particular music. A sign that advertises the "Best Deep-Dish Pizza in Chicago" is also making an argumentative claim about the quality of the pizza relative to the competition. Even prayers can be viewed as arguments: Some prayers represent direct appeals to God; others function as meditations directed toward self-understanding. In either case, those who pray are engaged in an argument for change—either in themselves or in the world around them.

As these examples suggest, arguments serve many purposes beyond confrontation or debate. Sometimes the purpose is to change minds and hearts or to win a decision; this is particularly true in politics, business, and law. But winning isn't always the goal of argument—especially in the academy, where writers focus on contributing to the scholarly conversation in their fields. Given this focus, students who bring a debate model of argumentation to academic writing often encounter problems. Think about the terminology used in debate: Debaters *attack* their *adversaries,* hoping to *demolish* their *opponents'* arguments so that they can *win* the judge's approval and claim *victory* in the contest. In academic arguments, the goal is inquiry and not conquest. Your teachers aren't interested in whether you can attack or demolish your opponents. Rather, they value your ability to examine an issue or a problem from multiple perspectives. They want you to make a commitment not to "winning" but to using clear reasoning and presenting substantial evidence.

Not all scholarly arguments are identical, however. Because they reflect the aims and methods of specific disciplines, they can vary in significant ways. For example, interpretation—whether of literary texts, artwork, or historical data—is central to arguments in the humanities. Scholars in the social sciences often argue about issues of policy; they also undertake studies that attempt to help readers better understand—and respond to—current issues and events. For instance, a sociologist might review and evaluate recent research on the effects of children's gender on parents' child-rearing practices and then present conclusions based on her own quantitative or qualitative study. Argument is also central to research in the natural sciences and applied sciences: Engineers who argue about how best to design and build trusses for a bridge or chemists who present new information about a particular chemical reaction are making claims that they must support with evidence and reasons.

Although scholarly arguments reflect disciplinary concerns, all scholars agree that the best arguments share the following traits:

1. They explore relevant ideas as fully as possible and from as many perspectives as possible.

2. They present their claims logically.

3. They include appropriate support for all significant claims.

These preferences distinguish academic arguments from other kinds of arguments. You and your friend might spend an hour on a Saturday night arguing about the merits of Mumford & Sons' new album, but your discussion would undoubtedly be fluid and improvisational, with many digressions. In academic argument, great value is placed on the careful, consistent, and logical exploration of ideas.

In a way, what is true of design is also true of academic arguments. (See the discussion of writing as design in Chapter 1.) Most academic arguments are open-ended and cannot be solved once and for all. Philosophers have been arguing for centuries, for instance, about whether it is possible to justify warfare, just as historians continue to argue about the significance and consequences of specific wars. In this sense, those writing academic essays are participating in an ongoing scholarly conversation.

The process of identifying problems is central to writers of academic arguments, just as it is for designers. A literary scholar who believes that other critics of Toni Morrison's *Beloved* have failed to recognize the importance of religious imagery in that novel is describing a problem. Since literary texts—like other complex data sets—are open to multiple interpretations, this critic's argument—her response to the problem—will depend in part on subjective value judgments. The same occurs when a historian argues that previous accounts of the fall of Saigon near the end of the Vietnam War overemphasize the Western media's role in this event.

Perhaps most important, those composing academic arguments are, like designers, concerned with what might, could, and should be. A biologist proposing a new method for protecting wetlands, a sociologist reporting the results of a new study on children in foster care, and a historian reconsidering previous studies of the spread of the Black Death in medieval Europe are all composing writing that *matters*—writing that addresses complex problems, expands the scholarly conversation, and makes a difference.

Exploring Aristotle's Three Appeals

thinking rhetorically

Academic writing places a high premium on the quality of ideas, evidence, and organization—that is, on logical appeals, or logos. This doesn't mean, however, that as a writer you should avoid emotional appeals (pathos) and ethical appeals (ethos). All writers—whether they're composing a letter to a friend, an editorial for the student newspaper, or an essay for a history class—need to establish their ethos, or credibility. Academic writers generally do so by demonstrating knowledge of their subject and of the methodologies that others in their field use to explore it. They reinforce their credibility when they explore their subject evenhandedly and show respect for their readers. Writers demonstrate this respect, for instance, when they anticipate readers' concerns and address possible counterarguments. In these and other ways, academic writers demonstrate *rhetorical sensitivity*. (For more on analyzing rhetorical situations and on Aristotle's three appeals, see Chapter 4.)

Just as all writers appeal to ethos, so too do they appeal to pathos—to emotions and shared values. Sometimes this type of appeal is obvious, as in requests for charitable contributions that feature heart-wrenching stories and images. Even texts that are relatively objective and that emphasize appeals to logos, as much academic writing does, nevertheless draw on and convey emotional appeals. An academic argument that uses formal diction and presents good reasons and evidence is sending readers a message based on pathos: "This subject is much too important for me to treat it frivolously. It requires the attention that only reasoned argument can give."

In academic writing, appeals to pathos can also emphasize just how much is at stake in understanding and addressing a problem or an event. Scholars writing about the Holocaust, for instance, often use vivid descriptions to encourage readers to connect personally with their texts. Moreover, to bring immediacy and impact to an argument, writers often employ figurative language, such as metaphors, similes, and analogies. (For example, some scholars who have written about the massacre that occurred when Nanking, China, fell to the Japanese on December 13, 1937, refer to this event as the Rape of Nanking.) They also may use images and graphics to lend visceral impact to their point.

Understanding the Role of Values and Beliefs in Argument

When you write an academic argument, you give reasons and evidence for your assertions. A student arguing against a Forest Service plan for a national forest might warn that increased timber harvesting will reduce access to the forest for campers and backpackers or that building more roads will adversely affect wildlife. This writer might also show that the Forest Service has failed to anticipate some problems with the plan and that cost-benefit calculations unfairly reflect logging and economic-development interests. These are all potentially good reasons for questioning the plan. Notice that these reasons necessarily imply certain values or beliefs. The argument against increasing the timber harvest and building more roads, for instance, reflects the belief that preserving wildlife habitats and wilderness lands is more important than the economic development of the resources.

Is this argument flawed because it appeals to values and beliefs? Of course not. When you argue, you can't suppress your own values and beliefs. After all, they provide links between yourself and the world you observe and experience.

Suppose that you and a friend are getting ready to go out for breakfast. You look out the window and notice some threatening clouds. You say, "Looks like rain. We'd better take umbrellas since we're walking. I hate getting soaked." "Oh, I don't know," your friend replies. "I don't think it looks so bad. I heard on the radio that it wasn't going to start raining until the afternoon. I think we're okay." Brief and informal as this exchange is, it constitutes an argument. Both you and your friend have observed something, analyzed it, and drawn conclusions—conclusions backed by reasons. Although you each cite different reasons, your conclusions reflect your different personal preferences. You're generally cautious, and you don't like getting caught unprepared in a downpour, so you opt for an umbrella. Your friend relies on expert opinion and might be more of a risk taker.

If your individual preferences, values, and beliefs shape a situation like this where only getting wet is at stake, imagine how crucial they are in more complicated situations, such as determining whether a controversial government proposal is right or wrong, just or unjust, effective or ineffective. Argument necessarily involves values and beliefs, held by both writer and reader, that cannot be denied or excluded — even in academic argument, with its emphasis on evidence and reasoned inquiry. The student arguing against the Forest Service plan can't avoid using values and beliefs as bridges between reasons and conclusions. And not all of these bridges can be explicitly stated; that would lead to an endless chain of reasons. The standards of academic argument require, however, that writers explicitly state and defend the most important values and beliefs undergirding their argument. In this case, then, the student opposing the Forest Service plan should at some point state and support the belief that preserving wildlife habitats and wilderness lands should take priority over economic development.

It's not easy to identify and analyze your own values and beliefs, but doing so is essential in academic argument. Values and beliefs are often held unconsciously, and they function as part of a larger network of assumptions and practices. Your opinions about the best way for the government to respond to unemployed individuals reflect your values and beliefs about family, the proper role of government, the nature of individual responsibility, and the importance of economic security. Thus if a political science instructor asks you to argue for or against programs requiring welfare recipients to work at state-mandated jobs in exchange for economic support, you need to analyze not just these workfare programs but also the role your values and beliefs play in your analysis. The guidelines on p. 135 will help you do so, thus enabling you to respond more effectively to the demands of academic argument.

thinking rhetorically

At the same time, when you argue, you must consider not only your own values and beliefs but also those of your readers. The student writing about the Forest Service plan would present one argument to a local branch of the Sierra Club (an organization that advocates for protecting the environment) and a very different argument to representatives of the Forest Service. In arguing to the Sierra Club, the student would expect readers to agree with his major warrants and therefore might focus on how the group could best oppose the plan and why members should devote time and energy to this particular project.

His argument to the Forest Service would be designed quite differently. Recognizing that members of the Forest Service would know the plan very well, would have spent a great deal of time working on it, and would be strongly committed to it, the student might focus on a limited number of points, especially those that the Forest Service might be willing to modify. The student would be wise to assume a tone that isn't aggressive or strident to avoid alienating his audience. He would articulate his most important

Guidelines for Analyzing Your Own Values and Beliefs

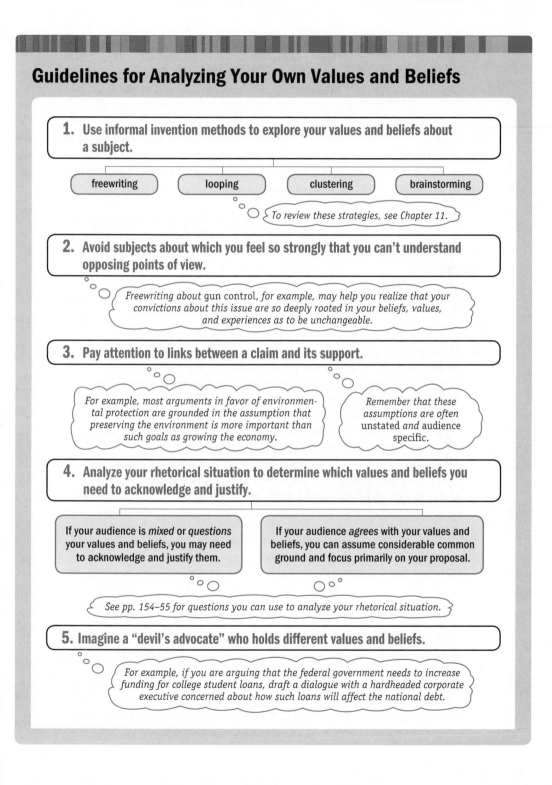

1. **Use informal invention methods to explore your values and beliefs about a subject.**

   freewriting   looping   clustering   brainstorming

   To review these strategies, see Chapter 11.

2. **Avoid subjects about which you feel so strongly that you can't understand opposing points of view.**

   Freewriting about gun control, *for example, may help you realize that your convictions about this issue are so deeply rooted in your beliefs, values, and experiences as to be unchangeable.*

3. **Pay attention to links between a claim and its support.**

   For example, most arguments in favor of environmental protection are grounded in the assumption that preserving the environment is more important than such goals as growing the economy.

   Remember that these assumptions are often unstated *and audience specific.*

4. **Analyze your rhetorical situation to determine which values and beliefs you need to acknowledge and justify.**

   If your audience is *mixed* or *questions* your values and beliefs, you may need to acknowledge and justify them.

   If your audience *agrees* with your values and beliefs, you can assume considerable common ground and focus primarily on your proposal.

   See pp. 154–55 for questions you can use to analyze your rhetorical situation.

5. **Imagine a "devil's advocate" who holds different values and beliefs.**

   For example, if you are arguing that the federal government needs to increase funding for college student loans, draft a dialogue with a hardheaded corporate executive concerned about how such loans will affect the national debt.

assumptions and align them whenever possible with the beliefs and values of those who work for the Forest Service.

In the case of the academic arguments you'll write as an undergraduate, of course, your reader is generally your instructor. In this rhetorical situation, the most useful approach is to consider values and beliefs that your instructor holds as a member of the academic community. In writing for an economics or a political science instructor, the student arguing against the Forest Service plan should provide logical, accurate, and appropriate evidence. He should avoid strong emotional appeals and harsh expressions of outrage or bitterness, focusing instead on developing a succinct, clearly organized, carefully reasoned essay.

The essays by Hope Leman (pp. 94–95) and Stevon Roberts (pp. 115–20) that appear in Chapter 5 are excellent examples of arguments that respect the values and beliefs that instructors hold as members of the academic community.

NOTE FOR MULTILINGUAL WRITERS

The standards of academic argument that are discussed in this book reflect the Western rhetorical tradition as it is taught in the United States—a tradition that you are learning if you are new to this country. This tradition encourages writers to clearly articulate and directly defend their values and beliefs. Other rhetorical traditions, including your own, may be different. Some traditions, for instance, encourage writers to convey their assumptions and values *indirectly*.

Try to identify any differences between the ways in which writers are encouraged to address their values and beliefs in your home culture and in the Western rhetorical tradition. If you discuss these differences with your teacher and classmates, you will enrich everyone's understanding of the way rhetorical practices differ in various contexts.

||||||||||||||||||||||||||||||||||||||||||||||||||||||||||||||||||||||||||||||||||||||||||||

FOR EXPLORATION

Think of an issue that concerns you, such as a campus controversy, a recent decision by your city council, or a broad national movement (e.g., to provide on-campus child-care facilities, house the homeless, or improve public transportation). After reflecting on this issue, use the guidelines presented on p. 135 to analyze your values and beliefs. Then respond to the following questions.

1. Given your values and beliefs, what challenges would writing an academic essay on this subject pose for you?

2. To what extent did your analysis help you understand that others might reasonably hold different views on this subject? Make a list of the possible opposing arguments. Then briefly describe the values and beliefs that underlie these counterarguments. How might you respond to these arguments?

3. Now write the major assertions or arguments that you would use to support your controlling idea, or thesis. Below each assertion, list the values or beliefs that your readers must share with you to accept that assertion.

4. How have the guidelines on p. 135 and this Exploration helped you understand how to write an effective academic argument? If you were to write an academic argument on this issue, how would you now organize and develop your ideas? What strategies would you use to respond to your readers' values and beliefs?

IIIIIIIIIIIIIIIIIIIIIIIIIIIIIIIIIIIIIIIIIIIIIIIIIIIIIIIIIIIIIIIIIIIIIIIIIIIIIIIIIIIIIIIIII

Mastering the Essential Moves in Academic Writing

Appeals to ethos and pathos play important roles in academic argument. For an academic argument to be effective, however, it must be firmly grounded in logos. The remainder of this chapter presents strategies that you can follow to meet the demands of academic writing. These strategies will help you to do the following:

1. Determine whether a claim can be argued

2. Develop a working thesis (an appropriately limited claim)

3. Provide good reasons and sound evidence for your argument

4. Acknowledge possible counterarguments

5. Frame your argument as part of the scholarly conversation

6. Consider whether visuals would strengthen your argument

Determining Whether a Claim Can Be Argued

You can't argue by yourself. If you disagree with a decision to increase school activity fees, you may mumble angry words to yourself, but you'd know that you're not arguing. To argue, you must argue *with* someone. Furthermore, the person must agree with you that an assertion raises an arguable issue. If you like hip-hop music, for example, and your friend, who prefers jazz, refuses to listen to (much less discuss) your favorite musician, you can hardly argue about her preferences. You'll both probably just wonder at the peculiarities of taste.

Similarly, in academic argument you and your reader (most often your instructor) must agree that an issue is worth arguing about if you're to argue successfully. Often this agreement involves sharing a common understanding of a problem, a process, or an idea. A student who writes an argument on the symbolism of Hester Prynne's scarlet *A* in *The Scarlet Letter*, for example, begins from a premise that she believes the teacher will share—that Hester's *A* has significance for the impact and significance of the novel.

The guidelines on p. 139 can help you compose an effective and arguable claim.

Developing a Working Thesis

Arguable claims must meet an additional criterion: They must be sufficiently limited so that both writer and reader can determine the major issues at stake and the lines of argument that best address them. In a late-night discussion with friends, you may easily slip from a heated exchange over the causes of the current unrest in world affairs to a friendly debate about whether Jessica Sanchez or Phillip Phillips deserved to win the *American Idol* competition in 2012.

In an academic argument, however, you must limit the discussion not just to a single issue but to a single thesis—a claim you will argue for. It's not enough, in other words, to decide that you want to write about nuclear energy or the need to protect the wilderness. Even limiting these subjects—writing about the Fukuyama nuclear plant or the Forest Service's Land Management Plan for the White Mountain National Forest—wouldn't help much. That's because your thesis must be an *assertion*—something, in other words, to argue about.

An appropriately limited thesis makes it clear (for you and for your reader) what's at stake in your argument. For this reason, many instructors and writers suggest that academic arguments should contain an explicit thesis statement—a single declarative sentence that asserts or denies something about the topic. The assertion "The U.S. Forest Service's Land Management Plan for the White Mountain National Forest fails to protect New Hampshire's wilderness areas adequately" is an example of a thesis statement.

Developing a clear, limited thesis statement can help you as a writer stay on track and include evidence or details relevant to the main point rather than extraneous or loosely related information. Readers—especially busy readers like your college instructors—also find thesis statements helpful. A clearly worded thesis statement helps instructors read your writing more efficiently and critically.

Guidelines for Developing an Arguable Claim

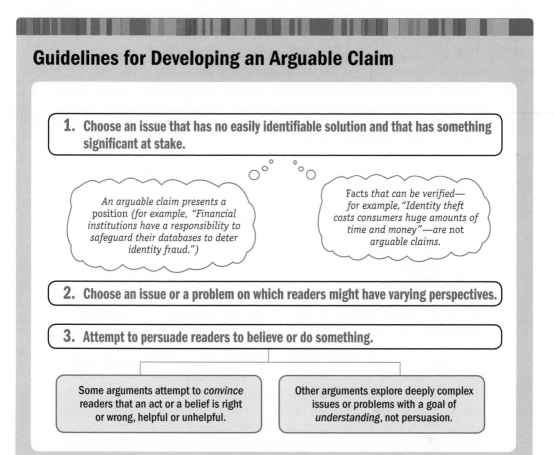

1. Choose an issue that has no easily identifiable solution and that has something significant at stake.

An arguable claim presents a position (for example, "Financial institutions have a responsibility to safeguard their databases to deter identity fraud.")

Facts *that can be verified—* for example, "Identity theft costs consumers huge amounts of time and money"—*are* not *arguable claims.*

2. Choose an issue or a problem on which readers might have varying perspectives.

3. Attempt to persuade readers to believe or do something.

Some arguments attempt to *convince* readers that an act or a belief is right or wrong, helpful or unhelpful.

Other arguments explore deeply complex issues or problems with a goal of *understanding*, not persuasion.

Here is the first paragraph of an essay written for a class on Latin American history. The thesis statement is highlighted. Notice how it clearly articulates the student's position on the topic, the role of multinational and transnational corporations in Central America.

Over the past fifty years, Latin American countries have worked hard to gain economic strength and well-being. To survive, however, these countries have been forced to rely on multinational and transnational corporations for money, jobs, and technological expertise. In doing so, they have lost needed economic independence and have left themselves vulnerable to exploitation by foreign financiers.

A clear thesis statement can help both writer and reader stay on track as they "compose" an essay.

Often, thesis statements appear early in an essay. In her analysis of the "mirror" and "flashlight" models of the role of journalists in American society that appears in Chapter 5, Hope Leman articulates an explicit thesis statement at the beginning of the second paragraph of her essay: "In this essay, I will argue that the 'flashlight' model provides a more accurate and complex understanding of the role of journalists in America than the 'mirror' model does" (p. 94). In "Digital and Online Technologies: Friend or Foe?" (also in Chapter 5), Amy Edwards states her thesis—that "as a culture we need to consider questions" such as the one raised in her title—at the end of her first paragraph (p. 124).

Stevon Roberts takes a different tack in his analysis of an excerpt from Etzioni's *The Limits of Privacy* in that same chapter. Roberts begins his essay by commenting on Etzioni's strong credibility as a writer and follows this by summarizing Etzioni's argument. Rather than introducing a thesis statement, Roberts concludes his second paragraph by raising the question that motivates and guides his analysis: "Is Etzioni justified in making his unconventional claims despite . . . [the] well-founded opposition" of civil libertarians and others concerned with privacy issues (p. 115)? As will be discussed more fully later in this chapter, Roberts spends the bulk of his essay carefully analyzing Etzioni's text, reserving final judgment until his concluding sentence, where he summarizes his analysis by arguing that ultimately the excerpt from Etzioni's text "leaves opponents (and critical readers) unsatisfied" (p. 120).

All three approaches represent thoughtful and effective responses to the writers' specific assignments. Hope Leman's and Amy Edwards's assignments required them to take a position on their topic, so it made sense for them to present their thesis statements early on. (Hope was also writing under time pressure since she was completing a take-home midterm.) Stevon Roberts's assignment was more general—to respond to and evaluate the excerpt from Etzioni's book. It thus made equally good sense for him to defer his final judgment until he completed this analysis and demonstrated his ability to engage Etzioni's ideas via his own critique.

Sometimes you may develop a working thesis early in your writing process. This is especially likely if your assignment requires you to take a stand and specifies the options available to you, as Hope Leman's assignment did. At times, however, you may have to think—and write—your way to a thesis. In situations like this, you'll develop your thesis and gather evidence recursively as you deepen your understanding of your topic and your rhetorical situation. This chapter concludes with a case study of one student writer, Daniel Stiepleman, whose argument evolved in this way. Reading Daniel's prewriting and drafts will help you better understand how to work through the process of making and supporting claims in academic arguments. Often you will discover, as Daniel did, that you need to explore your ideas at considerable length before determining your thesis.

Providing Good Reasons and Supporting Them with Evidence

To support a claim in a way that readers will find truly persuasive, you'll need to provide good reasons. Chapter 5 discusses two tools for analyzing and evaluating arguments: stasis theory and Aristotle's three appeals. You can use the same analytical tools to construct and revise your own arguments.

Let's say that you've drafted an argument challenging increased standardized testing in public schools. You're majoring in education, and you have strong feelings about federally mandated assessments, such as those required by the No Child Left Behind legislation. Your draft explores your ideas as freely and fully as possible. Now it's two days later—time to step back and evaluate the draft's effectiveness. So you turn to Aristotle's three appeals.

As you reread your draft with the appeals of ethos, pathos, and logos in mind, you realize that you've gathered a lot of evidence about the limitations of standardized testing—and thus made good use of appeals to logos. Your argument is much less successful in employing the appeals of ethos and pathos, however. Your rereading has helped you realize that the passion you bring to this subject caused you to write in a strident tone, which might make readers distrust your credibility and sense of fairness. You also haven't considered the advantages of standardized testing or the reasons that some people find it helpful and even necessary. Critical readers might well suspect that you've stacked the deck against standardized testing.

> thinking
> rhetorically

Clearly, you need to strengthen your argument's appeal to ethos. You revise your tone so that it's more evenhanded; you also consider multiple points of view by presenting and evaluating possible counterarguments. Perhaps in the process you'll discover some shared values and beliefs that can strengthen your argument. (You could acknowledge your opponents, for instance, for recognizing the importance of education as a national, and not just a local, concern.) You'll want to find as many ways as possible to demonstrate that you realize your subject is complex and that reasonable people might have different ideas on the best way to address it.

What about pathos? In rereading your essay, you realize that in gathering strong evidence to support your claim, you've failed to give your subject a human face. You've got plenty of statistics and expert testimony but little that demonstrates how standardized testing affects real students and teachers. Based on your own experiences and those of peers, you have good examples of how standardized testing can have a negative impact, so you write yourself a reminder to include at least one such example in your revised draft. You also look for other ways to remind readers that national debates over standardized assessment aren't about impersonal test scores but about the real-life learning and teaching experiences of students and teachers across America.

As this example suggests, such analytical tools as Aristotle's three appeals can play a key role in the construction of arguments. You may not use these tools to write the first draft of your argument, but once you have a rough draft you can use them to test your ideas and identify problems that need to be addressed and areas that need to be strengthened. The student who's arguing that increases in standardized testing threaten the quality of students' education, for instance, might find it helpful to identify the most important stasis questions at issue in her argument. Are they questions of fact? Definition? Interpretation? Value? Consequence? Policy?

In addition to using analytical tools, you can ask commonsense questions about the evidence that you include to support your claims. (See Questions for Evaluating Evidence, p. 143.)

|||||||||||||||||||||||||||||||||||||||||||||||||||||||||||||||||||||||||||||||||||||||

FOR EXPLORATION

Think again about the issue you analyzed in response to the Exploration on pp. 136–37. Formulate a tentative, or working, thesis statement that reflects your current position on this issue. Articulate two or three reasons or claims that support your thesis, and then list the major evidence you would use to support these claims. Finally, write a brief statement explaining why this evidence is appropriate, given your thesis statement, the reasons or claims that you have written, and your intended audience.

|||||||||||||||||||||||||||||||||||||||||||||||||||||||||||||||||||||||||||||||||||||||

Acknowledging Possible Counterarguments

Since academic argument is modeled on inquiry and dialogue rather than debate, as a writer you must consider multiple sides of an issue. Responding to counterarguments demonstrates that you've seriously analyzed an issue from a number of perspectives rather than simply marshalled evidence to support your predetermined position.

There are a number of ways to discover counterarguments. You could imagine dialogues with one or more "devil's advocates," or you could discuss your subject with a group of classmates. You might even interview someone who holds a different position. Being aware of your own values and beliefs can also help you identify counterarguments. The student arguing against the Forest Service plan might consider the views of someone with different values, perhaps a person who believes in the importance of economic development, such as the owner of a lumber company or individuals living in towns supported by the timber industry. Finally, reading and research can expose you to the ideas and arguments of others.

Questions for Evaluating Evidence

1. How *representative* are my examples?

> Will readers find these examples relevant to my argument?

2. Do I provide *enough* examples to make my point? (Do I provide too *many*, and risk overwhelming my audience?)

3. Is the *significance* of my examples clear? Are the connections between my examples and key points evident?

4. If I have used statistical evidence, was this evidence compiled by a *disinterested* source?

If *not*, do I have a good reason for presenting statistics from a source with an established position on my topic?

Are the statistics based on an *adequate sample*, and have I drawn *appropriate inferences* from them, given the sample size?

Have I considered *multiple interpretations* of this statistical evidence?

> Such sources can play a helpful role in your argument as long as you make it clear that the source is a stakeholder with a clearly established position on your topic.

5. What *authorities*, if any, do I draw on to support my argument?

Are these authorities *qualified* to comment on my topic?

Are any of them likely to be *biased*?

Are their comments *timely*?

Do I need to share the authorities' *credentials* with readers, or can I assume that readers already know and respect these sources?

> *Why?*

> If they are not — if I am citing an ancient authority on a contemporary topic, for instance — do I have a clear reason for why this authority's comment is relevant?

How you use counterarguments will depend on your subject and rhetorical situation. In some instances, counterarguments can play an important structural role in your essay. After introducing your topic and indicating your thesis, for example, you might present the major counterarguments to your position, refuting each in turn. You might also group the counterarguments, responding to them all at once or throughout your essay.

In his essay in Chapter 5 (pp. 115–20), which is organized around a point-by-point analysis of Amitai Etzioni's text, Stevon Roberts acknowledges counterarguments to many of the issues raised in his analysis. He is careful from the beginning to affirm the strong credibility that Etzioni, a former senior adviser to the White House, brings to his subject. He takes care, as well, to identify those elements of Etzioni's argument with which he is in agreement. On p. 116, for instance, Roberts comments that Etzioni's position on prenatal HIV testing represents "a well-documented and compelling argument." Although Roberts is critical of Etzioni's discussion of biometrics, he acknowledges that "to his credit, Etzioni is quick to follow up the drawbacks of biometrics with compelling statistics about the potential benefits" (p. 117). In these and other ways, Roberts makes it clear that rather than simply looking for reasons to disagree with Etzioni he is working hard to engage his ideas seriously and respectfully. The effect is to strengthen the presentation of his own position.

| | | | | | | | | | | | | | | | | | | | | | | | | | | | | | | | | | | | | | | | | | | | | | | | | | | | | | | | | | | | | | | | | | | | | | | | | | | | | | |

FOR COLLABORATION

This activity will help you recognize possible counterarguments to the thesis that you have been developing in this chapter. To prepare, be sure that you have a clear, easy-to-read statement of your working thesis and of the major evidence you would use to support it. Now spend five to ten minutes brainstorming a list of possible counterarguments.

Bring these written materials to your group's meeting. Determine how much time the group can spend per person if each student is to get help. Appoint a timekeeper. Then have each writer read his or her working thesis, evidence, and possible counterarguments. Members of the group should then suggest additional counterarguments that the writer has not considered. As you proceed, avoid getting bogged down in specific arguments; instead, focus on generating as many additional counterarguments as possible. Continue this procedure until your group has discussed each student's work.

| | | | | | | | | | | | | | | | | | | | | | | | | | | | | | | | | | | | | | | | | | | | | | | | | | | | | | | | | | | | | | | | | | | | | | | | | | | | | | |

Framing Your Argument as Part of the Scholarly Conversation

The previous discussion has emphasized the basic elements you need to understand in order to compose an effective academic argument. Whatever your topic or discipline, to argue effectively you need to do the following:

- Understand the role of values and beliefs in argument

- Determine whether a claim can be argued

- Develop a working thesis

- Provide good reasons and supporting evidence

- Acknowledge possible counterarguments

This section will discuss additional essential rhetorical "moves" that successful academic writers regularly employ — moves that signal to readers that the writers are familiar with the scholarly conversation of which their essays are a part.

In one way or another, for instance, most academic writers must find a meaningful way to *enter the conversation* that grounds or motivates their topic. In her essay in Chapter 5, for instance, Hope Leman begins her discussion by contrasting the "mirror" and the "flashlight" models of media theory, making it clear that her essay will represent her own take on this ongoing controversy. In her essay synthesizing the views and positions of Nicholas Carr and Sherry Turkle on the impact of digital and online technologies, also in Chapter 5, Amy Edwards uses the opportunity to engage essays by these authors to "reflect on the role of new technologies in my own life as a person and as a student" (p. 124). She enters the conversation that Carr's and Turkle's essays have helped establish, but she adds her own analysis of their essays and synthesizes them with her own experience and understanding.

Fostering the ability of students to enter into and contribute to the academic conversation is a major goal of this book. Chapter 5 and this chapter provide essential information on such topics as analysis, synthesis, and making and supporting claims. Daniel Stiepleman's essay, at the end of this chapter, provides a detailed example of how one student moved from an initial mixed response to a public service announcement (PSA) on literacy to a final position on this topic, one that required him to do a careful, in-depth reading of both the text and the visual design of that PSA. The material in Chapter 7, "Doing Research: Joining the Scholarly Conversation," also will help you master such strategies as summarizing, quoting, and interpreting sources that are integral to the scholarly exchange on your topic.

Although you may not realize it, you already have considerable experience with the kind of rhetorical strategies, or "moves," that play a key role in academic arguments. Imagine that you and a group of friends are trying to decide where to go out to eat one night. One friend explains that since she had pizza for lunch she doesn't want that for dinner. Another suggests the new Ethiopian restaurant in town, which she tried a few weeks ago. The others aren't sure they're feeling that adventurous, so the friend who wants to go to the Ethiopian restaurant uses her cell phone to check some online reviews of the restaurant and reads selected observations to the group, commenting as she reads. Other friends respond, raising issues about the cost, the atmosphere, and the spiciness of the food. In so doing, they add their own perspectives to the conversation. Finally the group agrees to try the restaurant.

You've had countless conversations like this. What you may not have realized is that in these conversations you are enacting some of the fundamental rhetorical moves of academic writing:

- Explaining
- Synthesizing
- Responding

In the previous example, for instance, the first friend *explained* why she didn't want pizza for dinner. The friend arguing for the Ethiopian restaurant went online, found reviews of the restaurant, and *synthesized* those evaluations of it. The rest of the group *responded* by raising additional issues and, finally, agreeing to give the restaurant a try.

Of course, in academic argument these moves can be a bit more complicated. A student who is *explaining* the ins and outs of a topic or an argument may do so by summarizing her own ideas or those of others by paraphrasing or quoting. In academic writing, the process of *synthesizing* most often involves identifying connections and contradictions within a text or group of texts that you have analyzed. And *responding* can take a wide variety of forms—from agreeing or disagreeing to granting part of an argument or a position but resisting another part and so forth. In academic argument and analysis, writers rely on these moves to locate themselves in the scholarly conversation to which they wish to contribute.

Chapter 4 includes an essay by Alia Sands titled "A Separate Education" (pp. 61–64). In the excerpts below, notice how the highlighted words call attention to the moves Alia makes as she articulates her response to Richard Rodriguez's chapter "Aria," from *Hunger of Memory: The Education of Richard Rodriguez.*

Explains two major positions on bilingual education she will address

> While some argue that students benefit from learning in their native languages, others, like writer Richard Rodriguez, argue that bilingual education deprives students of a shared public identity, which is critical to their full participation in civic life. (par. 1)

Unfortunately, our instructor did not speak Spanish and assumed that none of us spoke English. In fact, more than three-fourths of the students in the class were bilingual, and those who weren't bilingual only spoke English. (par. 5)

Responds to incorrect assumption her teacher made about students in her class and provides correct information

Unlike Rodriguez, before that class I had always had a sense of myself as part of the public community. (par. 12)

Distinguishes her experience from Rodriguez's and thus *responds to* his argument

As my experience and Rodriguez's demonstrate, schools play an active role in shaping students' sense of themselves as individuals. (par. 13)

Synthesizes her experience and Rodriguez's

Those engaged in scholarly conversation recognize that the ability to summarize the views of others accurately and fairly is an essential skill. In the following excerpt, the second paragraph from Stevon Roberts's essay "The Price of Public Safety" (pp. 115–20), Stevon demonstrates this ability. Note how the highlighted words and phrases call attention to the logic and organization of his summary.

Etzioni opens his argument by discussing recent HIV testing procedures in hospitals that may infringe on the rights of pregnant women. He then shifts gears and takes a brief look at public outrage from the Coalition for Constitutional Liberties regarding driver's license availability. Next, he gives us a crash course in "biometrics," a controversial new technology that could save billions of dollars lost to fraud every year. Finally, Etzioni addresses our fears (and those of other civil libertarians) that these and other procedures that are designed to increase our public health and safety will not be implemented justly and ethically. Etzioni admits, however, that a growing number of people and interest groups are not convinced that old laws—such as the Fourth Amendment, which protects the United States from becoming a military state—can protect us from new technology. We are left to wonder: Is Etzioni justified in making his unconventional claims despite such well-founded opposition?

Stevon's careful and respectful summary leads clearly to the major question he addresses in his analysis of Etzioni's argument and plays a central role in his effort to engage the scholarly conversation on public safety.

A final essential move in academic writing involves *showing what's at stake in your argument* — explaining why the issue you are discussing is important and why readers should care about it. In her essay on the "mirror" and the "flashlight" models of the role of journalists in Chapter 5, for instance, Hope Leman closes her essay by emphasizing that the power of the media makes it important for readers to have the richest possible understanding of the kinds of choices journalists make.

Whereas Hope makes this move at the end of her essay, Stevon Roberts emphasizes the significance of his argument early in his essay, when he comments that the events of September 11, 2001, "give an increased sense of urgency to Etzioni's message and consequently might make Americans more receptive to protocols that afford protection from public risks in general" (p. 115). Given this situation, this statement by Stevon suggests, it is all the more important to analyze clearly and carefully Etzioni's proposals to curtail protections of personal privacy.

This chapter began by discussing the model of argument that informs academic writing and emphasized that this model is based much more on inquiry than on debate: Rather than defeating opponents, the goal of academic argument is to enter the many rich scholarly conversations that occur in all the disciplines. The "moves" described thus far can help you enter these conversations in productive and rewarding ways.

||||||||||||||||||||||||||||||||||||||||||||||||||||||||||||||||||||||||||||||||||||||||||

FOR EXPLORATION

In this section, you read an excerpt from Stevon Roberts's essay "The Price of Public Safety" to see how he uses transitions and other sentence-level strategies to write an effective summary. Reread his entire essay, which appears on pp. 115–20, with an eye toward identifying other rhetorical "moves" discussed in this section of this chapter. Identify at least three moves Stevon makes that enable him to participate effectively in the scholarly conversation on his topic. Be prepared to share what you have learned with your classmates.

||||||||||||||||||||||||||||||||||||||||||||||||||||||||||||||||||||||||||||||||||||||||||

Using Visuals to Strengthen Your Argument

Images and graphics play an increasingly important role in communication today. Everywhere we turn — when we walk down the street, watch television, or surf the Web — images and graphics compete for our attention (and, often, for our money — think of the power of such logos as Target's red-and-white bull's-eye or McDonald's golden arches). Most news media rely heavily on photographs, audio clips, video clips, interactive graphics, and other emerging technologies to heighten the impact of their stories.

The use of multimedia and visually rich texts is not limited to professionals, though: Thanks to user-friendly software technologies, all of us can create texts that mix words, images, and graphics. But what role should such texts play in the academic writing you do as a student? ✲ Because academic argument typically emphasizes logos over ethos and pathos, rhetorical common sense suggests that you should use visuals when they strengthen the substance of your argument. Tables, charts, graphs, maps, and photographs can usefully present factual information that appeals to logos and helps the writer build credibility as well.

In writing about the collapse of the Tacoma Narrows Bridge in Tacoma, Washington, on November 7, 1940, for example, engineering student Brenda Shonkwiler used a number of images and graphics to good effect. In her essay, Brenda argues that engineers learned a number of key lessons from the bridge's failure and that engineering students should continue to study this dramatic event. Over the course of her argument, Brenda emphasizes that there had been many indications of a potential bridge failure: Indeed, the bridge had such a strong tendency to twist and turn in the wind that it earned the nickname "Galloping Gertie." To help readers visualize the bridge's failure, Brenda included three film stills of the bridge twisting and, ultimately, collapsing. One of these photos, which shows the center of the bridge undulating moments before the bridge collapsed, is presented on p. 150.

Brenda also included a diagram identifying the major features of a suspension bridge, as well as other charts, graphs, and tables. For example, her table on p. 151 provides basic information about suspension bridge failures throughout the world due to wind. Through use of these visual elements, Brenda strengthened the substance of her argument. The guidelines on p. 153 will help you make the most effective use of images and graphics in your academic writing.

✲ bedfordstmartins.com/rewriting
For several additional model essays incorporating research, click on **ModelDoc Central.**

thinking rhetorically

Shonkwiler   4

Fig. 2. <u>Film still of the Tacoma Narrows Bridge twisting</u>, 7 Nov. 1940, Tacoma Narrows Collection. Twisting just before failure.

Suspension bridges, in general, are more flexible than other types of bridges. To decrease the flexibility, suspension bridges are typically stabilized with stiffening trusses. Such stiffening trusses are frameworks consisting of many interconnected braces that allow wind to flow through them with relatively little resistance, while diminishing (dampening) vertical and torsional motions. The Tacoma Narrows Bridge had been stiffened with solid girders (horizontal beams) instead of trusses. (See Fig. 4.) Koughan says that the girders "were unusually shallow, only [eight feet] deep, in comparison

Student Essay Using Image for Evidence

Shonkwiler 9

expect the bridge to fail catastrophically the way it did. (161)

Actions Taken. According to Koughan, engineers tried several methods to minimize or eliminate the motion of the Tacoma Narrows Bridge, without success. First, they had tie-down cables strung from the plate girders to fifty-ton concrete blocks on the shore, but the cables soon snapped. They then installed inclined cables to attach the main cables to the bridge deck in the middle of the long span, but these cables failed to prevent the bridge from

Table 1
Suspension Bridge Failure Due to Wind

Bridge (location)	Span (ft.)	Failure Date
Dryburgh Abbey (Scotland)	260	1818
Union (England)	449	1821
Nassau (Germany)	245	1834
Brighton Chain Pier (England)	255	1836
Montrose (Scotland)	432	1838
Menai Strait (Wales)	580	1839
Roche-Bernard (France)	641	1852
Wheeling (United States)	1,010	1854
Niagara-Lewiston (USA--Canada)	1,041	1864
Niagara-Clifton (USA--Canada)	1,260	1889
Tacoma Narrows Bridge	2,800	1940

Source: Petroski 160.

Student Essay Using Table for Evidence

Composing an Academic Argument: A Case Study of One Student's Writing Process

thinking rhetorically
One of the major themes of this textbook is that written communication is situated within a particular context; therefore, there is no one-size-fits-all form of writing. Instead, just as designers must respond to the specifics of their situation, so too must writers respond to the specifics of their rhetorical situation. ✱ This book also emphasizes that writing is a *process*, one that often requires time and multiple iterations. This final section of Chapter 6 provides an extended case study of the process that one student, Daniel Stiepleman, followed in writing an academic argument.

When Daniel composed this essay, he was a student in a first-year writing class. Here is the assignment given to him and other students in the class:

> Write a two- to three-page analytical essay responding to an image of your choice. Be sure to choose an image that involves significant interaction between the text and graphics. Your essay should focus on how the words and graphics work together to generate the image's meaning and impact. Consider your instructor and your classmates to be the primary readers of your essay.

Daniel's first step after receiving his assignment was to look for an image that interested him. While he was flipping through the *Atlantic* magazine, a public service announcement (PSA) for the National Center for Family Literacy (NCFL) caught his eye. An aspiring English teacher, Daniel found the message of the PSA to be powerful, yet something about it that he couldn't quite put his finger on troubled him. In order to explore his initial response to the PSA, Daniel decided to annotate the text and image, using the Guidelines for Analyzing Visual Texts on pp. 284–85 as a guide. You can see the PSA with Daniel's annotations on p. 154.

When he first encountered the PSA, Daniel thought that the text's argument was easy to summarize: Literacy improves lives. While annotating, Daniel noticed some details that he didn't catch at first, such as the way the layout and type style underscore the simplicity of the PSA's message. The more he looked at his notes and re-examined the image and words, the more he wondered *why* simplicity was such a central part of the message. He also started to think about what the NCFL was trying to accomplish with the PSA and how other readers of the *Atlantic* might respond to it. And he still wasn't sure what it was about the message as a whole that troubled him.

✱ To review the concept of the rhetorical situation, see Chapter 4.

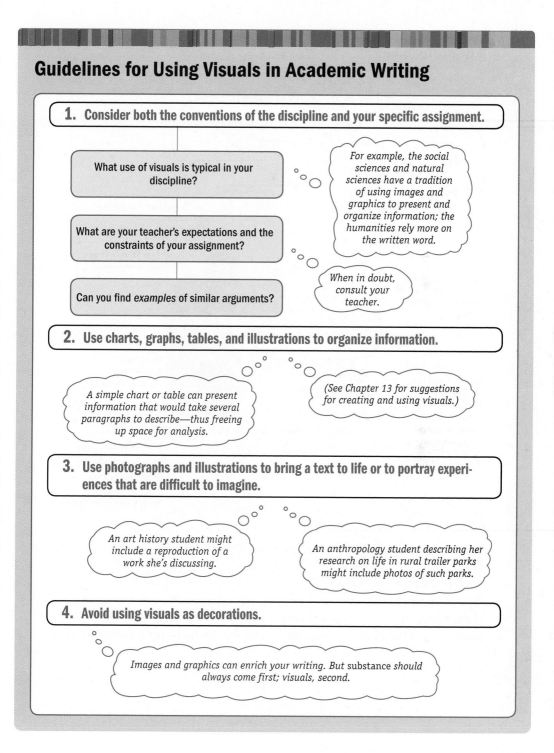

Guidelines for Using Visuals in Academic Writing

1. Consider both the conventions of the discipline and your specific assignment.

What use of visuals is typical in your discipline?

What are your teacher's expectations and the constraints of your assignment?

Can you find *examples* of similar arguments?

For example, the social sciences and natural sciences have a tradition of using images and graphics to present and organize information; the humanities rely more on the written word.

When in doubt, consult your teacher.

2. Use charts, graphs, tables, and illustrations to organize information.

A simple chart or table can present information that would take several paragraphs to describe—thus freeing up space for analysis.

(See Chapter 13 for suggestions for creating and using visuals.)

3. Use photographs and illustrations to bring a text to life or to portray experiences that are difficult to imagine.

An art history student might include a reproduction of a work she's discussing.

An anthropology student describing her research on life in rural trailer parks might include photos of such parks.

4. Avoid using visuals as decorations.

Images and graphics can enrich your writing. But substance should always come first; visuals, second.

Daniel Stiepleman's Annotation of the Public Service Announcement

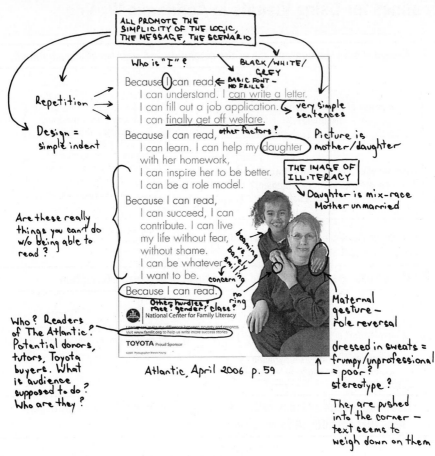

At this point in his writing process, Daniel's primary purpose was to engage as fully and critically as he could with the PSA that he had chosen to analyze. In order to explore his ideas more fully, Daniel decided to create a cluster on the word *illiteracy* to explore his response. ✳ After evaluating his cluster, Daniel realized that the causes and effects of illiteracy are more complicated than the PSA acknowledges — and that he had a promising topic for an essay.

✳ For more on invention strategies, see Chapter 11.

Daniel's Cluster

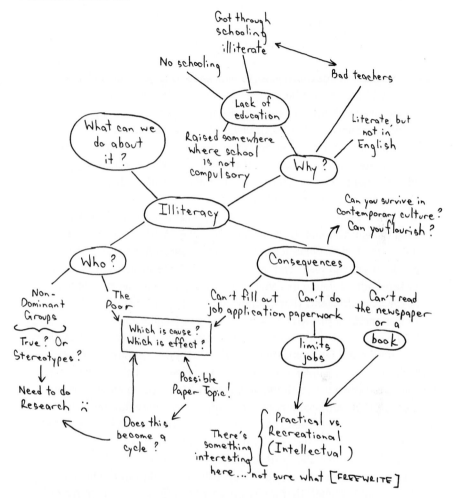

Thanks to these prewriting activities, Daniel had significantly deepened his understanding of the issues the PSA raised for him. He still did not feel ready to do a formal analysis of his rhetorical situation or to attempt a carefully structured first draft, so he decided to write a discovery draft.

Daniel's Discovery Draft

Literacy, often taken for granted, is a gift. The ability to read text not only offers opportunities for escape and entertainment but gives access to ideas that challenge our own limited worldviews, thus allowing each of us to expand our understandings of our lives on our own terms, at our own pace. The generation of text allows for the further development and sharing of our own ideas with others, at a time when much of the world has lost reverence for oral traditions. Literacy is a gift.

Several organizations exist to help share this gift, but they are underfunded and need help from the public. It is for this reason that groups like the National Center for Family Literacy (NCFL) print public service announcements (PSAs). Obviously these announcements, which appear in magazines and newspapers, are directed toward an educated and literate audience. The task of the men and women who design these advertisements is to convince readers to donate time and/or money toward the cause of literacy training.

In my essay, I want to analyze a PSA that appeared in the April 2006 issue of the *Atlantic* magazine. This PSA uses both text and an image to affect the emotions of the reader. The PSA consists of a series of "Because I can read" statements. The "I" is presumably the woman pictured with a young girl who seems to be the daughter mentioned in the advertisement, though they don't look that much alike. The woman pictured in the PSA stares directly at readers and explains some of the many real-world ways her life has improved because of literacy: "I can fill out a job application . . . I can help my daughter with her homework . . . I can be a role model." By using a first-person narrator, the advertisement is, I think, very successful at adding an emotional element that can inspire people to want to help more illiterate Americans improve their lives. Even though some of the things that are stated in the PSA may not be necessarily linked with literacy, such as when she says, "I can contribute" (certainly there are ways she could contribute to society even without being literate), I think this flaw in the logic of the PSA is subtle enough that an American who is flipping through his or her magazine would probably not notice it.

After reviewing his discovery draft, Daniel realized that while it represented a good start on his essay, he still had considerable work ahead of him. Here's what Daniel wrote about this draft in his journal.

Daniel's Journal Entry

Now that I've got some distance from this draft, I can see that it really is just a starting point. Right at the end something clicked with me: a flaw in the logic of the PSA. I tried to dismiss it; I even thought about deleting it because it would be easier for me to write about the value of literacy. But the fact of the matter is that the logic behind this ad really is problematic. This is going to be harder to write about, but it's also a more interesting and provocative idea. I think that I need to rewrite with this idea (or something like it) as my thesis. I'm a little frustrated at having to start over, but the truth is that I probably wouldn't have noticed this problem with the PSA if I hadn't written this draft.

Thanks to the preceding activities, which encouraged him to explore his response to the PSA, Daniel now felt ready to undertake a more formal exploration of his situation and goals as a writer. This was the moment, he decided, when it made sense for him to consider his controlling purpose and rhetorical situation and to do so in writing. Here is Daniel's analysis.

Daniel's Rhetorical Analysis

I am writing an analytical essay for my composition class. I want to persuade my readers — my instructor and my classmates — that there are some disturbing assumptions behind the National Center for Family Literacy's public service advertisement. If my readers are anything like I am, their first impressions will be that the ad must be good because it promotes literacy. I'm worried this will lead them to resist my argument that literacy isn't, as the ad implies, an easy solution to the problem of inequity. I've got to be convincing by using evidence, both from the text and from other sources.

thinking rhetorically

How will I persuade them to accept my argument? After all, I had to write my way to seeing it. What tone should I adopt — an objective tone or a passionate one? I'm inclined to try the latter, but I know our instructor said that being objective is usually a more effective strategy. Plus that may help it sound less like I'm arguing that the PSA's negative consequences are on purpose. I'll need to be careful in my analysis of the PSA.

Daniel also decided to develop a plan for his essay. As Daniel noted in his journal, he is a visual thinker, and so traditional outlines don't work well for him. So he came up with a visual map that helped him imagine how his essay might be organized (see p. 158). It includes several questions he thought he should address, reminders to himself, definitions of terms, and general comments. He used his plan to further explore his ideas and to determine the best organization for his essay. Although probably no one but Daniel could develop an essay from the diagrams and notes he created, the plan fulfilled his needs — and that's what counts.

Daniel's Plan for His Essay

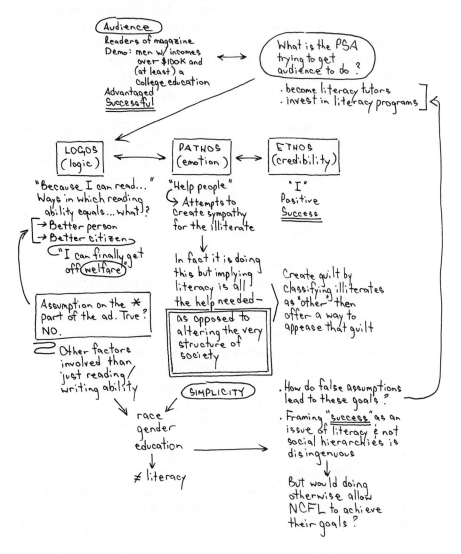

Daniel was now ready to write a formal draft. He had a clear controlling purpose: He wanted to critically examine the logic and design of the NCFL PSA and to convince his readers that although the ability to read and write is valuable, literacy cannot by itself solve the problem of poverty. Here is Daniel's first formal draft of his essay. (Note that for Daniel's first draft, he has not yet created the necessary works-cited page and his in-text citations are incomplete.)

Daniel's First Draft

Literacy, often taken for granted, is a gift. The ability to read text not only offers opportunities for escape and entertainment, but gives access to ideas that challenge our own limited worldviews, thus allowing each of us to expand our understandings of our lives on our own terms, at our own pace. The generation of text allows for the further development and sharing of our own ideas with others, at a time when much of the world has lost reverence for oral traditions. Literacy is a gift.

In recent years educational and other foundations have, in the print media especially, run literacy campaigns designed to persuade literate Americans to donate their time and/or money to the worthwhile cause of literacy education. These campaigns frequently create public service announcements (PSAs) to convey their message to the general public. One such PSA is produced by the National Center for Family Literacy (NCFL). Published in the April 2006 edition of the *Atlantic* magazine, the full-page advertisement essentially sets up a series of linked statements. It begins, "Because I can read," which is followed by a series of "I can . . ." statements, such as, "I can understand. I can write a letter. I can fill out a job application. I can finally get off welfare." At the bottom of the page is an invitation to help the person presented in this PSA and others like her get out of poverty by supporting the NCFL.

When I first read this PSA, I found it persuasive. But the more I thought about it, the more problematic the series of "I can" statements became. By asserting that the ability to read and write is tantamount to the ability to learn, be a role model, and contribute, the text also implies that people who are illiterate cannot learn, cannot be role models, and, worst of all, have nothing to contribute. Such persons, it seems, are utterly worthless without literacy.

The people reading the *Atlantic* are not illiterate. In fact, according to the magazine's Web site, the average reader of the *Atlantic* is a man in his early fifties with a college degree and a median household income of over $150,000. The image incorporated into the NCFL's "Because I can read" PSA is certainly not that of the typical reader of the *Atlantic*. The image is of a woman with an approximately ten-year-old girl, presumably her daughter, who is significantly darker skinned. What's more, the woman is not wearing a wedding ring. The image of illiteracy, then, is a single mother with a mixed-race child.

Can literacy solve this woman's problems? American society is immensely stratified; 58 percent of black and 62 percent of Hispanic children live in low-income households, as opposed to only 25 percent of white children (NCCP). According to the 1999 U.S. Census data, black and Hispanic Americans ("Hispanic" was still classified as a race in the 1999 census data) are twice as likely as European Americans to be unemployed. Those who work have a weekly income far less than whites — over $100 a week less for blacks, and almost $200 a week less for Hispanics (United States Census Bureau).

The NCFL PSA suggests that being able to read will magically get the woman portrayed in the ad off welfare. In reality, more highly educated black and Hispanic people are only slightly more likely to find work (as compared with equally educated whites) than their less-educated counterparts (United States Dept. of Education). Literacy does not equal social equality. Yet that is precisely what this PSA implies.

This PSA presents illiteracy as a problem of others who have not had the same advantages (role models, educational opportunities, membership in a dominant class or sex) as the readers. In so doing, it displays the inherent inequalities of our culture, but also offers an unrealistically simple solution to the problem — literacy. Given its purpose, the PSA is effective — but it is also a lie because it ignores the root causes of illiteracy. Granted, helping more Americans to become literate could be one step toward greater equality. So the question remains: Is the cumulative effect of this PSA harmful or good?

After writing this draft, Daniel knew that he would benefit from setting it aside for a while. After a day had passed, he decided to use the Questions for Evaluating Focus, Content, and Organization to analyze what he had written. ✱ Here is his analysis.

Focus: I think I do a good job of raising questions about the PSA. I wonder if I come on too strong, however. I also wonder if my focus is narrow and clear enough. I see that I don't write much about how the graphics and text interact. Our instructor specifically mentioned this in the assignment, so I need to pay more attention to that.

Content: I talk about how literacy affects income, and I think that's important. But looking back at the draft, I see that I don't really explain what other factors might cause a person to be poor. I definitely need to do some more research. I wonder, too, if I should include the PSA or describe it more thoroughly so that I can focus readers' attention on the parts of the PSA that are most important. I'd better go back to the PSA to decide which are the most important parts.

✱　See Chapter 14, pp. 341–42.

Organization: I'm not happy with my intro and conclusion. I kept the same introduction from my discovery draft mainly because I didn't want to worry about it. I'll need to change that. I like how I conclude with a question, but I wonder if it isn't more important to answer that question instead. There's still lots to do, but at least I can see that my ideas are taking shape.

When Daniel analyzed the first draft of his essay, he realized that while he had done a good job of exploring and raising questions about the PSA, his essay wasn't as effective as it could be. He worried that he didn't provide enough evidence to convince readers that his argument was valid, and he was unhappy with his introduction and conclusion. He also realized that he didn't analyze how the words and graphics worked together to create meaning in the PSA.

Fortunately for Daniel, his teacher included in-class peer response sessions for all major writing assignments in their class, so Daniel was able to revise his essay and share it with members of his writing group for feedback. His second draft is presented here, with some of the group members' comments. (Notice that his essay now has a title and that he has revised it in significant ways. This early draft includes some source citations, not yet in final MLA form.)

Daniel's Second Draft with Peer Comments

Daniel's second draft had many strengths, which members of his writing group acknowledge. But they had suggestions for improvement as well. A number of them commented on the evidence in paragraph 3, asking for more background on what Daniel meant by "the systematic stratification of American society." Several readers wanted to know more about the PSA's goals and suggested that Daniel's negative tone made his overall argument less convincing than it could be.

Literacy in America: Reading between the Lines

Daniel Stiepleman

A woman and girl look straight at us. Their relationship to one another is unclear, but the girl, maybe ten, stands over the woman with a hand on her shoulder — she seems, unexpectedly perhaps, almost maternal. Huddled together in the lower right-hand corner, they are cradled between a thin border and text. A series of connecting statements takes up the bulk of the page. "Because I can read," it begins in the opposite corner in simple, black font, which is followed, in slightly indented grey, by a series of "I can" statements: "I can understand. I can write a letter. I can fill out a job application. I can finally get off welfare." The call and response repeats: "Because I can read . . . Because I can read . . . Because I can read." This page, a public service announcement (PSA) by the National Center for Family Literacy (NCFL), appears in the *Atlantic* magazine. From its short diction to its basic design to its three-color scheme, everything about this ad reinforces the simplicity of its logic: "Because I can read, I can succeed." This simplicity is reassuring and hopeful, but it's more than that; it's deceptive.

In order for the woman portrayed in this PSA to gain her worth through literacy, we are urged to accept that without reading and writing she is worthless. Asserting that once she learns to read, she can "learn . . . be a role model . . . [and] contribute," the PSA implies that people who cannot read or write cannot learn, cannot be a role model, and, worst of all, have nothing to contribute. It is here where both the simplicity and the logic of the NCFL's message begin to fall apart. The message becomes that people who are illiterate are worthless, and that must be why she is still on welfare. But perhaps even more astonishingly, literacy is supposed to magically solve her problems.

This assertion ignores the systematic stratification of American society. Is illiteracy alone the reason why 58 percent of all black children and 62 percent of all Hispanic children in America currently live in poverty, while only 25 percent of white children do (National Center for Children in Poverty)? Will literacy training change the fact that, according to the 1999 U.S. Census data, black and Hispanic Americans are twice as likely as white Americans to be unemployed? Or that those who do work make an average of over $100 a week less than whites if they're black and almost $200 a week less if they're Hispanic? It seems unlikely that simply

---

Great opening!
–Parvin

Really compelling description. I like the idea that the simplicity of the design reflects the simplicity of the logic. But I'm having trouble imagining the design: Can you show a picture of it?
–Eric

It sounds like you're saying the NCFL is deliberately insulting the people they help, but I don't think that's what you mean. Maybe you could start by explaining what they're trying to do with the ad?
–Kyong

Good evidence. Are there similar statistics for women?
–Parvin

Where does this information come from?
–Kyong

"Because I [or any illiterate person] can read . . . I can succeed." The NCFL's suggestion otherwise is an unfortunate confirmation of the great American myth that anyone can pull him- or herself up by the bootstraps through simple, concerted effort, with only his or her ability and desire standing as obstacles in the way.

This PSA's potential for success relates directly to the degree to which it does not depict reality. The ad suggests that all the illiterate people in America need to achieve worth — based on its assumption that they are, without literacy, worthless — is to gain the ability to read and write; and it counts upon the readers' inexperience with both poverty and illiteracy to maintain its fiction. This is a safe bet as, according to the *Atlantic*'s Web site, the magazine's average reader is a man in his early fifties with a college degree and a median household income of over $150,000.

But the Census statistics portray a different image of America; it is a country in which the woman portrayed in the PSA will not so easily change her stake in the American dream. The injustice done by maintaining the myth of equal opportunity outweighs any good the NCFL can hope to accomplish with its ad. Looking at the woman more closely now, she seems somehow to know this. The girl is beaming, but there is a hesitance I see in the woman's smile. Am I projecting upon the image, or is there, in her face, concern? Her concern would be apt; she is shoved into the corner, held there, like so many Americans, beneath the weight of a text that would take the rich and daunting complexity of our multicultural society and give it short diction, basic design, and a three-color scheme. The illusion of simplicity.

> I'm not sure I follow you. What are the other reasons? Why wouldn't being able to read help a person succeed? Maybe you could answer the questions that start the paragraph.
> –Eric

> This sounds a little harsh.
> –Eric

> This is a strong conclusion. But your overall argument might be more effective if you acknowledged the positive aspects of the ad — maybe in the introduction?
> –Parvin

> I love how you circle back to the image in your conclusion.
> –Kyong

After Daniel contemplated his readers' responses, he recorded his reactions and ideas in his journal.

Daniel's Response to Peer Comments

At first, I had some resistance to my writing group's comments. I've worked hard on this essay and taken it quite far, given my first draft. But after reading their comments and taking some time to think, I can see that they pointed out problems that I was just too close to my essay to see. Most important, I think I need to work some more on my tone so readers understand that I'm questioning the PSA's assumptions, not the value of literacy itself or the work of the NCFL.

Several readers suggested that I include a new introductory paragraph that sets up the situation and explains what the PSA is trying to do. I thought quite a bit about this and tried out a few new paragraphs, but I kept coming back to the paragraph as it was. I really like this paragraph, so I decided to try to address their concerns by writing a new second paragraph.

Parvin commented that while I have evidence to support my claims, none of it cites the situation of women. Now that I think about it, this is very odd, given the nature of the PSA. I'll check additional sources of information so I can include that.

The rest of the comments seem relatively minor — less revision than editing. I need to fix citations in the text and prepare the works-cited page. Then I'll be really close to a final draft!

In reflecting on his group's responses, Daniel does a good job of taking their comments seriously while also holding to his own vision of his essay. It's not possible to show all the stages that Daniel's draft went through, for this process includes many scribbles, inserts, and crumpled papers. But the final draft demonstrates that his analysis of his readers' responses enabled him to revise his essay fully, to "see again" how he could most effectively make his point. Daniel's final draft begins on p. 165.

Daniel's Final Draft

In the process of writing his essay, Daniel was able to articulate what was at first only a vague sense of unease about the National Center for Family Literacy PSA. As he moved from his first draft to the second, Daniel was able to identify why the ad concerned him. He clarified the problems with the PSA's logic in his third draft, while also attending more carefully to the interplay of words and graphics in the PSA.

Daniel's final draft, you will probably agree, develops an argument that is not only persuasive but also stylish. His tone is more evenhanded, his paragraphs are more coherent, and his language is more polished. The effort that Daniel put into his essay more than paid off. This effort required planning: Daniel knew that he would have to work his way to a clear sense of purpose, audience, and organization, so he built in the necessary time for prewriting, drafting, and revising. The result is an engaged, persuasive analysis, and a good demonstration of the inseparable nature of academic analysis and argument.

Daniel Stiepleman
Professor Chang
English 100
20 March 2013

Literacy in America: Reading between the Lines

A woman and girl look straight at us. Though they look nothing alike, they are apparently mother and daughter. The girl, maybe ten, stands over the woman with a hand on her shoulder; it is she who seems maternal. Huddled together in the lower, right-hand corner of the page, they are cradled between a thin border and text. This text, presumably the words of the woman pictured, takes up the bulk of the page. "Because I can read" begins in the upper left-hand corner in simple, black font. This is followed, in slightly indented grey, by a series of "I can" statements: "I can understand. I can write a letter. I can fill out a job application. I can finally get off welfare." The call and response repeats: "Because I can read . . . Because I can read . . . Because I can read."

When I came across this page in the *Atlantic* magazine (see Fig. 1), the image of the girl and the woman was what first caught my eye, but it was the repeated statement "Because I can read" that captured my imagination. Its plainness was alluring. But as I read and reread the page, a public service announcement (PSA) designed to solicit donations of time and money for the National Center for Family Literacy (NCFL), I grew uncomfortable. The PSA, with its short diction, basic design, and black-and-white color scheme, reinforces the simplicity of its logic: "Because I can read, I can succeed." This simple message, though it promotes a mission I believe in, I fear does more harm than good.

The problem is with the underlying logic of this PSA. If we as readers believe the "Because I can read" statements, we must also believe that without literacy the woman in the PSA is worthless. Asserting that because a person can read, she "can learn . . . be a role model . . . [and] contribute," the PSA implies that people who cannot read or write cannot learn, cannot be role models, and, worst of all, have nothing to contribute to society. This is

Stronger introduction focuses readers on image being analyzed

New paragraph extends context

Copy of PSA included so readers can judge for themselves

Revised thesis statement is more balanced

Stiepleman 2

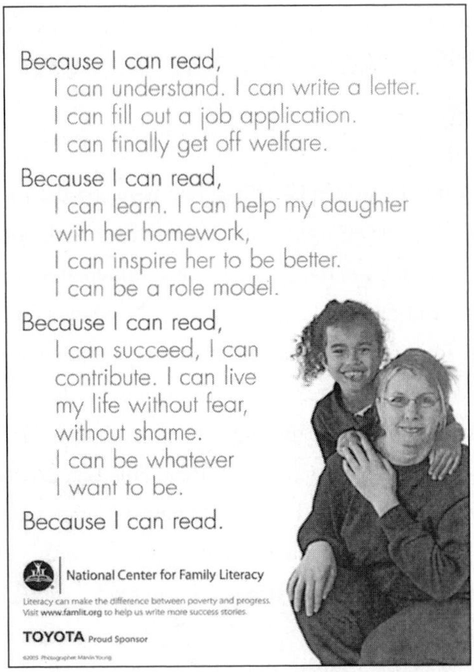

Because I can read,
    I can understand. I can write a letter.
    I can fill out a job application.
    I can finally get off welfare.
Because I can read,
    I can learn. I can help my daughter
    with her homework,
    I can inspire her to be better.
    I can be a role model.
Because I can read,
    I can succeed, I can
    contribute. I can live
    my life without fear,
    without shame.
    I can be whatever
    I want to be.
Because I can read.

National Center for Family Literacy
Literacy can make the difference between poverty and progress.
Visit www.famlit.org to help us write more success stories.
TOYOTA Proud Sponsor

Fig. 1. NCFL Public Service Announcement. *Atlantic*, April 2006. Print.

the real reason, the PSA suggests, why the woman portrayed in the photograph is still on welfare. But perhaps even more astonishing, literacy is supposed to be a quick fix to her problems.

New evidence added to strengthen argument

Sources are cited

This assertion ignores the systematic stratification of American society. Is illiteracy alone the reason why 60 percent of all black children and 61 percent of all Hispanic children in America currently live in poverty, while only 26 percent of white children do (National Center for Children in Poverty)? Will literacy training change the fact that, according to 1999 United States Census data, black and Hispanic Americans are twice as likely as white Americans to be unemployed? Or that those who do work make, on average, between $100 and 200 a week less than whites (406)? In the case of the woman pictured in the PSA, should literacy indeed lead her to a job, she is likely to make half as much money as a man with the same demographics

Stiepleman 3

who works in the same position (United States Dept. of Education). It is not my intent to undermine the value of being able to read and write, but given the other obstacles facing the disadvantaged in America, it seems unlikely that simply because someone learns to read, he or she "can succeed."

The benefits and opportunities for success extend well beyond a person's ability to fill out a job application. Race, class, and gender are powerful forces in our society, and the obstacles they present are self-perpetuating (Rothenberg 11–12). Even a well-educated person, if she is from a minority or low-income group, can find it overwhelmingly difficult to land a well-paying job with possibilities for advancement. The lack of simple things that middle-class readers of the *Atlantic* take for granted—the social connections of a network, the money for a professional wardrobe, a shared background with an interviewer—can cripple a job search. The NCFL's suggestion otherwise is an unfortunate reinforcement of the great American myth that anyone can pull him- or herself up by the bootstraps, with only his or her ability and desire standing as obstacles in the way.

The PSA suggests that all the illiterate people in America need to achieve worth is the ability to read and write. But Americans disadvantaged by race, class, or gender will not so easily alter their position in our stratified culture. As long as we continue to pretend otherwise, we have no hope of changing the inequities that continue to be an inherent part of our society. For this reason, as much as I value this PSA's emphasis on the importance of literacy, I question its underlying logic.

Looking at the woman portrayed in the PSA more closely now, she seems somehow to know that her and her daughter's lives cannot improve so easily. Though the girl is beaming, there is a hesitance I see in the woman's smile and concern in her face. And it is apt; she is shoved into the corner, held there, like so many Americans, beneath the weight of a text that would take the rich and daunting complexity of our multicultural society and give it the illusion of simplicity.

Less accusing tone wins readers over

New paragraph provides examples of obstacles that could prevent a literate person from succeeding

Language is more balanced

Stiepleman 4

Works Cited

National Center for Children in Poverty. *Low-Income Children in the United States*. New York: Columbia, Mailman School of Public Health, Sept. 2006. Web. 27 Feb. 2013.

National Center for Family Literacy. Advertisement. *The Atlantic*. Apr. 2006: 59. Print.

Rothenberg, Paula S. *Race, Class, and Gender in the United States: An Integrated Study*. 2nd ed. New York: St. Martin's, 1992. Print.

United States. Census Bureau. "Labor Force, Employment, and Earnings." *Statistical Abstract of the United States: 1999*. Census Bureau, 1999. Web. 5 Mar. 2013.

——. Dept. of Education. Inst. of Education Science. Natl. Center for Education Statistics. *1992 National Adult Literacy Survey*. NCES, 1992. Web. 2 Mar. 2013.

|||||||||||||||||||||||||||||||||||||||||||||||||||||||||||||||||||||||||||||||||||||

FOR THOUGHT, DISCUSSION, AND WRITING

1. This chapter has presented activities designed to improve your understanding of academic argument. The Exploration on pp. 136–37, for instance, asks you to identify the values and beliefs that have led you to hold strong views on an issue. The one on p. 142 asks you to formulate a working thesis and to list the major evidence you would use to support it. Finally, the group activity on p. 144 encourages you to acknowledge possible counterarguments to your thesis. Drawing on these activities, write an essay directed to an academic reader on the topic you have explored, revising your working thesis if necessary.

2. This chapter focuses on argumentative strategies that apply across the curriculum. Now that you have read it once, take a few moments to review the chapter to remind yourself of the topics and strategies covered. Then take five minutes to list the most important understandings that you have gained as a result of reading this chapter. Be prepared to share your thoughts with others in your class.

3. Newspaper editorials and opinion columns represent one common form of argument. If your college or university publishes a newspaper, read several issues in sequence, paying particular attention to the editori-

als and opinion columns. (If your school doesn't publish a newspaper, choose a local newspaper instead.) Choose one editorial or opinion column that you believe represents a successful argument; choose another that strikes you as suspect. Bring these texts to class, and be prepared to share your evaluations of them with your classmates.

||||||||||||||||||||||||||||||||||||||||||||||||||||||||||||||||||||||||||||||||

Doing Research: Joining the Scholarly Conversation

When you hear the word *research*, you probably think of looking for articles in the library or surfing the Web to find quotes to finish a paper or project. But, in fact, you are doing research any time you consult a source to answer a question, understand a concept, or solve a problem. When you check online reviews before upgrading your phone or ask a group of friends on Facebook for restaurant recommendations, you are conducting research.

You probably wrote research papers in high school. Some of the things you learned and some of the workflows you developed will continue to serve you well; others will not. To become an effective academic researcher, keep in mind what you learned from earlier chapters in this book: Writing for academic audiences means understanding how academics think about issues, how they frame questions, and what they value in terms of evidence. And this is not something you will just learn once. Scholars in different disciplines examine similar topics in different ways; what works in one course may not work in another. In addition, the tools we use to do research are changing quickly. We can do things on smartphones today that we couldn't do on computers a decade ago, and new pathways to information are opening up every day.

However, these advantages also bring challenges: To do academic research well, you need to make smart decisions about how to access and interact with texts, * you need to learn to sort efficiently through vast amounts of material in order to identify what you need, you need to understand how knowledge is created and distributed, and you need to learn how to leverage that understanding to find, use, evaluate, and manage information with purpose and intent. With today's tools, anyone can find sources to support a paper with little effort. It is up to you to decide if you want to distinguish your work from the rest, to go beyond the obvious to find unique, interesting, compelling sources that will push you, and your audience, to think in new ways. The strategies outlined in this chapter will help you do these things.

* See Chapter 2, "Rethinking Reading: Reading on Page and Screen," pp. 18–33.

The lessons you have learned about thinking rhetorically are central to the research process. In Chapter 1, rhetoric was defined as "a practical art that helps writers make effective choices . . . within specific rhetorical situations"; subsequent chapters helped you learn to think rhetorically as a reader and a writer and to use your rhetorical understanding to make appropriate choices as you navigate the reading and writing processes. Thinking rhetorically also makes you a better researcher and can help you make effective choices throughout the research process.

Questions for Analyzing Your Rhetorical Situation as a Researcher

1. What you are trying to accomplish in your research project?

2. What expectations (besides your own) do you need to consider?

3. How much freedom do you have to make choices in this rhetorical situation?

> Very little: Topic, format, style, sources, and time line are defined by the assignment's requirements.

or

> A great deal: I have the freedom to define my own standards.

4. Could you benefit from looking at examples of this kind of writing?

> *What conventions and common practices do authors who conduct this type of research follow?*

5. What image of yourself do you want to present in your final project?

> *How can the sources you choose help you present yourself in this way?*

The Questions for Analyzing Your Rhetorical Situation as a Researcher on p. 171 will guide you as you embark on any academic research project.

EXPLORING

The researcher-explorer . . .

- enjoys learning new things.

- considers multiple perspectives with an open mind.

- uses many types of sources.

- knows how to handle uncertainty.

For every research project, you need to search for information. How you search, though, varies depending on the type of research you need to do. If you want to find out how to program your thermostat, check weather conditions at the beach, or determine how much caffeine there is in green tea, a *lookup search* will get you answers.

If you need to start from scratch to learn everything about a new subject; synthesize information from several sources, including your own thoughts

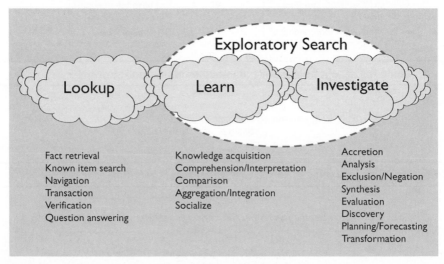

Diagram of Exploratory Search

and experiences; defend a position on a complicated topic and thought-fully respond to alternative perspectives; make a prediction about the fu-ture; or propose a new solution to an existing problem, then an *exploratory search* — not a lookup search — will help you meet these goals.

When you do a lookup search, your job is to figure out exactly what you need to know. Once you've done that, it's just a matter of looking in the right place, with the right search terms, to get an answer. An exploratory search is different. At the start of an exploratory search, you probably don't know exactly what you want to know. Your goal, therefore, is to find several re-sources that look interesting so that you can learn about your topic and fig-ure out where you want to go with it. Academic research requires exploratory searching.

Of course, at the beginning of the research process everything is uncer-tain: You don't know yet what you're going to argue or if you're going to be able to find the sources you need. It can be difficult to take the time to ex-plore widely — to read sources that might not be relevant once you develop your focus. But the time you spend in exploratory searching is anything but wasted. As discussed in Chapter 5, academic arguments are based on an open-minded exploration of the issues and a willingness to consider mul-tiple perspectives. Exploratory search — not lookup search — will help you meet these goals. The process of conducting exploratory search can be de-manding, but your gains in productivity will be significant.

Choosing a Topic

When you are asked to write an academic research paper, your freedom to choose a topic will vary greatly. Sometimes, you'll be assigned a topic to re-search and present; other times you may be told to choose anything you're interested in or passionate about. Choosing a topic can be one of the most difficult parts of the research process. Take the time to analyze the assign-ment carefully to make sure you choose an appropriate topic. Consider the amount of time you have, what you are being asked to do with the topic (to report, to analyze, to argue), and the types of sources you're being asked to use.

When you have the freedom to choose your own topic, try to select some-thing you want to learn more about. It can be difficult to search for something you don't know much about, so ask your instructor to recommend magazines or journals you can browse for ideas. Following links on *Wikipedia* can lead you to dozens of interesting topics. Sites like Newsmap (http://newsmap .jp) provide a visual interface for browsing the news. For a more scholarly browsing environment try Science Daily (http://www.sciencedaily.com), which will point you to interesting research from a variety of disciplines.

Browsing to find an interesting and relevant topic also means that you'll be more open to consider all sides of the issue. When you try to research something you already feel strongly about, maintaining the open-minded stance you need to explore broadly is difficult. Research shows that we tend to focus on information that is consistent with our previously held beliefs. In other words, we don't merely have trouble *accepting* information that challenges our beliefs; we have trouble even *noticing* it. It takes conscious effort, rigorous self-reflection, and mental discipline to make sure that we give information that challenges our beliefs the attention it deserves.

To explore any topic effectively, you need to take the time to think about and reflect on what you are reading in your sources, to identify areas where your beliefs are strong and difficult to change, and to ask yourself frequently whether your own beliefs are preventing you from seeing the value of new information.

Considering Multiple Perspectives

thinking
rhetorically

Exploring your topic requires you to think rhetorically about your project: to reflect on your needs and situation as a writer, to consider your readers' perspectives, and to recognize the different points of view expressed by sources on your topic. Your ethos ✱ in academic writing is closely connected with open- or fair-mindedness; exploration helps you demonstrate these qualities.

Think about the types of topics academic writers address. These are often big questions like "Should the government regulate hate speech?" or "Should there be cooperative international action against global warming?" On the surface, these may appear to be simple yes-or-no questions, but dig deeper and you will find that people who answer "yes" (or "no") to questions like these often have very different reasons for their position. As an academic writer, you want to explore all of these reasons in order to construct your own perspective. Doing so will allow you to present yourself as the kind of thinker who has carefully considered multiple perspectives on a topic and who is able to refine, revise, and expand your thinking as you encounter new ideas and evidence.

Finding a Focus

Your main goal in exploring a topic is to figure out what you think and what you want to argue — to find a *focus* for your research. It is important to recognize that the goal of academic research isn't to find a point of view you agree

✱ For more on Aristotle's appeals of logos, ethos, and pathos, see pp. 65–66, 106–10.

with and repeat it. You are not looking for a single source that gives you the "truth" about your topic. Instead, you're *constructing* your argument, building it out of the facts, figures, theories, concepts, ideas, and arguments that have been developed by a community of thinkers over the years. Your argument will still be original and creative, but it won't come out of nowhere.

The process of finding a focus works best when you think about research as a learning process, a chance to discover connections between new ideas and what you already know. If you approach research as a process of finding sources to support what you already believe, you guarantee that you won't learn anything new, that you won't discover anything interesting, and that your research will be, at best, boring (and, at worst, frustrating).

Start with a broad topic, explore it widely, and develop your own focused argument as you consider what you've found. The next section will discuss techniques you can use as you read and think about your sources to identify interesting ideas and connections. Your academic research process will probably not be simple or linear, but if you allow yourself to fully explore your topic and take the time you need to develop a focus, it will be productive.

| | | | | | | | | | | | | | | | | | | | | | | | | | | | | | | | | | | | | | | | | | | | | | | | | | | | | | | | | | | | | | | | | | | | | | | | | | | | | | | | | | | | | | | | | | |

FOR EXPLORATION

As you explore your research topic, write down ideas that you think you might want to talk about in your paper. Periodically, pull out your collection of ideas, lay it out, and look for connections. If you are a linear thinker, your idea map might look like an outline. If you are more visual, it might look like a cluster diagram. (See pp. 155, 298.) As you recognize recurring themes or ideas, assign each a color, and then use that color to categorize sources that address that theme. (Note: Post-it Notes in a variety of colors can be useful for tagging because they are easy to move around and you can fasten them directly to your articles or notes. But feel free to use any method that will allow you to arrange and rearrange your ideas easily: Note cards, spreadsheets, even a simple Word document will work.)

| | | | | | | | | | | | | | | | | | | | | | | | | | | | | | | | | | | | | | | | | | | | | | | | | | | | | | | | | | | | | | | | | | | | | | | | | | | | | | | | | | | | | | | | | | | | |

Looking at a Variety of Source Types

Professors often require students to use specific types of sources. This can be frustrating. But there is a reason for requirements like these. Sources are created for different reasons: A reporter writing a news article isn't trying to do the same thing as a researcher writing a scholarly journal article. By look-ing at a variety of source types, you are more likely to develop a broad under-standing of your topic and to consider it from multiple perspectives.

Reference Sources

Reference sources, like dictionaries, encyclopedias, and almanacs, are reli-able places to find objective, factual information. They might be general (like *Encyclopaedia Britannica*, *Wikipedia*, or *Webster's Dictionary*) or specific (like the *Dictionary of Financial Engineering* or the *Encyclopedia of Tudor England*). Reference sources offer a good place to get an overview of issues related to a topic or to look up facts and figures, but they shouldn't be the main sources you use to construct your argument.

A Note about *Wikipedia*

Some instructors question or even forbid the use of *Wikipedia* because it is a *wiki*, a Web site that anyone can edit. This makes it a very dynamic and com-prehensive source with articles on a wide variety of topics, while at the same time making it unreliable in some instructors' eyes, since virtually anyone, expert or not, can change the content. *Wikipedia* can nevertheless be an ex-cellent place to explore a topic for researchers who are aware of how it works and who understand that they will use different types of sources at differ-ent stages in their research process. *Wikipedia* can be especially helpful when you are doing exploratory research to identify and focus a topic.

If you consult *Wikipedia*, be sure to take advantage of its transparency. The View History link at the top of each article gives you access to every ver-sion of the article that has ever existed, so it is easy to track how a page has changed over time. The Talk tab, also at the top of each article, allows the ar-ticle editors to discuss their changes. Sometimes, these conversations are mundane, focusing on formatting issues. In other cases, they are very useful, showing how people with diverse values, beliefs, or points of view differ in their interpretation of the same facts.

Books

There are so many kinds of books that it is difficult to generalize about them, but they have one feature that is always true: Books give an author more room to examine a topic in-depth than any other type of source does. Because of this, books are likely to help you understand your topic *in context*. As you ex-plore, use books to understand where your topic fits — socially, geographi-cally, historically, or politically, for example — within a broader picture.

Periodicals

Periodicals, such as newspapers, magazines, and scholarly journals, are sources published at regular intervals. (Newspapers are generally published daily; magazines, weekly or monthly; and scholarly journals, monthly or quarterly.) Periodicals may be scholarly or popular, or they may be published for members of a profession (as is the case with trade journals).

ARTICLES IN SCHOLARLY JOURNALS Articles in scholarly journals are usually written by scholars and experts — people actively doing research and creating new knowledge; experts are also the primary audience for these articles. These articles are sometimes called "peer-reviewed" or "refereed." Scholarly articles may be difficult for the uninitiated to read and understand, but they are worth the effort. They are an important way to find out about recent discoveries related to your topic, and they will introduce you to the types of evidence that scholars find compelling.

ARTICLES IN NEWSPAPERS AND MAGAZINES Articles in newspapers and magazines are usually written for general audiences, but there are also specialized magazines that focus on particular activities (like cooking or hunting) or audiences (like parents or accountants). They focus on up-to-date information, but they may also include some historical or cultural context. Journalists place a high value on objectivity, but you will also find opinion pieces (editorials and op-eds) in both newspapers and magazines. Opinion pieces and news articles can give you a good sense of the issues surrounding your topic that are of interest to the general public.

Blogs

Blogs are frequently-updated Web sites that usually allow readers to make comments. Major media outlets (like newspapers or TV networks) use blogs to supplement their published content. Scholars use blogs to write informally about new research in their fields. Political observers use blogs to comment on the news of the day. Blogs can be excellent sources during research exploration: With reader comments, blog posts cover a variety of perspectives and also allow content to be published online very quickly, which makes them useful, but also may affect the quality of the content.

Government Documents

Government documents are produced by government agencies on topics that range from consumer protection to natural resource management and environmental quality. Some are written for the public and others for professionals in the field. Almost all documents produced by government agencies are available for free; today, most are posted online.

Moving from Exploring to Gathering

The process of finding a focus can be fun, challenging, frustrating, and interesting—sometimes all of these things at once. But when should you shift your focus from exploring sources to gathering them? At some point in your exploration, you might come across an idea that just makes sense to you. You might see a connection between that idea and others you have been exposed to or between two or more of your sources, or you might start grouping concepts together into an outline. These are all signs that it is time to shift away from broad exploration and to start gathering sources more intentionally.

GATHERING

The researcher-gatherer . . .

- finds an individual focus and point of view on a topic.
- plans an efficient research process.
- uses the right research tools for the job.
- thinks rhetorically about keywords.

Student researchers often report an upswing in confidence as they gain clarity about their argument and what they need to finish a project. Students who have found a good, meaningful focus for their work also feel interested and motivated to learn more. Once you have such a focus, you can start to gather sources with a specific purpose in mind. Some of the things you read during exploration will still be relevant and some will not. And as your argument develops and your information needs become more specific and precise, sources that didn't seem relevant at first might become very important. At times you might feel like you're backtracking, or spinning your wheels, so this can also be a frustrating time. But don't worry—this is a natural part of the research process.

Searching with Keywords

Keyword searches play a critical role in most students' research process, so it is important that you understand how to conduct effective keyword searches. Whenever you enter words or phrases that describe your topic into a search box—whether that box is in a search engine (like Google), a database (like Academic Search Complete, IMDb, or YouTube), or a library catalog, you're doing a *keyword search*. Whenever you do a keyword search, the following happens:

1. You choose a word or short phrase (your keywords).

2. You choose a research tool (a search engine, catalog, or database) and enter your keywords.

3. The computer scans all the documents the research tool indexes for those that include your keyword(s) and returns a list of results, documents that include your word or phrase, for you to review for appropriate resources.

There are things you can do at each stage to make your searches more effective. Let's examine the steps in the process of keyword searching more closely.

Choosing a Word or Phrase

To choose keywords (or search terms) effectively, you will need to think critically about your needs and about your rhetorical situation. Answering the questions in the chart on pp. 180–81 can make this process more effective.

thinking
rhetorically

Remember that the computer is going to look for documents that contain your exact keywords. So, essentially, you have to predict which terms will appear in those documents. The better you understand the rhetorical situation that produced your sources, the better able you are to predict the terms the authors were likely to have used.

Articles in scholarly journals are written for an audience of experts within an academic discipline or subdiscipline. Articles in newspapers may be written for residents of a particular town or community. Articles in magazines are written for people who share an interest (home decorating or auto repair, for example). Articles in trade publications are written for people working in a specific profession (such as advertising or school administration). Communities like these develop shared vocabularies; understanding those shared vocabularies will make your keyword searches more effective. For example, medical professionals use the term "hypertension" to describe the condition commonly called "high blood pressure." Thinking rhetorically, you would use the specialized term to search for articles written by and

Questions to Ask as You Brainstorm Keywords

1. **What are your needs at this stage in the research process?**

   Will your needs be served by broad keywords or by a more focused approach?

2. **In what rhetorical context was this source produced?**

   Are you interested in sources produced by or for a particular community?

   How do people in that community talk about your topic?

3. **Do different communities use specific or specialized terms to discuss your topic?**

4. **Are there resources you can use to identify specialized keywords?**

   Use subject headings or thesauri in library catalogs and databases.

   Look at articles you already found—did the authors provide keywords?

   Does your professor have any suggestions?

5. **Are you using a focused search tool (like Agricola or GeoRef) or something broad and cross-disciplinary (like Google Scholar or Academic Search Complete)?**

continued

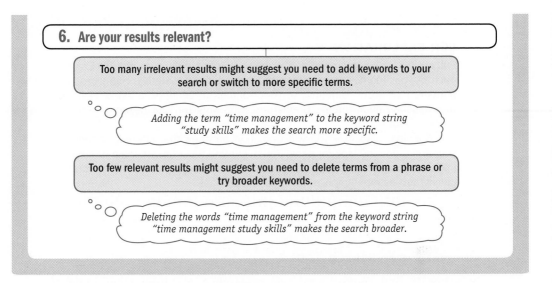

6. Are your results relevant?

Too many irrelevant results might suggest you need to add keywords to your search or switch to more specific terms.

Adding the term "time management" to the keyword string "study skills" makes the search more specific.

Too few relevant results might suggest you need to delete terms from a phrase or try broader keywords.

Deleting the words "time management" from the keyword string "time management study skills" makes the search broader.

for doctors and the more common term to search for newspaper articles written for the general public.

There are many places you can look for keywords. Academic journals often allow authors to add useful keywords to their articles; look for them. Librarians routinely add subject headings to catalog entries for sources. In addition, many professional communities (for example, medicine, psychology, and education) have developed specialized thesauri or classification systems that are embedded into their search tools. These are sometimes called "controlled vocabularies." Look for a list of limiting or narrowing options next to your search results to browse through relevant keywords, subject terms, or thesaurus terms for more ideas.

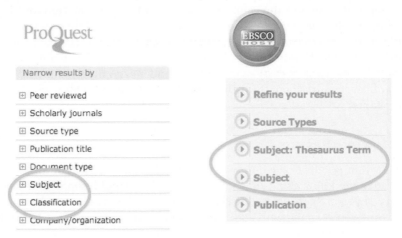

Examples of two databases that compile lists of subject terms or controlled vocabulary terms related to search results. The database user would click the arrow or plus sign to open up a browsable list of terms.

||||||||||||||||||||||||||||||||||||||||||||||||||||||||||||||||||||||||||||||||||||||||||

FOR EXPLORATION

Pull out the notes you made during the Exploration activity on p. 175. Examine each of your themes (or sections of your outline) separately. Use words and phrases that occur frequently in your sources to generate a list of keywords that describe each theme. Brainstorm synonyms for your keywords and add those to your list.

Consider also how you will transition between the different sections of your argument and look for gaps. You might find it useful to keep a running list of things you still need to figure out. Turn items from that list into keywords by pulling out the most important words and phrases.

||||||||||||||||||||||||||||||||||||||||||||||||||||||||||||||||||||||||||||||||||||||||||

Choosing a Research Tool

As a twenty-first-century academic researcher, you have a multitude of search tools available to you. Some tools, like Internet search engines, provide access to a huge variety of resources—resources on a variety of topics, created for a variety of reasons, by a variety of authors—and of varying quality. Others are more specialized, providing you access to one type of resource (such as newspaper articles, images, maps, books, or videos) or to resources on a specific topic. Luckily for you, as a member of your college or university community, you have access to many such resources.

In an academic research process, you can expect to use many different types of research tools as you gather your sources. You might check for books and videos in your library's catalog, scan for images at Flickr.com, and search for articles in a scholarly database. Think about your research tool, particularly its scope and coverage, as you choose keywords. For example, say you were interested in the economic impact of freeway construction. For a Google search, you would probably choose to include all of those terms: *freeway construction economic impacts*. In a database limited to articles from economics journals, however, the term *economic* would appear in almost every article. In that case, *freeway construction* would be an effective place to start. You will learn more about the different research tools available to you later in this chapter.

Reviewing Results

Review your results to see if they're relevant. If they are, great; if they're not, use what you know about how keywords work to troubleshoot your search terms. If you are getting results that are too broad, consider combining the keywords you're using with additional terms. Expect to do several searches testing different combinations. If your results include a few useful sources and several irrelevant texts, look closely at the relevant articles to see if they

Specialized Fields Available in Business Search Premier (EBSCO)

use different terms to describe your concepts. As discussed above, a student researching high blood pressure might notice that the term *hypertension* is preferred by medical professionals and repeat her search using that term.

At this point, it is useful to understand that most of the time the computer does not match your keywords against every word in the articles or books in its index. Computers store information in categories called *fields*. When you search for your keywords, the computer will focus on some fields and ignore others. For example, most article databases will look for your keywords in the *title*, *author*, *abstract*, and *subject heading* fields but not in the text of the article itself. Why? Because if your keywords appear in those main fields, the chances are good that the article will be relevant to your research. On the other hand, if your keywords appear just once in the text of a thirty-page article, it might be only tangentially related to your topic.

Most search tools will allow you to specify the field(s) you want to search. This is very useful when you want to narrow your search. Specialized databases will give you options that go well beyond the default options of title, author, and abstract. For example, in a business database, you can limit by industry code, ticker symbol, and more. Most databases will also allow you to search the full text of articles if you want a broader set of results than you get from the default search.

Using Common Research Tools

There are too many specific tools available to discuss them all, and what you need for your project is going to be specific to your rhetorical situation. The goal of this section is to give you a sense of what results are possible when you use different types of research tools.

Using Article (or Periodical) Databases

Most article databases (also sometimes called *periodical* databases) are proprietary: They are only accessible if you are a subscriber or if you are part of an institution that subscribes. As a college student, you probably have access to a good number of article databases at your library. (Some databases are also available through public libraries.)

The databases available on your library's Web site range from general purpose (for example, EBSCO's Academic Search Complete and ProQuest's Research Library), which include all types of articles and cover a variety of disciplines, to subject specific (such as Historical Abstracts or PubMed), which focus on articles published in scholarly journals in specific disciplines. In between, you will find databases like JSTOR and Web of Science, multidisciplinary databases of scholarly articles, and newspaper databases like LexisNexis or Ethnic News Watch. General-purpose databases are often a good starting point for an academic research project. But if you are taking an advanced class in your major, find out which databases are important in your field. Check your library's Web site for a list of *subject guides*. These guides, organized by discipline, should give you a sense of the tools used by professionals in your field.

Some article databases are just indexes, providing standard bibliographic information (title, author, subject, publication date, number of pages, etc.): They let you know that an article exists but require you to go elsewhere to find the actual text. Other databases include the full text of the article along with the bibliographic information. A third category provides full-text access to some articles and only bibliographic information about others. For questions to consider when using article databases, see below.

Questions to Consider When Using Article Databases

1. Is this a full-text database, or is it an index?

A full-text database includes articles in PDF or HTML format. Articles in PDF format generally include the illustrations from and formatting of the original article; articles in HTML format might be text only, or they might include figures and images as separate files.

2. **What does this database cover?**

> Does it include only magazines, newspapers, scholarly journals, or trade publications, or does it include a combination of source types?

> What are its dates of coverage? Can you use this database to find the most current articles? Does it include older back issues?

3. **Is this a general-purpose database or a subject-specific database that covers a particular discipline?**

> Is there an easy way to identify scholarly (or peer-reviewed) articles in this database?

4. **Does this database offer special tools, like citation formatting, that are useful in academic writing?**

Library Catalogs

Library catalogs are databases that let you search everything in a library's collection. Every library tries to tailor its collection to the needs of its students and faculty, and at almost all academic libraries, this means lots of books and journals. A school with a strong film studies program might offer a large film collection in the library; a school with a strong natural resources curriculum would purchase a lot of maps; and a chiropractic college might even provide bones and skeletons for checkout.

For questions to consider when using library catalogs, see p. 186.

Metasearch and Federated Search

Many academic libraries offer metasearch or federated search, tools that allow you to search for content in several databases and catalogs at the same time. The technology that makes these tools work varies from campus to campus, and the search boxes they offer are customized by the libraries that provide them, but you will usually find them posted prominently on the library's homepage. For example in the accompanying figure, notice how the search box, located in the header of the University of Pennsylvania

Questions to Consider When Using Library Catalogs

1. If your institution has multiple libraries, can you limit your search to the library you want to use?

2. If your institution has multiple campuses, can you search the holdings of all campus libraries at the same time?

3. If your institution belongs to a regional consortium of libraries, can you easily search the catalogs of all the libraries where you have borrowing privileges?

4. If you find a book at another branch or campus, how can you request it?

Libraries' Web site, defaults to search "Anywhere." This particular box lets the user search the library's catalogs, article databases, research guides, and selected pages of the library's Web site with a single search. Ask your librarian if your library has a tool like this and, if so, what it searches.

These tools are particularly useful early in the research process, when you want to scan broadly across source types and across academic disciplines. They are also very useful when you want to see whether your library provides access to a particular book or article: One search in a metasearch engine or federated search tool will let you scan most of your library's collection quickly.

Example of a One-Stop Search Tool on an Academic Library's Web Site

Search Engines

While there are some challengers, Google remains dominant in the area of Internet searches because of the huge amount of data it has indexed and because its ranking algorithm continues to deliver results that are perceived to be highly relevant by its users. In addition to Google Search (http://google.com), Google has two related search engines of particular interest to academic researchers: Google Books and Google Scholar.

Google Books (http://books.google.com) is a large, searchable database of digitized books. In some cases, you can download the full text of books; in others, you can look at several pages in "preview"; and in still others you can only access the snippet of text that includes your keywords.

Google Scholar (http://scholar.google.com) is Google's attempt to provide a focused search of scholarly sources. With this tool, you can quickly scan the scholarly literature on a topic across a variety of disciplines. You can set your preferences in Google Scholar so that your results will be connected to the holdings of your college library. Similarly, you can use a link in Google Books to find a book in a nearby library. This allows you to search broadly with these tools and then access the content using your library's subscriptions and holdings.

Google's dominance does not mean that it is the only Internet search option. There are a variety of alternatives available. Some of these will disappear quickly, and no doubt others will emerge. The list of available search engines maintained on *Wikipedia* (http://en.wikipedia.org/wiki/List_of_search_engines) is a useful starting point for those interested in exploring alternatives.

Getting the Full Text

As a student explores a variety of digital tools and sources, one question is particularly important: "How do I get the actual article?" As noted earlier, some databases provide you with the bibliographic information about an article without giving you access to the full text. Similarly, Internet search engines will frequently point you to articles or books that seem useful but are not available for free. It is frustrating to find a useful-looking article and click on the link only to find a price tag of $30, $40, or even $50.

As a member of a college or university community, it is very likely that your library can help you get the books and articles you need. Many libraries provide a tool, called a "link resolver," to help their users find the full text of articles in their databases. When you find a reference to an article in a database that does not have the full text available, these tools allow you to search for that article in the library's other databases with the click of a button. Like the one-stop search tools discussed above, these buttons are also customized by the libraries that use them. (See p. 188 for one example.) If your library does not provide a link resolver, don't despair! Ask your librarian for help finding your article. It may be available in another format.

1. Title: **The Economics of International Policy Agreements to Reduce Emissions from Deforestation and Degradation**
   Author(s): Kerr, Suzi C.
   Source: REVIEW OF ENVIRONMENTAL ECONOMICS AND POLICY Volume: **7** Issue: **1** Pages: **47-66**
   DOI: **10.1093/reep/res021** Published: **WIN 2013**
   Times Cited: 3 (from All Databases)
   ⊙ **Link to Full Text** ◄——————

Example of a Link-Resolver Button in an Article Database

If your library does not have the source you want in any form, find out whether your library offers an interlibrary loan service. Most academic libraries have developed agreements with other libraries to borrow items that your library doesn't have. To learn more about accessing articles that are not available through full-text databases, use the Guidelines for Getting the Full Text of Articles (below).

Guidelines for Getting the Full Text of Articles

1. Check for a link in the database to the full text of the article.

> This link might say "full text," it might be an icon, or it might be the PDF logo. You may have to hunt for it.

> Your library may provide a button or link resolver to help you retrieve the full text from another database.

2. If a copy of the article is not available through the database or through a link resolver, make a note of the title of the article and the title of the magazine or journal.

> You should also make a note of the publication date and the names of the authors.

3. Search the Web to find out if the article is available online for free.

> Enter the full article title and author(s)'s names into a search engine.
> Some authors archive their work on their own Web sites or in institutional
> repositories. If you find a version of the article this way, ask your
> instructor or a librarian for help formatting your citations.
> (If your article is not available for free, proceed to step 4.)

4. Use your library's interlibrary loan service to get a copy of the article.

> You may have to wait a bit for articles obtained through interlibrary loan,
> so plan accordingly.

Refining Your Searches

As your argument develops, you will notice ideas that you need to develop or questions you need to answer. Your assignment may also have specific requirements: For example, some professors require students to use specific source types (like scholarly journal articles), to use articles from a particular journal, or to use articles published after a certain year. By choosing keywords that reflect the rhetorical situation, you can start to focus your searches on the sources you most want to explore. But your library's research tools also include many features designed to help you refine your searches. Even Google Scholar includes some of these features.

The Advanced Search screen in your database or search engine will allow you to set some limits in advance. For example, you might limit results by any of the following:

Document type (articles in newspapers or in scholarly journals or book reviews, for example)

Publication date

Language

Full text

Most of the databases your library subscribes to will also allow you to set these limits after your initial search. This strategy—doing a broad search and then using the features mentioned above to refine or troubleshoot your results—can be very helpful. Google Scholar doesn't offer as many refining features as some of the proprietary databases, but it does allow you to refine by date or to filter out certain types of sources, like patents.

Discipline-specific databases usually offer more options for refining a search than multidisciplinary or general-purpose databases do. Recall the discussion of how databases work: They scan categories or fields of information (like title and abstract) to match your keywords. Specialized databases often include specialized fields, and these translate into powerful limits you can use to focus your searches. For example, ERIC, an education database, allows you to limit your search by educational level (such as kindergarten or Grade 8). Historical Abstracts allows you to limit results by historical period. As you progress through your studies, it is worth learning how to get the most out of the databases in your field.

Using Digital Workflows

For many years, information gathering was taught entirely separately from the writing process. In a world in which papers were typewritten and information sources were in print and housed in a library, that made sense. Today, such barriers are gone. We use the same tools to gather sources that we use to write our papers; journal articles and word processing programs are frequently open in side-by-side windows on computer screens. We know that the cognitive processes of reading, writing, analyzing, and synthesizing are intertwined, and in the digital landscape our workflows can reflect this. This also means, however, that our workflows must make sense in this new digital landscape.

Retrieving Content

When scholarly sources were all in print, knowing how to find them on the library's shelves was key to your success as a researcher. Now, searching online allows you to discover sources your library has access to but that aren't immediately available. So when you plan your research, you need to factor in time to retrieve content you want to use. The more you know about where your information is coming from, the better you can plan your process.

Look at your assignment requirements: As noted earlier, many instructors require writers to use specific types of sources in their papers, and these requirements can affect your time management. While there are huge amounts of information available immediately on the Web, some types of information are more readily available there than others. Current newspaper articles are usually easy to find (though as a story slips off the front page it may be harder to locate archived articles on the subject). Scholarly books and articles are also easy to find on the Web, but usually they can only be accessed for a price. You can get the same content from your library for free, but you may need to factor in delivery time if you request sources from other campuses or from other libraries.

There are many useful online tools designed to help you plan your time, such as the Assignment Calculator from the University of Minnesota Libraries (http://www.lib.umn.edu/apps/ac/), which has been adapted by libraries around the country.

Staying Organized

There are also a host of digital tools available to help you stay organized, several of which are discussed below. Each tool has different features; expect some trial and error as you figure out what works with your research and writing style. When choosing among digital tools, think about your workflow as a whole: How do you prefer to read? to write? to research? If you prefer to do all of these things in the same digital space—on your computer or tablet—then it might make sense to find one tool that will support all of those processes. If you prefer to do one or more of these things offline—maybe you sketch out concept maps by hand or take notes in the margins of your books—then you'll want to choose your tools accordingly. ✱

In a digital world, it is especially important that you develop workflows that allow you to easily find your sources again and to clearly distinguish source information from that of your own notes, thoughts, and ideas. This will protect you from unintentionally plagiarizing your sources, and it will also save you time. There is nothing more frustrating than spending hours attempting to refind a source the night before a paper is due.

Using Database Tools

Many academic databases feature built-in organizational tools that allow you to save articles or other sources to folders and then print or email the saved articles. They also allow you to specify a citation style for the sources you save, so you can cut and paste a formatted citation into your final paper (though you will want to double-check these citations for accuracy). But these tools are meant to help you save your research output only during a single session: Once you close your browser or leave the database, your folder disappears.

Academic database vendors (like Cambridge, EBSCO, or JSTOR) will also allow you to create an account so that, when you are logged in, you can save sources to permanent folders, save searches, and set up alerts that let

The discussion in Chapter 2 can help you make decisions like this. ✱ • • • • • • • • •

you know when new material on your topic is added to the database. Your log-in will work across all the databases your institution licenses from that vendor, so if your library licenses fifteen databases from EBSCO, you can save resources from all fifteen databases to your EBSCO account. Obviously, this type of account will not work across databases licensed from different vendors.

Using Citation Managers

Citation managers, also called reference managers, do work across databases from different vendors. But these tools, like Zotero (http://www .zotero.org), Mendeley (http://www.mendeley.com), and EndNote (http:// endnote.com), go one step further: They work seamlessly with word processing tools to streamline your use of sources while you write. You can save resources during the exploration phase, organize and save more during the gathering stage, take notes during the evaluation stage, and pull those sources back out into your paper during the creation (writing) stage.

They allow you to save resources from traditional academic research tools—like databases, library catalogs, and Internet search engines—and also from Web sites like Amazon.com, YouTube, and Flickr. You can organize the sources you find in a variety of ways: by adding labels to them, sorting them into folders, or building them into collections. These tools also allow you to work on many different projects from the same interface.

Using Cloud Storage

Increasingly, people need to manage information across multiple computers and devices. For example, you might have a laptop that is too heavy to carry to campus every day, so you also work on a computer in the library and on your smartphone. To store documents and sources somewhere that they can be accessed from any of these devices at any time, many people are turning to tools like Google Drive (https://drive.google.com), Dropbox (http://www .dropbox.com), and Evernote (http://evernote.com). These services allow you to save your documents "in the cloud" so that you have immediate access to the most recent version of them from any device. Tools like these, and like Zotero and EndNote mentioned above, also facilitate collaboration—when you save things online, it is much easier to share them with other people.

This landscape of organizational tools is extremely volatile: By the time the next edition of this book comes out, some of these tools will be gone, some will be more powerful than ever, and new tools and new functions that we haven't even begun to imagine will be available.

Conducting Field Research

Sometimes instead of relying on the research others have done, you will want to gather some original data yourself: You might want to interview an expert on your topic, conduct a survey, or observe an interaction or event firsthand. These kinds of activities are *field research*. Many students find that field research helps them build enthusiasm for learning because they are uncovering information that no one before has compiled in exactly the same way.

A note of caution is appropriate here. Any time you do research involving other people, you must treat your subjects ethically and with respect. You will have a great deal of latitude in interpreting what your subjects say in interviews, for example, so you must do so fairly and thoughtfully. For your field research to be valued by an academic audience, you must show that you have drawn your conclusions from your research, not from preconceived opinions. Your campus may have training or guidelines for students engaged in field research. Talk to your instructor, or investigate your school's Web site, to find out more.

Conducting Interviews

Interviews often provide information that is unavailable through other kinds of research. For a psychology project about child abuse, for example, you might interview a local caseworker who works with abused children. For a political science project on the Iraq War, you might interview a veteran of that war. If you do conduct interviews, keep in mind that a good interviewer is first of all a good listener—someone who is able to draw out the person being interviewed. Since interviews are more formal than most conversations, be sure to prepare carefully for them by doing some background research on the interviewee and by preparing a list of questions. The Guidelines for Conducting Interviews (p. 194) will help you get ready for a successful exchange.

Conducting Surveys

Surveys allow you to gather information from a large group of people at once. Depending on your questions, you can gather quantitative (numerical) or qualitative (open-ended) data. Some disciplines, like psychology and political science, use surveys and polling data to support broad claims about public attitudes, behaviors, and values. Designing, administering, and analyzing surveys like these takes years of training and practice. In introductory classes, students use surveys to identify possible themes or to understand different perspectives on a topic, but the information gathered from such questionnaires is not likely to be statistically valid or to reflect the population

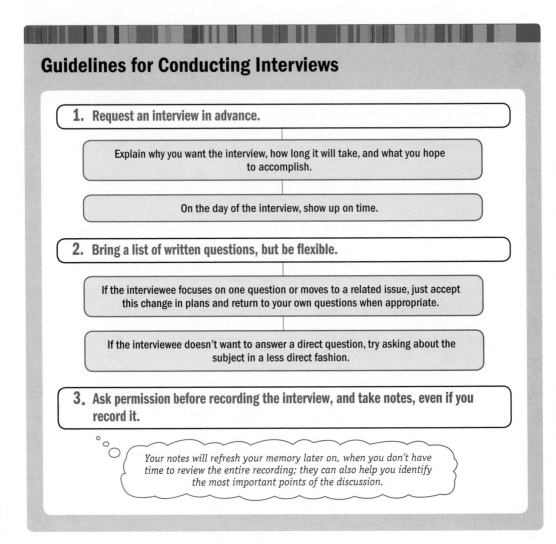

Guidelines for Conducting Interviews

1. Request an interview in advance.

Explain why you want the interview, how long it will take, and what you hope to accomplish.

On the day of the interview, show up on time.

2. Bring a list of written questions, but be flexible.

If the interviewee focuses on one question or moves to a related issue, just accept this change in plans and return to your own questions when appropriate.

If the interviewee doesn't want to answer a direct question, try asking about the subject in a less direct fashion.

3. Ask permission before recording the interview, and take notes, even if you record it.

Your notes will refresh your memory later on, when you don't have time to review the entire recording; they can also help you identify the most important points of the discussion.

generally, so it can serve only as anecdotal evidence. It should not be used to construct an argument about what *all* students believe or do.

The Guidelines for Designing and Using Surveys (pp. 195–96) has helpful suggestions for approaching this dynamic form of research.

Conducting Observations

Sociologists and anthropologists use firsthand observation to gather data. Sometimes they work as participant-observers, living in various communi-

Guidelines for Designing and Using Surveys

1. Explain the purpose of your survey briefly at the top.

Consider: How will the results tie in to the rest of your research project?

2. Decide who will receive the survey.

For a business paper, you might want to survey an entire small company, or a representative sample — say, every fifth employee from an alphabetized list — at a larger company.

3. Decide how you will distribute the survey and obtain responses.

Will you email it, send it by regular mail, or hand it out in person?

State clearly how surveys should be returned — via email, Facebook, or US Postal Service, for example — and provide a clear deadline.

4. Consider whether you need any demographic information, questions such as gender, income, marital status, age, or education.

If gathering opinions about the homeless for a sociology paper, the respondents' income levels may be relevant.

5. Write questions that are clear and to the point.

Most questions should be yes-or-no, multiple-choice, or ranking on a scale (say, from 1 to 5). Few people will complete long or complicated surveys.

continued

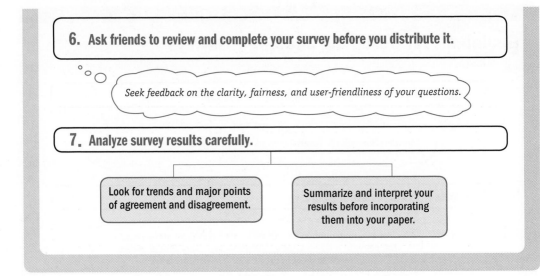

6. Ask friends to review and complete your survey before you distribute it.

Seek feedback on the clarity, fairness, and user-friendliness of your questions.

7. Analyze survey results carefully.

Look for trends and major points of agreement and disagreement.

Summarize and interpret your results before incorporating them into your paper.

ties to observe social customs and patterns of behavior. Scholars using this approach have gathered data on many types of groups, from day-care center users to corporate board members. While this type of research is beyond the scope of most undergraduate courses, you can still generate stimulating material by closely observing various activities or groups. If you're writing a paper on the effectiveness of your university's student senate, for example, you might attend several meetings, take careful notes, and act as a participant-observer during question-and-answer sessions.

The Guidelines for Conducting Observations (p. 197) will help you prepare for the unique challenges this research method entails.

Ethical Considerations

When you use any of the field research methods described above, you have an important responsibility to treat your research subjects with respect, ensuring that they consent to participate and protecting their privacy. When professional researchers study human subjects, they must prove that the research will be beneficial and adhere to a detailed set of ethical standards to minimize any risk to the participants. Before they can even begin research, their projects must be reviewed and approved by their institutional review board (IRB). For most classroom projects, you will not need to undergo formal review, but you may benefit from the educational materials and guidelines your university has prepared for research on human subjects. Search your school's Web site for *human subjects research* to see if guidelines have been posted, or ask your instructor for such guidelines.

Guidelines for Conducting Observations

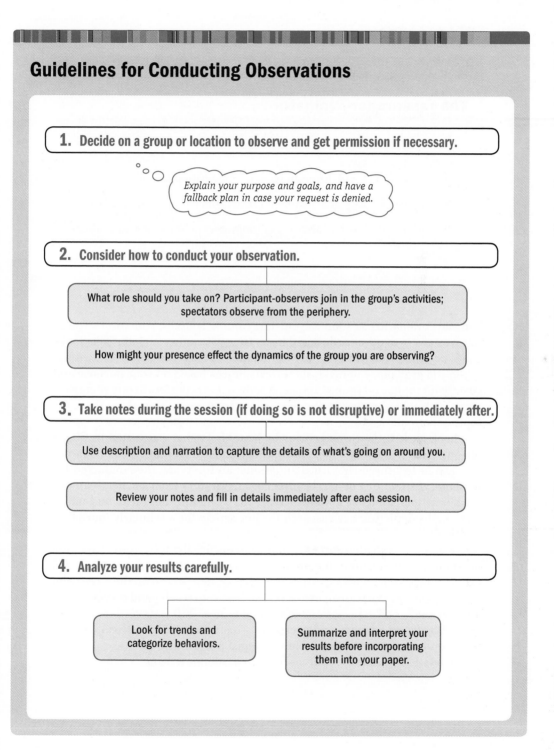

1. Decide on a group or location to observe and get permission if necessary.

Explain your purpose and goals, and have a fallback plan in case your request is denied.

2. Consider how to conduct your observation.

What role should you take on? Participant-observers join in the group's activities; spectators observe from the periphery.

How might your presence effect the dynamics of the group you are observing?

3. Take notes during the session (if doing so is not disruptive) or immediately after.

Use description and narration to capture the details of what's going on around you.

Review your notes and fill in details immediately after each session.

4. Analyze your results carefully.

Look for trends and categorize behaviors.

Summarize and interpret your results before incorporating them into your paper.

EVALUATING

The researcher-evaluator . . .

- makes rhetorical choices about sources throughout the research process.

- knows the value of different types of information sources.

- understands why information is created and how it is communicated.

- does additional research on authors and publications to evaluate sources effectively.

thinking rhetorically

You start evaluating as soon as you start finding sources; sometimes you're not even aware that you're doing it! Every time you say to yourself, "That looks good" or "That's too complex" or "I think that's a tangent," you're evaluating. When you evaluate, you make rhetorical choices based on your purpose and goals, your topic, and your audience. A source that is perfect in one rhetorical situation might not work in the next, even if you are writing about the same topic in both cases.

Look back at the three articles by Jean M. Twenge presented in Chapter 4 (pp. 74–79). Remember that Twenge chose different types of sources for each of her three rhetorical situations: an interview she conducted for her book written for a general audience, a news story from a college campus for her article aimed at a multidisciplinary academic audience, and tables and graphs depicting her research for her article for a scholarly journal in her field.

When you evaluate sources, you must consider them in context and understand how they fit into the broader picture. Are you quoting a recognized expert, a newcomer with a cutting-edge theory, or a person on the street who voices a common view in an apt way? The best sources depend on your goals and the needs and expectations of your audience. Will your readers be persuaded by famous names and prestigious institutions? Will charts, graphs, and numbers have an impact? These are just some of the questions you will ask yourself as you choose sources for your academic writing.

Evaluating for Relevance

The first type of evaluation you'll do is for yourself and your learning process: It is to determine whether the source is *relevant*. During exploration, many things will be relevant. Once you have found your focus, however, your assessment of which sources are relevant will change. At that point, you will look for sources that will help you understand, develop, support, or articulate your position. Of course, you may return to exploration as your argument develops, but the emphasis will remain on choosing sources that are relevant. Relevance is important, but it is not the only type of evaluation you want to do. To present your best face, and your best argument, you need to consider your readers' expectations as well as your own needs.

Evaluating for Quality

Students frequently complain that they feel disconnected from academic research because they have to find experts who agree with their ideas; they are frustrated that teachers won't accept students' reasons and logic alone. But consider what you learned in Chapter 6 about Aristotle's appeal to ethos, or credibility. ✴ The sources that you choose to include in your writing say as much about you as a writer as they do about your argument. In other words, you're not just relying on your authors' ethos when you use outside sources; you're also building your own. When you use a variety of source types reflecting multiple perspectives and rigorously gathered information, you are presenting yourself as someone who is careful, thoughtful, thorough, open-minded, and able to deal with complexity. In short, you are presenting yourself as an ideal academic writer.

Evaluating Different Types of Sources

You cannot evaluate all sources using the same set of rules. Let's use movies as an analogy here. You would expect a superhero movie to feature action sequences and high-budget special effects, and if someone asked you if *The Avengers* was good, you might comment on those things. On the other hand, if someone asked you the same question about *Anna Karenina*, you probably wouldn't say that there should have been more explosions because no one would go to a literary costume drama with that expectation.

The same logic holds true with academic information sources. You have to evaluate your sources in terms of what they are trying to do and by considering the standards for that type of discourse. You wouldn't expect a 500-page book and a 500-word blog post to display the same level of analysis; you

See pp. 132-33. ✴ • • • • • • • • •

shouldn't evaluate a scholarly journal article using the same standards you'd use to evaluate a newspaper article. Knowing how to recognize different types of sources is the first step in effective evaluation.

Recognizing Digital Sources

In a digital world, recognizing different types of sources is not an easy process. The physical characteristics that make a newspaper obviously different from a scholarly journal disappear when you find both of those sources in the same database. In the next section, we will talk about each of these source types and point out some things to look for as you evaluate. Before we do that, here are some tools you can use to identify different types of sources. First, most library resources will identify sources by type. (The screenshot below shows how one research tool displays such information.) This information isn't always accurate, so use your judgment, but making use of such a tool is an excellent place to start.

When you find articles online, in databases or with search engines, you should do a little research to discover more about them. Identify the name of the *periodical* (the journal, magazine, or newspaper) that published the article. For example, the first article in the screenshot below ("High School Sports Gender Equity Project") was published in the *Atlanta Journal/Atlanta Constitution*. A quick *Wikipedia* search of this publication tells you that it is a

High School Sports Gender Equity Project: A look at fairness in Georgia **high school sports**: Home Edition

The Atlanta Journal the Atlanta Constitution, 04/22/1999, p. JA.10
... Are **high school** boys and girls treated equally on the playing field? The Atlanta Journal-Constitution needs your help in researching **gender** equity in high...
Newspaper Article: Full Text Online

SPORT, GENDER-EQUITABLE ATTITUDES AND ABUSE PERPETRATION AMONG A SAMPLE OF **HIGH SCHOOL** STUDENT-ATHLETES

by McCauley, HL; Tancredi, D; Silverman, J; Decker, M; Virata, MC; O'Connor, B ...(more)
JOURNAL OF ADOLESCENT HEALTH, ISSN 1054-139X, 02/2013, Volume 52, Issue 2, p. S15
PSYCHOLOGY, DEVELOPMENTAL, PUBLIC, ENVIRONMENTAL & OCCUPATIONAL HEALTH, PEDIATRICS
Journal Article: Full Text Online

Source Types Identified in an Academic Research Tool

newspaper, that its official name is the *Atlanta Journal-Constitution*, and that it is important in its region.

Sometimes no matter how much you look, you won't be able to figure out what type of source you've found. Ask your instructor, or a librarian, for help if you are stumped.

Using Checklists

A common tool used to evaluate sources is a checklist. A checklist can provide useful questions to consider, but it will not answer them for you, and more important, it will not tell you what those answers mean. In other words, identifying a set of facts about a source (like the author, publisher, or publication date) is not the same as evaluating it. These facts are just your starting point. You will sometimes need to do additional research to find out more about an author or a publication; you always need to evaluate those facts in light of your rhetorical situation. The Framework for Evaluating Sources that follows on pp. 202–4 will help you do so.

thinking rhetorically

Understanding Peer Review

For many of the papers you write in college, your audience will expect you to consult peer-reviewed journal articles. *Peer review* is a collaborative process of quality control used by most academic journals to determine which articles should be published and which should not. Understanding this process will help you know what to expect from these articles and to recognize them when you see them. Here is a quick overview of the typical review process:

1. An author (or group of authors) has an idea for a study. He or she (or they) do the following:
   - gather information
   - analyze it
   - draw conclusions (*how* depends on the discipline, or field of study)
   - write an article describing the study and presenting the results
   - send the article to a journal in the discipline

2. The editor of the journal sends the article out to be reviewed by the author's peers: scholars and experts working in the same field.

A Framework for Evaluating Sources

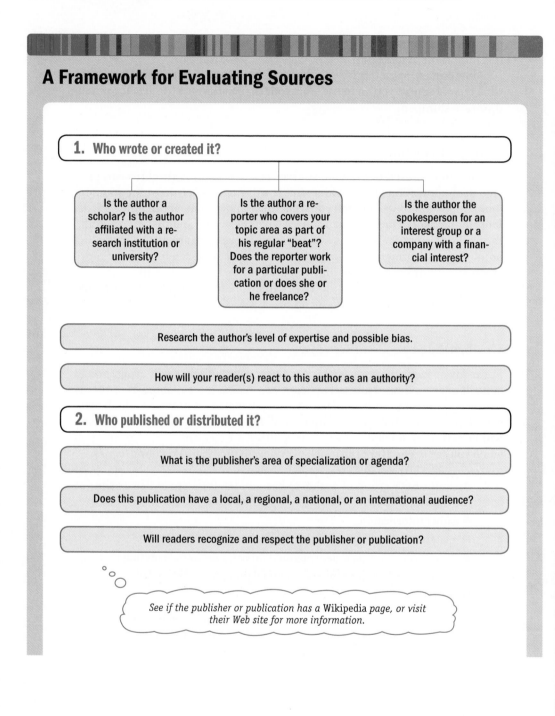

1. Who wrote or created it?

Is the author a scholar? Is the author affiliated with a research institution or university?

Is the author a reporter who covers your topic area as part of his regular "beat"? Does the reporter work for a particular publication or does she or he freelance?

Is the author the spokesperson for an interest group or a company with a financial interest?

Research the author's level of expertise and possible bias.

How will your reader(s) react to this author as an authority?

2. Who published or distributed it?

What is the publisher's area of specialization or agenda?

Does this publication have a local, a regional, a national, or an international audience?

Will readers recognize and respect the publisher or publication?

See if the publisher or publication has a Wikipedia *page, or visit their Web site for more information.*

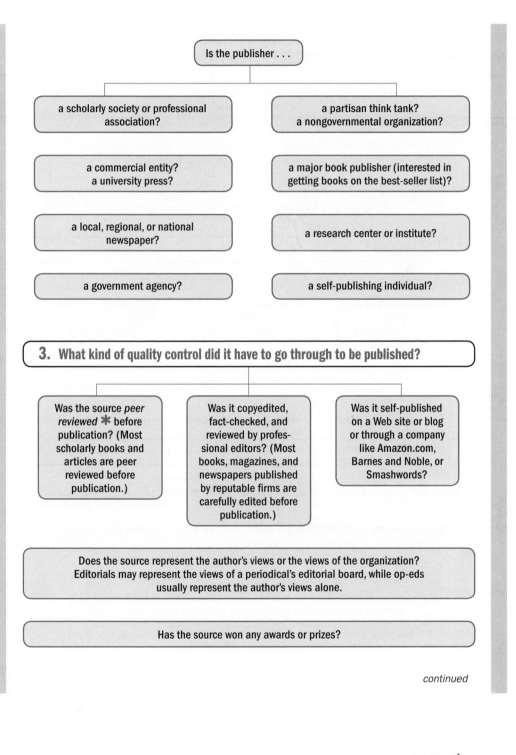

Is the publisher . . .

a scholarly society or professional association?

a partisan think tank?
a nongovernmental organization?

a commercial entity?
a university press?

a major book publisher (interested in getting books on the best-seller list)?

a local, regional, or national newspaper?

a research center or institute?

a government agency?

a self-publishing individual?

3. **What kind of quality control did it have to go through to be published?**

Was the source *peer reviewed* ✱ before publication? (Most scholarly books and articles are peer reviewed before publication.)

Was it copyedited, fact-checked, and reviewed by professional editors? (Most books, magazines, and newspapers published by reputable firms are carefully edited before publication.)

Was it self-published on a Web site or blog or through a company like Amazon.com, Barnes and Noble, or Smashwords?

Does the source represent the author's views or the views of the organization? Editorials may represent the views of a periodical's editorial board, while op-eds usually represent the author's views alone.

Has the source won any awards or prizes?

continued

For a discussion of peer review, see pp. 201–06. ✱

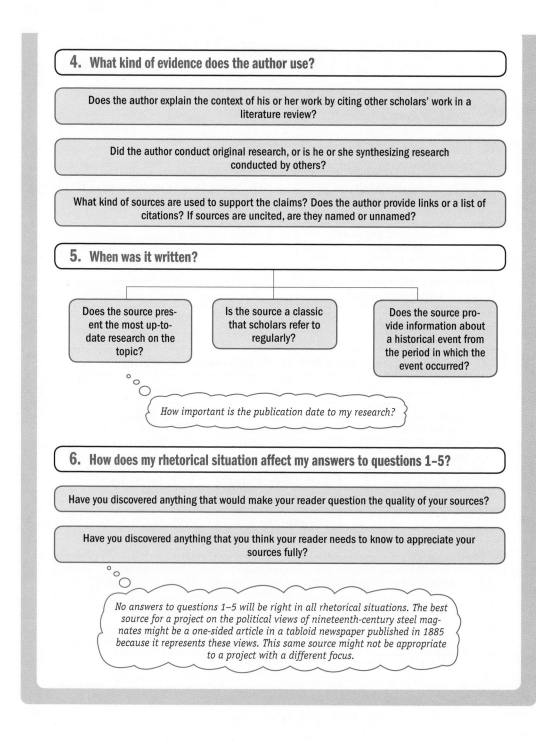

4. What kind of evidence does the author use?

Does the author explain the context of his or her work by citing other scholars' work in a literature review?

Did the author conduct original research, or is he or she synthesizing research conducted by others?

What kind of sources are used to support the claims? Does the author provide links or a list of citations? If sources are uncited, are they named or unnamed?

5. When was it written?

Does the source present the most up-to-date research on the topic?

Is the source a classic that scholars refer to regularly?

Does the source provide information about a historical event from the period in which the event occurred?

How important is the publication date to my research?

6. How does my rhetorical situation affect my answers to questions 1–5?

Have you discovered anything that would make your reader question the quality of your sources?

Have you discovered anything that you think your reader needs to know to appreciate your sources fully?

No answers to questions 1–5 will be right in all rhetorical situations. The best source for a project on the political views of nineteenth-century steel magnates might be a one-sided article in a tabloid newspaper published in 1885 because it represents these views. This same source might not be appropriate to a project with a different focus.

3. The reviewers examine the manuscript and recommend one of three outcomes to the editor:

   ■ publish

   ■ publish with revisions

   ■ reject

4. The editor sends the reviews to the author along with the reviewers' decisions.

   ■ If the decision is *publish with revisions*, then the author considers which changes to make, revises the manuscript, and sends it back to the editor for a final decision.

   ■ If the decision is *reject*, then the author may decide to submit the paper to a different journal and the process will begin again.

Peer review must be understood in context, and the context that is the most important is that of the academic *discipline*. Within a discipline, there is a set of shared assumptions that affect which articles get published and which do not. An author expects that reviewers understand these shared assumptions. A music theorist and a biochemist may be peers in terms of intellect, but they would not be asked to review each other's papers.

Peer reviewers have the expertise to determine whether the research methods employed in a study were appropriate and applied correctly. They can say that the results seem reasonable and evaluate whether the conclusions are supported by the results. They cannot know for sure, however, whether the results reported are valid and accurate or whether future researchers will be able to replicate them because they do not repeat the study themselves. When reviewers say an article should be published, they are saying that they think the research in that article will in some way inform or advance future research. They are not saying it is the last word on the topic; they expect that future researchers will reexamine, and build upon, the research being reported.

What does this mean for you? It means that you should not blindly accept a scholar's conclusions as "true" even if the article in which they appear has been peer reviewed. You should also try to find out where the conclusions fit within the larger context of the discipline:

■ Is an article responding to other researchers' findings?

■ Does it fill a gap in knowledge within the discipline, examining a question that hadn't been answered before?

■ Does it provide additional evidence for a theory or model that is important in the field?

The answers to these questions can help you understand how important an article is and how important it might be to your project.

So how can you tell if something has been peer reviewed? First, remember that peer review is a quality-control process that some academic journals use (and some do not). So your question really is *Was this article published in a journal that uses peer review for quality control?* To answer this question, go to the journal's Web site and look for a page titled "About this Journal" or "Instructions for Authors" for information about the journal's submission and review process.

Databases, especially those provided by professional societies, sometimes include a directory of journals. Look up your journal's name in this directory to find useful information about peer review as well as the journal's scope, its audience, the number of people who read it, and more. If your college library subscribes to Ulrichsweb, a directory of periodicals, use that as a one-stop spot to search for information about newspapers, magazines, and journals.

Evaluation is all about context: your context as you write your paper and the context(s) of your sources. You cannot evaluate your sources in a vacuum. Evaluation requires research, research that will help you understand where your sources fit into the broader conversation. One of the best, and quickest, ways to do research on a source you want to use is to ask your reader. In the case of academic writing, most often the reader is your professor. Most professors will be glad to respond to questions about the appropriateness of sources for your project.

CREATING

The researcher-creator . . .

- communicates effectively and appropriately for the audience and discipline.

- avoids plagiarism and respects the intellectual property of others.

- understands his or her rights as a content creator and exercises them.

- uses appropriate citation and presentation styles.

Look back at the "Diagram of Exploratory Search," on p. 172. Think about the processes described there: knowledge acquisition, analysis, synthesis, evaluation, transformation. These cognitive (thinking) processes require you to interact with the sources you find and to integrate what you learn with what you already know or believe; they require *synthesis*. The end result is something new — a new understanding of your topic and its complexity—which you share with your reader through your writing.

Using Sources: Synthesizing Information and Ideas

In Chapter 5, you learned that synthesis and analysis are closely related. In an academic research project you will do both: You will determine how a text, an object, or a body of data is structured and how its component parts work together. You will also synthesize information—explore connections and contradictions—among the ideas conveyed by a number of sources on your topic, indicating where (and why) you agree or disagree (or perhaps a bit of both) and drawing your own conclusions about the issues. By reading and thinking about several texts, you will notice common themes and trace related—and contradictory—ideas. These thoughts and ideas about your sources and what they mean may be based on the larger conversation taking place among your sources, but they are your original, creative ideas.

The Importance of Reading Critically

Doing the important work of synthesis takes time, so make sure that you give yourself time to read your sources and to analyze them carefully. Remember that academic sources may take longer to read than novels or magazine articles. Peer-reviewed articles and scholarly books are written for expert audiences, so you may need to read such material several times to pick up on the nuances of a researcher's argument, and you may need to look up some of the vocabulary and concepts the authors use. ✱

You will also want to take time to read your sources in conjunction with one another. You might compare works by multiple authors in one sitting, or you might take notes on each source and compare within their arguments and how they build on or respond to one another. You will also want to consider your composing style (see pp. 37–43) to make sure that your reading and writing processes work for you. A heavy reviser may do best reading and synthesizing sources at the same time, using the writing process to work out thoughts. A heavy planner, on the other hand, may prefer to read, take

✱ See Chapter 2 for more on the challenges of reading on a digital device.

careful notes, conduct a more formal analysis, and complete a synthesis chart (see the section below) before beginning to write a research paper.

As you dig more deeply into your sources, you may begin to feel as though you're having a conversation with the experts. And, indeed, this is the way good research works: You'll agree with some ideas, disagree with others, and begin to see trends in the information you gather. In other words, you'll be synthesizing information into something new, into something that reflects your thoughts and ideas.

Putting Things Together

Once you start identifying and analyzing ideas and information from sources on similar topics, you'll want to capture your thoughts. You probably already have a workflow for taking notes as you read: You might highlight key ideas; write summaries or paraphrases or copy and paste quotations into a citation manager (see p. 192), into your notes, or onto note cards; or make notes in the margins of printouts or on digital copies. These approaches to interacting with the text are valuable ways to figure out what your sources are saying. Synthesis, however, means taking this note taking to the next level — focusing on sources as wholes and drawing connections among them.

Some writers use a chart to organize their thoughts. When Alletta Brenner researched human trafficking in American garment manufacturing, for example, she began to see some major factors underlying human trafficking: violation by factory owners, available immigrant labor, and poor enforcement of laws. As she analyzed her sources, she organized them into a chart like the one below.

Topic	Source	My notes	Page #
Violations	*"Treated Like Slaves"*	¾ of textile manufacturing in NYC had substandard wages & working conditions	5
	Bonacich & Appelbaum	61% of garment manufacturers in LA violated wage/hour regs, underpaid workers $73 million per year	3
	Bonacich & Appelbaum	More than ½ firms inspected violated health/safety laws	3

Topic	Source	My notes	Page #
Available labor	USDOJ	⅔ of US trafficking cases involve foreign-born workers	75–91
	Bonacich & Appelbaum	In LA, 81% of garment workers are Asian & Latino immigrants	171–75
	Van Impe	Traffickers offer help, pose as employers, employment agencies, smugglers	114
	Parks	Manufacturers in the US territories can recruit and import thousands of workers from Asia & S. Am.	19–22

Notice that Alletta records page numbers along with her thoughts so that she can cite these sources as she writes. (Alletta's paper appears on pp. 221–31.) It may be that this kind of linear organization does not work for you as a writer, in which case creating a visual map may be more useful. ✱

Using Sources: Quoting, Paraphrasing, and Summarizing

Academic writers integrate sources into their writing in three main ways:

- By quoting a source's words exactly

- By paraphrasing a source, explaining its meaning using their own words and sentences

- By summarizing a source, restating its main ideas and key supporting examples in their own words

Many student writers tend to overquote from their sources. In other words, they use quotations instead of paraphrasing or summarizing, even when the language in question isn't very striking. For example, quoting a statement like this probably is not necessary: "From the year 1990 up until the present time, we have seen some modest improvement in the rate of adult literacy in the United States." Instead, you could paraphrase it: *According to Report A, the adult literacy rate in the United States has increased somewhat since 1990* (and end with an in-text citation of the source). The guidelines on p. 210 will help you decide when to quote, when to paraphrase, and when to summarize.

See the visual plan Daniel Stiepleman created on p. 158. ✱ • • • • • • • • •

Guidelines for Determining When to Quote, Paraphrase, or Summarize

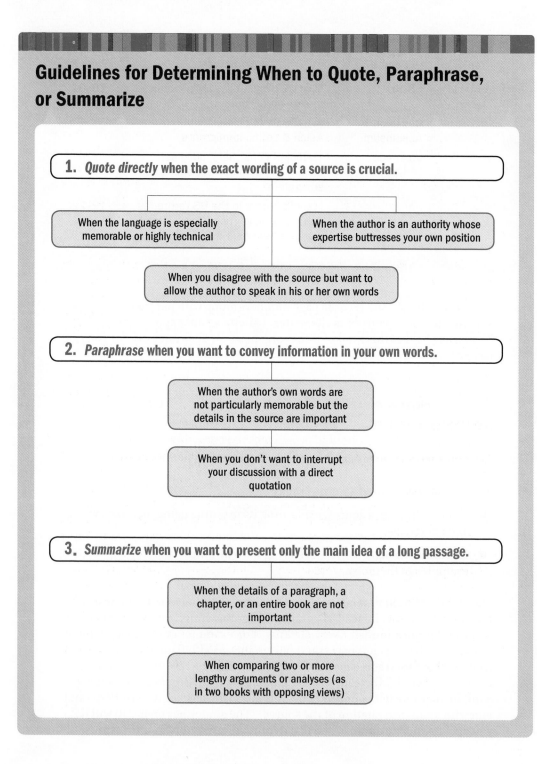

1. *Quote directly* when the exact wording of a source is crucial.

When the language is especially memorable or highly technical

When the author is an authority whose expertise buttresses your own position

When you disagree with the source but want to allow the author to speak in his or her own words

2. *Paraphrase* when you want to convey information in your own words.

When the author's own words are not particularly memorable but the details in the source are important

When you don't want to interrupt your discussion with a direct quotation

3. *Summarize* when you want to present only the main idea of a long passage.

When the details of a paragraph, a chapter, or an entire book are not important

When comparing two or more lengthy arguments or analyses (as in two books with opposing views)

Sometimes overquoting reflects a lack of confidence or the belief that it's always better to rely on the words of experts. Realize that in academic writing, since you must *always* cite your sources—whether you are quoting, paraphrasing, or summarizing—you can trust your citation to tell your reader that your ideas are supported, even if you do not use exact quotations. Sometimes overquoting occurs because quoting is easier than paraphrasing or summarizing: Transcribing a quotation requires less mental work. Regardless of the motivation, overquoting is often a sign that you haven't done enough thinking or that you're not clear on what *you* want to say. Try to limit your direct quotations to those situations in which capturing the author's voice is particularly important because of who he or she is, what he or she is saying, or how he or she says it.

Whether you quote, paraphrase, or summarize, it's essential to acknowledge sources accurately, both in the text of your paper and in the works cited (or references) list at the end of your paper. Within the text itself, you'll often want to use a *signal phrase* to introduce a source. A signal phrase includes the name(s) of the author(s) whose ideas you are discussing and a verb that communicates your attitude toward those ideas. For example, you might introduce a quotation from linguist Noam Chomsky with the signal phrase *Although Chomsky claims.* This phrase gives the reader the clear impression that you are going to disagree with Chomsky. *Chomsky clearly shows*, on the other hand, indicates that you agree with the ideas you are about to discuss. Signal phrases like *Chomsky believes* or *Chomsky's research suggests* are more neutral.

Engaging with your sources as you integrate them into your writing highlights the ways that academic research resembles an extended conversation. Be careful to use signal phrases that accurately reflect your stance toward your sources and to contextualize your sources with information that you discovered during evaluation. For example, you may want to mention in your signal phrase one or more of your reasons for including the source. If you were convinced by reading scholarly book reviews to use a particular book as a source, you might use a signal phrase like *In her well-reviewed book, Laurel Thatcher Ulrich introduced the concept.* You may also include your reasons for choosing a source or your explanation of how the source supports your claims in the analysis you provide following the quotation, paraphrase, or summary.

Make sure that your signal phrases enhance the readability of your argument and that you vary their location. They shouldn't always appear at the beginning of a sentence. Remember too that the documentation style you're following (MLA, APA, or others) will generally specify what to include in your signal phrases and in-text citations.

A Note about Citations

As noted above, as an academic writer you know that you must cite the sources you quote directly, but you may be less clear about whether you must cite reworded information or ideas taken from sources. You must, and there's a good reason why: Your ideas are grounded in the conversation represented by your sources, and your citations show how all the ideas—yours and your sources'—work together. Even when you paraphrase or summarize, you want to point to the authors who have informed your thinking, both in the text and in the works cited (or references) list.

Quoting Accurately

When you incorporate a quotation into your writing—for any reason—you must include the exact words from the source. The following original passage is from a classic essay about illiteracy in America. Read the original, and then see how one student used a short quotation from it in her research essay (following MLA style).

Original Passage

> Illiterates cannot travel freely. When they attempt to do so, they encounter risks that few of us can dream of. They cannot read traffic signs and, while they often learn to recognize and decipher symbols, they cannot manage street names which they haven't seen before. The same is true for bus and subway stops. While ingenuity can sometimes help a man or woman to discern direction from familiar landmarks, buildings, cemeteries, churches, and the like, most illiterates are virtually immobilized. They seldom wander past the streets and neighborhoods they know. Geographical paralysis becomes a bitter metaphor for their entire existence. They are immobilized in almost every sense we can imagine. They can't move up. They can't move out. They cannot see beyond.
>
> —Jonathan Kozol, "The Human Cost of an Illiterate Society"

Short Quotation

> Kozol points out that people who are illiterate often can't leave their own neighborhoods, which is "a bitter metaphor for their entire existence" (256).

The student who wrote this passage did three different things to effectively integrate the Kozol quotation:

1. She introduced the source with a signal phrase.

2. She used Kozol's words exactly and indicated the borrowed language with quotation marks.

3. She provided an in-text citation at the end of the sentence, pointing the reader to the page number where the quotation can be found in the original source and including that item in her list of works cited at the end of her paper. (Notice that the period appears after the page number in MLA style.)

Long Quotation

Indent longer quotations from the text as a block with no quotation marks. ✱ Introduce the quotation with a signal phrase, and include a page reference at the end, following the period.

> Although illiteracy creates serious problems in many aspects of a person's life, its effect on mobility is particularly devastating. Jonathan Kozol puts it this way:
>> Illiterates cannot travel freely. When they attempt to do so, they encounter risks that few of us can dream of. They cannot read traffic signs and, while they often learn to recognize and decipher symbols, they cannot manage street names which they haven't seen before. The same is true for bus and subway stops. While ingenuity can sometimes help a man or woman to discern directions from familiar landmarks, buildings, cemeteries, churches, and the like, most illiterates are virtually immobilized. (256)

Square Brackets and Ellipses

Use square brackets ([ ]) when you need to change a quotation to make it fit into your sentence, for example, to add a word, change a lowercase letter to a capital letter, and so on. Use ellipses (. . .) to eliminate words from the original. Be careful to use both techniques sparingly and to not change the meaning of the original quotation.

> Although illiteracy creates serious problems in many aspects of a person's life, its effect on mobility is particularly devastating. As Kozol puts it, "Illiterates cannot travel freely. . . . They cannot read traffic signs and . . . cannot manage street names which they haven't seen before. . . . [M]ost illiterates are virtually immobilized" (256).

Paraphrasing Effectively

A paraphrase expresses an author's ideas in your own words. To write an acceptable paraphrase, you should use different sentence structures and language from that of the original, but keep the overall length about the same. Consider the following paraphrases. One is an example of how to paraphrase appropriately, while the other contains several mistakes. Can you figure out which is which?

Paraphrase 1

> Jonathan Kozol, an expert on literacy, explains that illiterates are unable to travel on their own outside their immediate neighborhoods—and that it is hazardous for them to do so. People who can't read can't figure out most signs—for traffic, unfamiliar streets, bus stops, and so on. Most of the time, illiterates are unable to move very far from the area where they live. In a way, the inability to travel symbolizes the lives of illiterate people, who are frozen in their economic and social situation and thus lack hope about the future (256).

Paraphrase 2

> Jonathan Kozol, an expert on literacy, says that illiterate people cannot travel very easily. When they try to travel, they run into problems that most of us can't imagine. Illiterate people are unable to decipher traffic signs, unfamiliar street signs, and many other kinds of directional aids. Sometimes a familiar landmark or building may help an illiterate person figure out how to go somewhere, but most illiterate people remain immobilized in their own neighborhoods. They are, in a sense, geographically paralyzed. They can't move in any direction—or see the future. Because of these problems, the United States needs to take immediate steps to eliminate illiteracy in this country (256).

Appropriate Paraphrase

If you guessed that Example 1 was the appropriate paraphrase, you are correct. Both paraphrases introduce Kozol with a signal phrase and provide a page reference in an in-text citation at the end, but only the first paraphrase captures Kozol's ideas accurately, without borrowing Kozol's words, phrases, or sentence structure to do so. (Note that paraphrases may include key words or phrases from the original in quotation marks and everyday words or words for which there are no ready substitute—forms of the word *illiterate*, for example.) The appropriate paraphrase is also limited to conveying Kozol's ideas.

What to Avoid When Paraphrasing

Now let's analyze what went wrong in Example 2:

1. The author has borrowed much of Kozol's language, and some of the changes are so minor as to be irrelevant: changing "geographical paralysis" to "geographically paralyzed" does not make this striking phrase any less Kozol's.

2. The original sentence structure is preserved almost exactly.

3. The author adds his or her own ideas in the last sentence, without clearly marking them as such. This passage suggests that Kozol calls for "immediate steps to eliminate illiteracy," which is deceptive.

If you notice yourself "translating" a passage in this way, merely swapping in synonyms or turning words around, take a step back. It is likely that you haven't thought enough about the passage to figure out what meaning you really want to capture from it. (Note: Some instructors may consider this kind of sloppy paraphrase a form of plagiarism. For more information, see the section on plagiarism on p. 216.)

Summarizing

When you summarize, you condense a long passage—an excerpt, an article, or even a whole book—by conveying the main idea and key supporting points in your own words and sentence structures. Here is a summary of Jonathan Kozol's original paragraph on p. 212:

> Because illiterates cannot read signs and other directional aids, they cannot travel far from where they live. In much the same sense, they cannot move socially or economically to improve their lives (Kozol 256).

Summarizing is especially useful when writing evaluations or synthesizing ideas from several related sources. Whereas a paraphrase will be roughly the same length as the original text, a summary will be much shorter, including only the most important points. Accurately capturing the most essential ideas expressed in the source is key. Use these strategies to summarize:

1. Read the passage carefully to make sure you understand it completely, looking up unfamiliar words and concepts as necessary.

2. Identify and note the key ideas in the text. You might create an outline or underline the thesis statement and the topic sentences of key supporting paragraphs. Be sure to note how the ideas relate to each other.

3. Without looking at the source, draft the summary. If you find yourself getting too bogged down in detail—paraphrasing more than summarizing—take a break. When you come back you may find that the details have faded, leaving you free to focus on the main ideas.

4. Introduce the summary with a signal phrase, clearly indicating both the author's name and the title of the work you are summarizing. If you are only summarizing a chapter or an excerpt, make sure that this is clear to your readers. Provide an in-text citation at the end.

5. Double-check your summary against the source to make sure you have accurately captured the author's main points.

A Note about Plagiarism

Plagiarism is the intentional or unintentional use of others' words, ideas, or visuals as if they were your own. Plagiarism can have serious consequences. At some colleges, for example, students who plagiarize fail not only the assignment but also the entire course; at colleges that have honor codes, students may even be expelled. Plagiarism scandals happen outside school, too. Recently, professional authors, journalists, politicians, and news reporters alike have made public apologies and even lost their jobs after being caught using others' words as their own. Could it be that plagiarism is more common now than it used to be?

It is possible, but it is just as likely that it is easier to get caught today than it was in the past. Most people who plagiarize do so accidentally. Taking sloppy notes, forgetting where they saw an idea, writing a faulty paraphrase, failing to mark a quotation in an early draft—all of this is easier in the era of copying and pasting from digital texts, and any one of these mistakes can lead to inadvertent plagiarism. When most information sources were in print, it was easy for these mistakes to slip by. Even if something did not seem quite right, finding proof of plagiarism required diligence and a little bit of luck.

Now, with the Google Books project, a searchable database of almost any book a student might use in a paper is readily available online. If a text seems familiar or the language in a student's paper doesn't sound authentic, following up on that hunch is quick and easy. In addition, many campuses have implemented campus-wide licenses for plagiarism-detecting software. Two common examples are SafeAssign (http://safeassign.com) and Turnitin (http://turnitin.com). These programs allow faculty to compare student papers to published work as well as to other student papers.

The digital information landscape means that it is much easier to find interesting and useful sources than it used to be. It also means that keeping track of where sources come from and when and how material from sources gets used is crucial.

As mentioned earlier in this chapter (pp. 191–92) many article databases provided by college libraries allow you to create a permanent folder of sources, which you can easily access as you write. Some databases will also generate citations in a variety of documentation styles. Ask your librarian if you need help using these features. Bibliographic management tools like Zotero, Mendeley, and EndNote allow you to save resources, organize these resources into folders, take notes on your sources, and import passages as you write. The time it takes you to learn to use these tools is well worth the protection they afford from unintentional plagiarism. See the guidelines below for strategies for avoiding plagiarism.

Guidelines for Avoiding Plagiarism

1. Give yourself enough time to complete your paper without undue stress.

2. Develop a method for managing sources (using a working bibliography or an online reference management system), and make sure your bibliography is complete and accurate.

3. Develop a note-taking system that clearly identifies direct quotations and *use* it.

4. Write paraphrases and summaries in your own words.

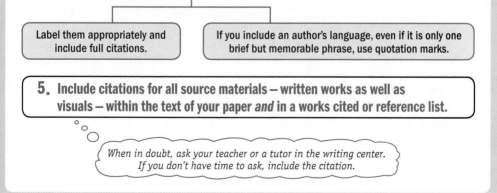

Label them appropriately and include full citations.

If you include an author's language, even if it is only one brief but memorable phrase, use quotation marks.

5. Include citations for all source materials — written works as well as visuals — within the text of your paper *and* in a works cited or reference list.

When in doubt, ask your teacher or a tutor in the writing center. If you don't have time to ask, include the citation.

Use these tools to keep track of your sources throughout your research process and to help you cite your sources ethically and accurately as you write. If your campus uses tools to detect plagiarism, it is in your interest to become familiar with them. They are not foolproof. In addition, you may be able to use them yourself to check your own writing before submitting it.

NOTE FOR MULTILINGUAL WRITERS

The concept of plagiarism is central to the modern Western intellectual tradition. It rests on the notion of intellectual property — the belief that language can be "owned" by writers who create original ideas. This belief contradicts the beliefs and practices of some other intellectual traditions. Indeed, in some countries, students are taught that using the words of others without citing them is a sign of respect, and writers in some countries assume that readers will recognize cited passages that are interwoven with the writer's own words. As a student at a North American institution, however, you need to follow Western documentation and citation practices. If you have questions or concerns about how to apply them, ask your instructor or a writing-center tutor.

Using Appropriate Citation Styles and Formatting

In Chapter 4, you learned the importance of understanding your audience's expectations and that readers from different academic disciplines have different expectations when it comes to research writing. As you think about how to present the information you collect, it is important to keep your readers' expectations in mind.

MLA (Modern Language Association) style and APA (American Psychological Association) style are two of the most frequently required styles for undergraduates. (*Chicago* and Council of Science Editors are two other popular styles.) MLA style is typically used in English and other areas of the humanities; APA is common in the social sciences. At the end of this chapter, you'll find a sample student essay using MLA documentation and formatting style (pp. 221–31). The documentation guidelines at the back of this book provide examples and explanations for MLA rules (pp. 367–99) and APA rules (pp. 400–22).

Understanding Your Rights as a Content Creator

There is a very good chance that you are already creating content for others to read and publishing it on the Web: Every time you tweet, update your Facebook status, or upload a video to YouTube, you're creating content. As an academic writer in the twenty-first century, you need to start thinking of yourself as a creator, not just a consumer, of information.

As a content creator, you have to decide how much control you want to assert over the things you create. Most online services allow you to decide how public you want your contributions to be. Still, even when you are allowed to adjust your privacy settings (as you can on Facebook), when you sign up for the service, you agree to share the rights to the intellectual property you create and publish on the site.

As you develop your skills as a researcher, you may be in a position to publish your own research, even as an undergraduate. When that happens, you will usually be asked to sign an agreement turning over some, or all, of your copyright to a publisher. Your professors and mentors can help guide you through this process.

There is no right answer to the question "How public should my intellectual property be?" There are arguments for keeping control of your intellectual property and arguments for sharing it. Your individual situation will determine what is right for you. One way that you can assert some control over content you do make public is by attaching a Creative Commons license to it (http://creativecommons.org). These licenses allow you to define, in advance, whether or not other people have permission to use your work, and they allow you to set conditions on that permission. There are a variety of licenses to choose from. These licenses do not eliminate your copyright, nor do they legally transfer ownership of your intellectual property to anyone else. They simply grant permission, in advance, to others who may want to use your work.

As a writer, you can also use Creative Commons licenses to ensure that you have the right to use images, music, and other intellectual property in your projects. Search engines like Google Images and services like Flickr allow you to do Creative Commons searches for content, so that you can find content with the appropriate license for your use.

Isn't There More to Say Here on Writing?

This final section might strike you as brief, when there's clearly so much to think about when writing with, and from, sources. Yet the brevity of this section illustrates something important about the recursive nature of the writing process and, indeed, of all rhetorical activities. While there's much to learn about how to do research, and while integrating sources into your writing takes practice, you will not (and should not) throw away everything you know about your writing process when you write with, and from, sources. The strategies you've explored throughout this book apply to research-based writing: Part One leads you to think broadly about reading, writing, and rhetoric; Part Two helps you accomplish specific kinds of reading and writing tasks; and Part Three gives you practical strategies for reading and writing effectively. So the short answer to the question posed in the heading above is that there *is* more to say — and you'll find it in the rest of the book.

Sample Research Essay Using MLA Documentation Style

Here is a research essay by Alletta Brenner, a student at the University of Oregon.

✱ bedfordstmartins.com/rewriting
  For additional sample research projects using MLA, APA, and other documentation styles, go to **Re:Writing** *and click on* **ModelDoc Central.**

Brenner 1

Alletta Brenner
Professor Clark
WR 222
9 May 2013

Sweatshop U.S.A.: Human Trafficking in the American

Garment-Manufacturing Industry

    In early 1999, Nguyen Thi Le, a Vietnamese mother of two, signed a four-year contract to work for a garment factory in American Samoa. The island is a US territory with a low minimum wage where enterprises seeking to benefit from cheap labor costs can produce items with a "Made in U.S.A." label. Dazzled by the opportunity to live in America and earn American wages, Nguyen eagerly looked forward to her new job, even though she would have to move an ocean away from her family and take out high-interest loans to cover the $5,000 fee for airfare and work permits. Despite these hardships, the job seemed to offer her the chance to earn wages more than twelve times those available at home. If she worked

Fig. 1. Two Vietnamese workers after they were beaten at the Daewoosa factory, American Samoa, 2000. National Labor Committee.

Brenner 2

abroad for just a few years, Nguyen believed, she could dramatically improve the quality of her family's life (Gittelsohn 16).

Opens with a narrative to engage readers' interest

However, upon arrival, Nguyen found a situation radically different from what she had expected. She and the other Daewoosa workers were paid only a fraction of the wages the garment factory had promised. The factory owner deducted high fees—sometimes half their monthly paychecks—for room and board that the contract had indicated would be "free," and when orders were slow, the owner didn't pay them at all. Kept in a guarded compound, Nguyen and her fellow garment sewers had to work sixteen- to eighteen-hour days under deplorable conditions. When they complained, they were often punished with violence, intimidation, and starvation (see figs. 1 and 2). According to the *New York Times*, when word of these abuses surfaced and the factory finally shut down in 2001, the women were left out on the streets with no means to return home (Greenhouse). Stuck in Samoa, Nguyen learned that back home, loan sharks were hounding her family to repay the debt she had incurred. Though Nguyen eventually received US government aid, which allowed her to move to the American mainland and

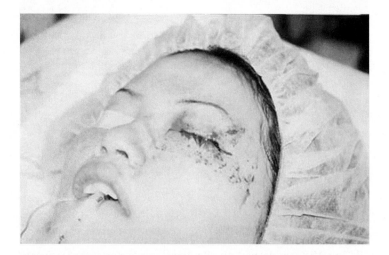

Fig. 2. Daewoosa woman worker who lost her eye after being brutally beaten on November 28, 2000. National Labor Committee.

Brenner 3

acquire a new job, it will take many years for her to recover from the damage to her personal and financial life (*"Made in the U.S.A."?*).

Human Trafficking: An Overview

Though what happened to Nguyen and the other workers may seem unusual to you, such occurrences are common in the United States today. Every year thousands of persons fall victim to human trafficking: they are transported either against their will or under false pretenses for the purpose of economic or sexual exploitation. In recent years, politicians as well as the media have paid more attention to human trafficking. Movies, newspaper articles, presidential speeches, and United Nations resolutions portray human trafficking as a negative consequence of globalization, capitalism, and immigration. Yet rarely do such accounts analyze the larger questions of how and why human trafficking exists. This essay will address some of these larger questions. In the American garment-manufacturing industry, three forces fuel human trafficking: violations by factory owners, an available immigrant labor force, and poor enforcement of laws. Before analyzing these factors, this discussion will take a closer look at the term *human trafficking* and the scope of its practice.

The official definition of the term *human trafficking* evolved in 2001 as a part of a United Nations treaty on transnational crime. The UN's *Protocol to Prevent, Suppress and Punish Trafficking in Persons* defines human trafficking as the "recruitment, transportation, transfer, harboring or receipt of persons by means of threat or use of force or other means of coercion, abduction, fraud, deception, abuse of power or position of vulnerability . . . for the purpose of exploitation" (Article 3). According to this definition, human trafficking has three components: 1) movement over geographical space, either across or within national borders; 2) the extraction of profits by the exploitation of victims' bodies or skills; and 3) the coercion of victims, which may include a wide range of tactics and forms (Gallagher 986–87).

How, then, does human trafficking work in practice? It can occur both within and across national borders and may involve a single perpetrator

Main topic of human trafficking introduced

States thesis and key questions for essay

Definition and background information provided

Brenner 4

or an organized criminal network of recruiters, transporters, sellers, and buyers. The victims of human trafficking usually want to migrate and seek new employment. Van Impe reports that human traffickers typically pose as employers, employment agencies, or smugglers, offering to help victims by assisting them in entering a country or providing a job (114). Once an individual accepts this help, the trafficker may keep up the charade for quite some time, so when victims eventually realize what has happened, they may feel there is no choice but to submit to the trafficker's demands. After individuals have moved and started working, human traffickers use abusive and illegitimate tactics to force victims to work. They may, for example, threaten victims with physical violence, deportation, or debt bondage, wherein traffickers claim that a victim owes them money for transport or other services and then force him or her to work off the debt (US, Dept. of State, *Trafficking* 21).

How widespread is human trafficking in the United States? Both because of its relative wealth, and because it is a destination country for millions of migrant workers every year, the United States is one of the primary destinations for trafficked persons worldwide ("Country Report"). The US Department of State estimates that between fourteen and eighteen thousand persons are trafficked in the United States each year (*Trafficking* 1–4); although the basis for these numbers is unclear, they appear to be consistent with global estimates on human trafficking. Not all victims are foreign-born, but immigrants are particularly vulnerable to such exploitation. In the United States, two-thirds of all human-trafficking cases investigated and brought to court since 2001 have involved foreign-born migrant workers, according to a recent report by the US Department of Justice (75–91).

Signal phrase for source at end of sentence, before in-text citation

Human Trafficking in American Garment Manufacturing

Some of the largest human trafficking cases uncovered to date in the United States have occurred in the garment-manufacturing industry. In addition to the Daewoosa factory in American Samoa, investigators have found large sweatshops utilizing human trafficking in California, New

Brenner 5

York, and the Northern Mariana Islands. Police discovered one of the worst cases in El Monte, California, in 1995, where they found seventy-two Thai immigrants in an apartment complex surrounded by razor wire and armed guards. Trafficked from Thailand, the men and women had endured eighteen-hour workdays, seven days a week for seven years, sewing clothing for some of the nation's best-known clothing companies. Constantly threatened by violence to themselves and their families at home, the victims were forced to live in the same tiny, filthy apartments in which they worked. Grossly underpaid and forced to buy food and other necessities from their captors at inflated prices, the workers were in constant debt. To make matters worse, when police discovered and raided the compound, they arrested the workers for immigration violations and put them in jail. Only when local leaders and nongovernmental organizations spurred public outrage over the case were the workers released on bond and able to begin normal lives in the America they had once envisioned (Ross 143–47).

Violations by factory owners are one reason human trafficking such as that in El Monte occurs. Because most American clothing companies outsource the production of their garments to factories around the world, US factories are under constant pressure to lower costs. Unfortunately, this pressure often translates into poorer wages and working conditions for those who produce clothing in this country and illegal activity on the part of their employers (Bonacich and Appelbaum 137). A common violation is the failure of factory owners to pay workers the legally mandated minimum wage. Unlike most US workers, garment workers earn a piece-rate wage rather than an hourly wage. Because the amount of available work and the going rate for items sewed constantly fluctuates, the amount workers earn often reflects downward pressure. Employers, however, are supposed to make up the difference so that workers still make the minimum wage. When employers fail to do so or attempt to comply with the law by forcing workers to speed up production, the result is substandard pay. Some workers in the

First subtopic: violations by factory owners

Brenner 6

American garment-manufacturing industry earn less than $4 an hour, and those who work from home make even less, sometimes as little as $2 per hour.

Studies of garment manufacturers throughout the United States have found that violations of wage, hours, and safety laws are the rule, not the exception. For example, one study of textile-manufacturing operations in the New York City area found that 75% of them were operating in the informal sector—not legally licensed or monitored—with substandard wages and working conditions (*"Treated Like Slaves"* 5). A different study described in *Behind the Label* found that 61% of garment manufacturers in Los Angeles were violating wage and hours regulations, underpaying their workers by an estimated $73 million every year. Yet another study found that in more than half of firms inspected, workers were in danger of serious injury or death as a result of health and safety law violations (Bonacich and Appelbaum 3).

Violations by factory owners, however, are only one part of the picture in the garment industry. Another factor is the availability of an immigrant labor force. Factories that produce clothing in the United States and its territories are heavily dependent on immigrants to meet their labor needs. For example, Bonacich and Appelbaum report that in Los Angeles, which has the highest concentration of garment manufacturers in the nation, 81% of workers are Asian and Latino immigrants (171–75). In American territories, immigrant labor is even more prevalent. In Saipan, the US territory with the largest number of garment factories, almost all garment workers are foreign-born. Because the indigenous populations of many territories are so small, most garment manufacturers could not survive without imported labor. For this reason, territories do not operate under the same immigration laws as the American mainland, where relatively few visas are available to low-skilled workers. Consequently, employers in US territories are able to legally recruit and import thousands of employees from Asia and South America (Parks 19–22).

Second subtopic: available immigrant labor force

Brenner 7

For a number of reasons, the use of a predominantly immigrant workforce makes it easier for unscrupulous manufacturers to coerce and exploit workers. First, immigrant workers facing economic hardships often have no choice but to take risks and accept poor treatment and pay. A book published by Human Rights Watch quotes one Guatemalan woman who stayed with her abusive employers for many years:

> I am the single mother of two daughters. The salary there
> [in Guatemala] is not sufficient for their studies, their food,
> their clothes. I want them to get ahead in life. . . . Sometimes
> one is pressured by the economic situation. It's terrible what
> one suffers. . . . Sometimes I ask myself why I put up with
> so much. It's for this, for my mother and my daughters.
> (Pier 9–10)

A second reason is that those who enter the country illegally fear deportation. Indeed, as Lelio points out, because of their status, illegal immigrants often work in the informal sector "under the table" in order to avoid authorities, which makes it much easier for traffickers to exploit them (68-69). These jobs may be within individual homes, or at businesses owned by other immigrants within tightly knit ethnic communities. The strong fear of deportation that permeates many such communities enables factory owners to effectively enforce a code of silence on their employees, legal and illegal immigrants alike (Bonacich and Appelbaum 144-47).

A third reason is that many immigrants lack English language skills and knowledge of American laws and culture. Thus they find it difficult to do anything about the situation they're in.

Even though most immigrant workers at garment factories in American territories are there legally, they are just as vulnerable to human trafficking. Like immigrant workers in the mainland United States, they are often under a great deal of pressure to support families back at home. Because most immigrant workers in the territories take out high-interest loans simply to get their jobs, they are even more likely to accept deplorable working conditions than are illegal immigrants on the mainland. When employers fail to pay their workers appropriately (or sometimes at all), they can prevent workers from paying off their debts and thereby keep them as virtual prisoners. Indeed, human rights organizations have reported that thousands of garment workers live in severe debt bondage throughout American territories in the Pacific (Clarren 35–36).

The incidence of human trafficking gets further impetus from the "guest worker" immigration laws. Because such workers' visas depend on their employment with a particular firm, leaving the employer with whom they are contracted would break the terms of their visa. Ironically, this places legal guest workers in a more precarious position than those who immigrate illegally, for guest workers who violate the terms of their visas face deportation. Though some workers do leave and turn to prostitution or other forms of black market work to survive, the fear of being sent back home is a constant one. As a result, most stay with their abusive employers, hoping to someday pay off their debts and leave (Clarren 38–41).

Third subtopic: poor enforcement of laws

A final factor that contributes to human trafficking in the garment industry is that where protective labor laws and standards do exist, their enforcement tends to be lax (Branigin 21–28). Despite the rampant violation of labor and safety laws throughout the industry, most garment manufacturers are able to avoid legal repercussions. Even when human-trafficking cases in the garment industry do occur, they tend to run much longer than other trafficking cases, averaging over six years in duration (US, Dept. of State, *Matrix* 6–9). This occurs for several reasons. First of all, as noted previously, many garment factories operate illegally. Because the Department of Labor only investigates such operations when someone makes an official complaint, traffickers who can control their victims are able to avoid detection. This is generally not a difficult task because victims of trafficking often lack the skills and knowledge required to take such action.

Second, inspectors from the Department of Labor and Occupational Safety and Health Administration rarely visit those factories that do operate legally. Even when workers complain, it can take up to a year for the government to open a case and make inspections. Moreover, when an investigation finally begins, owners often have advance warning, allowing them to conceal violations before the inspectors arrive. Some factory owners under investigation have been known to close up shop and disappear, leaving their employees out on the streets with months of back pay owed to them. These tendencies are especially prevalent in US territories because of the geographic and bureaucratic distance between the islands and the governmental bodies that are supposed to regulate them. With the enforcement of most laws left up to local officials and agencies, many of whom stand to profit from arrangements with factory owners, human traffickers find it easy to avoid government interference. The risk for such activity is thus relatively low (Ross 210–11).

Conclusion

In 2001, the same year that Nguyen's case hit the American media, President Bush proclaimed that the United States has a special duty to fight against "the trade in human misery" that human trafficking represents today. Since then, the United States has created a wide range of antitrafficking laws and measures, but little has changed in the lives of human-trafficking victims. Although the owner of the Daewoosa factory was eventually convicted of enslaving more than 250 workers in his factory, other garment manufacturers continue to operate much as they did a decade ago. Some high-profile American clothing companies, such as the Gap, have promised to stop contracting with factories that violate labor laws; however, the essential setup of the industry remains fully intact. Until these problems are directly addressed, human trafficking will continue to be a blemish on the American dream and, as President Bush recognized in a 2004 speech, "a shame to our country."

Conclusion restates the problem

Brenner 10

Works Cited

Bonacich, Edna, and Richard Appelbaum. *Behind the Label: Inequality in the Los Angeles Apparel Industry*. Berkeley: U of California P, 2000. Print.

Branigin, William. "A Life of Exhaustion, Beating and Isolation." *Washington Post* 5 Jan. 1999: A6. Print.

Bush, George W. National Training Conference on Combating Human Trafficking. Tampa Marriott Waterside Hotel, Tampa, FL. 16 July 2004. Address.

Clarren, Rebecca. "Paradise Lost." *Ms.* Spring 2006: 35–41. Print.

"Country Report—The United States." *The Protection Project*. The Protection Project, 2002. Web. 28 Apr. 2013.

Gallagher, Anne. "Human Rights and the New UN Protocols on Trafficking and Migrant Smuggling: A Preliminary Analysis." *Human Rights Quarterly* 23 (2001): 986–87. Print.

Gittelsohn, John. "U.S. Sends Strong Message to Those Who Traffic in Human Lives." *Global Issues: Responses to Human Trafficking* 8.2 (2003): 14–17. Web. 2 Apr. 2013.

Greenhouse, Steven. "Beatings and Other Abuses Cited at Samoan Apparel Plant That Supplied U.S. Retailers." *New York Times* 6 Feb. 2001: A14. Print.

Lelio, Marmora. *International Migration Policies and Programmes*. Geneva: Intl. Organization for Migration, 1999. Print.

"Made in the U.S.A."? Clothing for J.C. Penney, Sears and Target Made by Women Held under Conditions of Indentured Servitude at the Daewoosa Factory in American Samoa. New York: Natl. Labor Committee, 2001. Web. 2 Apr. 2013.

National Labor Committee. "Photos Related to Daewoosa in American Samoa." National Labor Committee, n.d. Web. 30 Apr. 2013.

Parks, Virginia. *The Geography of Immigrant Labor Markets: Space, Networks, and Gender*. New York: LFB Scholarly Publishing, 2005. Print.

Pier, Carol. *Hidden in the Home: Abuse of Domestic Workers with Special Visas in the United States*. New York: Human Rights Watch, 2001. Print.

Ross, Andrew, ed. *No Sweat: Fashion, Free Trade and the Rights of Garment Workers*. New York: Verso, 1997. Print.

"Treated Like Slaves": Donna Karan, Inc., Violates Women Workers' Human Rights. New York: Center for Economic and Social Rights, 1999. Print.

Heading centered

First line of each entry flush left, subsequent lines indented

List double-spaced throughout (single-spaced here for length)

Photographs obtained from Web site

Brenner 11

United Nations. Office on Drugs and Crime. *Protocol to Prevent, Suppress and Punish Trafficking in Persons, Especially Women and Children, Supplementing the United Nations Convention against Transnational Organized Crime.* New York: United Nations, 2000. Print.

United States. Dept. of Justice. *Report on Activities to Combat Human Trafficking: Fiscal Years 2001–2005.* DOJ, 2006. Web. 24 Apr. 2013.

———. Dept. of State. *Matrix of Some of the Major Trafficking Cases in the United States of the Last Eight Years.* DOS, May 2003. Web. 4 May 2013.

———. *Trafficking in Persons Report.* DOS, June 2004. Web. 4 May 2013.

Van Impe, Kristof. "People for Sale: The Need for a Multidisciplinary Approach toward Human Trafficking." *International Migration* 1 (2000): 114. Print.

Three works from same government; hyphens substituted for name

||||||||||||||||||||||||||||||||||||||||||||||||||||||||||||||||||||||||||||||||||||

FOR THOUGHT, DISCUSSION, AND WRITING

1. After reviewing this chapter's discussion of paraphrasing and summarizing, select one of the sample essays that appear in Chapter 8, "Writing in the Disciplines: Making Choices as You Write." Choose a paragraph from the essay—one that strikes you as particularly interesting or informative. After reading this paragraph carefully, first write a paraphrase of it, and then summarize the same passage. Finally, write a paragraph explaining why your paraphrase and summary of this passage are effective.

2. Identify an important journal for scholars in your major. You will probably have to ask someone (a major advisor, a professor, or a librarian) to recommend a journal that is important and useful in your field. If you do not have a major yet, ask the person who teaches your favorite class to recommend a journal of interest to scholars in that field.

   Now, browse through a copy of that journal, taking note of the articles and the topics it covers. As you browse, ask yourself the following:

   ■ How did you gain access to the journal? You might have found the journal online, if access is open. More likely, you needed to access the journal via your library. Think about access as an issue: How easy or difficult is it for people to use the content in this journal? What would the advantages and disadvantages be of changing its level of accessibility?

■ What do the articles tell you about how scholars in your field write? Do the articles have common characteristics (abstracts, section headings, citation styles)? Do the authors write in first person or third? Do they place their arguments into a context for you? What are some things they seem to assume you, as the reader, already know?

Write a paragraph reflecting on what you've learned.

3. Go to ScienceBlogs (http://scienceblogs.com) or ResearchBlogging (http://researchblogging.org). Find a post about an article written by a scholar in your major discipline or a post about an article on a topic discussed in one of your classes. Read the blog post and any responses to it. Take note of important issues or any points of controversy, and try to determine where this scholarly discussion fits within the larger field.

Now find and read the original article. (If the article is not available for free online—that is, if the link provided takes you to a fee-based site—search for the article through your library instead.) Compare the discussion on the blog about the article to the article itself. What information is available in both places? What information is available only in the post or only in the article? How might each source be useful in an academic research process?

Writing in the Disciplines: Making Choices as You Write

Part One of *The Academic Writer* began by asking this question: What does it mean to be a writer in the twenty-first century? Despite the increasing prevalence and power of visual and multimedia texts, writing does indeed still matter. In fact, those with access to computer and online technologies are writing more than ever before.

How can you negotiate the opportunities and challenges of twenty-first-century communication? As Part One emphasizes, you can draw on your understanding of rhetoric, the rhetorical situation, and the writing process. Part Two of *The Academic Writer* builds on the rhetorical approach to writing conveyed in Part One. It applies this approach to the essential intellectual skills needed in college writing. One of the challenges you face as an academic writer is learning how to apply these skills in a wide range of courses—from philosophy to chemistry to psychology. You can use your knowledge of rhetoric and of the writing process to negotiate the demands of academic writing in a broad variety of disciplines. This chapter will help you do so, and it will introduce you to the expectations and conventions of these disciplines.

thinking rhetorically

Meeting these expectations can be a significant challenge—especially when you take courses outside of your major. By thinking rhetorically about the nature and purpose of writing in the various academic disciplines, you can gain confidence, skill, and flexibility as a writer—attributes that will prove very useful when you graduate and begin a career. By learning how writing works in different fields, you can become a successful academic writer in *all* the courses you take in college.

Thinking Rhetorically about Writing in the Disciplines

The conventions of academic writing in different disciplines have histories worth noting. For example, scholars generally attribute the development of scientific writing to the rise of humanism and the scientific method during

thinking rhetorically

the Renaissance. When in 1660 a group of scientists in Great Britain founded the Royal Society (a body that still exists), they worked to standardize methods for reporting scientific results. Practitioners refined these textual conventions over time, but, as David Porush notes in *A Short Guide to Writing about Science*, "the basic outline of the scientific report has changed little in over a century."[1] There is no need for it to change because the scientific report still meets the day-to-day needs of working scientists: It encourages effective and efficient communication among scientists.

Textual conventions in the humanities, too, have a history. One particularly important impetus for those conventions was the desire to interpret religious texts, which has been a strong tradition in most of the world's major religions. Over time, interpretive practices for reading religious texts were applied to secular works as well. This tradition of textual interpretation is particularly important to such disciplines in the humanities as literature, philosophy, religious studies, and rhetoric, but it has influenced such other areas as history, music, and art.

Whereas scientists work to achieve objective and reliable results that others can replicate, those in the humanities often study questions for which there is no definitive answer. What constitutes a just war? How can we best interpret Shakespeare's *The Tempest* or best understand the concept of free will? Scholars in the humanities take it for granted that there are multiple ways to approach any topic. Though they hope that their writing will lead to a broader understanding of their subject, they don't expect that their research will result in the kind of knowledge generated by the scientific method. Indeed, in the humanities, originality is valued over replicability.

This brief discussion of the development of textual conventions in the humanities and sciences emphasizes that rather than being arbitrary forms to be filled in, the textual conventions that characterize different academic disciplines are deeply grounded in their history, nature, and goals. It is important to remember, however, that even though disciplines in these two broad areas share a number of general assumptions and practices, variations do exist. Moreover, disciplines in the social sciences, such as psychology, sociology, economics, anthropology, communication, and political science, include elements of both the sciences and the humanities, as does much writing in business.

As a college student, you can better understand your teachers' expectations as you move from, say, a chemistry class to a course in art appreciation by thinking rhetorically about the subject matter, methodology, and goals of the disciplines. The questions on p. 236 can guide this analysis.

---

[1]David Porush, *A Short Guide to Writing about Science* (New York: Harper, 1995), 8.

| | | | | | | | | | | | | | | | | | | | | | | | | | | | | | | | | | | | | | | | | | | | | | | | | | | | | | | | | | | | | | | | | | | | | | | | | | | | | | | | | |

FOR EXPLORATION

Take five minutes to write freely about your experience creating texts in various disciplines. Are you more confident writing for some disciplines than for others? Why? What questions seem most important to you as you anticipate writing in courses across the curriculum?

FOR COLLABORATION

Bring your response to the previous Exploration to class, and share it with a group of students. After each person has summarized his or her ideas, spend a few minutes noting common experiences and questions. Be prepared to report your results to the class.

| | | | | | | | | | | | | | | | | | | | | | | | | | | | | | | | | | | | | | | | | | | | | | | | | | | | | | | | | | | | | | | | | | | | | | | | | | | | | | | |

Writing in the Humanities

In a general sense, those studying the humanities are attempting to determine what something means or how it can best be understood or evaluated. For this reason, textual interpretation is central to the humanities. Depending on their discipline, scholars in the humanities may read the same or similar texts for different analytical and interpretive purposes. An art critic may analyze paintings by the American folk artist Grandma Moses (1860–1961) to study her use of brush strokes and color, while a historian might study her work to learn more about life in rural America in the mid-twentieth century.

Sample Student Essay in the Humanities*

Here is an essay written for an in-class exam in an American history course. The author, Elizabeth Ridlington, was responding to the following question: *During his presidency, did Lincoln primarily respond to public opinion, or did he shape public opinion more than he responded to it?* In analyzing her rhetorical situation, Elizabeth commented:

My teacher phrased this as an either/or question, inviting a strong and clear position statement at the outset. Because this is a history class, I knew that I needed to provide evidence from primary documents we'd read, offering the kind of specific and concrete details that historians value. I also needed

thinking
rhetorically

* bedfordstmartins.com/rewriting
   For a collection of dozens of sample student projects written for courses across the disciplines, go to Re:Writing *and then click on* **ModelDoc Central.**

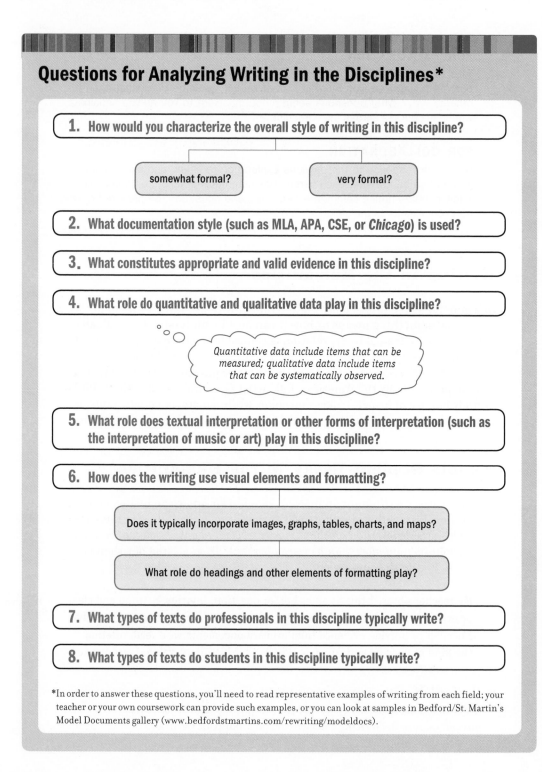

Questions for Analyzing Writing in the Disciplines*

1. **How would you characterize the overall style of writing in this discipline?**

   somewhat formal?   very formal?

2. **What documentation style (such as MLA, APA, CSE, or *Chicago*) is used?**

3. **What constitutes appropriate and valid evidence in this discipline?**

4. **What role do quantitative and qualitative data play in this discipline?**

   Quantitative data include items that can be measured; qualitative data include items that can be systematically observed.

5. **What role does textual interpretation or other forms of interpretation (such as the interpretation of music or art) play in this discipline?**

6. **How does the writing use visual elements and formatting?**

   Does it typically incorporate images, graphs, tables, charts, and maps?

   What role do headings and other elements of formatting play?

7. **What types of texts do professionals in this discipline typically write?**

8. **What types of texts do students in this discipline typically write?**

*In order to answer these questions, you'll need to read representative examples of writing from each field; your teacher or your own coursework can provide such examples, or you can look at samples in Bedford/St. Martin's Model Documents gallery (www.bedfordstmartins.com/rewriting/modeldocs).

to incorporate material from the lectures. In thinking about how to present information, I knew it was important not just to provide evidence but also to explain the logic behind my choice of details. Doing this makes for a more coherent essay in which every paragraph supports my initial thesis statement. Finally, looking at events and actions from multiple perspectives is very important for historians, so I explained Lincoln's decisions in a variety of circumstances essentially as a series of mini case studies.

Elizabeth Ridlington

Lincoln's Presidency and Public Opinion

This essay argues that Lincoln shaped public opinion more than he responded to it and examines the issues of military recruitment, Northern war goals, and emancipation as examples of Lincoln's interaction with public opinion.

Introduction frames response, lists supporting points

At the start of the war, Lincoln needed men for the military. Because of this, he could hardly ignore public opinion. But even as he responded in various ways to public opinion, he did not significantly modify his policy goals. Lincoln's first call for seventy-five thousand soldiers was filled through militias that were under state rather than federal control. As the war progressed, the federal government took more control of military recruitment. The government set quotas for each state and permitted the enlistment of African American soldiers via the Militia Act. Kentucky, a slave state, protested, and Lincoln waived the requirement that blacks be enlisted so long as Kentucky still filled its quota. In so doing, Lincoln responded to public opinion without changing his policy goal. Another example of this strategy occurred when the first federal draft produced riots in New York City. When the riots occurred, Lincoln relented temporarily and waited for the unrest to quiet down. Then he reinstated the federal draft. Again, Lincoln responded to a volatile situation and even temporarily withdrew the federal draft. But he ultimately reinstated the draft.

Multiple examples for first supporting point

Lincoln's efforts to shape public opinion in the North in favor of the war provide another example of his proactive stance. Whenever he discussed the war, Lincoln equated it with freedom and democracy. Northerners linked

Second supporting point

democracy with their personal freedom and daily well-being, and therefore Lincoln's linkage of the Union with democracy fostered Northern support for the war even when the conflict was bloody and Northern victory was anything but guaranteed. After the emancipation, Lincoln continued his effort to influence public opinion by connecting the abolition of slavery with democracy. The image of a "new birth of freedom" that Lincoln painted in his Gettysburg Address was part of this effort to overcome Northern racism and a reluctance to fight for the freedom of blacks.

The process that led to the emancipation provides perhaps the clearest example of Lincoln's determination to shape public opinion rather than simply respond to it. Lincoln's views on slavery were more progressive than those of many of his contemporaries. These views caused him personally to wish to abolish slavery. At the same time, Lincoln knew that winning the war was his highest priority. Consequently, retaining the border states early in the war was more important to Lincoln than emancipation, and for this reason he revoked Freemont's proclamation in the summer of 1861. In explaining this decision privately to Freemont, Lincoln admitted that he was concerned about public opinion in Kentucky since it would determine whether Kentucky stayed with the Union. However, in a letter that Lincoln knew might be made public, Lincoln denied that he had reacted to Kentucky's pressure and claimed that emancipation was not among his powers—a clear effort to gain public approval. Even when others such as Frederick Douglass (in a September 1861 speech) demanded emancipation, Lincoln did not change his policy. Not until July 1862 did Lincoln draft the preliminary emancipation proclamation. Rather than releasing it then, at the advice of his cabinet he waited for a time when it would have a more positive impact on public opinion.

Several primary sources cited to support third point

Lincoln realized that the timing of the Emancipation Proclamation was crucial. While he was waiting for an opportune time to release the document, Horace Greeley published his "Prayer of Twenty Million," calling on Lincoln to abolish slavery. Lincoln's response, a letter for publication, emphasized the importance of the Union and the secondary importance of the status of slavery. By taking this position, Lincoln hoped to shape public opinion. He wanted Northerners to believe that he saw the Union cause as

Final section cites primary sources, gives dates

foremost, so that the release of the proclamation would create as few racial concerns as possible. The Emancipation Proclamation was released on January 1, 1863. Once it was released, Lincoln stood by it despite strong public opposition. In 1864, when Democrats called for an armistice with the South, Lincoln stood by his decision to abolish slavery. He defended his position on military grounds, hoping voters would approve in the 1864 election.

As the examples I have just discussed indicate, Lincoln could not ignore public opinion, and at times he had to respond to it. But when Lincoln did so, this was always part of a larger effort to shape public opinion and to ensure Union victory.

Conclusion restates thesis

* bedfordstmartins.com/rewriting
For additional sample student projects written for the humanities, go to **Re:Writing** *and then click on* **ModelDoc Central**.

Writing in the Natural and Applied Sciences

Whatever their skill level, students in the humanities expect that writing will play a key role in their education. Those majoring in other areas, particularly the natural and applied sciences, sometimes assume otherwise. They're wrong. Here's what David Porush tells students to expect if they enter the sciences:

> You will write to report your research. You will write to communicate with colleagues at other institutions. You will write to request financial support for your work. You will write to colleagues, managers, and subordinates in your own institutional setting. You will write instructions and memos, and keep lab notebooks.[2]

Porush's argument is supported by other scientists. Victoria McMillan, author of *Writing Papers in the Biological Sciences*, points out that "no experiment,

---

[2]David Porush, *A Short Guide to Writing about Science* (New York: Harper, 1995), xxi–xxii.

however brilliant, can contribute to the existing fund of scientific knowledge unless it has been described to others working in the same field."[3]

Because established formats for scientific writing encourage efficient communication and facilitate replication of experiments, scientists use them whenever possible. At the same time, they pay particular attention to the effective presentation of data, often using figures, tables, images, and models. This attention to format and document design is equally important in student writing in the sciences.

Scientists write a variety of kinds of texts. Since maintaining and operating labs can be costly, scientists spend considerable time writing proposals to fund research projects. Most research proposals follow this format: title page, introduction, purpose, significance of the study, methods, timeline, budget, and references. The format for research reports and journal articles is generally as follows: title, author(s), abstract, introduction, literature review, materials and methods, results, discussion, and references.

Sample Student Essay in the Natural and Applied Sciences

Scientists value precision, clarity, and objectivity. The following essay, an undergraduate research proposal by Tara Gupta, demonstrates these traits. Note that Tara uses headings to mark the various sections of her proposal. She also uses the documentation style required by the Council of Science Editors (CSE). For details on this reference style, consult its handbook, *Scientific Style and Format: The CSE Manual for Authors, Editors, and Publishers,* 7th ed. (2006).

---

[3]Victoria McMillan, *Writing Papers in the Biological Sciences,* 4th ed. (Boston: Bedford, 2006), 1.

Field Measurements of
Photosynthesis and Transpiration
Rates in Dwarf Snapdragon
(*Chaenorrhinum minus* Lange):
An Investigation of Water Stress
Adaptations

Complete title,
specific and
informative

Tara Gupta

Proposal for a
Summer Research
Fellowship
Colgate University
March 12, 2013

Water Stress Adaptations 2

Introduction

Dwarf snapdragon (*Chaenorrhinum minus*) is a weedy pioneer plant found growing in central New York during spring and summer. The distribution of this species has been limited almost exclusively to the cinder ballast of railroad tracks,[1] a harsh environment characterized by intense sunlight and poor soil water retention. Given such environmental conditions, one would expect *C. minus* to exhibit anatomical features similar to those of xeromorphic plants (species adapted to arid habitats).

However, this is not the case. T. Gupta and R. Arnold (unpublished) have found that the leaves and stems of *C. minus* are not covered by a thick, waxy cuticle but rather with a thin cuticle that is less effective in inhibiting water loss through diffusion. The root system is not long and thick, capable of reaching deeper, moister soils; instead, it is thin and diffuse, permeating only the topmost (and driest) soil horizon. Moreover, in contrast to many xeromorphic plants, the stomata (pores regulating gas exchange) are not found in sunken crypts or cavities in the epidermis that retard water loss from transpiration.

Despite a lack of these morphological adaptations to water stress, *C. minus* continues to grow and reproduce when morning dew has been its only source of water for up to five weeks (R. Arnold, personal communication). Such growth involves fixation of carbon by photosynthesis and requires that the stomata be open to admit sufficient carbon dioxide. Given the dry, sunny environment, the time required for adequate carbon fixation must also mean a significant loss of water through transpiration as open stomata exchange carbon dioxide with water. How does *C. minus* balance the need for carbon with the need to conserve water?

Aims of the Proposed Study

The above observations have led me to an exploration of the extent to which *C. minus* is able to photosynthesize under conditions of low water availability. It is my hypothesis that *C. minus* adapts to these conditions by photosynthesizing in the early morning and late afternoon, when leaf and air temperatures are lower and transpirational water loss is reduced. I predict

---

Margin annotations:

Shortened title and page number

Headings throughout help organize proposal

Introduction states scientific issue, gives background information, cites relevant studies

Personal letter cited in parentheses, not included in references

Aims and scope of proposed study

Water Stress Adaptations 3

that its photosynthetic rate may be very low, perhaps even zero, on hot, sunny afternoons. Similar diurnal changes in photosynthetic rate in response to midday water deficits have been described in crop plants.[2,3] There is only one comparable study[4] on noncrop species in their natural habitats.

Thus, the research proposed here aims to help explain the apparent paradox of an organism that thrives in water-stressed conditions despite a lack of morphological adaptations. This summer's work will also serve as a basis for controlled experiments in a plant growth chamber on the individual effects of temperature, light intensity, soil water availability, and other environmental factors on photosynthesis and transpiration rates. These experiments are planned for the coming fall semester.

Methods

Simultaneous measurements of photosynthesis and transpiration rates will indicate the balance *C. minus* has achieved in acquiring the energy it needs while retaining the water available to it. These measurements will be taken daily at field sites in the Hamilton, NY, area, using an LI-6220 portable photosynthesis system (LICOR, Inc., Lincoln, NE). Basic methodology and use of correction factors will be similar to that described in related studies.[5-7] Data will be collected at regular intervals throughout the daylight hours and will be related to measurements of ambient air temperature, leaf temperature, relative humidity, light intensity, wind velocity, and cloud cover.

Budget

1 kg soda lime	$56.00
(for absorption of CO_2 in photosynthesis analyzer)	
1 kg anhydrous magnesium perchlorate	$280.75
(used as desiccant for photosynthesis analyzer)	
Shipping of chemicals (estimate)	$15.00
Estimated 500 miles travel to field sites in own car	$207.15
@ $0.405/mile	
CO_2 cylinder, 80 days rental	$100.00
(for calibration of photosynthesis analyzer)	
TOTAL REQUEST	$658.90

Margin annotations:

CSE documentation, citation-sequence format

States significance of study

Connects study to future research projects

Methodology described briefly

Itemized budget gives details

Water Stress Adaptations 4

References

1. Widrlechner MP. Historical and phenological observations of the spread of *Chaenorrhinum minus* across North America. Can J Bot 1983;61(1):179–87.
2. Manhas JG, Sukumaran NP. Diurnal changes in net photosynthetic rate in potato in two environments. Potato Res. 1988;31:375–8.
3. Yordanov I, Tsonev T, Velikova V, Georgieva K, Ivanov P, Tsenov N, Petrova T. Changes in CO_2 assimilation, transpiration and stomatal resistance in different wheat cultivars experiencing drought under field conditions. Bulg J Plant Physiol. 2001;27(3–4):20–33.
4. Chaves MM, Pereira JS, Maroco J, Rodrigues ML, Ricardo CP, Osório ML, Carvalho I, Faria T, Pinheiro C. How plants cope with water stress in the field: photosynthesis and growth. Ann Bot. 2002;89(Jun): 907–916.
5. Jarvis A, Davies W. The coupled response of stomatal conductance to photosynthesis and transpiration. J Exp Bot. 1998;49(Mar):399–406.
6. Kallarackal J, Milburn JA, Baker DA. Water relations of the banana. III. Effects of controlled water stress on water potential, transpiration, photosynthesis and leaf growth. Aust J Plant Physiol. 1990;17(1):79–90.
7. Idso SB, Allen SG, Kimball BA, Choudhury BJ. Problems with porometry: measuring net photosynthesis by leaf chamber techniques. Agron J. 1989;81(4):475–9.

Numbered references relate to citation order in text

Before embarking on her grant proposal, Tara spent time analyzing her rhetorical situation. Here is her analysis:

thinking rhetorically

I am writing to persuade a committee to grant me funds for working on my scientific project. Because I want the readers (scientists) to notice my ideas and not the medium, and because I want to convince them of my scientific merit and training, I will use the traditional medium and style for scientists — a written research proposal. A research proposal follows a standard format. Hence, I would say that my role as a writer, and my product, is relatively fixed. In the end, I want readers to hear the voice of a fellow scientist who is hardworking, trustworthy, and a creative observer.

To be persuasive, I need to understand the behaviors, motivations, and values of scientists. I expect the readers, as scientists, to immediately begin formulating questions and hypotheses as I present the background information — scientists instinctively do this. My job is to give them the best information to help them form the questions I would like them to be thinking about. In addition, it is important to include all logical steps in proceeding with my idea and background knowledge, especially since the scientists reading my proposal are not all in my research field and cannot fill in the information gaps. Nothing is more boring or painful for a scientist than reading something that has flawed logic which they have trouble following or understanding. I also need credibility, so I will have references for all background information.

Scientists value communication that is succinct, concrete, logical, accurate, and above all, *objective*. For example, if I want to discuss the environmental conditions these plants live in, I will not write a subjective account of how I've grown up in this area and know how hot and dry it can be in the summer. Instead, I will present an objective account of the environmental conditions using specific language (location, temperatures, moisture). In science, the hardest information to write about is ambiguous information, since it can be difficult to be succinct, concrete, logical, accurate, or objective; though in the end, this ambiguity is where the next experiment is and where the real work is to be done.

In reading Tara's analysis, you might be surprised by how extensive and complex her thinking is. After all, scientists just follow the conventions of scientific writing, don't they? Tara's analysis is a powerful demonstration of the kind of rhetorical sensitivity that scientists draw on when they write proposals, lab reports, and other scientific documents.

Writing in the Social Sciences*

The social sciences, disciplines such as sociology, psychology, anthropology, communications, political science, and economics, draw from both the sciences and the humanities. Many scholars in the social sciences address questions that interest humanities scholars, but their methods of investigating these questions differ. Consider the topic of aging. An English professor might study several novels with elderly characters to see how they are

* bedfordstmartins.com/rewriting
For additional sample student projects written for the natural and applied sciences, go to **Re:Writing** *and then click on* **ModelDoc Central**.

represented. A philosopher might consider the moral and political issues surrounding aging and longevity. A sociologist, on the other hand, might explore the ways in which the elderly are treated in a particular community and evaluate the impact such treatment has on elders' moods, and activity levels.

In general, social scientists explore questions through controlled methods, including the following:

- Surveys and questionnaires
- Experiments
- Observation
- Interviews
- Case studies
- Ethnographic field work

Careful observation is central to all these methods, for, like scientists, social scientists value the development of objective and reliable knowledge. As a result, they ground their arguments in quantitative data (data based on statistics) or qualitative data (data based on observations). An economist studying the effect of aging on earning power might gather statistics that enable him to generate a hypothesis about their relationship. A sociologist might use one or more surveys, interviews, and case studies to gain a nuanced understanding of the impact of aging on self-perception and self-esteem.

Writing is as important in the social sciences as it is in the natural and applied sciences and humanities. As Deidre McCloskey, internationally known economist and author of *Economical Writing*, points out, a person trained in economics "is likely to spend most of her working life writing papers, reports, memoranda, proposals, columns, and letters. Economics depends much more on writing (and on speaking, another neglected art) than on the statistics and mathematics usually touted as the tools of the trade."[4] In her book, McCloskey argues for the value of a rhetorical approach to writing in economics.

---

[4] Deidre McCloskey, *Economical Writing*, 2nd ed. (Long Grove: Waveland Press, 2000), 5.

Sample Student Essay in the Social Sciences

Pages 248–56 present an example of effective writing in the social sciences. Tawnya Redding wrote this essay for an upper-level psychology class in clinical research methods. A major assignment for the class was to write a review of the literature on a possible theoretical experiment. Tawnya chose to write her review on music preference and the risk for depression and suicide in adolescents. Note that this essay uses APA documentation style, required for this course.[5] For details on this reference style, see the APA Documentation Guidelines section at the back of this book.

---

[5] The formatting shown in the sample paper that follows is consistent with typical APA requirements for undergraduate writing. Formatting guidelines for papers prepared for publication differ in some respects; see pp. 400–22.

"Running head:"
followed by
shortened title in
all caps and page
number

Running head: MOOD MUSIC   1

Title, double-
spaced

Mood Music:

Music Preference and the Risk for Depression and Suicide in Adolescents

Name and
affiliation,
double-spaced

Tawnya Redding

Psychology 480

Professor Bernieri

February 25, 2013

MOOD MUSIC   2

Abstract

The last 20 years have shown a growing concern for the effects that certain genres of music (such as heavy metal and country) have on youth. While a correlational link between these problematic genres and increased risk for depression and suicide in adolescents has been established, researchers have been unable to pinpoint what is responsible for this link, and a causal relationship has not been determined. This paper will begin by discussing correlational literature concerning music preference and increased risk for depression and suicide, as well as the possible reasons for this link. Finally, studies concerning the effects of music on mood will be discussed. This examination of the literature on music and increased risk for depression and suicide points out the limitations of previous research and suggests the need for new research establishing a causal relationship for this link as well as research into the specific factors that may contribute to an increased risk for depression and suicide in adolescents.

Heading, centered

Summary of literature review

Double-spaced

MOOD MUSIC   3

Mood Music: Music Preference and

the Risk for Depression and Suicide in Adolescents

Music is a significant part of American culture. Since the explosion of rock 'n' roll in the 1950s there has been a concern for the effects that music may have on those who choose to listen and especially for the youth of society. The genres most likely to come under suspicion in recent decades have included heavy metal, country, and even blues. These genres have been suspected of having adverse effects on the mood and behavior of young listeners. But can music really alter the disposition and create self-destructive behaviors in listeners? And if so, what genres and aspects of these genres are responsible?

The following review of the literature will establish the correlation between potentially problematic genres of music, such as heavy metal and country, and depression and suicide risk. First, correlational studies concerning music preference and suicide risk will be discussed, followed by a discussion of the literature concerning the possible reasons for this link. Finally, studies concerning the effects of music on mood will be discussed. Despite the link between genres such as heavy metal and country and suicide risk, previous research has been unable to establish the causal nature of this link.

The Correlation between Music and Depression and Suicide Risk

Studies over the past two decades have set out to establish the causal nature of the link between music and mood by examining the correlation between youth music preference and risk for depression and suicide. A large number of these studies have focused on heavy metal and country music as the main genre culprits in association with youth suicidality and depression (Lacourse, Claes, & Villeneuve, 2001; Scheel & Westefeld, 1999; Stack & Gundlach, 1992). Stack and Gundlach (1992) examined the radio airtime devoted to country music in 49 metropolitan areas and found that the higher the percentages of country music airtime, the higher the incidence of suicides among whites. Stack and Gundlach (1992) hypothesized that themes in

---

Margin annotations:

Full title, centered, not bold

Opening sentences set context for study, argue for significance

Questions frame focus of report

Second paragraph outlines paper's purpose, structure, and conclusion

Heading, centered and boldface

Opening sets chronological context

APA-style parenthetical citation of three studies

Source named in the body of the text

MOOD MUSIC   4

country music (such as alcohol abuse) promote audience identification and
reinforce preexisting suicidal mood and that the themes associated with
country music were responsible for the elevated suicide rates. Similarly,
Scheel and Westefeld (1999) found a correlation between heavy metal music
listeners and an increased risk for suicide, as did Lacourse et al. (2001).

Reasons for the Link: Characteristics of Those
Who Listen to Problematic Music

Unfortunately, previous studies concerning music preference and
suicide risk have been unable to determine a causal relationship and have
focused mainly on establishing a correlation between suicide risk and music
preference. This leaves the question open as to whether an individual at risk
for depression and suicide is attracted to certain genres of music or whether
the music helps induce the mood, or both.

Some studies have suggested that music preference may simply be a
reflection of other underlying problems associated with increased risk for
suicide (Lacourse et al., 2001; Scheel & Westefeld, 1999). For example, in
research done by Scheel and Westefeld (1999), adolescents who listened
to heavy metal were found to have lower scores on Linehan, Goodstein,
Nielsen, and Chiles's Reasons for Living Inventory (1983) and several of
its subscales, a self-report measure designed to assess potential reasons for
not committing suicide. These adolescents were also found to have lower
scores on several subscales of the Reason for Living Inventory, including
responsibility to family along with survival and coping beliefs.

Other risk factors associated with suicide and suicidal behaviors
include poor family relationships, depression, alienation, anomie, and drug
and alcohol abuse (Bobakova, Madarasova Geckova, Reijneveld, & Van
Dijk, 2012; Lacourse et al., 2001). Lacourse et al. (2001) examined 275
adolescents in the Montreal region with a preference for heavy metal and
found that this preference was not significantly related to suicide risk when
other risk factors were controlled for. This was also the conclusion of Scheel
and Westefeld (1999), in which music preference for heavy metal was

Headings organize literature review; section discusses studies that fail to establish music as causal factor in suicide risk

Identifies an important psychological measurement tool

thought to be a red flag for suicide vulnerability but which suggested that the source of the problem may lie more in personal and familial characteristics.

George, Stickle, Rachid and Wopnford (2007) further explored the correlation between suicide risk and music preference by attempting to identify the personality characteristics of those with a preference for different genres of music. A community sample of 358 individuals was assessed for preference of 30 different styles of music, along with a number of personality characteristics including self-esteem, intelligence, spirituality, social skills, locus of control, openness, conscientiousness, extraversion, agreeableness, emotional stability, hostility, and depression (George et al., 2007). The 30 styles of music were then sorted into eight categories: rebellious (for example, punk and heavy metal), classical, rhythmic and intense (including hip-hop, rap, pop), easy listening, fringe (for example, techno), contemporary Christian, jazz and blues, and traditional Christian. The results revealed an almost comprehensively negative personality profile for those who preferred to listen to the rebellious and rhythmic and intense categories, while those who preferred classical music tended to have a comprehensively positive profile. Like Scheel and Westefeld (1999) and Lacourse et al. (2001), this study also supports the theory that youth are drawn to certain genres of music based on already existing factors, whether they be related to personality or situational variables.

Reasons for the Link: Characteristics of Problematic Music

Another possible explanation for the correlation between suicide risk and music preference is that the lyrics and themes of the music have a negative effect on listeners. In this scenario, music is thought to exacerbate an already depressed mood and hence contribute to an increased risk for suicide. This was the proposed reasoning behind higher suicide rates in whites in Stack and Gundlach's (1992) study linking country music to suicide risk. In this case, the themes associated with country music were thought to promote audience identification and reinforce preexisting behaviors associated with suicidality (such as alcohol consumption).

Transitional
sentence
announces
discussion of
new group of
studies

MOOD MUSIC   6

Stack (2000) also studied individuals with a musical preference for blues to determine whether the themes in blues music could increase the level of suicide acceptability. The results demonstrated that blues fans were no more accepting of suicide than nonfans, but that blues listeners were found to have lowered religiosity levels, an important factor for suicide acceptability (Stack, 2000). Despite this link between possible suicidal behavior and a preference for blues music, the actual suicide behavior of blues fans has not been explored, and thus no concrete associations can be made.

Year distinguishes this study from previously cited study conducted by same researcher

The Effect of Music on Mood

While studies examining the relationship between music genres such as heavy metal, country, and blues have been able to establish a correlation between music preference and suicide risk, it is still unclear from these studies what effect music has on the mood of the listener. Previous research has suggested that some forms of music can both improve and depress mood (Johnson, 2009; Lai, 1999; Siedliecki & Good, 2006; Smith & Noon, 1998).

Heading and transitional sentence identify problem not yet answered by research

Lai (1999) found that changes in mood were more likely to be found in an experimental group of depressed women versus a control group. The physiological variables of heart rate, respiratory rate, blood pressure, and immediate mood state were measured before and after the experimental group had listened to music of their choice for 30 minutes and the control group had listened to pink sound (similar to white noise) for 30 minutes. It was found that music listening had a greater effect on participants' physiological conditions, as decreases in heart rate, blood pressure, and respiratory rate were greater in the experiment group than the control group (Lai, 1999). This study suggests that music can have a positive effect on depressed individuals when they are allowed to choose the music they are listening to.

In a similar study, Siedliecki and Good (2006) found that music can increase a listener's sense of power and decrease depression, pain, and disability. Researchers randomly assigned 60 African American and

MOOD MUSIC 7

Caucasian participants with chronic nonmalignant pain to either a standard music group (offered a choice of instrumental music between piano, jazz, orchestra, harp, and synthesizer), a patterning music group (asked to choose between music to ease muscle tension, facilitate sleep, or decrease anxiety), or a control group. There were no statistically significant differences between the two music groups. However, the music groups had significantly less pain, depression, and disability than the control group.

On the other hand, Martin, Clark and Pearce (1993) identified a subgroup of heavy metal fans who reported feeling worse after listening to their music of choice. Although this subgroup did exist, there was also evidence that listening to heavy metal results in more positive affect for some, and it was hypothesized that those who experience negative affect after listening to their preferred genre of heavy metal may be most at risk for suicidal behaviors.

Smith and Noon (1998) also determined that music can have a negative effect on mood. Six songs were selected for the particular theme they embodied: (1) vigorous, (2) fatigued, (3) angry, (4) depressed, (5) tense, and (6) all moods. The results indicated that selections 3–6 had significant effects on the mood of participants, with selection 6 (all moods) resulting in the greatest positive change in mood while selection 5 (tense) resulted in the greatest negative change in mood. Selection 4 (depressed) was found to sap the vigor and increase anger/hostility in participants, while selection 5 (tense) significantly depressed participants and made them more anxious. Although this study did not specifically comment on the effects of different genres on mood, the results do indicate that certain themes can indeed depress mood. The participants for this study were undergraduate students who were not depressed, and thus it seems that certain types of music can have a negative effect on the mood of healthy individuals.

Is There Evidence for a Causal Relationship?

Despite the correlation between certain music genres (especially that of heavy metal) and an increased risk for depression and suicidal behaviors

---

Mentions seemingly contradictory research findings

MOOD MUSIC   8

in adolescents, it remains unclear whether these types of music can alter the mood of at-risk youth in a negative way. This view of the correlation between music and suicide risk is supported by a meta-analysis done by Baker and Bor (2008), in which the authors assert that most studies reject the notion that music is a causal factor and suggest that music preference is more indicative of emotional vulnerability. However, it is still unknown whether these genres can negatively alter mood at all, and if they can, whether it is the themes and lyrics associated with the music that are responsible. Clearly, more research is needed to further examine this correlation, as a causal link between these genres of music and suicide risk has yet to be shown. However, even if the theory put forth by Baker and Bor (2008) and other researchers is true, it is still important to investigate the effects that music can have on those who may be at risk for suicide and depression. Even if music is not the ultimate cause of suicidal behavior, it may act as a catalyst that further pushes individuals into a state of depression and increased risk for suicidal behavior.

Heading and transitional sentence emphasize inconclusive nature of studies

Emphasizes need for further research and suggests direction research might take

References begin
new page

First line of each
entry begins
at left margin;
subsequent lines
indent ½ inch

Online
document
identified with
URL

Citation follows
APA style for
print journal
article

Article from
database
identified with
the article's doi
(Digital Object
Identifier)

References
double-spaced
(single-spaced
here for length)

References

Baker, F., & Bor, W. (2008). Can music preference indicate mental health status in young people? *Australasian Psychiatry, 16*, 284–288.

Bobakova, D., Madarasova Geckova, A., Reijneveld, S. A., & Van Dijik, J. P. (2012). Subculture affiliation is associated with substance use of adolescents. *Addiction Research, 18*, 91–96.

George, D., Stickle, K., Rachid, F., & Wopnford, A. (2007). The association between types of music enjoyed and cognitive, behavioral, and personality factors of those who listen. *Psychomusicology, 19*(2), 32–56.

Johnson, F. D. (2009). The effects of music on temporary disposition. Retrieved from http://clearinghouse.missouriwestern.edu /manuscripts/260.php

Lacourse, E., Claes, M., & Villeneuve, M. (2001). Heavy metal music and adolescent suicidal risk. *Journal of Youth and Adolescence, 30*, 321–332.

Lai, Y. (1999). Effects of music listening on depressed women in Taiwan. *Issues in Mental Health Nursing, 20*, 229–246. doi: 10.1080/016128499248637

Linehan, M. M., Goodstein, J. L., Nielsen, S. L., & Chiles, J. A. (1983). Reasons for staying alive when you are thinking of killing yourself: The Reasons for Living Inventory. *Journal of Consulting and Clinical Psychology, 51*, 276–286. doi:10.1037/0022–006X.51.2.276

Martin, G., Clark, M., & Pearce, C. (1993). Adolescent suicide: Music preference as an indicator of vulnerability. *Journal of the American Academy of Child and Adolescent Psychiatry, 32*, 530–535.

Scheel, K., & Westefeld, J. (1999). Heavy metal music and adolescent suicidality: An empirical investigation. *Adolescence, 34*, 253–273.

Siedliecki, S., & Good, M. (2006). Effect of music on power, pain, depression and disability. *Journal of Advanced Nursing, 54*, 553–562. doi:10.1111/j.1365-2648.2006.03860.x

Smith, J. L., & Noon, J. (1998). Objective measurement of mood change induced by contemporary music. *Journal of Psychiatric & Mental Health Nursing, 5*, 403–408.

Snipes, J., & Maguire, E. (1995). Country music, suicide, and spuriousness. *Social Forces, 74*, 327–329.

Stack, S. (2000). Blues fans and suicide acceptability. *Death Studies, 24*, 223–231. doi:10.1080/074811800200559

Stack, S., & Gundlach, J. (1992). The effect of country music on suicide. *Social Forces, 71*, 211–218.

In reflecting on her experience writing this essay, Tawnya had this to say:

thinking
rhetorically

> My assignment was to write a literature review on a topic of my choice.
> Since the literature review is a fairly standard genre in psychology, my
> role as a writer was both fixed and flexible. It was fixed in that I had to
> follow the conventions for literature reviews; this includes conveying the
> tone of a serious scholar, in part by using the statement-oriented third
> person rather than the first person. But it was flexible in that I was able to
> determine what material to include in the review, the conclusions I drew
> from my analysis, and my suggestions for future research. My professor was
> the intended reader for this essay, but I also had a more general critical
> reader in mind as I wrote. I wanted to encourage readers to think critically
> about the studies being presented. What are the strengths and weaknesses
> of the studies? How might they be improved? What information is lacking
> in the current research? What problem has previous research not yet
> addressed, and how might future research do so? The constraints of the
> literature review were actually enabling in that I was able to build on this
> foundation to go beyond simply conveying information to raising important
> questions about my topic and the research that has investigated it.

✱ bedfordstmartins.com/rewriting
For additional sample student projects written for the social sciences, go to **Re:Writing**
and then click on **ModelDoc Central**.

Writing in Business

Historians of business writing emphasize the roles that the spread of literacy
in the Middle Ages and the invention of the printing press in the Renaissance played in this history. According to Malcolm Richardson, a contributor
to *Studies in the History of Business Writing*, even before capitalism developed
in Europe there were scribes and scriveners, who played a key role in both
government and private communication.[6] In the fourteenth century, what
some historians believe to be the first business writing school opened in
England, and in the sixteenth century, Angell Day's *The English Secretary or
Method of Writing Epistles and Letters*, one of the earliest texts on business
communication (which at that time primarily took the form of letter writing)
appeared.

---

[6]George H. Douglas and Herbert William Hildebrandt, eds., *Studies in the History of Business Writing* (Ur-
bana, IL: Association for Business Communication, 1985).

The conventions that characterize modern business writing—particularly the preference for clear, concise, goal- and audience-oriented communication and an easy-to-read visual design—developed slowly but steadily. With the growth of the middle class and the increase of commerce, businesspersons needed to be able to communicate with both internal and external audiences. Basic forms of business writing, such as memos, letters, proposals, and reports, became more standard. As layers of management evolved and departments proliferated, written internal communication became increasingly important, as did changes in the technologies of communication. The typewriter and carbon paper (and, later, dictaphones and photocopiers) transformed the office through the mid-twentieth century.

Developments in online, electronic, and digital communication are once again effecting powerful changes in business writing. Today's business writers communicate online, as well as in traditional print environments. They must be able to work effectively in teams, and they need to be able to respond to the demands of working in a global environment. The essential characteristics of effective business writing, however, remain grounded in basic issues of rhetorical sensitivity. When writing for business, it's especially important to consider the differing needs—and situations—of your readers. You may need to consider readers spread geographically or across an organization chart, and, in some cases, you may even need to consider future readers.

Sample Student Email for Business Writing

The email message memo shown on p. 259 was written by Michelle Rosowsky and Carina Abernathy, two students in a business class. Their email message presents an analysis and recommendation to help an employer make a decision. As you read, notice how the opening paragraph provides necessary background information and clearly states the email's purpose. Even if this email is forwarded to others, the subject line will make its purpose clear. Michelle and Carina are also careful to follow the traditional memo design format and to use bold type to emphasize the most important information.

This assignment took the form of a case study. The students' teacher provided them with a series of hypothetical facts about a potential business transaction. Their job was to analyze this information, determine their recommendations, and communicate them in the most effective form possible.

In reflecting on their email message, Michelle and Carina commented that the first and most important step in their writing process involved analyzing both the information that they were given and their rhetorical situation.

thinking
rhetorically

We first had to analyze the facts of the case to come up with an appropriate recommendation and then present the recommendation within the format of a typical business email. Because it's written for a busy manager, we wrote the email as concisely as possible so that the information would be available at a glance. We also put the most critical calculation, the manufacturing cost, at the beginning of the email and in bold so that the manager could find it easily and refer back to it later if necessary. We go on to make a recommendation about a bidding price and then provide a few other relevant facts since the goal of the email is to enable the manager to make her own decision. The succinctness of the email message also reflects our confidence in the analysis, which gives us a strong and positive ethos and helps establish our reliability and competence.

FW: Taylor Nursery Bid - Message (HTML)		

From: Rosowsky, Michelle **Sent:** Fri 4/12/2013 1:13 PM
To: Donahue, Rosa
Cc: Abernathy, Carina
Subject: Taylor Nursery Bid

As you know, Taylor Nursery has requested bids on a 25,000-pound order of private label fertilizer. Taylor Nursery is one of the largest distributors of our Fertikil product. The following is our analysis of Jenco's costs to fill this special order and a recommendation for the bidding price.

The total costs for manufacturing 25,000 pounds of private label brand for Taylor Nursery is $44,075. The cost includes the following:
- Direct material
- Direct labor
- Variable manufacturing overhead

Although our current equipment and facilities provide adequate capacity for processing this special order, the job will involve an excess in labor hours. The overtime labor rate has been factored into our costs.

The absolute minimum price that Jenco could bid for this product without losing money is $44,075 (our cost). Applying our standard markup of 40% results in a price of $61,705. Thus you could reasonably establish a price anywhere within that range.

In making the final assessment, we advise you to consider factors relevant to this decision. Taylor Nursery has stated that this is a one-time order. Therefore, the effort to fill this special order will not bring long-term benefits.

Finally, Taylor Nursery has requested bids from several competitors. One rival, Eclipse Fertilizers, is submitting a bid of $60,000 on this order. Therefore, our recommendation is to underbid Eclipse slightly with a price of $58,000, representing a markup of approximately 32%.

Please let us know if we can be of further assistance in your decision on the Taylor Nursery bid.

Michelle Rosowsky | Sales Associate
Carina Abernathy | Sales Associate
❖ Jenco ❖

Subject line clearly indicates topic

Paragraphs flush left

Bold type highlights most important financial information

Double-spaced between paragraphs

Options presented and background given

Final recommendation

Closing offers further assistance

✴ bedfordstmartins.com/rewriting
For additional student samples of business writing, go to **Re:Writing** *and then click on* **ModelDoc Central**.

||||||||||||||||||||||||||||||||||||||||||||||||||||||||||||||||||||||||||||||||||

FOR THOUGHT, DISCUSSION, AND WRITING

1. Although you may not have determined your major area of study yet, you probably have some idea of whether you want to major in the humanities, social sciences, sciences, or business. Meet with a group of classmates who share your general interests. Working together, first make a list of the reasons you all find this area interesting. Next, make a list of the writing challenges that students in this area face. Finally, choose two of these challenges and brainstorm productive ways that students can respond to them. Be prepared to share the results of your discussion with the entire class.

2. Write an essay in which you reflect on the reasons you are drawn to a particular discipline or general area of study. How long-standing is your interest in this discipline? What do you see as its challenges and rewards? (Before writing this essay, you might like to read Brandon Barrett's essay on his decision to major in chemistry, which appears on pp. 68–69.)

3. Choose one of the student essays presented in this chapter, and analyze it to determine what features reflect the disciplinary preferences described in this chapter. Alternatively, choose an essay you have written for a class in the sciences, social sciences, humanities, or business, and similarly analyze it. In studying either your own essay or an essay that appears in this chapter, be sure to consider its vocabulary, style, method of proof, and use of conventional formats.

||||||||||||||||||||||||||||||||||||||||||||||||||||||||||||||||||||||||||||||||||

Strategies for Reading

Why—and how—do people read? Not surprisingly, they read for as many different reasons and in as many different contexts as they write. They read to gain information—to learn how to program their DVR, to decide whether to attend a movie, or to explore ideas for writing. They read for pleasure, whether checking in on Facebook, browsing through a magazine, or enjoying a novel. They read to engage in extended conversations about issues of importance to them, such as ecology, U.S. foreign policy, or contemporary music. In all of these ways, people read to experience new ways of thinking, being, and acting.

Reading and writing are in some respects parallel processes. The process of reading a complex written work for the first time—of grappling with it to determine where the writer is going and why—is similar to the process of writing a rough draft. When you reread an essay to examine the strategies used or the arguments made, you're "revising" your original reading, much as you revise a written draft. Because writing requires the physical activity of drafting, you may be more aware of the active role you play as writer than as reader. Reading is, however, an equally active process. Like writing, it is an act of *composing,* of constructing meaning through language and images.

Applying Rhetorical Sensitivity to Your Reading

Reading, like writing, is a *situated* activity. When you read, whether you're reading traditional print or multimedia texts, you draw not only on the printed words and images but also on your own experiences to make cultural, social, and rhetorical judgments. The purposes you bring to your reading, the processes you use to scrutinize a text, your understanding of the significance of what you read—these and other aspects of your reading grow out of the relationships among writer, reader, text, and medium. ✳

An example might help to clarify this point. Imagine two people reading and drinking tea in a café. One person is reading an accounting textbook for a course she's taking; the other is browsing blogs and online magazines

(thinking rhetorically)

To review the discussion of the rhetorical situation, see Chapter 4, pp. 52–64. ✳

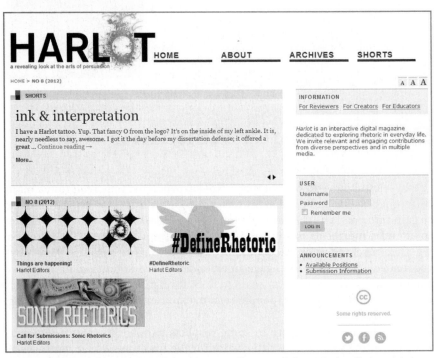

Harlot: A Revealing Look at the Arts of Persuasion, an Online Journal (http://harlotofthehearts.org)

(or *e-zines*) on his laptop. Both individuals are reading texts—but they are undoubtedly reading them in quite different ways.

The accounting student has many reasons for believing her textbook is authoritative and therefore reads it slowly and with care. If asked what she's doing, she might say she's studying rather than reading. The person browsing blogs and e-zines, on the other hand, knows that they can be put out by anyone with the time and inclination and can range from well-written and thought-provoking reflections on contemporary issues to poorly written diatribes. Before diving in, then, he skims the contents quickly to see if the topics are interesting and the writing worth reading. (He ends up spending a good deal of time on *Harlot: A Revealing Look at the Arts of Persuasion*, a well-written, interactive e-zine that explores the role of rhetoric in everyday life.)

Recognizing the Importance of Genre

The differences between how these two people read reflect their purposes as well as their social and cultural understandings of the texts. These readers are also, however, influenced by the texts' *genre*—that is, by the kinds of text

BOOK STALKER

ABOUT ME   THE PLAN   BOOKSTALKED   BIRTHDAY   ROUNDUPS   BOOK RECS

Adelle Waldman's hot-off-the-press debut novel, THE LOVE AFFAIRS OF NATHANIEL P., may help answer that age-old dating question: *WTF?* For anyone who's been confused by the current dating scene (ahem, me), Adelle illuminates the perspective of the young, modern, sensitive-yet-jerkish male through main character Nate Piven. A literary breakout in Brooklyn, Nate faces a plethora of potential relationships but fails to navigate any of them smoothly.

Adelle's book has been named a NYT Editors Choice, a B&N Discover Great New Writers Selection, and an Amazon Best Book of July. Critics have lauded her wry humor and have called the tale "a smart, engaging 21st-century comedy of manners." Adelle agreed to chat about her reading experiences thus far, which (unsurprisingly) contain the same level of observation and humor that can be found in her fiction.

Search Keywords

All about the NYC lit scene. I'm Julia Bartz, a writer and editor living in Brooklyn, NY. Email me at juliabartz@gmail.com.

Blogroll

Beatrice

Book Riot

Book Slut

The Contextual Life

Electric Literature

Five Chapters

Screenshot from the blog *Book Stalker*

or the category to which they belong, such as textbook, blog, e-zine, scholarly article or book chapter, Facebook post, or newspaper article. When we recognize that a text belongs to a certain genre, we make assumptions about the form of the writing and about its purposes and subject matter.

For example, a businessperson reading a company's annual report understands that it is a serious document and that it must follow specific conventions, including those of standard written English. When the same person goes online to read *Book Stalker*, a blog about contemporary fiction, he brings quite different expectations to his reading. *Book Stalker* uses slang and has a tone that would be inappropriate in business writing, but he not only accepts but also enjoys its use in *Book Stalker*.

As a student, and in your general reading, you will be a stronger, more effective reader if you are attentive to genre. The following are some common genres with selected examples:

Personal writing: letters, blogs, Facebook posts, personal essays

Academic writing: textbooks, scholarly articles and books, lab reports, essay exams, research papers

Popular writing: articles in mass-market magazines, reviews, fan publications

Civic writing: editorials, letters to the editor, advocacy Web sites

Professional writing: technical and scientific articles and books, job applications, business memos

Creative or literary writing: poetry, stories, novels

> • Genre has/have histories.
>
> • Some genres change over time.

nportant to remember several important s have histories: They are not static forms esponses to the specific needs of writers to note that while some genres, such as lab time, others are more fluid. Think, for in- that exist today—everything from personal er of the author's friends and family mem- on Post that circulate widely in ways similar

daily lives, we intuitively understand many ppropriately as readers: For example, we read instructions for our new HD television differently than we read a scholarly article for a class or the news feed on Facebook. As a college student, however, you need to develop a sophisticated response to an array of academic genres. A textbook written for students in an introduction to sociology course is very different from a scholarly article or book published in this same area.

Particularly as you take courses in various disciplines, you will find it helpful to ask yourself what the defining features are of the genre you are reading. The questions on p. 265 will help you.

||||||||||||||||||||||||||||||||||||||||||||||||||||||||||||||||||||||||||||||||||||||

FOR EXPLORATION

Consider the different ways you read texts. Start by making a list of the different kinds of texts you read, such as textbooks, newspaper editorials, Web sites, graphic novels, Facebook pages, and popular magazines. Then think about how your approach to these texts changes according to what they are and why you're reading them. For instance, do you read the introduction to a psychology text differently than you do your Facebook news feed or the sports page in your local newspaper? Freewrite for five minutes about the reading strategies you already use.

||||||||||||||||||||||||||||||||||||||||||||||||||||||||||||||||||||||||||||||||||||||

Questions to Ask about Genres

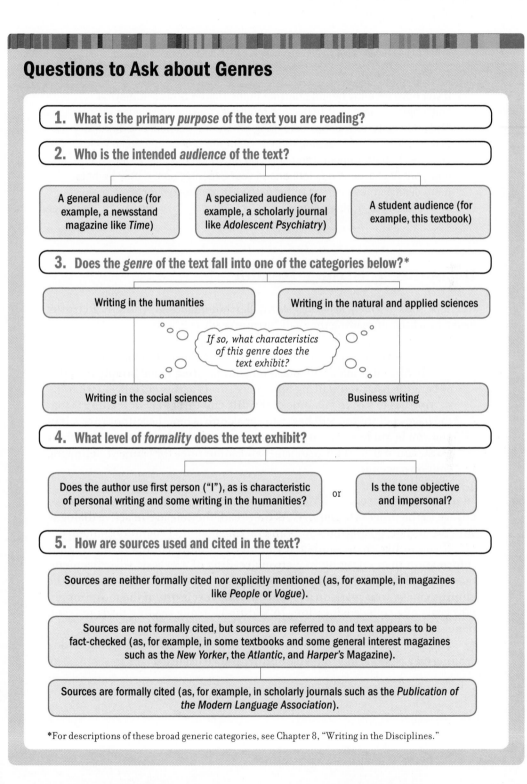

1. What is the primary *purpose* of the text you are reading?

2. Who is the intended *audience* of the text?

- A general audience (for example, a newsstand magazine like *Time*)
- A specialized audience (for example, a scholarly journal like *Adolescent Psychiatry*)
- A student audience (for example, this textbook)

3. Does the *genre* of the text fall into one of the categories below?*

- Writing in the humanities
- Writing in the natural and applied sciences

If so, what characteristics of this genre does the text exhibit?

- Writing in the social sciences
- Business writing

4. What level of *formality* does the text exhibit?

- Does the author use first person ("I"), as is characteristic of personal writing and some writing in the humanities?

or

- Is the tone objective and impersonal?

5. How are sources used and cited in the text?

- Sources are neither formally cited nor explicitly mentioned (as, for example, in magazines like *People* or *Vogue*).

- Sources are not formally cited, but sources are referred to and text appears to be fact-checked (as, for example, in some textbooks and some general interest magazines such as the *New Yorker*, the *Atlantic*, and *Harper's* Magazine).

- Sources are formally cited (as, for example, in scholarly journals such as the *Publication of the Modern Language Association*).

*For descriptions of these broad generic categories, see Chapter 8, "Writing in the Disciplines."

NOTE FOR MULTILINGUAL WRITERS

If you have recently begun studying in the United States, it may be challenging to interpret texts that require extensive knowledge about American culture. You may also bring different rhetorical and cultural expectations to your reading than many of the other students in your classes. To better understand how you approach reading, reflect on how your background has influenced your expectations. It may be helpful to discuss these expectations with your teacher, your classmates, or a tutor in the writing center.

Becoming a Strong Reader

In their book *Ways of Reading,* David Bartholomae and Anthony Petrosky describe a kind of reading they call "strong reading":

> Reading involves a fair measure of push and shove. You make your mark on a book and it makes its mark on you. Reading is not simply a matter of hanging back and waiting for a piece, or its author, to tell you what the writing has to say. In fact, one of the difficult things about reading is that the pages before you will begin to speak only when the authors are silent and you begin to speak in their place, sometimes for them—doing their work, continuing their projects—and sometimes for yourself, following your own agenda.[1]

In other words, strong readers read not simply to gain information but to engage in the process of inquiry. As they read, they engage in active dialogue with the author, posing questions and raising potential counterarguments.

If you're like many students, you may feel more confident reading for information than engaging in a strong reading of an essay, advertisement, poem, political treatise, engineering report, or Web site. Yet gaining the ability to make your mark on a verbal or visual text is one of the most important goals of a college education. In addition, strong reading leads to—and benefits—writing.

The guidelines on pp. 267–69 provide suggestions for practicing strong reading on a wide variety of print, online, and visual texts.

---

[1]David Bartholomae and Anthony Petrosky, *Ways of Reading,* 9th ed. (Boston: Bedford, 2010), 1.

Guidelines for Strong Reading

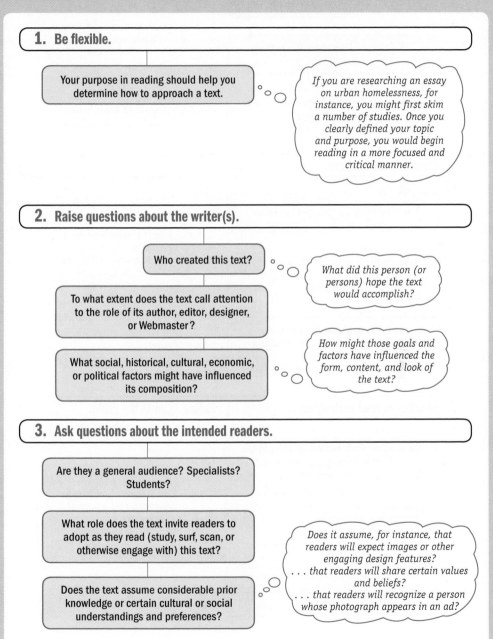

1. Be flexible.

Your purpose in reading should help you determine how to approach a text.

If you are researching an essay on urban homelessness, for instance, you might first skim a number of studies. Once you clearly defined your topic and purpose, you would begin reading in a more focused and critical manner.

2. Raise questions about the writer(s).

Who created this text?

What did this person (or persons) hope the text would accomplish?

To what extent does the text call attention to the role of its author, editor, designer, or Webmaster?

What social, historical, cultural, economic, or political factors might have influenced its composition?

How might those goals and factors have influenced the form, content, and look of the text?

3. Ask questions about the intended readers.

Are they a general audience? Specialists? Students?

What role does the text invite readers to adopt as they read (study, surf, scan, or otherwise engage with) this text?

Does the text assume considerable prior knowledge or certain cultural or social understandings and preferences?

Does it assume, for instance, that readers will expect images or other engaging design features?
. . . that readers will share certain values and beliefs?
. . . that readers will recognize a person whose photograph appears in an ad?

continued

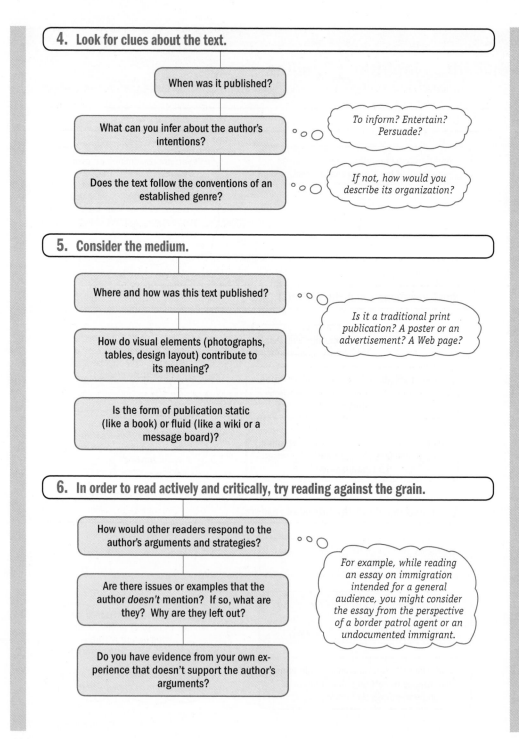

4. Look for clues about the text.

When was it published?

What can you infer about the author's intentions?

To inform? Entertain? Persuade?

Does the text follow the conventions of an established genre?

If not, how would you describe its organization?

5. Consider the medium.

Where and how was this text published?

Is it a traditional print publication? A poster or an advertisement? A Web page?

How do visual elements (photographs, tables, design layout) contribute to its meaning?

Is the form of publication static (like a book) or fluid (like a wiki or a message board)?

6. In order to read actively and critically, try reading against the grain.

How would other readers respond to the author's arguments and strategies?

For example, while reading an essay on immigration intended for a general audience, you might consider the essay from the perspective of a border patrol agent or an undocumented immigrant.

Are there issues or examples that the author *doesn't* mention? If so, what are they? Why are they left out?

Do you have evidence from your own experience that doesn't support the author's arguments?

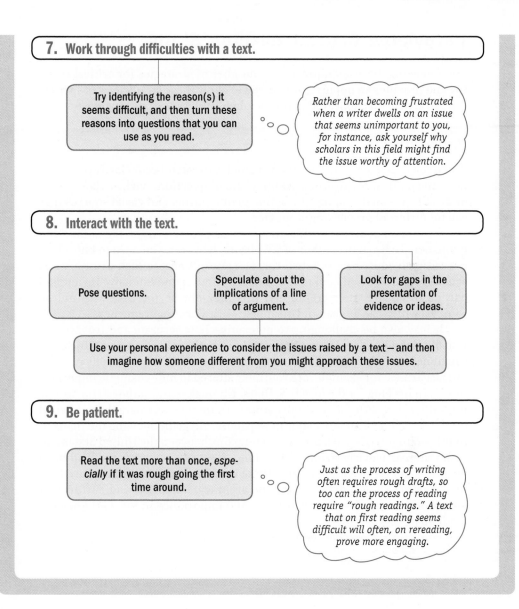

7. Work through difficulties with a text.

Try identifying the reason(s) it seems difficult, and then turn these reasons into questions that you can use as you read.

Rather than becoming frustrated when a writer dwells on an issue that seems unimportant to you, for instance, ask yourself why scholars in this field might find the issue worthy of attention.

8. Interact with the text.

Pose questions.

Speculate about the implications of a line of argument.

Look for gaps in the presentation of evidence or ideas.

Use your personal experience to consider the issues raised by a text — and then imagine how someone different from you might approach these issues.

9. Be patient.

Read the text more than once, *especially* if it was rough going the first time around.

Just as the process of writing often requires rough drafts, so too can the process of reading require "rough readings." A text that on first reading seems difficult will often, on rereading, prove more engaging.

Developing Critical Reading Skills

The following discussion presents a number of strategies for critical read-ing and provides an opportunity for you to apply these strategies to a specific text, an article that appeared in the October 2012 issue of the *Atlantic*.

Previewing

When you preview a text, you survey it quickly to establish or clarify your pur-pose and context for reading, asking yourself questions such as those listed on p. 271. As you do so, recognize that print, online, and visual sources may call for different previewing strategies.

With print sources, for instance, it's easy to determine the author and publisher. To learn the author of a Web site, however, you need to know how to read Web addresses and drill through sites. Whereas such print texts as scholarly journals and books have generally undergone extensive review and editing to ensure their credibility, this may not be the case with online sources, which can appear and disappear with alarming frequency.

It may also be challenging to determine how accurate and trustworthy visually rich texts are. Many photographs, whether they appear online or in a national magazine, have been manipulated for effect (photographs in fash-ion magazines, for example, are routinely altered to hide cosmetic imperfec-tions). In his blog for the *New York Times*, filmmaker and author Errol Morris presents a fascinating discussion of one (in)famous "fauxtograph" published on July 10, 2008, by many major newspapers, allegedly showing the firing of four Iranian missiles, at a time when tensions between the United States and Iran were particularly strong.[2] The photo, it was soon discovered, had been doctored and was fraudulent; only three missiles had actually been fired. As this example shows, determining the accuracy, authority, and currency of online and visual resources can be of vital importance in the world beyond academia.

---

[2]See Errol Morris, "Photography as a Weapon," August 11, 2008, http://opinionator.blogs.nytimes.com/2008/08/11/photography-as-a-weapon/.

Questions for Previewing a Text

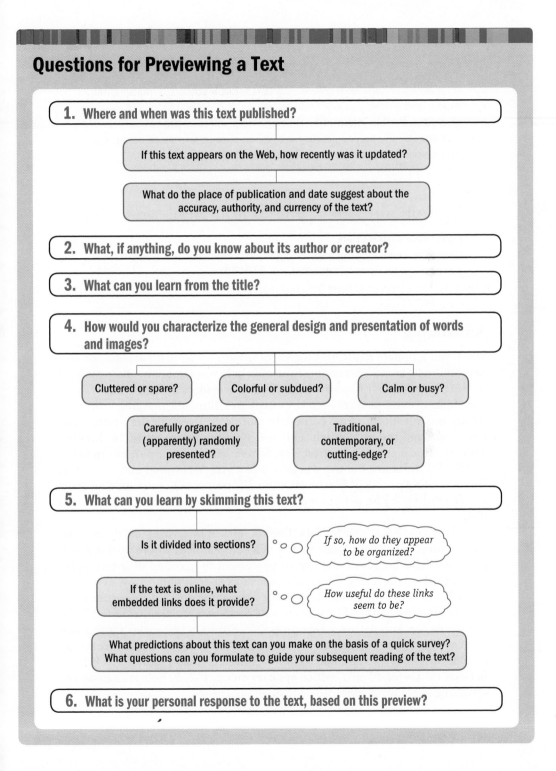

1. Where and when was this text published?

> If this text appears on the Web, how recently was it updated?

> What do the place of publication and date suggest about the accuracy, authority, and currency of the text?

2. What, if anything, do you know about its author or creator?

3. What can you learn from the title?

4. How would you characterize the general design and presentation of words and images?

> Cluttered or spare?

> Colorful or subdued?

> Calm or busy?

> Carefully organized or (apparently) randomly presented?

> Traditional, contemporary, or cutting-edge?

5. What can you learn by skimming this text?

> Is it divided into sections?

> *If so, how do they appear to be organized?*

> If the text is online, what embedded links does it provide?

> *How useful do these links seem to be?*

> What predictions about this text can you make on the basis of a quick survey? What questions can you formulate to guide your subsequent reading of the text?

6. What is your personal response to the text, based on this preview?

NOTE FOR MULTILINGUAL WRITERS

All readers benefit from previewing texts, but if you are a multilingual reader and writer, you will find previewing particularly helpful. It will give you valuable information that can help you read the text efficiently and effectively. As you preview a text, be sure to formulate questions about specialized terms or about the text's general approach.

||||||||||||||||||||||||||||||||||||||||||||||||||||||||||||||||||||||||||||||||||

FOR EXPLORATION
Using the Questions for Previewing a Text, preview "The Selfish Meme," the article by Frank Rose reprinted on pp. 273–74.

||||||||||||||||||||||||||||||||||||||||||||||||||||||||||||||||||||||||||||||||||

Annotating

When you annotate a text, you highlight important words, passages, or images and write comments or questions that help you establish a dialogue with the text or remember important points. Some readers are heavy annotators, highlighting many passages and key words and filling the margins with comments and questions. Others annotate more selectively, preferring to write few comments and to highlight only the most important parts. In thinking about your own annotating strategies, remember that your purpose in reading should influence the way you annotate a text. You would annotate a text you're reading primarily for information differently than you would an essay you're reading for an assignment or a novel you're reading for a literature class.

Many readers annotate texts directly, either by writing on them or by using a program like Annotate Pro or XPX Annotator. If you're working with print and have borrowed the text or prefer not to mark up your own copy, you can use sticky notes, a separate piece of paper, a photocopy, or a computer file to copy or highlight important passages and to write questions and comments. How can you know the most effective way to annotate a text? The Questions for Annotating a Text on p. 275 can help you make appropriate choices as you read and respond to texts. (See p. 276 for an excerpt from student Stevon Roberts's annotated copy of Amitai Etzioni's essay "Less Privacy Is Good for Us (and You)," which appears on pp. 102–5. Roberts's essay responding to Etzioni's work can be read on pp. 115–20.)

The Selfish Meme

Twitter, dopamine, and the evolutionary advantages of talking about oneself

FRANK ROSE | SEP 19 2012, 8:56 PM ET |

Nicholas Blechman

THIS SPRING, a couple of neuroscience researchers at Harvard published a study that finally explained why we like to talk about ourselves so much: sharing our thoughts, it turns out, activates the brain's reward system. As if to demonstrate the thesis, journalists and bloggers promptly seized the occasion to share their own thoughts about the study, often at a considerable cost to accuracy. "Oversharing on Facebook as Satisfying as Sex?" the Web site for the *Today* show asked.

Well, not really. The study, which combined a series of behavioral experiments and brain scans, didn't suggest that anyone, in the lab or elsewhere, had found sharing on Facebook to be an orgasmic experience. What it did suggest was that humans may get a neurochemical reward from sharing information, and a significantly bigger reward from disclosing their own thoughts and feelings than from reporting someone else's.

The Harvard researchers—Diana Tamir, a grad student in psychology, and Jason Mitchell, her adviser—performed functional MRI scans on 212 subjects while asking them about their own opinions and personality traits, and about other people's. Neuroimaging of this sort can reveal which parts of the brain are being activated; in this case, the researchers found that the mesolimbic dopamine system—the seat of the brain's reward mechanism—was more engaged by questions about the test subject's own opinions and attitudes than by questions about the opinions and attitudes of other people. The system has long been known to respond to both primary rewards (food and sex) and secondary rewards (money), but this was the first time it's been shown to light up in response to, as the researchers put it, "self-disclosure."

What the study really illustrated, then, was a paradox: when it comes to information, sharing is mostly about *me*. The researchers weren't trying to answer the thornier question of *why*—why, as they wrote, our species might have "an intrinsic drive to disclose thoughts to others." The paper nonetheless points to an intriguing possibility: that this drive might give us humans an adaptive advantage.

Researchers have previously shown that certain online activities—such as checking your e-mail or Twitter stream—stimulate the brain's reward system. Like playing a slot machine, engaging in these activities sends the animal brain into a frenzy as it anticipates a possible reward: often nothing, but sometimes a small prize, and occasionally an enormous jackpot. The response to this unpredictable pattern seems to be deeply ingrained, and for the most basic of reasons: precisely the same cycle of suspense and excitement motivates animals to keep hunting for food. E-mail inboxes and slot machines simply tap into an attention-focusing mechanism that's perfectly designed to make sure we don't lose interest in Job No. 1, which is to keep ourselves alive.

However unrelated food and Facebook may seem, this foraging impulse sheds light on why, by one count, 96 percent of the country's online population uses social-networking sites: we get high from being on the receiving end of social media. But that's only half the story. The Harvard study helps clarify why we are so eager to be on the sharing side as well. "This would certainly explain the barroom bore, wouldn't it?" said Brian Boyd, the author of the literary Darwinist treatise *On the Origin of Stories*, when I asked him about the brain's response to acts of self-disclosure. What about estimates that, while 30 to 40 percent of ordinary conversation consists of people talking about themselves, some 80 percent of social-media updates fall in the same category? "Ordinarily, in a social context, we get feedback from other people," Boyd told me. "They might roll their eyes to indicate they don't want to hear so much about us. But online, you don't have that."

At first blush, the notion that the self-disclosure impulse is somehow good for the species might seem counterintuitive. If all we did was prattle on about ourselves, we'd soon bore one another to extinction. Why would we have evolved to get a rush of pleasure from hearing ourselves talk?

A closer look at the advantages conferred by storytelling offers some clues: by telling stories effectively, we gain status, obtain social feedback, and strengthen our bonds with other people. And on the flip side, all of this nattering—or tweeting—by our fellow humans ensures that we don't have to discover everything on our own. We have no end of people competing to tell us what's what. Hence the *real* paradox of sharing: what feels good for *me* probably ends up benefiting us all.

Questions for Annotating a Text

1. **What is your purpose in reading this text?**

   What do you need to annotate to accomplish this purpose?

2. **Where does the writer identify the text's purpose and thesis (or main idea)?**

3. **What are the main points, definitions, and examples?**

   Would it be useful to number the main points or make a scratch outline in the margin?

4. **What questions does this text suggest to you?**

5. **What key words play an important role in the discussion?**

   Does the text provide enough information so that you can understand these key words and appreciate their significance, or do you need further explanation?

6. **What passages seem particularly crucial?**

   What is your response to these passages?

7. **What role, if any, do images and graphics play?**

   Are they primary or secondary in creating meaning?

   Do they reinforce, challenge, or in other ways complicate the written words?

8. **Do your personal experience, values, or knowledge of the subject cause you to question the author's assertions, evidence, or method?**

Congress passed the buck by asking the Institute of Medicine (IOM) to conduct a study of the matter. The IOM committee, dominated by politically correct people, just reported its recommendations. It suggested that all pregnant women be asked to consent to HIV testing as part of routine prenatal care. There is little wrong with such a recommendation other than it does not deal with many of the mothers who are drug addicts or otherwise live at society's margins. Many of these women do not show up for prenatal care, and they are particularly prone to HIV, according to a study published in the American Health Association's *Journal of School Health*. To save the lives of their children, they must be tested at delivery and treated even if this entails a violation of mothers' privacy.

Recently a suggestion to use driver's licenses to curb illegal immigration has sent the Coalition for Constitutional Liberties, a large group of libertarians, civil libertarians, and privacy advocates, into higher orbit than John Glenn ever traversed. The coalition wrote:

> This plan pushed us to the brink of tyranny, where citizens will not be allowed to travel, open bank accounts, obtain health care, get a job, or purchase firearms without first presenting the proper government papers.
>
> The authorizing section of the law . . . is reminiscent of the totalitarian dictates by Politburo members in the former Soviet Union, not the Congress of the United States of America.

Meanwhile, Wells Fargo is introducing a new device that allows a person to cash checks at its ATM machines because the machines recognize faces. Rapidly coming is a whole new industry of so-called biometrics that uses natural features such as voice, hand design, and eye pattern to recognize a person with the same extremely high reliability provided by the new DNA tests.

It's true that as biometrics catches on, it will practically strip Americans of anonymity, an important part of privacy. In the near future, a person who acquired a poor reputation in one part of the country will find it much more difficult to move to another part, change his name, and gain a whole fresh start. Biometrics see right through such assumed identities. One may hope that future communities will become more tolerant of such people, especially if they openly acknowledge the mistakes of their past and truly seek to lead a more prosocial life. But they will no longer be able to hide their pasts.

Above all, while biometrics clearly undermines privacy, the social benefits it promises are very substantial. Specifically, each year at least half a million criminals become fugitives, avoiding trial, incarceration, or serving their full sentences, often committing additional crimes while on the lam. People who fraudulently file for multiple income tax refunds using fake identities and multiple Social Security numbers cost

Handwritten annotations:

I wonder if these groups would put themselves into these categories

inflammatory & dismissive

maybe alarmist

what's the cost & who pays for it? Is it worth it?

not likely

This is a fantasy!

speculation — sounds like someone is trying to sell me on something... (oh right, they ARE :")

Stevon Roberts's Annotations of "Less Privacy Is Good for Us (and You)"

||||||||||||||||||||||||||||||||||||||||||||||||||||||||||||||||||||||||||||||||

FOR EXPLORATION
Annotate "The Selfish Meme" by Frank Rose (pp. 273–74) as if you expected to write an essay responding to it for your composition class.

FOR COLLABORATION
Working in small groups, compare your annotations of the article. List all the various annotating strategies that group members used. To what extent did group members rely on similar strategies? What can individual differences tell you about your own strengths and limitations as an annotator?

||||||||||||||||||||||||||||||||||||||||||||||||||||||||||||||||||||||||||||||||

Summarizing

Never underestimate the usefulness of writing clear, concise summaries of texts. Writing a summary allows you to restate the major points of a book or an essay in your own words. Summarizing is a skill worth developing, for it requires you to master the material you're reading and make it your own. Summaries can vary in length, depending on the complexity and length of the text. Ideally, however, they should be as brief as possible, certainly no longer than a paragraph or two. The guidelines on pp. 278–79 offer suggestions for writing your own summaries.

||||||||||||||||||||||||||||||||||||||||||||||||||||||||||||||||||||||||||||||||

FOR EXPLORATION
Following the guidelines on pp. 278–79, write a one-paragraph summary of "The Selfish Meme" (pp. 273–74).

||||||||||||||||||||||||||||||||||||||||||||||||||||||||||||||||||||||||||||||||

Analyzing Lines of Argument

Previewing, analyzing visuals, annotating, and summarizing can all help you determine the central points in a text. Sometimes the central argument is explicitly stated. In the last paragraph of "The Selfish Meme," Frank Rose answers the question he raises in the first paragraph, telling us that "we like to talk about ourselves so much" because "by telling stories effectively, we gain status, obtain social feedback, and strengthen our bonds with other people. . . . Hence the *real* paradox of sharing: what feels good for *me* probably ends up benefiting us all."

Not all authors are so direct. Someone writing about the role of feminism in contemporary North America may raise questions rather than provide answers or make strong assertions. Whether an author articulates a clear

Guidelines for Summarizing a Text

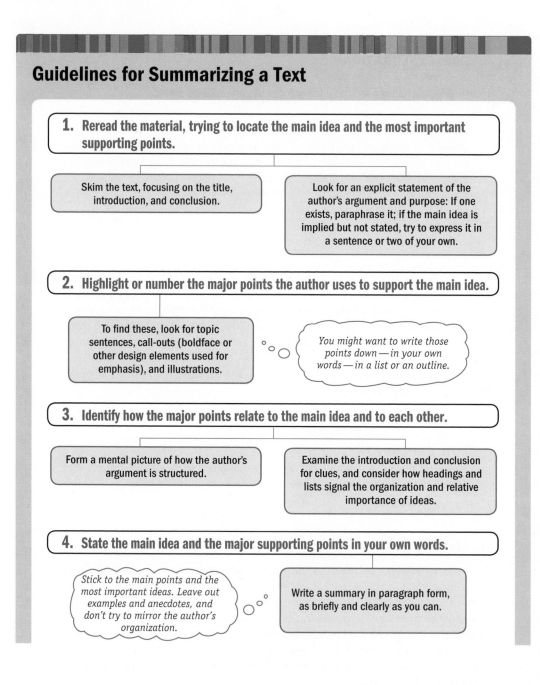

1. Reread the material, trying to locate the main idea and the most important supporting points.

Skim the text, focusing on the title, introduction, and conclusion.

Look for an explicit statement of the author's argument and purpose: If one exists, paraphrase it; if the main idea is implied but not stated, try to express it in a sentence or two of your own.

2. Highlight or number the major points the author uses to support the main idea.

To find these, look for topic sentences, call-outs (boldface or other design elements used for emphasis), and illustrations.

You might want to write those points down — in your own words — in a list or an outline.

3. Identify how the major points relate to the main idea and to each other.

Form a mental picture of how the author's argument is structured.

Examine the introduction and conclusion for clues, and consider how headings and lists signal the organization and relative importance of ideas.

4. State the main idea and the major supporting points in your own words.

Stick to the main points and the most important ideas. Leave out examples and anecdotes, and don't try to mirror the author's organization.

Write a summary in paragraph form, as briefly and clearly as you can.

5. Resist the urge to quote or paraphrase sentences or phrases from the original text.

It may help to put the original out of sight and work from memory and notes, referring back to the text for accuracy only after you have drafted the summary.

6. Be objective.

Your purpose is to distill the main idea and supporting points, not to record your reaction to the piece or to express your opinion of its merits.

position on a subject or poses a question for consideration, critical readers attempt to determine if the author's analysis is valid—that is, if the author provides good reasons in support of a position or line of analysis.

The questions on pp. 280–81 provide an introduction to analyzing the argument of a text. For a fuller discussion of this and related issues, see Part Two, "Writing in College."

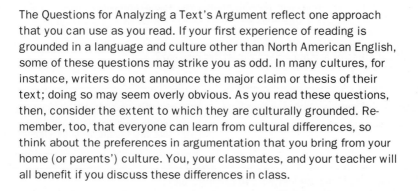

NOTE FOR MULTILINGUAL WRITERS

The Questions for Analyzing a Text's Argument reflect one approach that you can use as you read. If your first experience of reading is grounded in a language and culture other than North American English, some of these questions may strike you as odd. In many cultures, for instance, writers do not announce the major claim or thesis of their text; doing so may seem overly obvious. As you read these questions, then, consider the extent to which they are culturally grounded. Remember, too, that everyone can learn from cultural differences, so think about the preferences in argumentation that you bring from your home (or parents') culture. You, your classmates, and your teacher will all benefit if you discuss these differences in class.

Questions for Analyzing a Text's Argument

1. What is the major claim or thesis of this text?

Is it explicitly stated, or is it implicit, requiring you to read between the lines?

2. What interests or values may have caused the writer to develop this thesis?

Information about the writer from other sources, as well as clues from the writing itself, may help you determine this.

3. What values and beliefs about the subject do you bring to your reading of this text?

How might these values and beliefs affect your response to the writer's argument?

4. Does the writer define key terms?

If not, what role do these unstated definitions play in the argument?

5. What other assumptions does the writer rely on in setting up or working through the argument?

In texts on the Web, for instance, what choices and organizing principles do the links suggest?

6. What kinds of evidence does the writer present?

Is the evidence used logically and fairly?

Has the writer failed to consider any significant evidence, particularly evidence that might refute his or her claims?

7. What role, if any, do images and graphics play?

8. In what ways does the writer try to put the reader in a receptive frame of mind?

> *Does the writer attempt to persuade the reader through inappropriately manipulative emotional appeals?*

9. How does the writer establish his or her credibility?*

> *What self-image does the writer create?*

*For more on what makes a text credible, see Chapter 5, pp. 106–10, and Chapter 7, p. 199.

FOR EXPLORATION

Using the Questions for Analyzing a Text's Argument, analyze "The Selfish Meme" (pp. 273–74). Be sure to answer all the questions.

FOR COLLABORATION

By comparing your responses to this chapter's Exploration questions with those of your peers, you can gain perspective on the effectiveness of your critical reading strategies. You can also better understand how different purposes and practices influence the reading of and responses to texts.

Bring your responses to the Exploration questions in this chapter to class. Meeting with a group, compare your responses. After doing so, work together to describe briefly the extent to which your responses are similar or dissimilar. Then discuss what these similarities and differences have helped you understand about the process of critical reading, and try to come to two or three conclusions to share with your classmates.

FOR THOUGHT, DISCUSSION, AND WRITING

1. Analyze the first chapter of two textbooks you are reading this term (including this one, if you like). Do these textbooks share certain textual conventions? How do you think the writers of these textbooks have analyzed their rhetorical situation? These textbooks are written for you and other students. How effective are they in reaching you? How might they be more effective?

2. Pick a text that you have read recently (a traditional printed work, a visually rich text, or an electronic document of any length), and freewrite for five minutes about your experience reading it. How did your rhetorical sensitivity affect the way you read it? To what extent did your expectations and previous experiences as a reader influence your interaction with the text? How would you approach it differently if you were to read it again?

3. Earlier in this chapter, you read "The Selfish Meme" by Frank Rose (pp. 273–74). If you haven't already, use the questions and guidelines in this chapter to preview, annotate, summarize, and analyze Rose's argument. Then answer the following questions.

   ▪ As you skimmed this text, what were your expectations? To what extent did the form of the text and your knowledge of its original place of publication influence your expectations?

   ▪ After reading the text more carefully, what was your response? To what extent did this response represent a deepening of or shift from your earlier expectations?

   ▪ How did your own assumptions and values about social networking sites such as Facebook influence your reading?

   ▪ How would you describe the author's stance or relationship with readers? What role does the text invite you to play as reader?

   ▪ How did reading this text influence your own views about social networking sites?

4. Choose one or two of the critical reading skills discussed in this chapter that you haven't used in the past, and try them as you work on a current reading assignment. If you have time, discuss this experiment with some classmates. Then write a brief analysis of which skills work best for you and why.

||||||||||||||||||||||||||||||||||||||||||||||||||||||||||||||||||||||||||||||||||||||||

Strategies for Analyzing Visual Texts

Why is it important to be able to read visual images and to understand the role that design and visual elements can play in written texts? Perhaps the most important reason has to do with the increasingly pervasive role that images have come to play in modern life. Driving down the street, watching television, skimming a magazine, reading online: In these and other situations, we're continually presented with images and visual texts, many of which are designed to persuade us to purchase, believe, or do certain things. Often these images can be a source of pleasure and entertainment. But given the persuasive intent of many images, critical readers need to develop ways to read visual texts with the same insight they bring to written texts — at least if they want to be informed consumers and engaged citizens.

As an academic writer, you will frequently be asked to analyze traditional print texts. Increasingly, however, the ability to analyze *visual* texts — that is, texts that rely partly or completely on illustrations, photos, and visual design to convey their meanings — is gaining importance in academic writing.

If you haven't done so before, writing about visual texts can seem intimidating at first: How can you "get enough out of" a simple photograph, for example, to write about it? How do you go about understanding the relationship between text and image? The guidelines on pp. 284–85 will give you a place to start.

thinking
rhetorically

Guidelines for Analyzing Visual Texts

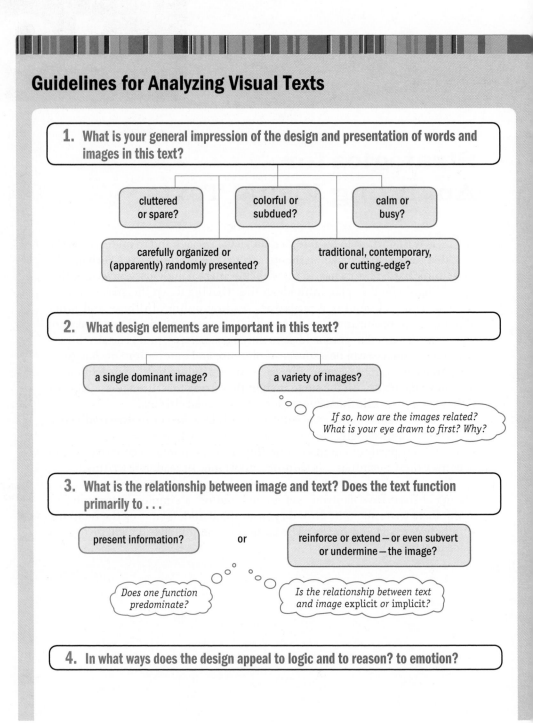

1. **What is your general impression of the design and presentation of words and images in this text?**

cluttered or spare?

colorful or subdued?

calm or busy?

carefully organized or (apparently) randomly presented?

traditional, contemporary, or cutting-edge?

2. **What design elements are important in this text?**

a single dominant image?

a variety of images?

If so, how are the images related? What is your eye drawn to first? Why?

3. **What is the relationship between image and text? Does the text function primarily to . . .**

present information?

or

reinforce or extend — or even subvert or undermine — the image?

Does one function predominate?

Is the relationship between text and image explicit or implicit?

4. **In what ways does the design appeal to logic and to reason? to emotion?**

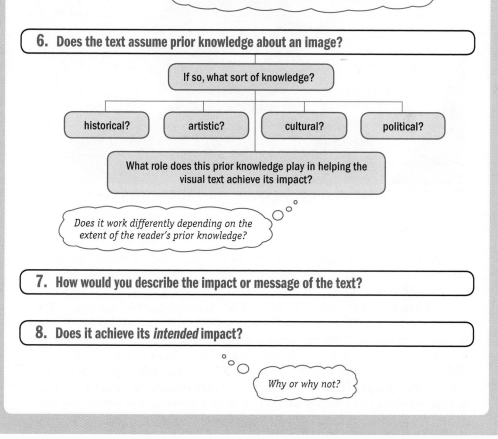

5. What role (if any) does the credibility of a company or an individual play in this text?

Does the text assume that readers would recognize a trademark or corporate name, for instance, or a photograph or drawing of a well-known figure?

6. Does the text assume prior knowledge about an image?

If so, what sort of knowledge?

historical? artistic? cultural? political?

What role does this prior knowledge play in helping the visual text achieve its impact?

Does it work differently depending on the extent of the reader's prior knowledge?

7. How would you describe the impact or message of the text?

8. Does it achieve its *intended* impact?

Why or why not?

Ernesto "Che" Guevara, Photographed by Alberto Korda on March 5, 1960

Even apparently simple visual texts can have rich cultural histories. Above, for instance, is a well-known photograph of the Marxist revolutionary Che Guevara.

An Argentinian by birth, Ernesto "Che" Guevara played a key role in the Cuban revolution. This photo of Guevara was taken by photographer Alberto Korda on March 5, 1960, in Havana, Cuba. Korda recognized the power of the photo, but it was not distributed broadly until after Guevara's October 9, 1967, execution. After Guevara's death, this photograph quickly achieved near mythic status. Today, this image—and manipulations of it—persist in global culture as a powerful symbol of countercultural and political resistance. On p. 287, for instance, is a stylized version of the original photograph available as public domain clip art via www.wpclipart.com.

In this rendering, the historical Guevara has become, literally, an icon, which appears today in countless reproductions in every imaginable context, adorning posters, T-shirts, bumper stickers, Cuban currency, and even ice cream wrappers, wine labels, and condoms.[1] Guevara's image has also become a popular tattoo, sported by Angelina Jolie and Mike Tyson, among

---

[1]For additional examples accompanied by intelligent discussion, see author Michael Casey's Web site companion to his book *Che's Afterlife* at http://www.chesafterlife.com/images/.

"Che" Clip Art

many, many others. (For an entertaining sampling, try searching Google images for "Che tattoo.")

Some uses of the image employ irreverence or outright mockery to resist the heroic image of Guevara promoted by his admirers. For example, "LiberaChe" by artist Christopher Nash morphs Guevara, usually the epitome of machismo, into a likeness of the flamboyant, rhinestone-bedecked entertainer Liberace, who was especially popular in the mid-twentieth century.

The widespread use of Guevara's image has also given rise recently to "meta-" references to its popularity—that is, to uses of the image that make tongue-in-cheek reference to how frequently the image is used. For instance, a T-shirt sold online by the *Onion* depicts Guevara wearing a T-shirt with his own image. In a similar vein, the cartoon from the *New Yorker* on the next page depends on readers recognizing not only Che Guevara's iconic image but also that of Bart Simpson (an image that vies with Guevara's image in terms of its ubiquity).

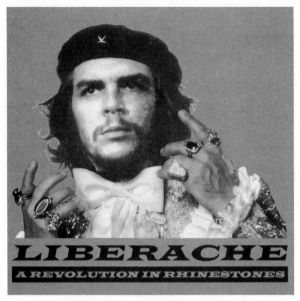

"LiberaChe," by Artist Christopher Nash

Cartoon: Che and Bart

As "meta-" references, these uses of Guevara's image call into question the ways in which the image has been and continues to be used. Rather than invoking Guevara as a symbol of countercultural and political resistance, they seem to be suggesting something about the image's commercialization — about its (mis)appropriation as a fashion statement and a means of perpetuating a consumer culture that the historical Guevara rejected.

|||||||||||||||||||||||||||||||||||||||||||||||||||||||||||||||||||||||||||||||||||

FOR EXPLORATION

Find a visual text that you believe has a rich cultural history. That history could be serious or humorous, high culture or pop culture. Take ten minutes to brainstorm everything you can think of about this visual text:

- What makes it interesting culturally?

- What are the specifics of its history?

- How has it been used in various contexts?

- What can it help writers better understand about how images and other visual elements create meaning?

Be prepared to share your visual text and brainstormed notes with others.

FOR COLLABORATION

Bring your visual text and brainstormed notes to class. Meet with a group of peers, dividing the time your instructor has allotted for this collaborative activity so that each student has roughly the same amount of time to present his or her visual text and brainstormed notes. Be sure to reserve at least five minutes for general group discussion about what you have learned as a result of this activity. Appoint a recorder/reporter who will share your group's results with the class. What has this activity helped you better understand about analyzing visual texts?

|||||||||||||||||||||||||||||||||||||||||||||||||||||||||||||||||||||||||||||||||||

Chapter 6 presents an extended case study of one student's analysis of a visual text, a public service ad (PSA) for the National Center for Family Literacy. This case study shows student Daniel Stiepleman moving from his early explorations of this PSA through planning, drafting, and revision. Daniel struggled at times with his analysis, as is clear from the two rough drafts included in the chapter. But his effort more than paid off; his final essay, presented on pages 165–68, represents a thought-provoking and engaging analysis of a visual text, one where image, text, and design work together in powerful ways.

||||||||||||||||||||||||||||||||||||||||||||||||||||||||||||||||||||||||||||||||||

FOR THOUGHT, DISCUSSION, AND WRITING

1. Take a look at the public service announcement (p. 291) on treatment for drug addiction. Using the Guidelines for Analyzing Visual Texts (pp. 284–85), write a response to each question. Finally, write one or two paragraphs about what you have learned as a result of this analysis.

2. Turn to "Literacy in America: Reading between the Lines" (pp. 165–68), by Daniel Stiepleman, in which he analyzes a public service announcement by the National Center for Family Literacy. Much of his analysis focuses on the layout and design of the PSA. After reading Stiepleman's essay, write a few paragraphs reflecting on the extent to which you agree or disagree with his analysis.

3. Find a PSA that interests you (or use one of the PSA's that appear on pp. 86–89) and write your own two- to three-page analysis of how the words and graphics work together to generate the PSA's meaning and impact.

4. You may be familiar with Pinterest.com, an online pinboard that enables users to share favorite images, recipes, crafts, and more. Pinterest's goal, as articulated in its mission statement, is "to connect everyone in the world through the 'things' they find interesting." If you are already familiar with Pinterest and regularly "pin" and "follow" on Pinterest, write an essay about why you find this experience satisfying and what your preferences reveal about your own interests and sense of style. Alternatively, write an essay about Pinterest in which you address an audience of peers who are unfamiliar with it. Be sure to explain what the site is and how readers might (or might not) benefit by participating on it.

||||||||||||||||||||||||||||||||||||||||||||||||||||||||||||||||||||||||||||||||||

Are we making strides in the fight against meth? **Absolutely.**

Law enforcement officials, professionals in drug prevention and treatment, and many others have been working hard to eliminate meth from people's lives. And it's working—meth use has declined among young adults since 2002.[1]

There is still much work to be done, however. In areas across the country where meth use and production continue, this drug leaves a path of destruction that rips apart communities and families, endangers children and overburdens police forces.

Left untreated, drug addiction costs communities millions of dollars and places untold burdens on families. But treatment for addiction, including for meth, works.[2] Not only does it work, but it's a no-nonsense way to fight the disease of addiction and break the cycle of drug abuse and crime often associated with meth.

Just ask Josh.

Josh's first encounter with meth at the age of 17 spiraled into a full-blown addiction. It cost him his job at a car dealership, his house, and the trust of his family. Soon after, Josh was arrested for meth possession. Through a drug court in Dunklin County, MO, Josh was provided the treatment, structure and accountability he needed to turn his life around. His recovery is an ongoing process that continues today; Josh now works as a junior drug counselor and lives with his wife and kids.

DRUG ADDICTION TREATMENT IS COST-EFFECTIVE
For every $1 invested in drug treatment programs there's a $12 savings in crime and health care costs.[3]

People can—and do—recover from meth addiction.
Find out about substance abuse treatment, and support meth treatment in your community.

National Association of Drug Court Professionals
National Association of Attorneys General
Major Cities Chiefs Association
Community Anti-Drug Coalitions of America (CADCA)
Partnership for a Drug-Free America

Visit methresources.gov
or call 1-800-662-HELP

Office of National Drug Control Policy

11

Strategies for Invention

Like many writers, you may feel that finding ideas to write about is the most mysterious part of the writing process. Where do ideas come from? How can you draw a blank one minute and suddenly know the right way to support your argument or describe your experience the next? Is it possible to increase your ability to think and write creatively? Writers and speakers have been concerned with questions such as these for centuries. Ancient Greek and Roman rhetoricians, in fact, were among the first to investigate the process of discovering and exploring ideas. The classical Roman rhetoricians called this process *inventio,* for "invention" or "discovery." Contemporary writers, drawing on this Latin term, often refer to this process as *invention.*

In practice, invention usually involves both individual inquiry and dialogue with others. In working on a lab report, for example, you might spend most of your time writing alone, but the experiment you're writing about might have been undertaken by a group of students working together; you might look up some related research to be sure you understand the principles you're writing about; you might also ask other students or your instructor for advice in putting the report together. Every time you talk with others about ideas, or consult print or online materials for information, you're entering into a conversation with others about your topic, and, like all writers, you can benefit from their support and insights.

The strategies discussed in this chapter aim to help you invent successfully, whether you're having a conversation with yourself as you think through and write about ideas or working with classmates or friends. These methods can help you discover what you know — and don't know — about a subject. They can also guide you as you plan, draft, and revise your writing.

Most writers find that some of the following methods work better for them than others. That's fine. Just be sure you give each method a fair chance before deciding which ones to rely on.

Discovering Ideas

Successful writers are pragmatists. Understanding that different writing tasks call for different approaches, they develop a repertoire of strategies to find ideas and explore those ideas in writing.

Read this section with a writer's eye. Which of these strategies do you already use? Which ones could you use more effectively? What other strategies might extend your range or strengthen your writing abilities? As you read about and experiment with these strategies, remember to assess their usefulness based on your own needs and preferences as a writer as well as on your particular writing situation.

NOTE FOR MULTILINGUAL WRITERS

When you practice the methods of invention, you're focusing on generating ideas — not on being perfectly correct. There's no need to interrupt the flow of your ideas by stopping to edit your grammar, spelling, vocabulary, or punctuation. Feel free, in fact, to invent in your first or home language — or even to mix languages — if it increases your fluency and helps you generate ideas.

Freewriting

Freewriting is the practice of writing as freely as possible without stopping. It's a simple but powerful strategy for exploring important issues and problems. Here is a description of freewriting by Peter Elbow, from his book *Writing with Power: Techniques for Mastering the Writing Process*:

> To do a freewriting exercise, simply force yourself to write without stopping for [a certain number] of minutes. . . . If you can't think of anything to write, write about how that feels or repeat over and over "I have nothing to write" or "Nonsense" or "No." If you get stuck in the middle of a sentence or thought, just repeat the last word or phrase till something comes along. The only point is to keep writing.[1]

Freewriting may at first seem *too* simple to achieve very powerful results, but in fact it can help you discover ideas that you couldn't reach through more conscious and logical means. Because it helps you generate a great deal of

---

[1]Peter Elbow, *Writing with Power: Techniques for Mastering the Writing Process* (New York: Oxford University Press, 1981), 13.

material, freewriting is also an excellent antidote for the anxiety many writers feel at the start of a project. It can also improve the speed and ease with which you write.

Freewriting is potentially powerful in a variety of writing situations. Writing quickly without censoring your thoughts can help you explore your personal experience, for example, by enabling you to gain access to images, events, and emotions that you've forgotten or suppressed. Freewriting can also help you experiment with more complex topics without having to assess the worthiness of individual ideas. The following shows how one student used five minutes of freewriting to explore and focus her ideas for a political science paper on low voter turnout:

> I just don't get it. As soon as I could register I did — it felt like a really important day. I'd watched my mother vote and my sisters vote and now it was my turn. But why do I vote; guess I should ask myself that question — and why don't other people? Do I feel that my vote makes a difference? There have been some close elections but not all that many, so my vote doesn't literally count, doesn't decide if we pay a new tax or elect a new senator. Part of it's the feeling I get. When I go to vote I know the people at the polling booth; they're my neighbors. I often know the people who are running for office in local elections, and for state and national elections — well, I just feel that I should. But the statistics on voter turnout tell me I'm unusual. I want to go beyond statistics. I want to understand *why* people don't vote. Seems like I need to look not only at research in political science, but also maybe in sociology. (Check journals in economics too?) I wonder if it'd be okay for me to interview some students, maybe some staff and faculty, about voting — better check. But wait a minute; this is a small college in a small town, like the town I'm from. I wonder if people in cities would feel differently — they might. Maybe what I need to look at in my paper is rural/small town versus urban voting patterns.

This student's freewriting not only helped her explore her ideas but also identified a possible question to address and sources she could draw on as she worked on her project.

Looping

Looping, an extended or directed form of freewriting, alternates freewriting with analysis and reflection. Begin looping by first establishing a subject for your freewriting and then freewriting for five or ten minutes. This is your first loop. After completing this loop, read what you have written and look for the center of gravity or "heart" of your ideas — the image, detail, issue, or problem that seems richest or most intriguing, compelling, or productive. Select or write a sentence that summarizes this understanding; this sentence will become the starting point of your second loop. The student who wrote about low voter turnout, for example, might decide to use looping to reflect on this sentence: "I want to understand *why* people don't vote."

There is no predetermined number of loops that will work: Keep looping as many times as you like, or until you feel you've exhausted a subject.

When you loop, you don't know where your freewriting and reflection will take you; you don't worry about the final product. Your final essay might not even discuss the ideas generated by your efforts. That's fine; the goal in freewriting and looping is not to produce a draft of an essay but to discover and explore ideas, images, and sometimes even words, phrases, and sentences that you can use in your writing.

|||||||||||||||||||||||||||||||||||||||||||||||||||||||||||||||||||||||||||||||||||||

FOR EXPLORATION

Choose a question, an idea, or a subject that interests you, and freewrite for five or ten minutes. Then stop and read your freewriting. What comments most interest or surprise you? Write a statement that best expresses this center of gravity, or "heart," of your freewriting. Use this comment to begin a second loop by freewriting for five minutes more.

After completing the second freewriting, stop and reread both passages. What did you learn from your freewriting? Does your freewriting suggest possible ideas for an essay? Finally, reflect on the process itself. Did you find the experience of looping helpful? Would you use freewriting and looping in the future as a means of generating ideas and exploring your experiences?

|||||||||||||||||||||||||||||||||||||||||||||||||||||||||||||||||||||||||||||||||||||

Brainstorming

Like freewriting and looping, brainstorming is a simple but productive invention strategy. When you brainstorm, you list as quickly as possible all the thoughts about a subject that occur to you without censoring or stopping to reflect on them. Brainstorming can help you discover and explore a number of ideas in a short time. Not all of them will be worth using in a piece of writing, of course. The premise of brainstorming is that the more ideas you can generate, the better your chances will be of coming up with good ones.

Alex Osborn, the person generally credited with naming this technique, originally envisioned brainstorming as a group, not an individual, activity. Osborn believed that the enthusiasm generated by the group helped spark ideas. Group brainstorming can be used for a variety of purposes. If your class has just been assigned a broad topic, for instance, your group could brainstorm a list of ways to approach or limit this topic. Or the group could use email, an online discussion board, a wiki, or a blog to generate possible arguments in support of or in opposition to a specific thesis. (See the guidelines on the next page for group brainstorming.)

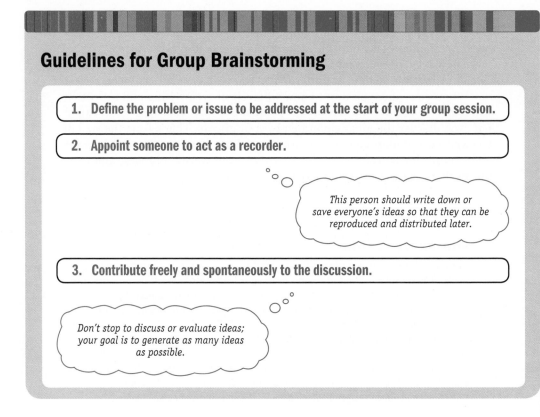

Guidelines for Group Brainstorming

1. Define the problem or issue to be addressed at the start of your group session.

2. Appoint someone to act as a recorder.

This person should write down or save everyone's ideas so that they can be reproduced and distributed later.

3. Contribute freely and spontaneously to the discussion.

Don't stop to discuss or evaluate ideas; your goal is to generate as many ideas as possible.

There are also brainstorming resources available online that you may find useful. Some software, including Thinkature and Bubbl.us, allows you to brainstorm and diagram relationships between ideas.

Those who regularly write with teams or groups cite increased intellectual stimulation and improved quality of ideas as major benefits of brainstorming together, but solitary brainstorming can be just as productive. To brainstorm alone, take a few moments at the start to formulate your goal, purpose, or problem. Then list your ideas as quickly as you can. Include everything that comes to mind, from facts to images, memories, fragments of conversations, and other general impressions and responses. (You are the only one who needs to be able to decipher what you've written, so your brainstorming can be as messy or as organized as you like.) Then review your brainstorming to identify the most promising or helpful ideas.

After freewriting about low voter turnout, for example, the student whose writing you read on p. 294 decided to brainstorm a list of possible reasons people might not vote. Here is part of her list:

Some people (young people?) mistrust politicians

Alienated from the political process

Many political issues are highly polarized — abortion, research using stem cells, war, drugs, death penalty, health care, etc.

People in the middle may feel left out of the discussion

Don't know enough about the issues — or the candidates — to decide

"My vote won't make a difference"

Her brainstorming also raised several important questions:

What role does voter registration play?

Is the problem getting people to register — or getting registered voters to vote?

What's the connection between voting and other forms of community and civic engagement?

This student will need to explore her ideas further via both analysis and research, but her brainstormed list has raised important issues and questions for her to consider.

||||||||||||||||||||||||||||||||||||||||||||||||||||||||||||||||||||||||||||||||||||||||||||

FOR EXPLORATION

Reread the freewriting you did earlier, and then choose one issue or question you'd like to explore further. Write a single sentence summarizing this issue or question, and then brainstorm for five to ten minutes. After brainstorming, return to your list. Put an asterisk (*) beside those ideas or images that didn't appear in your earlier freewriting. How do these new ideas or images add to your understanding of your subject?

||||||||||||||||||||||||||||||||||||||||||||||||||||||||||||||||||||||||||||||||||||||||||||

Clustering

Like freewriting, looping, and brainstorming, clustering emphasizes spontaneity. The goal of all four strategies is to generate as many ideas as possible, but clustering differs in that it uses visual means to generate ideas. Some writers find that it enables them to explore their ideas more deeply and creatively. (See p. 298 for a cluster done by the student whose writing appears on pp. 294 and 297.)

Start with a single word or phrase that best summarizes or evokes your topic. Write this word in the center of a page of blank paper and circle it.

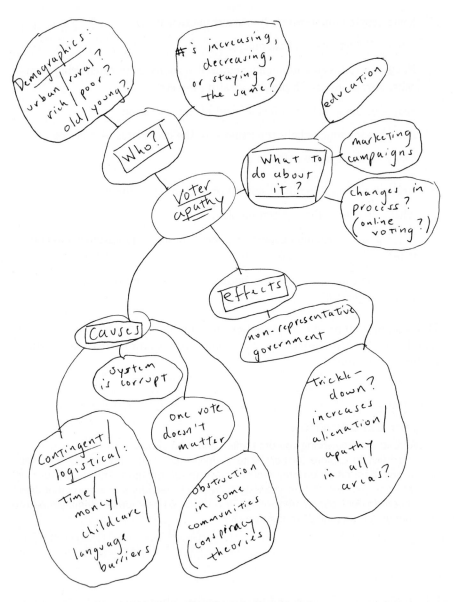

"Voter Apathy" Brainstorming Cluster

Now fill in the page by adding ideas connected with this word. Don't censor your ideas or force your cluster to assume a certain shape—your goal is to be as spontaneous as possible. Simply circle your key ideas and connect them either to the first word or to other related ideas. After clustering, put the material you've generated aside for a bit and then return to it so that you can evaluate it more objectively. When you do return to it, try to find the cluster's center of gravity—the idea or image that seems richest and most compelling. ✱

|||||||||||||||||||||||||||||||||||||||||||||||||||||||||||||||||||||||||||||||||||||||||

FOR EXPLORATION
Reread the freewriting, looping, and brainstorming you have written thus far. Then choose one word that seems especially important for your subject, and use it as the center of a cluster. Without planning or worrying about what shape it's taking, fill in your cluster by branching out from this central word. Then take a moment to reflect on what you have learned.

|||||||||||||||||||||||||||||||||||||||||||||||||||||||||||||||||||||||||||||||||||||||||

Asking the Journalist's Questions

If you have taken a journalism class or written for a newspaper, you know that journalists are taught to answer six questions in articles they write: *who, what, when, where, why,* and *how.* By answering these questions, journalists can be sure that they have provided the most important information about an event, an issue, or a problem for their readers. And because they probe several aspects of a topic, the journalist's questions can help you discover not just what you know about but also what you *don't* know—and thus alert you to the need for additional research.

You may find these questions particularly useful when describing an event or writing an informative essay. Suppose that your political science instructor has assigned an essay on the political conflict in Syria. Using the journalist's questions as headings, you could begin working on this assignment by asking yourself the following:

■ *Who* is involved in this conflict?

■ *What* issues most clearly divide those engaged in this dispute?

■ *When* did the conflict begin, and how has it developed over the last few years?

■ *Where* does the conflict seem most heated or violent?

For another example of a cluster, see pp. 155. ✱ • • • • • • • • •

■ *Why* have those living in this area found it so difficult to resolve the situation?

■ *How* might this conflict be resolved?

Although you might discover much the same information by simply brainstorming, using the journalist's questions ensures that you have covered all the major points.

|||||||||||||||||||||||||||||||||||||||||||||||||||||||||||||||||||||||||||||||||||||||

FOR EXPLORATION

Using the journalist's questions, explore the subject that you have investigated in preceding Explorations in this chapter. (If you feel that you have exhausted this subject, feel free to choose a different topic.)

    Once you have employed this method, take a few moments to reflect on this experience. To what extent did the strategy help you organize and review what you already know, and to what extent did it define what you still need to find out?

|||||||||||||||||||||||||||||||||||||||||||||||||||||||||||||||||||||||||||||||||||||||

Exploring Ideas

The previous invention strategies have a number of advantages. They're easy to use, and they can help you generate a reassuringly large volume of material when you're just beginning to work on an essay. Sometimes, however, you may want to use more systematic methods to explore a topic. This is especially true when you've identified a potential topic but aren't sure that you have enough to say about it.

Asking the Topical Questions

One of the most helpful methods for developing ideas is based on the topics of classical rhetoric. In his *Rhetoric*, Aristotle describes the topics as potential lines of argument, or places (*topos* means "place" in Greek) where speakers and writers can find evidence or arguments. Aristotle defined twenty-eight topics, but the list is generally abbreviated to five: *definition, comparison, relationship, circumstance,* and *testimony.*

    The classical topics represent natural ways of thinking about ideas. When confronted by an intellectual problem, we all instinctively ask such questions as these:

■ What is it? (*definition*)

■ What is it like or unlike? (*comparison*)

- What caused it? (*relationship*)

- What is possible or impossible? (*circumstance*)

- What have others said about it? (*testimony*)

Aristotle's topics build on these natural mental habits. The topical questions can help you pinpoint alternative approaches to a subject or probe one subject systematically, organizing what you know already and identifying gaps that require additional reading or research. Simply pose each question in turn about your subject, writing down as many responses as possible. You might also try answering the expanded list of questions for exploring a topic on pp. 302–3.

|||||||||||||||||||||||||||||||||||||||||||||||||||||||||||||||||||||||||||||||||||||||||||

FOR EXPLORATION

Use the topical questions on pp. 300–301 to continue your investigation of the subject that you explored with the journalist's questions in the Exploration on p. 300. What new information or ideas do the topical questions generate? How would you compare these methods?

|||||||||||||||||||||||||||||||||||||||||||||||||||||||||||||||||||||||||||||||||||||||||||

Researching

You're probably already aware that many writing projects are based on research. The formal research paper, however, is not the only kind of writing that can benefit from looking at how others have approached a topic. Whatever kind of writing you're doing, a quick survey of published materials can give you a sense of the issues surrounding a topic, fill gaps in your knowledge, and spark new ideas and questions.

Chapter 7 covers the formal research process in detail. At the invention stage, however, loose, informal research is generally more effective. If you're interested in writing about skydiving, for example, you could pick up a copy of *Skydiving* magazine or spend a half hour or so browsing Web sites devoted to the sport to get a better feel for current trends and issues.

To cite another example, imagine that you're writing about the Americans with Disabilities Act (ADA) for a political science assignment. After freewriting and asking yourself the journalist's questions, you find yourself wondering if the fact that President Franklin Delano Roosevelt was afflicted with polio had any influence on accessibility legislation. You type "FDR" and "disability" into a search engine, and, browsing the first few hits, you learn that while FDR is now considered an inspiration for Americans with disabilities, he spent years trying to keep his wheelchair hidden from public view. Realizing that you're very interested in this shift in attitude, you decide

Questions for Exploring a Topic

Questions about Physical Objects

What are the physical characteristics of the object (shape, dimensions, materials, and so on)?

What sort of structure does it have?

What other object is it similar to?

How does it differ from things that resemble it?

Who or what produced it?

Who uses it? For what?

Questions about Events

Exactly what happened? (who? what? when? where? why? how?)

What were its causes?

What were its consequences?

How was the event like or unlike similar events?

To what other events was it connected?

How might the event have been changed or avoided?

Note: These questions are based on those first proposed by Edward P. J. Corbett, *The Little Rhetoric and Handbook* (Glenview, IL: Scott, Foresman, 1982).

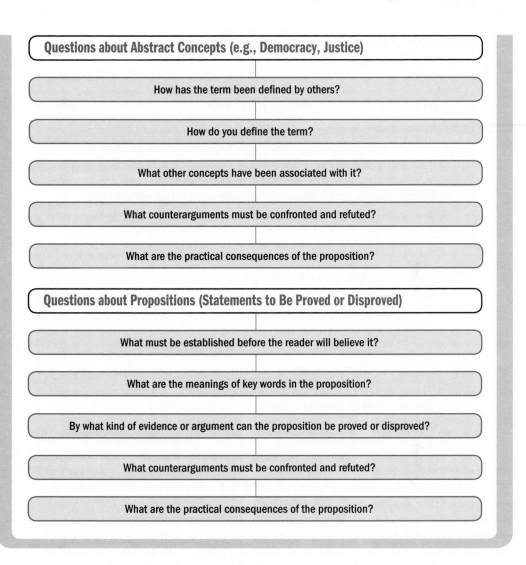

Questions about Abstract Concepts (e.g., Democracy, Justice)

How has the term been defined by others?

How do you define the term?

What other concepts have been associated with it?

What counterarguments must be confronted and refuted?

What are the practical consequences of the proposition?

Questions about Propositions (Statements to Be Proved or Disproved)

What must be established before the reader will believe it?

What are the meanings of key words in the proposition?

By what kind of evidence or argument can the proposition be proved or disproved?

What counterarguments must be confronted and refuted?

What are the practical consequences of the proposition?

to focus on the question of how the ADA has influenced public perceptions of disability. A few keystrokes have given you a valuable idea.

NOTE FOR MULTILINGUAL WRITERS

If you write in languages other than English, you may have learned ways of discovering and exploring ideas that are different from those discussed in this chapter. How are they different? If you have been educated in another culture, do the invention methods used in that culture reflect different rhetorical and cultural values? If there are significant differences, how have you dealt with them?

---

* **bedfordstmartins.com/rewriting**

For more advice and resources for beginning informal research, go to **Re:Writing** *and then click on* **The Bedford Research Room**.

Writing a Discovery Draft

Sometimes the best way to develop and explore ideas is to write a very rough draft and see, in effect, what you think about your topic. This strategy, which is sometimes called *discovery drafting*, can work well as long as you recognize that your draft will need extensive analysis and revision.

Writing a discovery draft is a lot like freewriting, although the process tends to be more focused and usually takes more time. As you write, stick to your topic as best you can, but expect that your thoughts may veer off in unexpected directions. The goal is not to produce a polished—or even a coherent—essay, but to put your ideas into written form so that you can evaluate them. Once you have completed a discovery draft, you can use it to identify and fine-tune your most promising ideas, to clarify your goals, and to determine what remains to be done. In order to do so, you will need to put your draft aside for a bit so you can look at it objectively when you return to it. *

FOR COLLABORATION

Meet with a group of classmates to discuss the methods of discovering and developing ideas. Begin by having group members briefly describe the advantages and disadvantages they experienced with these methods. (Appoint a recorder to summarize each person's statements.) Then, as a group, discuss your responses to these questions: (1) How might different students'

---

* For an example of one student's discovery draft, see pp. 155–56.

preferences for one or more of these strategies be connected to different learning, composing, and cultural preferences? (2) What influence might situational factors (such as the nature of the assignment or the amount of time available for working on an essay) have on the decision to use one or more of these strategies? Be prepared to discuss your conclusions with your classmates.

FOR THOUGHT, DISCUSSION, AND WRITING

1. Early in this chapter, you used freewriting, looping, brainstorming, clustering, and the journalist's questions to investigate a subject of interest to you. Continue your exploration of this topic by conducting some informal research and drawing on the topical questions. ✴ Then use the material you have gathered to write a discovery draft on your subject.

2. Observe a group of your classmates as they brainstorm (either in person or online), and make notes about what you see. It may be helpful to record how often each member of the group participates in the discussion, for example. Pay attention, too, to group dynamics. Is the group working effectively? Why or why not? What could group members do to interact more effectively? Summarize the results of your observations in a report addressed to the group. Be sure to suggest several ways that the group could work more effectively in the future.

3. Choose one of the strategies discussed in this chapter that you have not used in the past, and try it as you work on your current writing assignment. If you have time, discuss this experiment with some classmates. Then write a brief analysis of why this strategy did or did not work well for you.

|||||||||||||||||||||||||||||||||||||||||||||||||||||||||||||||||||||||||||||||||

See pp. 300–303. ✴

12

Strategies for Planning and Drafting

Although it can be intensely rewarding, writing is not easy for anyone. Even professional writers struggle, but they are willing to work through moments of frustration to achieve the insights that make writing worthwhile. Writing is a complex, dynamic process that challenges you to draw on all your re-sources and to be open to change as your thoughts — and your drafts — take unpredictable twists and turns.

The processes of thinking and writing are too variable and too depen-dent on context to be reduced to rules or formulas. As Chapter 3 points out, different people have different composing styles, and many factors can af-fect the processes of planning and drafting, from the time available to the complexity of the writing task. **✻** No matter what your situation, however, the keys to successful writing are preparation and flexibility. There are also specific strategies you can learn that will make the challenge of composing a draft more manageable. You'll learn about those strategies in this chapter.

Understanding the Process of Planning

It may be helpful to think of planning as involving waves of play and work. When you're discovering and exploring ideas, for example, you're in a sense playing — pushing your ideas as far as you can without worrying about how useful they'll be later. Most people can't write an essay based on a brain-storming list or thirty minutes of freewriting, however. At some point, they need to settle down to work and formulate a plan for the project.

The planning activities described in this section generally require more discipline than the play of invention does. Because much of the crafting of your essay occurs as a result of these activities, however, this work can be intensely rewarding.

✻ For more on composing styles, see pp. 39–42.

Establishing a Working Thesis

You can't establish a workable plan for your essay without having a tentative sense of the goals you hope to achieve by writing. These goals may change along the way, but they represent an important starting point for guiding your work in progress. Before you start to draft, then, try to establish a *working thesis* for your essay.

A working thesis reflects an essay's topic but also the point you wish to make and the effect you wish to have on your readers. An effective working thesis narrows your topic, helps you organize your ideas, enables you to determine what you want to say and *can* say, helps you decide if you have enough information to support your assertions, and points to the most effective way to present your ideas.

A few examples may help clarify this concept. Suppose that you're writing an editorial for your campus newspaper. "What are you going to write about?" a friend asks. "The library," you reply. You've just stated your topic, but this statement doesn't satisfy your friend. "What about the library? What's your point?" "Oh," you say, "I'm going to argue that students should petition library services to extend the number of hours it is open each week. The current hours are too limited, which is inconvenient and unfair to students who work long hours to finance their education." This second statement, which specifies both the point you want to make and its desired effect on readers, is a clearly defined working thesis. Further, because the newspaper editorial is an established genre with specific writing conventions, you know before you start that your argument will need to be brief, explicit, and backed up with concrete details.

You can best understand and establish a working thesis by analyzing the elements of your rhetorical situation: writer, reader, text, and medium. This process (which is described in detail in Chapter 4) should give you a clearer understanding of both your reasons for writing and also the most appropriate means to communicate your ideas. In some cases, you may be able to analyze your rhetorical situation and establish a working thesis early in the writing process by asking yourself the questions on p. 308. In many other instances, however, you'll have to think and write your way into understanding what you want to say.

A working thesis will help you structure your plan and guide your draft, but you should view it as preliminary and subject to revision. After you've worked on an essay for a while, your working thesis may evolve to reflect the understanding you gain through further planning and drafting. You may even discover that your working thesis isn't feasible. In either case, the time you spend thinking about your preliminary working thesis isn't wasted, for it has enabled you to begin the process of organizing and testing your ideas.

thinking rhetorically

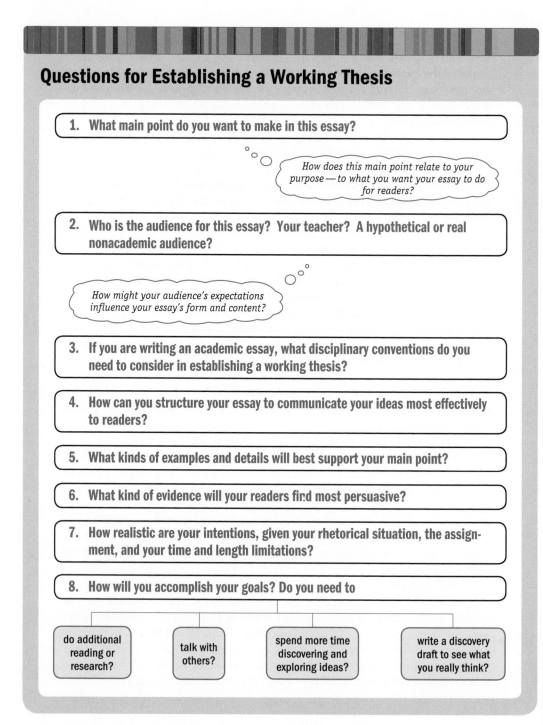

Questions for Establishing a Working Thesis

1. **What main point do you want to make in this essay?**

   How does this main point relate to your purpose — to what you want your essay to do for readers?

2. **Who is the audience for this essay? Your teacher? A hypothetical or real nonacademic audience?**

   How might your audience's expectations influence your essay's form and content?

3. **If you are writing an academic essay, what disciplinary conventions do you need to consider in establishing a working thesis?**

4. **How can you structure your essay to communicate your ideas most effectively to readers?**

5. **What kinds of examples and details will best support your main point?**

6. **What kind of evidence will your readers find most persuasive?**

7. **How realistic are your intentions, given your rhetorical situation, the assignment, and your time and length limitations?**

8. **How will you accomplish your goals? Do you need to**

   - do additional reading or research?
   - talk with others?
   - spend more time discovering and exploring ideas?
   - write a discovery draft to see what you really think?

Formulating a Workable Plan

Once you have established a working thesis, you should be able to develop a plan that can guide you as you work. As the discussion of differing composing styles in Chapter 3 indicates, people plan in different ways. Some develop detailed written plans; others rely on mental plans; others might freewrite and determine their goals by reflecting on their own written text.

As a college student, you will often find written plans helpful. Some writers develop carefully structured, detailed outlines. Others find that quick notes and diagrams are equally effective. Developing a plan—whether a jotted list of notes or a formal outline—is an efficient way to try out ideas and engage your unconscious mind in the writing process. In fact, many students find that by articulating their goals on paper or on-screen they can more effectively critique their own ideas—an important but often difficult part of the writing process.

There is no such thing as an ideal one-size-fits-all plan. An effective plan is one that works for you. Plans are utilitarian, meant to be used *and* revised. In working on an essay, you may draw up a general plan only to revise it as you write. Nevertheless, if it helps you begin drafting, your first plan will fulfill its function well.

Consider, for example, one student's actual plan, below. Lisa DeArmand, a first-year student majoring in business, was writing an informal essay reviewing three popular pizza parlors near campus. She had already decided that the most effective way to approach her essay would be to compare the three restaurants, and she had detailed notes, including interviews with

	BOBBIE'S PIZZA	PIZZA-IN-A-HURRY	PIZZA ROMA
Cost for large pie (one topping)	$15.50	$18.00	$19.50
Positives	close to campus cheapest	coupons decent number of toppings	best pizza! two kinds of crust unusual toppings spicy and mild sauces
Negatives	limited hours delivery charge pizza OK but not great	crust thin and soggy tastes like frozen pizza	most expensive

Lisa DeArmand's Plan ✳

For Daniel Stiepleman's plan for his essay on a public service announcement, see p. 158.

students, parts of which she planned to incorporate in her essay. Because Lisa had such a clear mental image of what she wanted to say and how she wanted to say it, she didn't need a highly detailed written plan—instead, she drafted a simple table.

NOTE FOR MULTILINGUAL WRITERS

You may find it helpful to consider how your knowledge of multiple languages or dialects affects the way you formulate plans. Is it easier and more productive to formulate plans in your first or home language and then translate these plans into English? Or is it more helpful to formulate plans in English because doing so encourages you to keep North American rules and expectations in mind? You may want to experiment with both approaches so that you can determine the planning process that works best for you.

||||||||||||||||||||||||||||||||||||||||||||||||||||||||||||||||||||||||||||||

FOR EXPLORATION

If you have ever created a plan for an essay or a school project, what kinds of plans have you typically drawn up? Do you formulate detailed, carefully structured plans, or do you prefer less structured ones? Do you use diagrams or other visuals? Or do you just start writing? Use these questions to think about the plans you have (or have not) used in the past; then spend ten minutes writing about how you might develop more useful plans in the future.

||||||||||||||||||||||||||||||||||||||||||||||||||||||||||||||||||||||||||||||

Developing Effective Strategies for Drafting

The British writer E. M. Forster once asked, "How can I know what I think until I see what I say?" You can see what he means if you take the writing process seriously: By working through drafts of your work, you gradually learn what you think about your subject. Although your process may begin with freewriting or brainstorming, drafting is the point in the process when you explore your ideas more fully and deeply, and it is through drafting that you create a text that embodies your preliminary goals.

Managing the Drafting Process

When you sit down to begin writing, it can be hard to imagine the satisfaction of completing a rough draft. Just picking up pen or pencil or turning on your computer can seem daunting. Once you pass the initial hurdle of getting started, you'll probably experience the drafting process as a series of ebbs and flows. You may write intensely for a short period, stop and review what you've written, make a few notes about how to proceed, and then draft again more slowly, pausing now and then to reread what you've written. It's important to keep your eye on the prize, though: Very few writers, if in fact any at all, can produce anything worth reading without going through this messy, sometimes painful, process. (If, like most writers, you experience moments of writer's block, try the block-busting strategies suggested on p. 312 to get back on track.)

While no two people approach drafting the same way—indeed, even a single person will take different approaches at different times—the strategies discussed in this section can help make your process more efficient and productive.

OVERCOMING RESISTANCE TO GETTING STARTED.   All writers experience some resistance to drafting; however, there are ways to overcome this resistance. Many writers rely on rituals to get started, such as clearing their writing space of clutter, gathering notes and other materials in a handy place, or queuing up a favorite song or playlist. Personal predispositions affect writing habits as well. Some people write best early in the morning; others, late at night. Some require a quiet atmosphere; others find the absence of noise distracting. Some find it easier to draft if they're doing something else at the same time; others shut down email and Facebook so they can focus. The trick is to figure out what works best for you.

Reading through early notes is an effective way to begin drafting. It can be reassuring to remind yourself that you're not starting from scratch, and you may find yourself turning fragmentary notes into full sentences or grouping them into paragraphs—that is, drafting—before you know it.

Perhaps the best motivation is to remind yourself that a draft doesn't have to be perfect. Your initial goal should simply be to *get something down* in writing. If you can't think of a way to open your essay, for instance, don't force yourself; just begin writing whatever you're ready to write and return to the introduction later.

BUILDING MOMENTUM.   While it might seem easier said than done, it's important to keep at it—to keep producing something, *anything*—so that the momentum can help you move steadily toward your goal. Accept that your draft will be imperfect, even incomplete, and just focus on putting your thoughts into words. By giving yourself permission to create a messy draft, you free yourself to explore ideas and discover what you want to say.

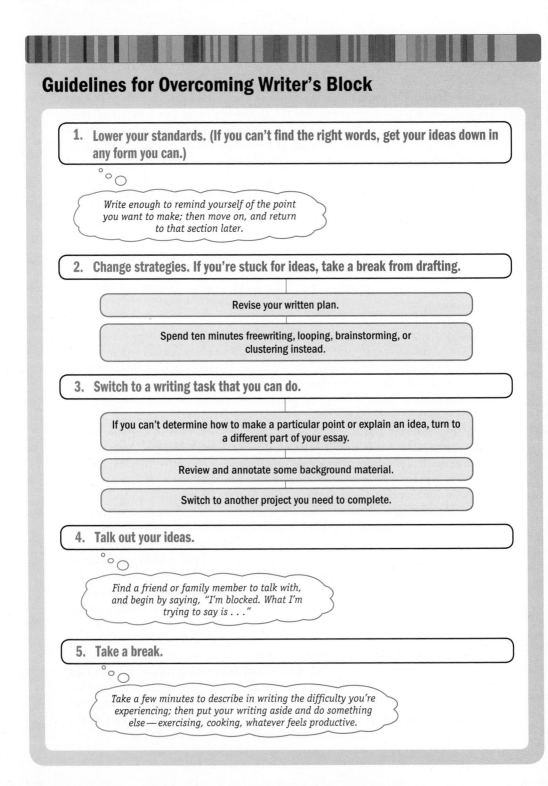

Guidelines for Overcoming Writer's Block

1. **Lower your standards. (If you can't find the right words, get your ideas down in any form you can.)**

   Write enough to remind yourself of the point you want to make; then move on, and return to that section later.

2. **Change strategies. If you're stuck for ideas, take a break from drafting.**

   Revise your written plan.

   Spend ten minutes freewriting, looping, brainstorming, or clustering instead.

3. **Switch to a writing task that you can do.**

   If you can't determine how to make a particular point or explain an idea, turn to a different part of your essay.

   Review and annotate some background material.

   Switch to another project you need to complete.

4. **Talk out your ideas.**

   Find a friend or family member to talk with, and begin by saying, "I'm blocked. What I'm trying to say is . . ."

5. **Take a break.**

   Take a few minutes to describe in writing the difficulty you're experiencing; then put your writing aside and do something else — exercising, cooking, whatever feels productive.

Don't try to correct or polish your writing in the drafting stage: Stopping to check spelling or grammar can interrupt your momentum and throw you off balance. Furthermore, it's easier to delete unnecessary or repetitive material when you revise than it is to add new material. If you can't quite articulate an argument or formulate an example, write yourself a note and keep drafting. When you return to your draft, you can fill in these gaps.

Finally, be aware that most word-processing programs offer a number of features that can make writing easier and more productive. If you're drafting quickly and wish to maintain your momentum but also remember a question or an idea, for example, you can insert comments as you write and return to them in a later drafting session. The guidelines for drafting on a computer on p. 314 offer tips on additional useful features. (Always be careful, of course, not to let your computer's capabilities distract you from the task of drafting itself.)

KEEPING IN TOUCH WITH YOUR "FELT SENSE." You attend to many things when you draft. You stop and reread; you reflect about your topic and assignment; you think about your readers. If you're an effective writer, you also look at what you've written not just to see what's on the page but also to consider what *might* be there — that is, you take stock periodically and evaluate how what you've written so far measures up to the meaning you want to get across. Professor Sondra Perl calls this sort of awareness *felt sense*. This felt sense, Perl argues, encourages us to become aware "of what is just on the edge of our thinking but not yet articulated in words."[1]

The ability to develop and maintain felt sense doesn't require magical gifts. Rather, you need to draft for long enough periods so that you can become immersed in your writing. Additionally, as you write words, sentences, and paragraphs, you need to pause periodically to reflect on the extent to which your draft responds to readers' needs and expectations; it's also a good idea to jot down notes on these reflections.

ALLOWING TIME FOR INCUBATION. Ideally, you'll come to a natural stopping point, a moment when you feel that you've solved a problem you've been wrestling with or concluded a section you've been working on. At this point, take a few moments to jot down notes about what you've accomplished as well as about what you still need to do. You may also wish to ask yourself a few questions: "What's the best transition here?" "Which examples should I use next?" If you're like many writers, your subconscious mind will present appropriate answers when you next sit down to draft.

---

[1]Sondra Perl, *Felt Sense: Writing with the Body* (Portsmouth, NH: Boynton/Cook, 2004), xii.

Guidelines for Drafting on a Computer

1. *Use the* WINDOW *or* SPLIT BAR *function* to work on multiple documents (or multiple versions of a single document) at the same time.

> *You might, for example, place a freewrite, an outline, or a plan in one window and write your draft in the other, or you might keep your introduction in view as you write later sections.*

2. *Use* TRACK CHANGES, COMMENT, *and* MARKUP *functions* to write notes or compare versions of a draft.

> *These features allow you to interact with your own and others' writing without cluttering drafts with comments that need to be deleted later.*

3. *Use the* SAVE AS *function* to experiment without losing critical material.

> *Give each new attempt at a draft a different name or number, so all earlier versions will still be there if you change your mind.*

4. *Protect your work* by using the SAVE function frequently, making backup copies of your drafts and saving them in the cloud or on a flash drive, and printing hard copies.

Sometimes it helps to *stop* thinking consciously about your ideas and just let them develop in your mind while you relax, sleep, or occupy yourself with other projects. After this period of incubation, you'll often spontaneously recognize how to resolve a problem or answer a question. (Don't confuse incubation with procrastination, however. *Procrastination* means avoiding the writing process; *incubation* means recognizing and using the fluctuations of the process to your advantage.)

|||||||||||||||||||||||||||||||||||||||||||||||||||||||||||||||||||||||||||||||||

FOR EXPLORATION

How do you typically draft an essay? How long do your drafting sessions usually last? What do you do when you run into problems? Could one or more of the suggestions presented here enable you to draft more productively? How might you best implement these suggestions? Spend five or ten minutes freewriting in response to these questions.

|||||||||||||||||||||||||||||||||||||||||||||||||||||||||||||||||||||||||||||||||

Developing and Organizing Your Ideas

As you draft, you'll become more aware of what you have to say about a subject. Consequently, you'll also become increasingly engaged with issues of organization and structure. "What do I think about this subject?" becomes less important than "How can I best present my ideas to my readers?" This section suggests strategies for responding to the second question. Keep in mind that these strategies are only suggestions; your use of them should be based on your understanding of your assignment, purpose, and rhetorical situation.

thinking rhetorically

Using a Thesis Statement

North American readers quickly become irritated if writers violate their expectations about how certain kinds of writing should be organized. In general, readers expect writing that is straightforward and to the point. For this reason, sharing your working thesis with readers and providing cues about how you will support it are essential.

How to share your working thesis most effectively depends on a number of factors. If you're working on a take-home essay exam for a history class or an analytical essay for a mass media class, for example, you may wish to include in your introduction a *thesis statement*, usually a single sentence that states the main point of your essay. ✱ Your introduction may also preview the main lines of argument you'll use to support your position.

For more on thesis statements, see Chapter 6, pp. 138–41. ✱ • • • • • • • • • • •

Much academic writing benefits from the inclusion of a thesis statement, but it is not always necessary or even desirable to include an explicit statement of your main point. If you're writing a personal essay for your first-year writing class about what the word *family* means to you, for example, you might decide that you don't want to articulate the main point of your essay in a single sentence. Instead, you might begin with an example that will create interest in your essay and show, rather than tell, what *family* means to you.

Whether or not you include a thesis statement, what's important is that you have a clear working thesis and that readers can figure it out easily. As you work on your draft, having a working thesis in mind—even if it's not expressed directly—will help you organize your thoughts; it will also help ensure that readers will stay with you. ✳

Developing Ideas

It's a good idea to begin each new drafting session by reviewing the material you've already generated, looking for ideas and details to add or develop more fully. Often in rereading these explorations and early drafts, writers realize that they've relied on words that have meaning for themselves but not necessarily for their readers. Learning to recognize and expand, or "unpack," such words in your own writing can help you develop your ideas so that their significance is clear to readers.

Here is a paragraph from one student's freewriting about what the word *family* means to her. While rereading her writing, she recognized a number of general and abstract words, which she underlined.

> When I think of the good things about my family, Christmas comes most quickly to mind. Our house was filled with such <u>warmth</u> and <u>joy</u>. Mom was busy, but she was <u>happy</u>. Dad seemed less absorbed in his work. In the weeks before Christmas he almost never worked late at the office, and he often arrived with brightly wrapped presents that he would tantalizingly show us—before whisking them off to their hiding place. And at night we did <u>fun</u> things together to prepare for the big day.

Words like *warmth* and *joy* undoubtedly have many strong connotations for the writer; most readers, however, would find these terms vague. This writer realized that in drafting she would have to provide plenty of concrete, specific details to enable readers to visualize what she means.

✳ bedfordstmartins.com/rewriting
For more help developing a thesis statement for an academic project, go to **Re:Writing** *and then click on* **The Bedford Research Room**.

Following Textual Conventions

When you draft, you don't have to come up with an organizational structure from scratch. Instead, you can draw on conventional methods of organization, methods that reflect common ways of analyzing and explaining information. Your subject may naturally lend itself to one or more methods of organization.

Suppose, for example, that you're writing an essay about political and economic changes in Eastern Europe and Asia in recent decades. Perhaps in your reading you were struck by the different responses of Russian and Chinese citizens to economic privatization. You might draw on conventional methods of *comparing and contrasting* to organize such an analysis. Or perhaps you wish to discuss the impact that severe industrial pollution in China could have on the development of a Western-style economy. After *classifying* the most prevalent forms of industrial pollution, you might discuss the consequences of this pollution for China's economy. In some cases, you may be able to use a single method of organization—such as *comparison*, *definition*, *cause and effect*, or *problem-solution*—to organize your entire essay. More often, however, you'll draw on several methods to present your ideas.

In considering how best to draw on conventional methods of organizing information, remember that you shouldn't impose them formulaically. Begin thinking about how to organize your writing by reflecting on your goals as a writer and on your rhetorical situation. If your analysis suggests that one or more methods of organizing information represent commonsensical, logical ways of approaching your subject, use them in drafting. But remember that the organization or structure you choose should complement your ideas, not be imposed on them.

thinking rhetorically

||||||||||||||||||||||||||||||||||||||||||||||||||||||||||||||||||||||||||||||||||||||||

FOR THOUGHT, DISCUSSION, AND WRITING

1. Choose a writing assignment that you have just begun. After reflecting on your ideas, develop and write a workable plan. While drafting, keep a record of your activities. How helpful was your plan? Was it realistic? Did you revise your plan as you wrote? What can you learn about your writing process from this experience? Be prepared to discuss this experience with your class.

2. Interview someone who works in the field that you hope to enter after graduation, and ask the following questions about how he or she plans and drafts on-the-job writing.

   ■ What kinds of plans do you typically construct?
   ■ In what ways have new technologies influenced your planning and drafting strategies?
   ■ Do you experience writer's block? If the answer is yes, what block-busting strategies work best for you?

- How do your profession and work schedule influence your planning and drafting?
- How often do you write alone? As a member of a group or team?
- What advice about writing would you give to a student who hopes to enter this field?

Write an essay summarizing the results of your interview.

3. Think of a time when you simply couldn't get started writing. What did you do to move beyond this block? How well did your efforts work—and why? After reflecting on your experience, write an essay (humorous or serious) about how you cope with writer's block.

| | | | | | | | | | | | | | | | | | | | | | | | | | | | | | | | | | | | | | | | | | | | | | | | | | | | | | | | | | | | | | | | | | | | | | | | | | | | | | | | | | | | | | | | | | | | | | |

Strategies for Designing Pages and Screens

Until relatively recently, few academic writers concerned themselves with the visual look of a text. Although advertising copy, magazines and newspapers, and business and technical texts have long been influenced by design concerns, just twenty years ago most college writers produced simply formatted pages of straight prose, either in longhand or at the typewriter. Students were typically required to use specific margins, headings, blue or black ink, and appropriate paper, and to follow other basic formatting rules. But these were the only visual elements that students needed to be concerned about.

Today's digital technologies allow writers to make many more decisions about texts than they did in the past. Someone who wants to share her passion for black Labrador retrievers, for instance, could create a Web site, PowerPoint-based lecture, or a video about this popular breed. Each medium would require her to be as concerned with the visual as with the verbal, for in all of these media the verbal and visual are interdependent.

Even when writing more traditional text-based papers, writers have a significant array of options, including the use of color, fonts, design templates, and software that allows them to create and incorporate drawings, photographs, charts, and graphs. With access to the Web, writers can also easily (if not always legally) download or create texts, images, and audio or video clips and integrate them into their writing. It is increasingly common for college students to develop texts that take full advantage of these options for document design.

In fact, document design is fundamental to creating readable, clearly organized, and engaging texts. Your goal for your academic projects should be an appropriate final design, one that creates a consistent overall impression and that is best suited to the kind of document you are creating.

This chapter will help you answer basic questions about designing effective texts, online and in print. (Note that your instructor may specify a particular document design or format. If you're unsure about instructors' preferences, don't hesitate to ask.)

Looking at Design and the Rhetorical Situation

Questions about document design are, in fact, *rhetorical* questions—questions, that is, that depend on your particular rhetorical situation, involving you as a writer, your audience, the ideas you want to convey, and the medium you use to deliver these ideas. ✱ For any writing project, you should analyze your situation to make informed decisions about document design and other visual elements of communication.

||||||||||||||||||||||||||||||||||||||||||||||||||||||||||||||||||||||

FOR EXPLORATION

How attuned are you to the visual elements in texts you read in print and online? Take a few moments to think about the many different texts that you read—textbooks, magazines, newspapers, advertisements, Web sites, blog posts, Facebook, email, tweets, just to name a few. Next, freewrite in response to these questions:

■ How much do design elements and images influence your response to and understanding of a text? Can you think of examples from a text you've read recently?

■ How does a magazine or Web site intended for twenty-somethings differentiate itself visually from one intended for a different readership? Try to provide examples, if possible from two texts that are similar in purpose but clearly intended for different audiences.

■ Do you have strong preferences about such visual features as type font, color, and images? If so, what are they?

||||||||||||||||||||||||||||||||||||||||||||||||||||||||||||||||||||||

NOTE FOR MULTILINGUAL WRITERS

Most cultures have their own preferences about written texts, visual texts, and visual design principles. If you are an international student or come from a North American community that uses a language other than English, you may have noticed that newspapers in your home country or home community look considerably different from English-language North American newspapers. These differences reflect cultural preferences about visual design.

Take a few moments to consider these differences. How might such design preferences influence your decisions as a writer of academic texts? Which elements of your home community's or culture's visual design preferences might enrich your academic writing, and vice versa?

✱   For more on rhetorical situation, see Chapter 4.

Imagine two students who are working on different projects: One student is writing a fifteen-page paper for an art history class on the nineteenth-century British artists called the Pre-Raphaelites; the other is writing a four-page analysis for an English class of a poem by the contemporary American poet Mary Oliver. Both have access to online content and images (such as reproductions of paintings by various Pre-Raphaelites or photographs of Mary Oliver). But should they use these images? If so, how?

A rhetorical response to these questions would consider the students' particular situations. Though they're writing different kinds of essays, both are writing *academic* essays, so any visual elements they use should reflect the seriousness and formality that characterize academic writing. Because ideas are central in academic writing, any image, chart, or other visual element should be essential to the intellectual richness and impact of the writing.

As you have perhaps already realized, both students do need to consider some visual elements. Because the paper about the Pre-Raphaelites is long, headings will help orient readers to critical divisions within the paper. Even more important, however, is the role that reproductions of art by the Pre-Raphaelites could play in this student's analysis. Such reproductions would enable readers to understand and evaluate the student's analysis of various paintings without having to refer to other sources. The student might also include photographs of the Pre-Raphaelites themselves if he's sure that the photos will enrich his analysis—for example, if he's discussing the historical, cultural, or social role of this movement in nineteenth-century England.

The student writing an analysis of one of Oliver's poems would need to attend to visual elements such as the use of white space, fonts, page numbers, and headings, which are important for any academic essay. But unless some aspect of the analysis specifically requires visual support, this student probably wouldn't include photographs or other visuals. They would add little to the development of her ideas and might even distract readers.

As these examples suggest, a rhetorical approach to document design encourages you to ask questions about your reader, your text, your medium, and yourself. (See the guidelines on pp. 322–23.) ✻

Understanding the Basic Principles of Design

Once you know the basic principles of document design, you can create accessible, inviting texts that share information, lead readers smoothly through your presentation, and achieve your purpose. Whether you're creating a print text or a digital or online text, certain fundamental design principles are essential: These include *alignment*, *proximity*, *repetition*, and *contrast*.

✻ bedfordstmartins.com/rewriting
For a tutorial on designing effective Web texts, go to **Re:Writing** *and then click on* **Tutorial Nation**.

thinking
rhetorically

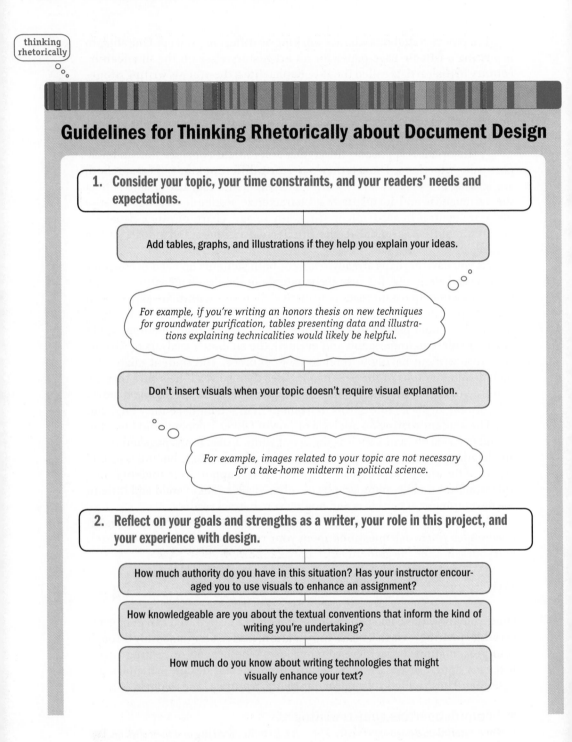

Guidelines for Thinking Rhetorically about Document Design

1. **Consider your topic, your time constraints, and your readers' needs and expectations.**

   Add tables, graphs, and illustrations if they help you explain your ideas.

   For example, if you're writing an honors thesis on new techniques for groundwater purification, tables presenting data and illustrations explaining technicalities would likely be helpful.

   Don't insert visuals when your topic doesn't require visual explanation.

   For example, images related to your topic are not necessary for a take-home midterm in political science.

2. **Reflect on your goals and strengths as a writer, your role in this project, and your experience with design.**

   How much authority do you have in this situation? Has your instructor encouraged you to use visuals to enhance an assignment?

   How knowledgeable are you about the textual conventions that inform the kind of writing you're undertaking?

   How much do you know about writing technologies that might visually enhance your text?

3. Gather information about textual conventions.

Memos, for example, are formatted in certain ways, and they often include headings.

In many of the sciences, tables and figures are common; other conventions include headings in lab reports and grant proposals.

In traditionally text-based disciplines such as English and philosophy, tables are rarely used, and figures — photographs, graphs, and other images — are used infrequently.

If you're unsure about the conventions ask your instructor.

4. Consider the requirements and limitations of your medium.

If the assignment doesn't specify a medium, consider whether the one you've chosen will appeal to readers and effectively convey your intended meaning.

If the medium is assigned — research essay, Web site, PowerPoint slideshow, or poster, for example — attend to any requirements about size or format.

If the medium is online, consider the following:

- Will your text require updates?
- Will you need to request permission to publish online any sources or visuals you've used?
- Do you have access to — and skills for working with — the appropriate software?
- Do you need access to a high-speed Internet connection, color printer, scanner, or other hardware to complete your project successfully?

Alignment

This principle relates to the way words or visuals on a page or screen are lined up vertically and horizontally. Horizontally, the options are to present text as flush left, flush right, justified, or centered. (The text you're reading right now is horizontally justified—that is, the spacing between words and letters is adjusted so that each full line of text begins and ends precisely at the margins set for the page.) Vertically, text can be aligned with the top or bottom of the page, centered, or justified. (This text is vertically top-aligned, though in page layout, considerable effort is expended on filling out every page as fully as possible.) Your goal in designing your text should be to maintain a clear, consistent alignment so that readers can follow it without becoming distracted. You should be aware that lack of alignment is a very common Web design problem, so be sure that you don't mix alignments within a design.

Proximity

A page or screen makes effective use of the design principle of proximity when the relationships between text elements (such as headings, subheadings, captions, and items in a list) and visual elements (such as illustrations, charts, and tables) are clear. Your goal should be to position related points, chunks of text, and visual elements together so that your reader's understanding of your meaning is unimpeded.

An easy way to evaluate your text's use of proximity is to squint your eyes and see how the page or screen looks. Does your eye move logically from one part to another? If not, you'll want to work on the internal relationships.

Repetition

This principle is important for creating a sense of coherence: A consistent design gives a unified look and helps guide readers through the text.

Repetition can involve elements that are visual, verbal, or both. For example, you'll want to be consistent in the design of typefaces you choose, the placement and use of color, and the positioning of graphic elements, such as a navigational banner on a homepage. One example of repetition in a text-based document is the practice of indenting paragraphs: The seemingly subtle half-inch actually signals the start of a new topic or subtopic and helps your reader keep track of your argument.

Contrast

A page or screen effectively employs contrast when the design attracts the reader's eye and draws him or her in. Contrast helps organize and orient the reader's interactions with a text, guiding the reader around the elements on a page and making the information accessible. Even the simplest, text-based documents employ contrast in the interplay between white space and text. Margins, double-spacing, and unused space around headings or graphics, for instance, frame the text and guide the reader through it. (Take a look at the white space on this page, and try to imagine how the page would look without it and how difficult it would be to read word after word presented uninterrupted and extending to the borders of the page on all sides.)

Focal points play an important role in establishing contrast. A focal point—a point that the eye travels to first and that the mind uses to organize the other elements in the composition—may be an image, a logo, or a dominant set of words. When you design a page or a screen, you should organize the elements so that the flow of information starts with this point. White space can also create effective contrast.

Formatting and Layout

There are so many formatting and layout elements to consider when designing a document that it's sometimes hard to choose the best elements for a particular layout. There is no one right answer for all situations; what works well in one situation isn't necessarily appropriate in another. The following advice will help you make appropriate decisions, but remember that your assignment or the genre you're working in may have specific requirements.

Color

Color can add visual appeal and impact, so it can play an important role in document design. In brochures, Web pages, newsletters, and similar documents, using color is not only acceptable but also expected. In academic papers, however, most instructors still require that texts be printed only in black ink. If you do plan to use color, see the Guidelines for Using Color Effectively on pp. 326–27.

Fonts and Typefaces

With computers and digital media, writers have a dazzling—but potentially bewildering—array of fonts to choose from, and they can display them in any size. How can you make the best use of them? For academic assignments, a standard, easy-to-read font such as Times New Roman in an 11- or 12-point type size is best:

This is 11-point Times New Roman.

This is 12-point Times New Roman.

But what if you're composing a brochure, newsletter, or Web site? In keeping with the conventions of those genres, you may want to use a variety of typefaces.

First, you should consider whether to use a *serif* or *sans serif* typeface for particular elements. Serif fonts add small, decorative embellishments to the basic form of the characters.

Guidelines for Using Color Effectively

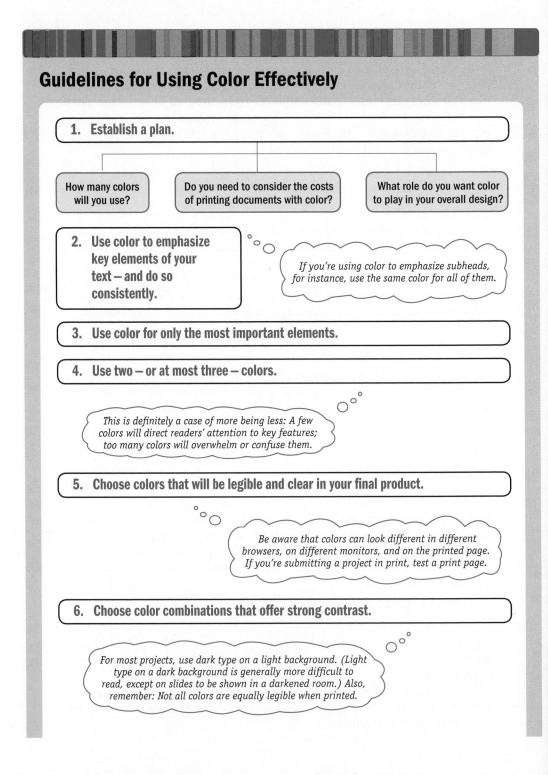

1. Establish a plan.

How many colors will you use?

Do you need to consider the costs of printing documents with color?

What role do you want color to play in your overall design?

2. Use color to emphasize key elements of your text — and do so consistently.

If you're using color to emphasize subheads, for instance, use the same color for all of them.

3. Use color for only the most important elements.

4. Use two — or at most three — colors.

This is definitely a case of more being less: A few colors will direct readers' attention to key features; too many colors will overwhelm or confuse them.

5. Choose colors that will be legible and clear in your final product.

Be aware that colors can look different in different browsers, on different monitors, and on the printed page. If you're submitting a project in print, test a print page.

6. Choose color combinations that offer strong contrast.

For most projects, use dark type on a light background. (Light type on a dark background is generally more difficult to read, except on slides to be shown in a darkened room.) Also, remember: Not all colors are equally legible when printed.

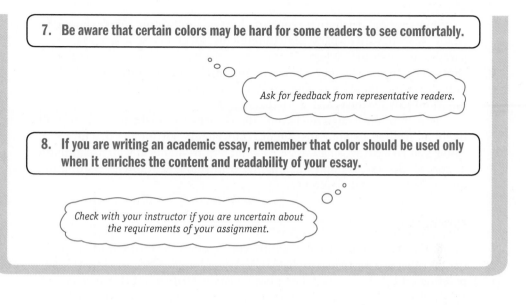

7. **Be aware that certain colors may be hard for some readers to see comfortably.**

Ask for feedback from representative readers.

8. **If you are writing an academic essay, remember that color should be used only when it enriches the content and readability of your essay.**

Check with your instructor if you are uncertain about the requirements of your assignment.

E (serif)   **E** (sans serif)

Many readers find serif typefaces (such as Times New Roman or Filosofia, which is used for the main text of this book) easier to read for printed texts and sans serif ones (such as Arial, Helvetica, or Verdana) easier to read online and for headings. In some situations, you may want to consider using an unusual font such as **Impact** or Century Gothic to create a particular tone. Remember, though, that script, handwriting, or decorative typefaces call attention to themselves and should be used sparingly.

Even in types of writing that call for the use of multiple fonts, you'll probably want to limit yourself to two or at most three fonts in a single document. If you shift fonts and sizes too often within a document, you'll distract readers from focusing on your text.

Spacing

Margins and the spacing of elements on a page are important for determining whether your text looks dense or readable. White space—in the margins, between paragraphs and sentences, and around visual or textual elements such as figures and lists—helps draw the reader's eye to the appropriate text or visual elements. For most academic writing, your text should be double-spaced, with one-inch margins and paragraphs indented one-half inch.

Some genres, including résumés, letters, and online texts, should be single-spaced, with no paragraph indents (use an extra line of space between paragraphs instead). When writing in still other genres, including brochures and flyers, you may want to choose different margins, use columns, or include additional white space around visual elements to draw attention to them and balance the visuals with the text. ✱

As with other design decisions, the choices you make for spacing will likely be limited by your instructor, your supervisor, or the discipline in which you're writing, so always check the requirements of your assignment or course. See the examples in Chapter 8 for models of the formatting required by different disciplines.

Pagination

Academic assignments usually require you to follow the formatting and pagination rules of a particular style (MLA, APA, *Chicago*, CSE, and others), depending on the discipline. (For sample papers that show MLA formatting, see pp. 165–68 and 221–31. For a sample APA-style paper, see pp. 248–56.) Cover pages or first pages need clear identifying information—usually including the title of your paper, your name, the date, your instructor's name, and the course title. Since subsequent pages can become disconnected, they should also have identifying information—usually either a shortened version of the title or your last name, along with a page number.

For online texts, the information that would appear on a printed page's header should appear in a navigation bar that unifies the electronic pages and makes it easy for users to locate parts of the text. Additional information that you can attach to each part of an online text includes your name, the date of publication, and links to the text's homepage.

If you haven't received specific information about how to handle the page number and other pagination information for your document, or if you aren't sure, check with your instructor.

Choosing Effective Headings

Headings provide structure to a text and help readers find the information they need. For some academic writing, there are required headings (*Works Cited* or *Abstract*, for example) and guidelines for their typeface and positioning. When you have flexibility in choosing headings, you should consider *wording*, *type size* and *style*, and *positioning*.

✱ bedfordstmartins.com/rewriting
   For more help creating effective layouts using your word processor, go to **Re:Writing** *and then click on* **Tutorial Nation**.

Wording

Make headings concise yet informative. They can be single nouns (*Literacy*), a noun phrase (*Literacy in Families*), a gerund phrase (*Testing for Literacy*), or a question or statement (*How Can Literacy Be Measured?*). Make all headings at the same level consistent throughout your text—for example, by using all single nouns or all gerund phrases. Avoid using headings that simply state the name of the section of text (such as *Conclusion*).

Type Size and Style

For academic writing in MLA or APA style, headings need to be set in the same font as the rest of the text. For documents where you have some choice, you can distinguish headings by using color, bold or italics, and type size and style. Using only type, you might distinguish among levels using capitals, bold, and italics, as here:

FIRST-LEVEL HEADING
Second-Level Heading
Third-Level Heading

Positioning

Place headings consistently throughout your text. Centered headings are common for the first level; for secondary-level headings, you may indent, set flush left, or run them in to the text (that is, you can start the section's text on the same line as the heading).

Using Visuals Effectively

Visuals can add to a text's persuasiveness. They're best used when a text truly *needs* them—that is, when they can present information more succinctly and clearly than words alone. ✱ Visuals fall into two broad categories: *tables* and *figures*. Tables summarize data, usually in clearly labeled horizontal rows and vertical columns. Figures include all other visuals: pie charts, line and bar graphs, drawings, diagrams, maps, photographs, and other illustrations. Whether you're using tables or figures, rhetorical common sense can help you make a number of important decisions. (See the guidelines on pp. 330–31.)

See also "Using Visuals to Strengthen Your Argument," pp. 148–51. ✱

Guidelines for Using Visuals Effectively

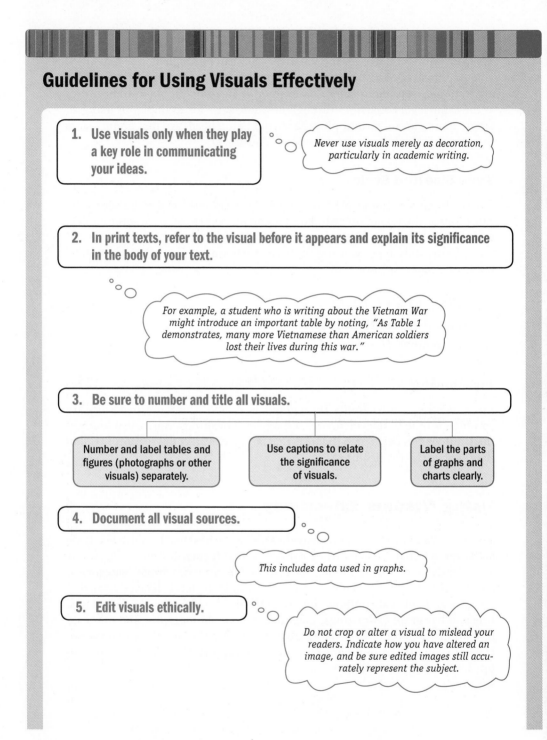

1. **Use visuals only when they play a key role in communicating your ideas.**

   Never use visuals merely as decoration, particularly in academic writing.

2. **In print texts, refer to the visual before it appears and explain its significance in the body of your text.**

   For example, a student who is writing about the Vietnam War might introduce an important table by noting, "As Table 1 demonstrates, many more Vietnamese than American soldiers lost their lives during this war."

3. **Be sure to number and title all visuals.**

   | Number and label tables and figures (photographs or other visuals) separately. | Use captions to relate the significance of visuals. | Label the parts of graphs and charts clearly. |

4. **Document all visual sources.**

   This includes data used in graphs.

5. **Edit visuals ethically.**

   Do not crop or alter a visual to mislead your readers. Indicate how you have altered an image, and be sure edited images still accurately represent the subject.

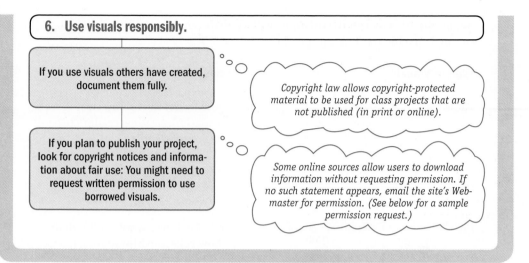

6. Use visuals responsibly.

If you use visuals others have created, document them fully.

Copyright law allows copyright-protected material to be used for class projects that are not published (in print or online).

If you plan to publish your project, look for copyright notices and information about fair use: You might need to request written permission to use borrowed visuals.

Some online sources allow users to download information without requesting permission. If no such statement appears, email the site's Webmaster for permission. (See below for a sample permission request.)

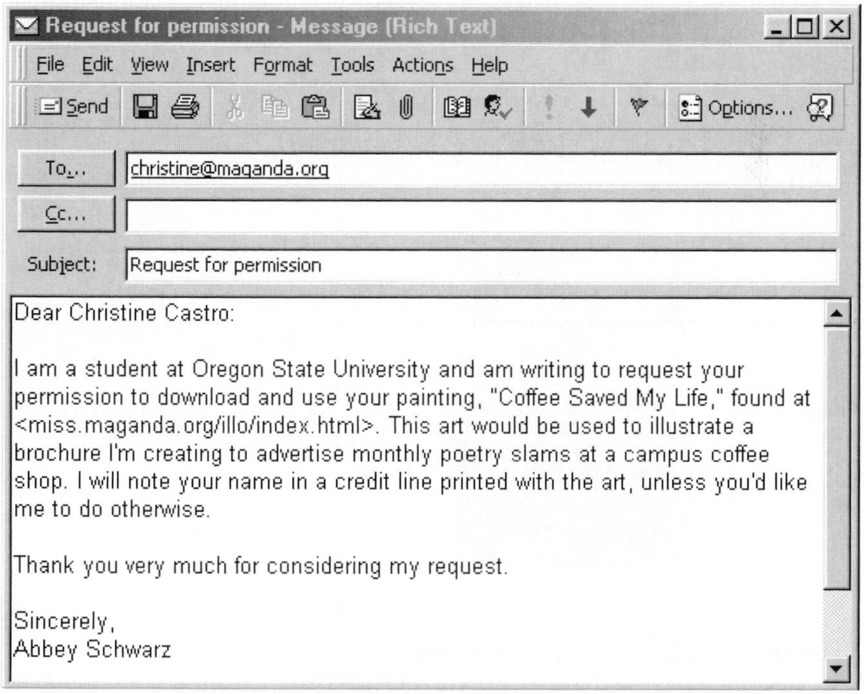

�✉ **Request for permission - Message (Rich Text)** _ ☐ ✕

File Edit View Insert Format Tools Actions Help

≡ Send | 🖫 🖨 | ✂ 🖻 🖺 | 🖳 📎 | 📖 ❗ | ! ↓ ❦ | 🔡 Options... 🔊

To... | christine@maganda.org

Cc... |

Subject: | Request for permission

Dear Christine Castro:

I am a student at Oregon State University and am writing to request your permission to download and use your painting, "Coffee Saved My Life," found at <miss.maganda.org/illo/index.html>. This art would be used to illustrate a brochure I'm creating to advertise monthly poetry slams at a campus coffee shop. I will note your name in a credit line printed with the art, unless you'd like me to do otherwise.

Thank you very much for considering my request.

Sincerely,
Abbey Schwarz

Permission Request Email

Remember that different situations call for different visuals. Use visuals that are appropriate to your situation and purpose. ✱

Type of Visual		Purpose
Table		To convey detailed numerical information; to allow readers to make comparisons
Pie Chart	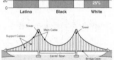	To display how a whole is divided; to show relationships among parts
Bar Graph or Line Graph		To call attention to relationships among data; to show change over time
Diagram or Drawing		To call attention to details; to show processes
Map		To call attention to locations and spatial relationships
Photograph		To show people, objects, or an event; to convey an emotion or support an argument

✱ bedfordstmartins.com/rewriting
For more help creating effective visuals, go to **Re:Writing** *and then click on* **Tutorial Nation**.

|||||||||||||||||||||||||||||||||||||||||||||||||||||||||||||||||||||||||||||||||||||||||

FOR EXPLORATION

Review Alletta Brenner's research essay on human trafficking in the garment-manufacturing industry in Chapter 7 (pp. 221–31). As you reread this essay, pay particular attention to its visuals (two photographs). How do these visual elements contribute to her essay's effectiveness? How does Alletta follow the conventions of copyright law in acknowledging the sources of these visuals?

|||||||||||||||||||||||||||||||||||||||||||||||||||||||||||||||||||||||||||||||||||||||||

Making Effective Decisions about Design: Sample Documents

One way to learn how to make effective decisions about document design is to study the decision-making process that others have followed. Collected on pp. 333–35 are sample documents that make effective design moves, annotated with some tips to help you create your own documents.

Distinct typefaces used in heading to differentiate important elements

The Craft of Writing Series Presents:

Bryan Ko

"Showing & Telling: Designing a Career in Picture Books"

April 19, 2013
4:00pm
Journey Room
Memorial Union

Central illustration draws attention and relates to speaker's topic

Bryan Ko is an OSU graduate and a passionate new author of picture books. He combines elements of Graphic Design with Fine Arts in his unique vision of children's literature. He graduated in 2005 from Oregon State University's Honors College with a Bachelor's Degree in Fine Arts. His undergraduate thesis, a picture book titled Eddie's World, is being considered for publication.

Bryan Ko joins us to share his experiences, his insights, and his vision with the OSU community and the public.

This event is free and open to the public.
Sponsored by The Center for Writing and Learning,
The Craft of Writing Series, and The Visiting Artists Series.

Boxed time and location information set off prominently

Related information grouped together

Flyer

Tall, narrow
bifold design

Title in clear,
prominent type

Clear, bold
headings

Bulleted lists
give questions
to ask, steps
to take

**Questions to ask your local beach
health monitoring official:**

- Which beaches do you monitor and how often?

- What do you test for?

- Where can I see the test results and who can
explain them to me?

- What are the primary sources of pollution that
affect this beach?

**What to do if your beach is not
monitored regularly:**

- Avoid swimming after a heavy rain.

- Look for storm drains along the beach. Don't
swim near them.

- If the waters of your beach have been designated
as a no-discharge zone for vessel sewage, check
to see if boat pumpout facilities are available and
working.

- Look for trash and such other signs of pollution
as oil slicks in the water. These kinds of
pollutants may indicate the presence of disease-
causing microorganisms that may also have been
washed into the water.

- If you think your beach water is contaminated,
contact your local health or environmental
protection officials. It is important for them to
know about suspected
beach water
contamination so they
can protect citizens
from exposure.

- Work with your local
authorities to create a
monitoring program.

*In celebration of the 30th anniversary
of the Clean Water Act, EPA presents*

Before You Go
to the Beach...

★ 2002 ★
THE YEAR OF
CLEAN WATER

Images layered to draw in reader

Brochure

Logo in distinctive font

Decorative background (used sparingly)

Menu

Major heading in large type

Additional spacing between paragraphs

Subsections with distinct type treatments

Links to photos, documents, and further information

First Page of a Web Text

| | | | | | | | | | | | | | | | | | | | | | | | | | | | | | | | | | | | | | | | | | | | | | | | | | | | | | | | | | | | | | | | | | | | | | | | | | | | | | | | | | | | | | | | | | | |

FOR THOUGHT, DISCUSSION, AND WRITING

1. Look at the introductions to the three selections by Jean Twenge presented in Chapter 4 on pp. 74–79. Chapter 4's discussion of these selections touches on issues of document design, noting, for instance, that the selection intended for the broadest audience uses an intentionally provocative cover. But it doesn't discuss the design of these selections in depth. Drawing on the guidelines presented in this chapter, analyze the visual design of the Twenge selections and relate the elements of each design to the intended audience.

2. The textbook you're reading right now has, like most books, been designed by a team of editors, designers, and artists. The book's design uses elements such as type fonts and sizes, white space, headings, color, and visuals to increase the text's readability and effectiveness. Drawing on the principles of design discussed in this chapter and also on your own design preferences, write a paragraph in which you evaluate the design of this textbook. Conclude your analysis with one or two suggestions for improving the book's design in future editions.

3. For a community, church, civic, or other group project in which you are currently involved, develop a flyer, brochure, newsletter, or Web page that your group will use as an internal document or share with others. If you aren't currently involved in such a project, develop a document that relates to a project that interests you.

4. "Putin? Never Heard of Her" (p. 337) is from the July 2007 issue of *Wired* magazine. *Wired* is known for its cutting-edge page design, and in this piece the editors developed visuals to represent results from a recent study on Americans' knowledge of current events conducted by an independent research group. Read the text and examine the visuals carefully. In what ways are these visuals effective? What kind of information might be missing? Your instructor may ask you to write several paragraphs analyzing this page.

| | | | | | | | | | | | | | | | | | | | | | | | | | | | | | | | | | | | | | | | | | | | | | | | | | | | | | | | | | | | | | | | | | | | | | | | | | | | | | | | | | | | | | | | | | | |

Putin? Never Heard of Her.

Despite the Internet explosion, Americans remain woefully ill-informed.

More than a decade after the Internet went mainstream, the world's richest information source hasn't necessarily made its users any more informed. A new study from the Pew Research Center for the People & the Press shows that Americans, on average, are less able to correctly answer questions about current events than they were in 1989. Citizens who call the Internet their primary news source know slightly less than fans of TV and radio news. Hmmm ... maybe a little less Perez Hilton and a little more Jim Lehrer. —PATRICK DI JUSTO

Americans now know less about politics than they did in 1989.

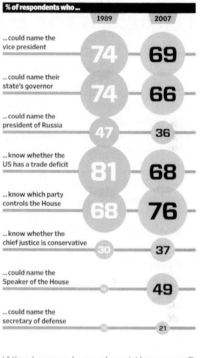

Daily Show viewers are more up on current events than Fox News fans.

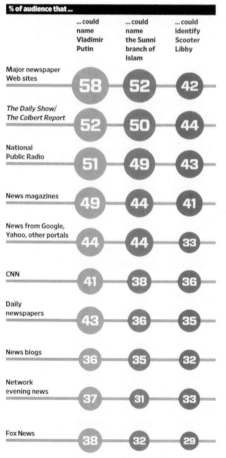

Who knows less about the news? Pretty much everyone.

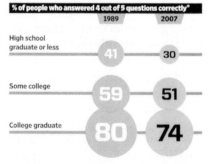

'The five questions: Who is the vice president? Who is your state's governor? Does the US have a trade deficit or surplus? Which party controls the House of Representatives? Is the chief justice of the Supreme Court a liberal, moderate, or conservative?

SOURCE: THE PEW RESEARCH CENTER FOR THE PEOPLE & THE PRESS

14

Strategies for Revision

Revising can be the most rewarding part of the writing process: It gives you the satisfaction of bringing your ideas to completion in an appropriate form. Revision challenges you to look at your work from a dual perspective: to read your work with your own intentions in mind and also to consider your readers' perspectives. Although revision occurs throughout the writing process, you'll probably revise most intensively after completing a rough draft that serves as a preliminary statement of your ideas.

This chapter focuses first on revision as a process, explaining how revision differs from editing, or correcting mistakes, and offering strategies for reading your work more objectively so that you can recognize strengths and weaknesses. Next, the chapter describes strategies for revising effectively and efficiently and shows how you can use responses to your draft to help establish priorities for revision. The last section offers ideas for improving your essay's structure and style.

Revising through Re-Vision

You can learn a great deal about revision just by considering the word itself. *Revision* combines the root word *vision* with the prefix *re-*, meaning "again." When you revise, you "see again": You develop a new vision of your essay's logic and organization or of the best way to improve the way it flows.

Revision is very different from editing, which generally occurs at the end of the writing process. Editing is essentially tidying up: When you edit, you're concerned mainly with correctness—with issues of grammar, punctuation, spelling, word choice, and sentence structure.

Unlike editing, revision is a process of discovery where much more than correctness is at stake. Because it generates growth and change, revision sometimes requires you to take risks. Often these risks are minor. If you attempt to fine-tune the details in a paragraph, for instance, you need spend only a little time and can easily revert back to the original version. Sometimes when you revise, however, you make large-scale decisions with more significant consequences. You might conclude that a different organization

Guidelines for Revising Objectively

1. Plan at least a short break between writing and revising.

It's difficult to critique your rough draft when you've just finished composing it; taking a break before revising can help you gain distance and objectivity.

2. Prepare mentally for a revising session.

Review your assignment and the analysis of your rhetorical situation.

Reread your draft and ask yourself the following questions:
- What state is your draft in—how rough or near completion?
- To what extent does your draft respond to the assignment and your rhetorical situation?
- How well does your draft meet the goals you established for it?
- What goals should you establish for this revising session, and how can you fulfill them? What should you work on first?

3. Revise from typed or printed copy.

It's generally easier, both for you and for anyone who might be reviewing your draft, to see stylistic and organizational problems in printed drafts.

4. Try reading your work out loud.

If you (or a reader) falter over a phrase or have to read a sentence several times before it makes sense, that may indicate a problem of style or logic.

is in order, decide to rework your thesis statement, or consider a new approach to your topic altogether. Trying major changes such as these often requires rewriting or discarding whole sections of a draft, but a willingness to experiment can also lead to choices that make revising easier and less frustrating.

See the guidelines for revising objectively on p. 339.

|||||||||||||||||||||||||||||||||||||||||||||||||||||||||||||||||||||||||||||||||||||||||

FOR EXPLORATION

Think back to earlier writing experiences and freewrite on them for five or ten minutes.

- When, and for what reasons, have you revised your work, instead of just editing it?

- How would you characterize these revision experiences? Were they satisfying? Frustrating? Why?

|||||||||||||||||||||||||||||||||||||||||||||||||||||||||||||||||||||||||||||||||||||||||

Asking the Big Questions: Revising for Focus, Content, and Organization

When you revise a draft, begin by asking the big, important questions — questions about how well your essay has responded to your rhetorical situation and how successfully you've achieved your purpose. If you discover — as writers often do — that your essay hasn't achieved its original purpose or that your purpose evolved into a different one as you wrote, you'll want to make major changes in your draft.

Examining Your Own Writing

From the moment you begin thinking about a writing project until you make your last revision, you must be an analyst and a decision maker. When you examine your work, you look for strengths to build on and weaknesses to remedy. Consequently, you must think about not just what is in your text but also what is *not* there and what *could be* there. You must read the part (the introduction, say, or several paragraphs) while still keeping in mind the whole.

Asking the Questions for Evaluating Focus, Content, and Organization (pp. 341–42) first is a practical approach to revising. Once you're confident that the overall focus, content, and organization of your essay are satisfactory, you'll be better able to recognize less significant but still important stylistic problems.

Questions for Evaluating Focus, Content, and Organization

Focus

What do you hope to accomplish in this essay? How clearly have you defined — and communicated — your working thesis?

How well does your essay respond to your rhetorical situation? If it is an academic essay, does it fulfill the requirements of the assignment?

Have you tried to do too much in this essay? Or are your goals too limited or inconsequential?

How does your essay respond to the needs, interests, and expectations of your readers?

Content

How effectively does your essay fulfill the commitment stated or implied by your working thesis? Do you need to develop it further?

What supporting details and evidence have you provided? Do they relate clearly to your working thesis and to each other?

What additional details, evidence, or counterarguments might strengthen your essay?

Have you included any material that is irrelevant to your working thesis?

How could your introduction and conclusion be more effective?

continued

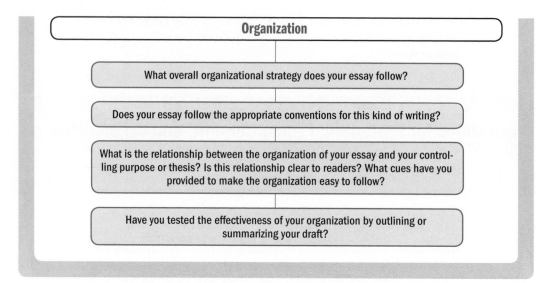

Organization

What overall organizational strategy does your essay follow?

Does your essay follow the appropriate conventions for this kind of writing?

What is the relationship between the organization of your essay and your controlling purpose or thesis? Is this relationship clear to readers? What cues have you provided to make the organization easy to follow?

Have you tested the effectiveness of your organization by outlining or summarizing your draft?

| | | | | | | | | | | | | | | | | | | | | | | | | | | | | | | | | | | | | | | | | | | | | | | | | | | | | | | | | | | | | | | | | | | | | | | | | | | | | | | | | | | | | | | | |

FOR EXPLORATION

Use the Questions for Evaluating Focus, Content, and Organization to evaluate the draft of an essay you are currently working on. Respond as specifically and as concretely as possible, and then take a few moments to reflect on what you have learned about your draft. Use your responses to make a list of goals for revising.

| | | | | | | | | | | | | | | | | | | | | | | | | | | | | | | | | | | | | | | | | | | | | | | | | | | | | | | | | | | | | | | | | | | | | | | | | | | | | | | | | | | | | | | | |

One Student Writer's Revision for Focus, Content, and Organization

Here is how one writer, Stevon Roberts, used the Questions for Evaluating Focus, Content, and Organization to establish goals for his revision. For an introductory composition class, Stevon was assigned a four- to five-page essay that proposed a solution to a contemporary problem. Stevon decided to write on something he was truly interested in: Internet privacy. This interest was sparked in part by personal experience and in part by his analysis of Amitai Etzioni's "Less Privacy Is Good for Us (and You)." ✳

Stevon spent some time discussing the problem with friends and conducted research online, taking notes as he did so. He reread his notes and then did a freewrite (see p. 343) to determine his rhetorical situation and figure out what he really wanted to get across.

✳ See pp. 102–5.

I am writing an essay for my composition class in which I'm supposed to propose a solution to a contemporary problem. I've decided to tackle the problem of Internet privacy. Since my readers — my instructor and classmates — almost certainly spend at least some time online, I think they'll be familiar with the general context of my discussion. Since the things we do online vary so widely, though, I've decided to narrow my focus to social media — Facebook, blogs, Twitter, and so on. I do have some practical recommendations to make for ways we can protect our privacy, but I've realized in talking with people and doing some research that making concrete recommendations is not always very helpful: rapid changes in technology mean that they'll rapidly become obsolete. For this reason, I've decided primarily to raise awareness of the problem, emphasizing the need for every person who uses technology to understand the dangers of providing personal information online and be alert to new threats.

Stevon's Early Draft

My name is Stevon Roberts. I'm a videographer, a blogger, a student, and a tech enthusiast (at least, that's what it says on my Twitter profile). My last known location was on the corner of NW Beca Avenue and NW 20th Street, at a place called Coffee Culture, in Corvallis, Oregon.

In the past, I would have guarded this kind of information to prevent marketers, hackers, and identity thieves from building a profile to exploit. Identity thieves have gotten very good at compiling seemingly innocuous pieces of information and using them for purposes like credit card fraud. These threats are still very real, and I still take some measures to protect myself. You probably do, too. Most of us know by now how to recognize phishing scams and other threats to our personal security. But with the advent of social media, we've seen huge changes in the way this information is obtained.

Most of us just give information away for free on Facebook, Twitter, blogs, and other social media services, often compromising security. In the same way that the automobile revolutionized transportation, social media have fundamentally shifted the way we manage our personal information. We learned to mitigate our risks on the road by using safety belts and obeying traffic laws, but most of us probably don't yet have a good understanding of the appropriate precautions for social media. As these services become more integral to our lifestyles, and more revealing of our identities, protecting our identities will become more critical, both online and in real life.

Other security concerns in the digital realm haven't gone away. Spam, for example, has become so pervasive that world spending for anti-spam software was expected to exceed $1.7 billion in 2008, up from $300 million in 2003 ("Anti-Spam Spending Set to Soar," *Global Secure Systems* 24 Feb. 2005). Apart from reducing the annoyance factor, this can also protect from more serious security threats, such as phishing scams, wherein unsuspecting victims will reply to fraudulent emails with personal information — sometimes even giving away bank account numbers!

Clearly, these security issues are still at the forefront of people's minds, and we're taking steps toward better solutions. But let's put the risks in context, and compare our relative response. As of the writing of this essay, Facebook had approximately 300 million users. Many of them are content to settle for the default privacy settings, which aren't all that private. Additionally, many Facebook users will add "applications," including games, quizzes, etc., which have access to many parts of your user profile that you may not want to share. In fact, in a twist of irony, the ACLU has added a quiz that you can take to explain exactly what is exposed when you add these sorts of quizzes (aclunc_privacy_quiz/). The quiz offers some suggestions for changing the privacy settings to protect personal information, but many people simply aren't aware, or don't take the time, to make these adjustments.

But let's not focus on Facebook at the expense of an even larger context. Location services, such as Brightkite, allow you to pinpoint your location on a map. You'd probably be happy to share this information with friends whom you'd like to join you, but you likely wouldn't want to share this information with a stalker, or even an angry ex-boyfriend or -girlfriend. Would you broadcast the location of your home address? Most of us would probably think twice before doing that, but the lines can quickly become blurry. Is it okay to broadcast your location from a friend's house? Your classroom, or your office?

With its instructional tagline "What are you doing?" Twitter gives its users 140 characters to broadcast activities, locations, Web site URLs, and even pictures (via helper services). An individual post, or "tweet," might cost you a job if, for example, you tell your friends you took a job only for its "fatty paycheck" (Snell). You might risk being overlooked for an interview if you posted a picture from a drinking party.

Similarly, your political views and feelings may be called into question if you endeavor to start a blog, as I have. My blog is not especially personal, but it occurred to me when I started writing that this might be another potential vector for increased risk. It bothered me so much that I wrote to one of my favorite bloggers (Leo Babauta of Zenhabits .net), asking him whether he was concerned about security. He wrote back (via Twitter), "No, I haven't faced security or privacy issues as a blogger (yet). My readers are 100% really cool, nice (and sexy) people." It's worth pointing out that his blog has over a hundred thousand subscribers.

Still . . . social media, location services, and blogs: These new services all allow you to compromise your own personal identity and security in ways that are unprecedented. And at the same time, participation in all of these environments is almost obligatory. Very few of my friends have not yet succumbed to the peer pressure to be available on Facebook, despite security concerns. And if you're trying to run a business (or promote your blog), avoiding Twitter is tantamount to professional suicide — these venues are key ingredients for successful marketing. In short, your personal name and profile have almost become like a kind of brand that is expected to be proliferated and maintained in cyberspace. And yet censorship levels must be very high to avoid getting passed over for the next opportunity, because heaven forbid that your future employer doesn't agree with you about the last hot political topic (or whatever).

Along with the members of his peer response group, Stevon used the Questions for Evaluating Focus, Content, and Organization to analyze his draft. The following analysis reflects both Stevon's own observations and those of his writing group.

Focus: Some of my readers were confused about my main focus. I think I can correct this by revising my introduction and explaining more clearly that we (my instructor, classmates, and I) are all probably too sophisticated now for the "Nigerian royalty" email scams — we've all been there and learned our lessons — but other dangers exist, and we might not all be aware of them: specifically, the dangers presented in giving personal information away while using social media, which many of us are virtually addicted to.

I made one point that readers found really important — the idea that cutting social media off completely is not really an option for most of us, because it's too important for our social and even professional lives — late in the essay; I think I'll move it up closer to the beginning.

Some of my readers wanted more concrete recommendations for what to do to protect themselves. I have to make it clear from the outset that I think awareness and seeking out solutions that work for you is really the only universal solution anyone can offer — there's too much variety in the kinds of technology people use and it all changes really, really fast. I'm trying to teach them to fish, I guess, instead of giving them fish.

Content: Some of my readers were confused about my opening (where I give away private information about myself — what's my point there, exactly?). I think I just need to make the point more clearly in the second paragraph.

A couple of my readers didn't know what "phishing" was — I have to be careful about assuming too much common knowledge in technical terminology.

I realized on rereading one of my sources that a statistic it offered was a bit out-of-date, so I found a more current source.

I need to provide some more examples of some of the risks that people didn't entirely "get," like how having a blog could cost you a job.

Probably most critical is the fact that my readers didn't like my conclusion: They felt like the discussion just dropped off without really "concluding." I think adding a stronger conclusion, reminding readers of my major points, will make the essay much stronger.

Organization: I did try outlining my draft; it worked out OK, but I realize that I do ping-pong a bit, especially in the beginning, between old threats like spam and new threats like Facebook quizzes. I need to work on transitions to make what I'm doing there clearer (because that's where some of the confusion about my focus crept in, I think).

I also have to add some clearer transitions between the different kinds of risks I discuss (the usual stuff with marketers and scam artists, and then other, even scarier stuff, like losing a job or being stalked). In the discussion of the latter risks (like stalkers), I lost some readers when I started out talking about Brightkite (it uses GPS technology but my readers didn't immediately know what I was talking about), so I think I'll reorder the presentation of topics here, and start with Twitter and blogs (which people are more familiar with).

Stevon used this analysis to completely rework his essay. The result follows on pp. 347–51.

Roberts 1

Stevon Roberts
Dr. Mallon
Comp 101
Oct. 17, 2013

Identity, Rebooted

When you're doing stuff online, you should behave as if you're doing it in public—because increasingly, it is.—Cornell University computer science professor Jon Kleinberg (qtd. in Lohr)

My name is Stevon Roberts. I'm a videographer, a blogger, a student, and a tech enthusiast (at least, that's what it says on my Twitter profile). My last known location was on the corner of NW Beca Avenue and NW 20th Street, at a place called Coffee Culture, in Corvallis, Oregon.

If someone had told me even five years ago that I would one day regularly broadcast this kind of information about myself to people I didn't know, I wouldn't have believed it. If someone I didn't know had asked me back then for information like this, I would have refused to give it, to prevent unscrupulous people from exploiting it. I was well aware of how expert marketers, hackers, and identity thieves had become at compiling such seemingly innocuous pieces of information and using them for unwanted sales pitches, or even worse, for credit card scams and other kinds of fraud.

These threats are still very real, and I take some measures to protect myself against them. You probably do, too: Most of us are wary of filling out surveys from dubious sources, for example, and most of us know by now how to recognize obvious email scams like the ones purporting to be from "Nigerian royalty." But with the advent of social media, many of us find ourselves in a bind: We want to be connected, so many of us regularly give confidential—and potentially damaging—information away on Facebook, Twitter, blogs, and other social-media services.

Added title to prepare readers for content of essay

Added new epigraph to provide thought-provoking expert commentary

Revised pars. 2 and 3 to reflect rhetorical situation—writing to media-savvy readers in age of Facebook—and explained focus to make readers aware of privacy concerns

Replaced the term "phishing," with example that would be more familiar to readers

Moved up important aspect of argument: Social media matter because we want to be connected

Roberts 2

In the same way that the automobile revolutionized transportation, social media have fundamentally shifted the way we communicate and share personal information. We learned to mitigate our risks on the road by using safety belts and obeying traffic laws, but most of us probably don't yet have a good understanding of appropriate precautions for social media. As these services become more integral to our lifestyles, protecting our identities from those who might use them for nefarious ends will become even more critical. Given the speed with which social media are developing and changing, it's difficult to give specific recommendations. An important first step, however, is becoming aware of the risks you run in broadcasting personal information.

These new concerns about privacy and safety in the digital realm have arrived on the heels of older problems that haven't gone away. Spam, for example, has become so pervasive that, according to a 2009 estimate by Ferris Research, annual spending that year for antispam software, hardware, and personnel would reach $6.5 billion — $2.1 billion in the United States alone (Jennings). As these figures show, though, in the case of spam, most of us can and do fight back: Antispam software eliminates or at least reduces the amount of unwanted email we receive, and it can protect us well from security threats like the "Nigerian royalty" scam mentioned above, wherein unsuspecting victims will reply to fraudulent emails with personal information — sometimes even giving away bank account numbers.

Most of us are not yet doing anything about the threats posed by the information we publish via social media, however, and many of us are not even fully aware of them. In order to put the problem in context, let's take a closer look at the kinds of social media we're talking about and the nature and extent of the risks they pose. Participation in social networks like Facebook, Twitter, Flickr, and others has exploded in the last few years: As of the writing of this essay, Facebook alone had over one billion users. Most of those who participate don't think twice about privacy issues, or they assume that the systems' default privacy settings will protect them. Yet recent studies done by researchers at M.I.T., Carnegie Mellon, and the University of Texas have demonstrated that it's possible to determine sexual orientation, match identities to "anonymously" stated preferences, and even

---

Margin annotations:

Clarified and limited primary goal of essay

Updated statistics and synthesized these with his own experience to provide concrete examples of problems that remain

Clarified transition, moving from spam (older security concern) to social media

Synthesized experience with information about recent studies to specify "threats to privacy"

Roberts 3

piece together Social Security numbers from profile information on Facebook and other social networks (Lohr).

As if putting basic profile information out there weren't enough, many Facebook users will add applications like games and quizzes that allow outside parties unmediated access to unrelated information from their profiles. In an attempt to raise awareness of the issue, the ACLU has added a quiz(!) to Facebook that explains exactly what is exposed when you add these sorts of quizzes (Conley; see also http://apps.facebook.com/aclunc _privacy_quiz/). The ACLU's quiz offers some suggestions for changing Facebook privacy settings to protect personal information.

The risks you take in revealing personal information via social media go beyond its possible misuse by marketers, hackers, and identity thieves. For example, with its tagline, "What are you doing?" Twitter gives its users 140 characters to broadcast activities, locations, Web site URLs, and even pictures (via helper services). A single post, or "tweet," however, might cost you a job, as it did the woman who openly expressed her concerns about taking a job she disliked for a "fatty paycheck" (Snell). You might risk being turned down for an interview if you post a picture from a wild drinking party.

Similarly, your views and opinions, political and otherwise, may become an issue if you start a blog. I have a blog that's not especially personal, but it occurred to me when I started writing that this might be a potential source of risk: What if my boss saw what I wrote, disagreed, and started treating me differently at work? What if my landlord was bothered enough to refuse to renew my lease? I began to worry so much about it that I wrote to one of my favorite bloggers (Leo Babauta of Zenhabits.net), asking him whether he was concerned about security. He wrote back (via Twitter), "No, I haven't faced security or privacy issues as a blogger (yet). My readers are 100% really cool, nice (and sexy) people." It's worth pointing out that his blog has over a hundred thousand subscribers, so maybe I'm worried over nothing. On the other hand, Mr. Babauta lives on the island of Guam, works for himself, and likely doesn't face many of the same identity expectations that I would as a student and young professional.

Added transition to clarify move from one kind of risk to another; also reorganized section, moving Twitter and blogs to beginning as they were likely to be more familiar to readers

Provided some examples to clarify kinds of risks he might be taking in posting blog

Responded to question about why readers should be concerned if Babauta wasn't

Roberts 4

One last service that's become a recent phenomenon is the use of Global Positioning System (GPS) technology in cell phones. Many cell phones now have GPS receivers built in, and as with some Twitter applications, location services such as Brightkite allow you to pinpoint your location on a map with startling accuracy. Broadcasting your location is optional, but many people do so because the technology's there and they don't see how it could hurt. It could hurt: When you broadcast your location, everyone, not just your friends, will know where you are. How about angry ex-boyfriends or -girlfriends or potential stalkers? What if someone were casing your home for a break-in and were able to determine via one of these services that you were away?

Clearly, social media allow you to reveal aspects of your identity and (therefore) compromise your security in ways that are unprecedented. At the same time, for many of us participation in these environments is tempting and at times almost obligatory. Very few of my friends have not yet succumbed to the peer pressure to be available on Facebook, for example. If you're trying to run a business (or promote your blog), avoiding Twitter is tantamount to professional suicide—these venues are key ingredients for successful marketing. In short, your personal name and profile have become a brand that you're expected to proliferate and maintain in cyberspace: Without them, you're nothing. Yet, as I have discussed, the risks that accompany this self-promotion are high.

Because the explosion in social media is relatively new, best practices for mitigating these risks are not clearly identified yet. One friend and professional colleague argues that it's simply impossible to manage your identity online because much of it is revealed by others—your friends will post the embarrassing party pictures for you, school or work will post documents detailing your achievements, and Google will determine what appears in the search results when you type your name in. M.I.T. professor Harold Abelson agrees: "Personal privacy is no longer an individual thing. . . . In today's online world, what your mother told you is true, only more so: people really can judge you by your friends" (qtd. in Lohr).

Roberts 5

The most positive spin on this perspective is to think of your online identity in terms of a "signal-to-noise" ratio: Assuming you know what you're doing, you are in charge of the "signal" (the information you yourself tweet or allow to appear on Facebook), and this signal will usually be stronger than the "noise" generated by your friends or others who broadcast information you'd rather not share. The key phrase there is "assuming you know what you're doing," and that's where all of us could use some pointers. If you're going to put your faith in your ability to create a strong, positive signal, you need to follow a few key rules. First, realize that there's a potential problem every time you post something private online. Next, make yourself thoroughly acquainted with the privacy settings of any and all social media you interact with. The default settings for any of these programs are almost certainly inadequate because my security concerns aren't the same as Leo Babauta's, and they're not the same as yours. Finally, keep talking (and blogging and Googling) about the issue and sharing any best practices you discover. We need to work together to understand and manage these risks if we want to retain control of the "brand" that is us.

Works Cited

Babauta, Leo. "Re: Security Concerns?" Message to the author. 11 Oct. 2013. Tweet.

Conley, Chris. "Quiz: What Do Facebook Quizzes Know about You?" *Blog of Rights*. ACLU, 11 June 2009. Web. 10 Oct. 2013.

Jennings, Richi. "Cost of Spam Is Flattening—Our 2009 Predictions." *Ferris.com*. Ferris Research, 28 Jan. 2009. Web. 7 Oct. 2013.

Lohr, Steve. "How Privacy Vanishes Online." *New York Times*. New York Times, 16 Mar. 2010. Web. 8 Oct. 2013.

Snell, Jason. "Think before You Tweet." *Macworld*. Mac Publishing, 18 Mar. 2009. Web. 9 Oct. 2013.

The Works Cited page includes all sources in correct MLA format. (*Note:* in an actual MLA-style paper, works-cited entries start on a new page.)

Benefiting from Responses to Work in Progress

You may write alone a good deal of the time, but writing needn't be a lonely process. You can draw on the responses of others to help you re-see your writing and to gain support. When you ask others to respond to your writing, you're asking for feedback so that you can see your writing in fresh and different ways.

Responses can take a number of forms. Sometimes you may find it helpful to ask others simply to describe your writing for you. You might, for example, ask them to summarize in their own words how they understand your main point or what they think you're getting at. Similarly, you might ask them what parts of your draft stood out for them, and what they felt was missing.

On other occasions, you may find more analytical responses helpful. You might ask readers to comment on your essay's organization or how well it responds to their needs and interests. If you're writing an argumentative essay, you might ask readers to look for potential weaknesses in its structure or logic.

To determine what kind of feedback will be most helpful, think commonsensically about your writing. Where are you in your composing process? How do you feel about your draft and the kind of writing you're working on? If you've just completed a rough draft, for instance, you might find descriptive feedback most helpful. After you've worked longer on the essay, you might invite more analytical responses.

As a student, you can turn to many people for feedback. The differences in their situations will influence how they respond; these differences should also influence how you use their responses. No matter whom you approach for feedback, though, learn to distinguish between your writing and yourself. Try not to respond defensively to suggestions for improvement, and don't argue with readers' responses. Instead, use them to gain insight into your writing. Ultimately you are the one who must decide how to interpret and apply other people's comments and criticisms.

NOTE FOR MULTILINGUAL WRITERS

If you were educated in another culture, the process of revising multiple drafts may be new to you. Revising is meant to help you rework your writing to make sure it is as effective and clear as possible. If receiving (and giving) comments on drafts is new to you, be assured that the suggestions and questions from peer and other reviewers should lead to constructive collaboration.

Responses from Friends and Family Members

You can certainly ask the people close to you to respond to your writing, but you should understand their strengths and weaknesses as readers. One important strength is that you trust them. Even if you spend time filling them in, however, friends and family members won't understand the nature of your assignment or your instructor's standards for evaluation; they're also likely to be less objective than other readers. All the same, friends and family members can provide useful responses to your writing if you choose such respondents carefully and draw on their strengths as outsiders. Rather than asking them to respond in detail, you might ask them to give a general impression or a descriptive response to your work. If their understanding of the main idea or controlling purpose of your essay differs substantially from your own, you've gained very useful information.

Responses from Classmates

Because your classmates know your instructor and the assignment as insiders, they can provide particularly effective responses to work in progress. Classmates don't need to be experts to provide helpful responses. They simply need to be attentive, honest, supportive readers. Classmates can also read your work more objectively than family members and friends can. To ensure that you and your classmates provide a helpful balance of support and criticism, you and they should follow the Guidelines for Responses from Classmates on pp. 354–55.

||||||||||||||||||||||||||||||||||||||||||||||||||||||||||||||||||||||||||||||||||||||||||||||||

FOR EXPLORATION

Think about responses to your work that you have received from classmates. Freewrite for five or ten minutes about these experiences, and then draw up a list of statements describing the kinds of responses that have been most helpful.

Meet with a group of your classmates. Begin by having each group member read his or her list. Then, working together, list all the suggestions for responses from classmates. Have one student record all the suggestions and distribute them to everyone in the group for future use.

||||||||||||||||||||||||||||||||||||||||||||||||||||||||||||||||||||||||||||||||||||||||||||||||

Guidelines for Responses from Classmates

Advice for Writers

Prepare for response meetings.

Carefully formulate the questions about your work that you most need to have answered.

Bring a legible draft to class.

Be sure to bring a working draft, not a jumble of brainstorming ideas, free-writing, and notes.

Explain your rhetorical situation.

If you are addressing a specific audience — members of a certain organization, for example, or readers of a particular magazine — be sure to let your classmates know.

Maintain your own authority as the writer.

Your fellow students' responses are just that: responses. Treat their comments seriously, but remember that you must always decide what advice to accept and what to reject.

Advice for Readers

Follow the golden rule.

Respond to the writing of others as you would like them to respond to your own work.

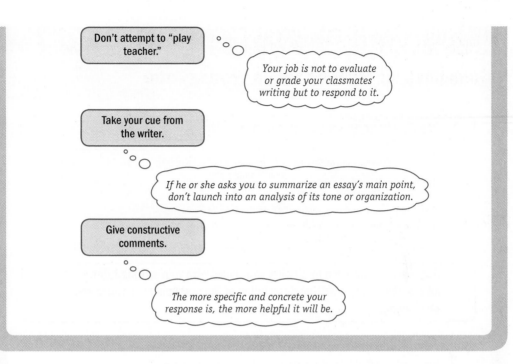

Responses from Writing Center Tutors

Many colleges and universities have writing centers staffed by undergraduate and graduate writing assistants or tutors. Tutors are not professional editors, nor are they faculty aides standing in for instructors who are unavailable or too busy to meet with students. Writing tutors are simply good writers who have been formally trained to respond to peers' work and to make suggestions for improvement. Tutors can provide excellent responses to work in progress. If your college or university has a writing center, be sure to take advantage of its services. For guidelines on meeting with a tutor, see p. 356.

Responses from Your Instructor and Others

Because your instructor is such an important reader for your written assignments, you want to make good use of any written comments he or she provides. For guidelines on making the most of them, see p. 357.

Friends, family members, classmates, writing tutors, instructors—all can provide helpful responses to your writing. None of these responses, whether criticism or praise, should take the place of your own judgment, however. Your job is to *interpret* and *evaluate* these responses, using them along with your own assessment of your rough draft to establish goals for revising.

Guidelines for Meeting with a Writing Tutor

1. Identify your goals before meeting with a tutor.

Reread your writing and ask yourself what kind of help you would benefit most from:

- A discussion of your essay's organization
- An examination of a section of your draft
- Some other activity, such as brainstorming ideas or evaluating possible evidence for your position

2. Begin your conference by sharing your goals with your writing tutor. If at all possible, bring a written description of the assignment to which you are responding.

You might also find it helpful to tell the writing tutor where you are in your process—in the early stages of drafting, for instance, or in the process of final editing.

3. Be realistic about what you can accomplish in the time available.

Recognize, as well, that the writing tutor's job is to respond and advise, not to correct or rewrite your draft.

Keeping Your Readers on Track: Revising for Style

"Proper words in proper places"—that's how the eighteenth-century writer Jonathan Swift defined style. As Swift suggests, writing style reflects all the choices a writer makes, from global questions of approach and organization to the smallest details about punctuation and grammar. When, in writing, you put the proper words in their proper places, readers will be able to follow your ideas with understanding and interest. In addition, they will probably gain some sense of the person behind the words—that is, of the writer's presence.

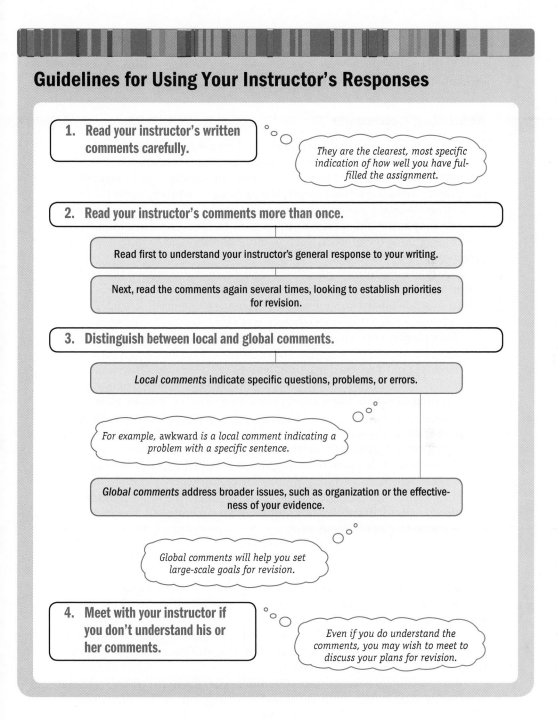

Guidelines for Using Your Instructor's Responses

1. **Read your instructor's written comments carefully.**

   They are the clearest, most specific indication of how well you have fulfilled the assignment.

2. **Read your instructor's comments more than once.**

   Read first to understand your instructor's general response to your writing.

   Next, read the comments again several times, looking to establish priorities for revision.

3. **Distinguish between local and global comments.**

   Local comments indicate specific questions, problems, or errors.

   For example, awkward *is a local comment indicating a problem with a specific sentence.*

   Global comments address broader issues, such as organization or the effectiveness of your evidence.

   Global comments will help you set large-scale goals for revision.

4. **Meet with your instructor if you don't understand his or her comments.**

   Even if you do understand the comments, you may wish to meet to discuss your plans for revision.

Most writers concern themselves with style *after* writing a rough draft and determining that the essay's focus, content, and organization are effective. At this point, the writer can make changes that enable readers to move through the writing easily and enjoyably.

Achieving Coherence

Most writers are aware that paragraphs and essays need to be *unified*—that is, that they should focus on a single topic. Writing is *coherent* when readers can move easily from word to word, sentence to sentence, and paragraph to paragraph. There are various means of achieving coherence. Some methods, such as *repeating key words and sentence structures* and *using pronouns*, reinforce or emphasize the logical development of ideas. Another method involves *using transitional words* such as *but, although*, and *because* to provide directional cues for readers.

The following introduction to "Home Town," an essay by the popular writer Ian Frazier, uses all of these methods to keep readers on track. The most important means of achieving coherence are italicized.

> *When glaciers* covered much of northern Ohio, the land around Hudson, the town where I grew up, lay under one. *Glaciers* came and went several times, the most recent departing about 14,000 years ago. *When* we studied *glaciers* in an Ohio-history class in grade school, I imagined our *glacier* receding smoothly, like a sheet pulled off a new car. *Actually, glaciers* can move forward *but* they don't back up—*they* melt in place. *Most likely* the *glacier* above Hudson softened, *and* began to trickle underneath; rocks on its surface absorbed sunlight and melted tunnels into *it; it* rotted, *it* dwindled, *it* dripped, *it* ticked; *then it* dropped a pile of the sand and rocks *it* had been carrying around for centuries onto the ground in a heap. Hudson's landscape was hundreds of these little heaps—hills rarely big enough to sled down, a random arrangement made by gravity and smoothed by weather and time.
>
> — Ian Frazier, "Home Town"

When you read your own writing to determine how to strengthen its coherence, use common sense. Your writing is coherent if readers know where they have been and where they are going as they read. Don't assume that your writing will be more coherent if you simply sprinkle key words, pronouns, and transitions throughout your prose. If the logic of your discussion is clear without such devices, don't add them.

Revision for coherence proceeds most effectively if you look first at large-scale issues, such as the relationship among your essay's introduction, body, and conclusion, before considering smaller concerns. For guidelines on revising for coherence, see p. 359.

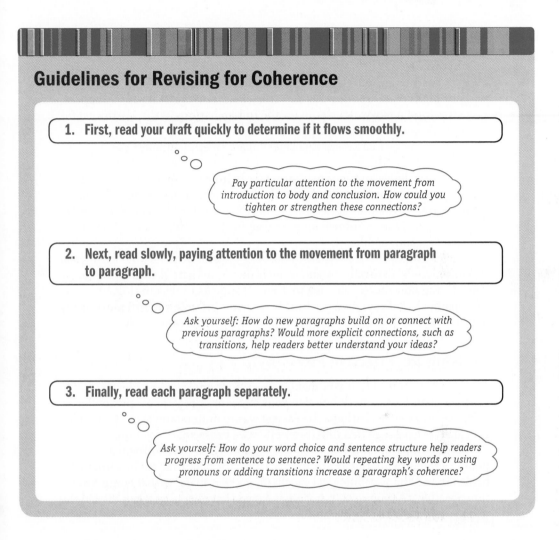

Guidelines for Revising for Coherence

1. First, read your draft quickly to determine if it flows smoothly.

Pay particular attention to the movement from introduction to body and conclusion. How could you tighten or strengthen these connections?

2. Next, read slowly, paying attention to the movement from paragraph to paragraph.

Ask yourself: How do new paragraphs build on or connect with previous paragraphs? Would more explicit connections, such as transitions, help readers better understand your ideas?

3. Finally, read each paragraph separately.

Ask yourself: How do your word choice and sentence structure help readers progress from sentence to sentence? Would repeating key words or using pronouns or adding transitions increase a paragraph's coherence?

Finding an Appropriate Voice

A writer's style reflects his or her individual taste and sensibility. But just as people dress differently for different occasions, so too do effective writers vary their style, depending on their rhetorical situation. As they do so, they are particularly attentive to the *persona*, or voice, they want to convey through their writing.

Sometimes writers present strong and distinctive voices. Here, for instance, is the beginning of an essay by the novelist Ken Kesey on the Pendleton Round-Up, a Northwest rodeo.

My father took me up the Gorge and over the hills to my first one thirty-five years ago. It was on my fourteenth birthday. I had to miss a couple of days' school plus the possibility of suiting up for the varsity game that Friday night. Gives you some idea of the importance Daddy placed on this event.

For this is more than just a world-class rodeo. It is a week-long shindig, a yearly rendezvous dating back beyond the first white trappers, a traditional powwow ground for the Indian nations of the Northwest for nobody knows how many centuries.

— Ken Kesey, "The Blue-Ribbon American Beauty Rose of Rodeo"

Kesey's word choice and sentence structure help create an image of the writer as folksy, relaxed, and yet also forceful—just the right insider to write about a famous rodeo. In other situations, writers may prefer a less personal voice, as is often the case in informative writing for textbooks, academic articles, newspapers, and the like.

If you think rhetorically, always asking questions about your rhetorical situation, you'll naturally consider such major stylistic issues as voice. By considering how much you wish to draw on appeals to reason (logos), emotion (pathos), and your own credibility as writer (ethos), you will more easily determine your own voice and your relationship with readers. ✳

Revising for Effective Prose Style

The stylistic choices that you make as you draft and revise reflect not only your rhetorical awareness but also your awareness of general principles of effective prose style. Perhaps the easiest way to understand these principles is to analyze a passage that illustrates effective prose style in action.

Here is a paragraph from the first chapter of a psycholinguistics textbook. (Psycholinguistics is an interdisciplinary field that studies linguistic behavior and the psychological mechanisms that make verbal communication possible.) As you read it, imagine that you have been assigned to read the textbook for a course in psycholinguistics.

Language stands at the center of human affairs, from the most prosaic to the most profound. It is used for haggling with store clerks, telling off umpires, and gossiping with friends as well as for negotiating contracts, discussing ethics, and explaining religious beliefs. It is the medium through which the manners, morals, and mythology of a society are passed on to the next generation. Indeed, it is a basic ingredient in virtually every social situation. The thread that runs through all these activities is communication, people trying to put their ideas over to others. As the main vehicle of human communication, language is indispensable.

— Herbert H. Clark and Eve V. Clark, *Psychology and Language*

✳   See pp. 52–56, 65–67, 106–10.

This paragraph, you would probably agree, embodies effective prose style. It's clearly organized and begins with a topic sentence, which the rest of the paragraph explains. The paragraph is also coherent, with pronouns, key words, and sentence patterns helping readers proceed. But what most distinguishes this paragraph, what makes it so effective, is the authors' use of concrete, precise, economical language and carefully crafted sentences.

Suppose that the paragraph were revised as follows. What would be lost?

> Language stands at the center of human affairs, from the most prosaic to the most profound. It is a means of human communication. It is a means of cultural change and regeneration. It is found in every social situation. The element that characterizes all these activities is communication. As the main vehicle of human communication, language is indispensable.

This revision communicates roughly the same ideas as the original paragraph, but it lacks that paragraph's liveliness and interest. Instead of presenting vivid examples—"haggling with store clerks, telling off umpires, and gossiping with friends"—these sentences state only vague generalities. Moreover, they're short and monotonous. Also lost in the revision is any sense of the authors' personalities, as revealed in their writing.

As this example demonstrates, effective prose style doesn't have to be flashy or call attention to itself. The focus in the original passage is on the *ideas* being discussed. The authors don't want readers to stop and think, "My, what a lovely sentence." But they do want their readers to become interested in and engaged with their ideas. So they use strong verbs and vivid, concrete examples whenever possible. They pay careful attention to sentence structure, alternating sequences of sentences with parallel structures with other, more varied sentences. They make sure that the relationships among ideas are clear. As a result of these and other choices, this paragraph succeeds in being both economical and emphatic.

Exploring your stylistic options—developing a style that reflects your understanding of yourself and the world and your feel for language—is one of the pleasures of writing. The Guidelines for Effective Prose Style on p. 362 describe just a few of the ways you can revise your own writing to improve its style.

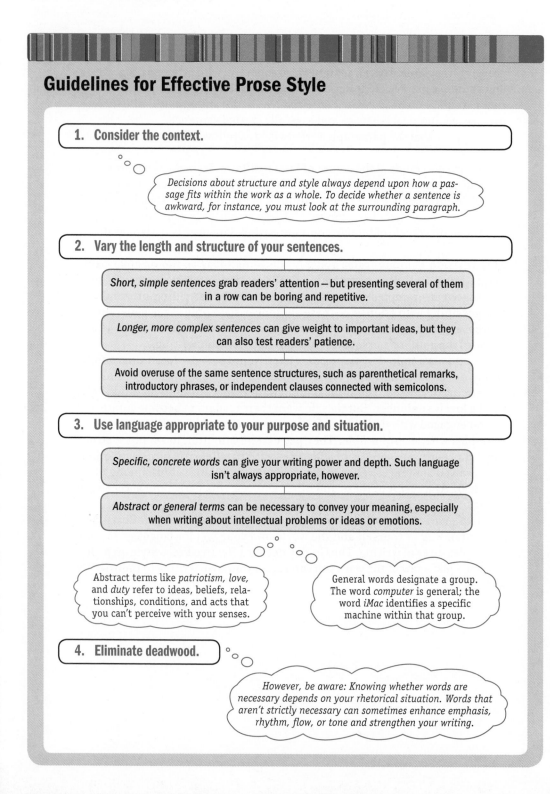

Guidelines for Effective Prose Style

1. Consider the context.

Decisions about structure and style always depend upon how a passage fits within the work as a whole. To decide whether a sentence is awkward, for instance, you must look at the surrounding paragraph.

2. Vary the length and structure of your sentences.

Short, simple sentences grab readers' attention — but presenting several of them in a row can be boring and repetitive.

Longer, more complex sentences can give weight to important ideas, but they can also test readers' patience.

Avoid overuse of the same sentence structures, such as parenthetical remarks, introductory phrases, or independent clauses connected with semicolons.

3. Use language appropriate to your purpose and situation.

Specific, concrete words can give your writing power and depth. Such language isn't always appropriate, however.

Abstract or general terms can be necessary to convey your meaning, especially when writing about intellectual problems or ideas or emotions.

Abstract terms like *patriotism, love,* and *duty* refer to ideas, beliefs, relationships, conditions, and acts that you can't perceive with your senses.

General words designate a group. The word *computer* is general; the word *iMac* identifies a specific machine within that group.

4. Eliminate deadwood.

However, be aware: Knowing whether words are necessary depends on your rhetorical situation. Words that aren't strictly necessary can sometimes enhance emphasis, rhythm, flow, or tone and strengthen your writing.

|||||||||||||||||||||||||||||||||||||||||||||||||||||||||||||||||||||||||||||||||||||||||||||||||

FOR THOUGHT, DISCUSSION, AND WRITING

1. To study your own revision process, number and save all your plans, drafts, and revisions for a paper that you're currently writing or have written recently. After you have completed the paper, review these materials, paying particular attention to the revisions you made. Can you describe the revision strategies that you followed and identify ways to improve the effectiveness of this process? Your instructor may ask you to write an essay discussing what you have learned as a result of this analysis.

2. Interview two students in your class about their revision strategies. How do their strategies reflect their preferred composing styles? How are their strategies similar to and different from your own? How do these students feel about revising, and how do their feelings compare with your own? Can you apply any of their strategies to your own writing? What can you learn from these interviews? Your instructor may ask you to write an essay summarizing the results of your interviews.

3. From an essay you are currently working on, choose two or three paragraphs that you suspect could be more coherent or stylistically effective. Using this chapter's discussion as a guide, revise these paragraphs.

4. Read the essay by Frank Rose on pp. 273–74 (or choose another essay in this book that interests you), and then answer the following questions.

   ■ How would you describe the general style of this essay? Write three or four sentences describing its style.

   ■ How would you describe the persona, or voice, conveyed by this essay? List at least three characteristics of the writer's voice, and then indicate several passages that exemplify these characteristics.

   ■ Find three passages that demonstrate the principles of effective prose style as discussed in this chapter. Indicate why you believe each passage is stylistically effective.

   ■ What additional comments could you make about the structure and style of this essay? Did anything about the style surprise you? Formulate at least one additional comment about the essay's structure and style.

|||||||||||||||||||||||||||||||||||||||||||||||||||||||||||||||||||||||||||||||||||||||||||||||||

Writers' References

MLA Documentation Guidelines

The Modern Language Association (MLA) recommends the following format for the manuscript of a research-based essay or project. It's always a good idea, however, to check with your instructor about formatting issues before preparing your final draft.

For detailed guidelines on formatting a list of works cited, see p. 373. For sample student essays in MLA style, see pp. 61, 115, 165, 221, and 347.

- *First page and title page.* The MLA does not require a title page. Type each of the following items on a separate line on the first page, beginning one inch from the top and flush with the left margin: your name, the instructor's name, the course name and number, and the date. Double-space between each item; then double-space again and center the title. Double-space between the title and the beginning of the text.

- *Margins and spacing.* Leave one-inch margins at the top and bottom and on both sides of each page. Double-space the entire text, including set-off quotations, notes, and the list of works cited. Indent the first line of a paragraph one-half inch.

- *Page numbers.* Include your last name and the page number on each page, one-half inch below the top and flush with the right margin.

- *Long quotations.* Set off a long quotation (more than four typed lines) in block format by starting it on a new line and indenting each line one inch from the left margin. Do not enclose the passage in quotation marks.

- *Headings.* MLA style allows, but does not require, headings. Many students and instructors find them helpful. (See pp. 328–29 for guidelines on using headings.)

- *Visuals.* Place tables, photographs, drawings, charts, graphs, and other figures as near as possible to the relevant text. (See pp. 330–31 for advice on incorporating visuals into your text.) Tables should have a label and number (*Table 1*) and a clear caption. The label and caption should be aligned on the left, on separate lines. Give the source information below the table. All other visuals should be labeled *Figure* (abbreviated *Fig.*), numbered, and captioned. The label and caption should appear on the same line, followed by the source information. Remember to refer to each visual in your text, indicating how it contributes to the point(s) you are making.

In-Text Citations

MLA style requires a citation in the text of an essay for every quotation, paraphrase, summary, or other material requiring documentation. In-text citations document material from other sources with both signal phrases and parenthetical references. Parenthetical references should include the information your readers need to locate the full reference in the list of works cited at the end of the text (see pp. 373–99). An in-text citation in MLA style aims to give the reader two kinds of information: (1) It indicates *which source* on the works-cited page the writer is referring to, and (2) it explains *where in the source* the material quoted, paraphrased, or summarized can be found, if the source has page numbers or other numbered sections.

The basic MLA in-text citation includes the author's last name either in a signal phrase introducing the source material (see p. 369) or in parentheses at the end of the sentence. For print sources, it also includes the page number in parentheses at the end of the sentence.

Directory to MLA style for in-text citations

In his discussion of *Monty Python* routines, Crystal notes that the group relished "breaking the normal rules" of language (107).

SAMPLE PARENTHETICAL CITATION

A noted linguist explains that *Monty Python* humor often relied on "bizarre linguistic interactions" (Crystal 108).

Note in the following examples where punctuation is placed in relation to the parentheses.

1. AUTHOR NAMED IN A SIGNAL PHRASE The MLA recommends using the author's name in a signal phrase to introduce the material and citing the page number(s), if any, in parentheses.

Lee claims that his comic-book creation, Thor, was "the first regularly published superhero to speak in a consistently archaic manner" (199).

2. AUTHOR NAMED IN A PARENTHETICAL REFERENCE When you do not mention the author in a signal phrase, include the author's last name before the page number(s) in the parentheses. Use no punctuation between the author's name and the page number(s).

The word *Bollywood* is sometimes considered an insult because it implies that Indian movies are merely "a derivative of the American film industry" (Chopra 9).

3. TWO OR THREE AUTHORS Use all the authors' last names in a signal phrase or in parentheses.

Gortner, Hebrun, and Nicolson maintain that "opinion leaders" influence other people in an organization because they are respected, not because they hold high positions (175).

4. FOUR OR MORE AUTHORS Use the first author's name and *et al.* ("and others"), or to give credit to all authors, name all the authors in a signal phrase or in parentheses.

Similarly, as Belenky et al. assert, examining the lives of women expands our understanding of human development (7).

Similarly, as Belenky, Clinchy, Tarule, and Goldberger assert, examining the lives of women expands our understanding of human development (7).

5. ORGANIZATION AS AUTHOR Give the group's full name or a shortened form of it in a signal phrase or in parentheses.

Any study of social welfare involves a close analysis of "the impacts, the benefits, and the costs" of its policies (Social Research Corporation iii).

6. UNKNOWN AUTHOR Use the full title, if it is brief, in your text—or a shortened version of the title in parentheses.

> One analysis defines *hype* as "an artificially engendered atmosphere of hysteria" ("Today's Marketplace" 51).

7. AUTHOR OF TWO OR MORE WORKS CITED IN THE SAME PROJECT If your list of works cited has more than one work by the same author, include a shortened version of the title of the work you are citing in a signal phrase or in parentheses to prevent reader confusion.

> Gardner shows readers their own silliness in his description of a "pointless, ridiculous monster, crouched in the shadows, stinking of dead men, murdered children, and martyred cows" (*Grendel* 2).

8. TWO OR MORE AUTHORS WITH THE SAME LAST NAME Include the author's first *and* last names in a signal phrase or first initial and last name in a parenthetical reference.

> Children will learn to write if they are allowed to choose their own subjects, James Britton asserts, citing the Schools Council study of the 1960s (37-42).

9. INDIRECT SOURCE (AUTHOR QUOTING SOMEONE ELSE) Use the abbreviation *qtd. in* to indicate that you are quoting from someone else's report of a source.

> As Arthur Miller says, "When somebody is destroyed everybody finally contributes to it, but in Willy's case, the end product would be virtually the same" (qtd. in Martin and Meyer 375).

10. MULTIVOLUME WORK In a parenthetical reference, note the volume number first and then the page number(s), with a colon and one space between them.

> Modernist writers prized experimentation and gradually even sought to blur the line between poetry and prose, according to Forster (3: 150).

If you name only one volume of the work in your list of works cited, include only the page number in the parentheses.

11. LITERARY WORK Because literary works are often available in many different editions, cite the page number(s) from the edition you used followed by a semicolon; then give other identifying information that will lead readers to the passage in any edition. Indicate the act and / or scene in a play (*37; sc. 1*). For a novel, indicate the part or chapter (*175; ch. 4*).

> In utter despair, Dostoyevsky's character Mitya wonders aloud about the "terrible tragedies realism inflicts on people" (376; bk. 8, ch. 2).

For a poem, cite the part (if there is one) and line(s), separated by a period. If you are citing only line numbers, use the word *line(s)* in the first reference (*lines 33-34*).

> Whitman speculates, "All goes onward and outward, nothing collapses, /
> And to die is different from what anyone supposed, and luckier" (6.129-30).

For a verse play, give only the act, scene, and line numbers, separated by periods.

> The witches greet Banquo as "Lesser than Macbeth, and greater" (1.3.65).

12. WORK IN AN ANTHOLOGY OR COLLECTION For an essay, short story, or other piece of prose reprinted in an anthology, use the name of the author of the work, not the editor of the anthology, but use the page number(s) from the anthology.

> Narratives of captivity play a major role in early writing by women in the United States, as demonstrated by Silko (219).

13. SACRED TEXT To cite a sacred text such as the Qur'an or the Bible, give the title of the edition you used, the book, and the chapter and verse (or their equivalent), separated by a period. In your text, spell out the names of books. In parenthetical references, use abbreviations for books with names of five or more letters (*Gen.* for *Genesis*).

> He ignored the admonition "Pride goes before destruction, and a haughty spirit before a fall" (*New Oxford Annotated Bible*, Prov. 16.18).

14. ENCYCLOPEDIA OR DICTIONARY ENTRY An entry from a reference work—such as an encyclopedia or dictionary—without an author will appear on the works-cited list under the entry's title. Enclose the title in quotation marks and place it in parentheses. Omit the page number for reference works that arrange entries alphabetically.

> The term *prion* was coined by Stanley B. Prusiner from the words *proteinaceous* and *infectious* and a suffix meaning *particle* ("Prion").

15. GOVERNMENT SOURCE WITH NO AUTHOR NAMED Because entries for sources authored by government agencies will appear on your list of works cited under the name of the country (see item 68, p. 397), your in-text citation for such a source should include the name of the country as well as the name of the agency responsible for the source.

> To reduce the agricultural runoff into the Chesapeake Bay, the United States Environmental Protection Agency has argued that "[h]igh nutrient loading crops, such as corn and soybean, should be replaced with alternatives in environmentally sensitive areas" (2-26).

16. ELECTRONIC OR NONPRINT SOURCE Give enough information in a signal phrase or in parentheses for readers to locate the source in your list of works cited. Many works found online or in electronic databases lack stable page numbers; you can omit the page number in such cases. However, if you are citing a work with stable pagination, such as an article in PDF format, include the page number in parentheses.

> As a *Slate* analysis has noted, "Prominent sports psychologists get praised for their successes and don't get grief for their failures" (Engber).

> The source, an article on a Web site, does not have stable pagination.

> According to Whitmarsh, the British military had experimented with using balloons for observation as far back as 1879 (328).

> The source, an online PDF of a print article, includes stable page numbers.

If the source includes numbered sections, paragraphs, or screens, include the abbreviation for section (*sec.*), paragraph (*par.*), or screen (*scr.*) and the number in parentheses.

> Sherman notes that the "immediate, interactive, and on-the-spot" nature of Internet information can make nondigital media seem outdated (sec. 32).

17. ENTIRE WORK Include the reference in the text, without any page numbers.

> Jon Krakauer's *Into the Wild* both criticizes and admires the solitary impulses of its young hero, which end up killing him.

18. TWO OR MORE SOURCES IN ONE CITATION Separate the information with semicolons.

> Economists recommend that *employment* be redefined to include unpaid domestic labor (Clark 148; Nevins 39).

Explanatory and Bibliographic Notes

MLA style recommends explanatory notes for information or commentary that would not readily fit into your text but is needed for clarification or further explanation. In addition, MLA style permits bibliographic notes for citing several sources for one point and for offering thanks to, information about, or evaluation of a source. Use superscript numbers in the text to refer readers to the notes, which may appear as endnotes (typed under the heading *Notes* on a separate page after the text but before the list of works cited) or as footnotes at the bottom of the page (typed four lines below the last text line).

SUPERSCRIPT NUMBER IN TEXT

> Stewart emphasizes the existence of social contacts in Hawthorne's life so that the audience will accept a different Hawthorne, one more attuned to modern times than the figure in Woodberry.[3]

[3] Woodberry does, however, show that Hawthorne *was* often an unsociable individual. He emphasizes the seclusion of Hawthorne's mother, who separated herself from her family after the death of her husband, often even taking meals alone (28). Woodberry seems to imply that Mrs. Hawthorne's isolation rubbed off on her son.

List of Works Cited

A list of works cited is an alphabetical list of the sources you have referred to in your essay. (If your instructor asks you to list everything you have read as background, call the list *Works Consulted*.)

- Start your list on a separate page after the text of your essay and any notes.
- Continue the consecutive numbering of pages.
- Center the heading *Works Cited* (not italicized or in quotation marks) one inch from the top of the page.
- Start each entry flush with the left margin; indent subsequent lines for the entry one-half inch. Double-space the entire list.
- List sources alphabetically by the first word. Start with the author's name, if available; if not, use the editor's name, if available. If no author or editor is given, start with the title.
- Italicize titles of books and long works, but put titles of articles and other short works in quotation marks.

Guidelines for Author Listings

The list of works cited is arranged alphabetically. The in-text citations in your writing point readers toward particular sources on the list (see p. 368).

NAME CITED IN SIGNAL PHRASE IN TEXT

Crystal explains . . . .

NAME IN PARENTHETICAL CITATION IN TEXT

. . . (Crystal 107).

BEGINNING OF ENTRY ON LIST OF WORKS CITED

Crystal, David.

Directory to MLA style for works-cited entries

1. ONE AUTHOR Put the last name first, followed by a comma, the first name (and initial, if any), and a period.

Crystal, David.

2. MULTIPLE AUTHORS List the first author with the last name first (see model 1). Give the names of any other authors with the first name first. Separate authors' names with commas, and include the word *and* before the last person's name.

Martineau, Jane, Desmond Shawe-Taylor, and Jonathan Bate.

For four or more authors, either list all the names or list the first author followed by a comma and *et al.* ("and others").

Lupton, Ellen, Jennifer Tobias, Alicia Imperiale, Grace Jeffers, and
    Randi Mates.

Lupton, Ellen, et al.

3. ORGANIZATION OR GROUP AUTHOR Give the name of the group, government agency, corporation, or other organization listed as the author.

Getty Trust.

United States. Government Accountability Office.

4. UNKNOWN AUTHOR When the author is not identified, begin the entry with the title, and alphabetize by the first important word. Italicize titles of books and long works, but put titles of articles and other short works in quotation marks.

"California Sues EPA over Emissions."

New Concise World Atlas.

5. TWO OR MORE WORKS BY THE SAME AUTHOR Arrange the entries alphabetically by title. Include the author's name in the first entry, but in subsequent entries, use three hyphens followed by a period. (For the basic format for citing a book, see model 6. For the basic format for citing an article from an online newspaper, see model 35.)

> Chopra, Anupama. "Bollywood Princess, Hollywood Hopeful." *New York Times*. New York Times, 10 Feb. 2008. Web. 13 Feb. 2008.

> ---. *King of Bollywood: Shah Rukh Khan and the Seductive World of Indian Cinema*. New York: Warner, 2007. Print.

Note: Use three hyphens only when the work is by *exactly* the same author(s) as the previous entry.

BOOKS

6. BASIC FORMAT FOR A BOOK Begin with the author name(s). (See models 1–5.) Then include the title and subtitle, the city of publication, the publisher, and the publication date. The source map on pp. 378–79 shows where to find this information in a typical book.

> Crystal, David. *Language Play*. Chicago: U of Chicago P, 1998. Print.

Note: Place a period and a space after the name, title, and date. Place a colon after the city and a comma after the publisher, and shorten the publisher's name—omit *Co.* or *Inc.*, and abbreviate *University Press* to *UP*.

7. AUTHOR AND EDITOR BOTH NAMED

> Bangs, Lester. *Psychotic Reactions and Carburetor Dung*. Ed. Greil Marcus. New York: Knopf, 1988. Print.

Note: To cite the editor's contribution instead, begin the entry with the editor's name.

> Marcus, Greil, ed. *Psychotic Reactions and Carburetor Dung*. By Lester Bangs. New York: Knopf, 1988. Print.

8. EDITOR, NO AUTHOR NAMED

> Wall, Cheryl A., ed. *Changing Our Own Words: Essays on Criticism, Theory, and Writing by Black Women*. New Brunswick: Rutgers UP, 1989. Print.

9. ANTHOLOGY Cite an entire anthology the same way you would cite a book with an editor and no named author (see model 8).

> Walker, Dale L., ed. *Westward: A Fictional History of the American West*. New York: Forge, 2003. Print.

10. WORK IN AN ANTHOLOGY OR CHAPTER IN A BOOK WITH AN EDITOR List the author(s) of the selection or chapter; its title, in quotation marks; the title of the book, italicized; *Ed.* and the name(s) of the editor(s); publication information; and the selection's page numbers.

> Komunyakaa, Yusef. "Facing It." *The Seagull Reader*. Ed. Joseph Kelly. New York: Norton, 2000. 126-27. Print.

For a reprinted selection, add original publication information after the title.

> Byatt, A. S. "The Thing in the Forest." *New Yorker* 3 June 2002: 80-89. Rpt. in *The O. Henry Prize Stories 2003*. Ed. Laura Furman. New York: Anchor, 2003. 3-22. Print.

11. TWO OR MORE ITEMS FROM THE SAME ANTHOLOGY List the anthology as one entry (see model 9). Also list each selection separately with a cross-reference to the anthology.

> Salzer, Susan K. "Miss Libbie Tells All." Walker 199-212. Print.

12. TRANSLATION

> Bolaño, Roberto. *2666*. Trans. Natasha Wimmer. New York: Farrar, 2008. Print.

13. BOOK WITH BOTH TRANSLATOR AND EDITOR List the editor's and translator's names after the title, in the order they appear on the title page.

> Kant, Immanuel. *"Toward Perpetual Peace" and Other Writings on Politics, Peace, and History*. Ed. Pauline Kleingeld. Trans. David L. Colclasure. New Haven: Yale UP, 2006. Print.

14. BOOK IN A LANGUAGE OTHER THAN ENGLISH Include a translation of the title in brackets, if necessary.

> Bendetti, Mario. *La borra del café [The Coffee Grind]*. Buenos Aires: Sudamericana, 2000. Print.

15. GRAPHIC NARRATIVE If the words and images are created by the same person, cite a graphic narrative just as you would a book (model 6).

> Bechdel, Alison. *Fun Home: A Family Tragicomic*. New York: Houghton, 2006. Print.

For a collaboration, list the author or illustrator who is most important to your research before the title, and list other contributors after the title; label each person's contribution.

> Stavans, Ilan, writer. *Latino USA: A Cartoon History*. Illus. Lalo Arcaraz. New York: Basic, 2000. Print.

MLA SOURCE MAP: Books

Take information from the book's title page and copyright page (on the reverse side of the title page), not from the book's cover or a library catalog.

(1) Author. List the last name first. End with a period. For variations, see models 2–5.

(2) Title. Italicize the title and any subtitle; capitalize all major words. End with a period.

(3) City of publication. If more than one city is given, use the first one listed. For foreign cities, add an abbreviation of the country or province (*Cork, Ire.*). Follow it with a colon.

(4) Publisher. Give a shortened version of the publisher's name (*Oxford UP* for *Oxford University Press*). Follow it with a comma.

(5) Year of publication. If more than one copyright date is given, use the most recent one. End with a period.

(6) Medium of publication. End with the medium (*Print*) followed by a period.

A citation for the work on p. 379 would look like this:

```
        1                              2
┌───┴───┐ ┌─────────────────────────┴──────────────────────┐
```

Patel, Raj. *The Value of Nothing: How to Reshape Market Society and Redefine*

```
                3        4       5       6
        ┌───────┴──┐ ┌───┴──┐ ┌──┴──┐ ┌──┴──┐
```
Democracy. New York: Picador, 2009. Print.

THE VALUE OF NOTHING

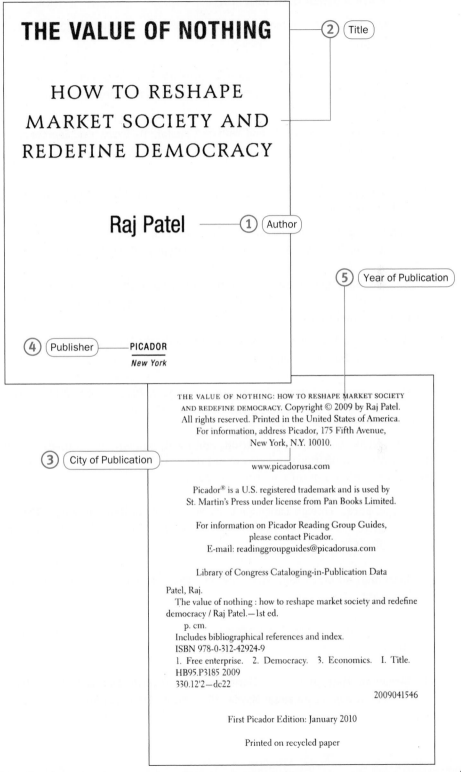

② Title

HOW TO RESHAPE MARKET SOCIETY AND REDEFINE DEMOCRACY

Raj Patel ① Author

⑤ Year of Publication

④ Publisher **PICADOR**
New York

③ City of Publication

THE VALUE OF NOTHING: HOW TO RESHAPE MARKET SOCIETY AND REDEFINE DEMOCRACY. Copyright © 2009 by Raj Patel. All rights reserved. Printed in the United States of America. For information, address Picador, 175 Fifth Avenue, New York, N.Y. 10010.

www.picadorusa.com

Picador® is a U.S. registered trademark and is used by St. Martin's Press under license from Pan Books Limited.

For information on Picador Reading Group Guides, please contact Picador.
E-mail: readinggroupguides@picadorusa.com

Library of Congress Cataloging-in-Publication Data

Patel, Raj.
   The value of nothing : how to reshape market society and redefine democracy / Raj Patel.—1st ed.
      p. cm.
   Includes bibliographical references and index.
   ISBN 978-0-312-42924-9
   1. Free enterprise.   2. Democracy.   3. Economics.   I. Title.
   HB95.P3185 2009
   330.12'2—dc22

                                          2009041546

First Picador Edition: January 2010

Printed on recycled paper

16. EDITION OTHER THAN THE FIRST

Walker, John A. *Art in the Age of Mass Media*. 3rd ed. London: Pluto, 2001. Print.

17. MULTIVOLUME WORK

If you cite only one volume, give the number of the volume cited after the title. Including the total number of volumes after the medium is optional.

Ch'oe, Yong-Ho, Peter Lee, and William Theodore De Barry, eds. *Sources of Korean Tradition*. Vol. 2. New York: Columbia UP, 2000. Print. 2 vols.

If you cite two or more volumes, give the number of volumes in the complete work after the title.

Ch'oe, Yong-Ho, Peter Lee, and William Theodore De Barry, eds. *Sources of Korean Tradition*. 2 vols. New York: Columbia UP, 2000. Print.

18. PREFACE, FOREWORD, INTRODUCTION, OR AFTERWORD

After the writer's name, describe the contribution. After the title, indicate the book's author (with *By*) or editor (with *Ed.*).

Atwan, Robert. Foreword. *The Best American Essays 2002*. Ed. Stephen Jay Gould. Boston: Houghton, 2002. viii-xii. Print.

Moore, Thurston. Introduction. *Confusion Is Next: The Sonic Youth Story*. By Alec Foege. New York: St. Martin's, 1994. xi. Print.

19. ENTRY IN A REFERENCE BOOK

For a well-known encyclopedia, note the edition (if identified) and year of publication. If the entries are alphabetized, omit publication information and page number.

Judge, Erica. "Foreign-Language Daily Newspapers in New York City." *The Encyclopedia of New York City*. Ed. Kenneth T. Jackson. New Haven: Yale UP, 1995.

Kettering, Alison McNeil. "Art Nouveau." *World Book Encyclopedia*. 2002 ed. Print.

20. BOOK THAT IS PART OF A SERIES

Cite the series name (and number, if any) from the title page.

Nichanian, Marc, and Vartan Matiossian, eds. *Yeghishe Charents: Poet of the Revolution*. Costa Mesa: Mazda, 2003. Print. Armenian Studies Ser. 5.

21. REPUBLICATION (MODERN EDITION OF AN OLDER BOOK) Indicate the original publication date after the title.

> Austen, Jane. *Sense and Sensibility*. 1813. New York: Dover, 1966. Print.

22. PUBLISHER'S IMPRINT If the title page gives a publisher's imprint, hyphenate the imprint and the publisher's name.

> Hornby, Nick. *About a Boy*. New York: Riverhead-Penguin Putnam, 1998. Print.

23. BOOK WITH A TITLE WITHIN THE TITLE Do not italicize a book title within a title. For an article title within a title, italicize as usual and place the article title in quotation marks.

> Mullaney, Julie. *Arundhati Roy's* The God of Small Things: *A Reader's Guide*. New York: Continuum, 2002. Print.

> Rhynes, Martha. *"I, Too, Sing America": The Story of Langston Hughes*. Greensboro: Morgan, 2002. Print.

24. SACRED TEXT To cite individual published editions of sacred books, begin the entry with the title. If you are not citing a particular edition, do not include sacred texts in the list of works cited.

> *Qur'an: The Final Testament (Authorized English Version) with Arabic Text*. Trans. Rashad Khalifa. Fremont: Universal Unity, 2000. Print.

PRINT PERIODICALS

Begin with the author name(s). (See models 1–5.) Then include the article title, the title of the periodical, the date or volume information, and the page numbers. The source map on pp. 382–84 shows where to find this information in a sample periodical.

25. ARTICLE IN A JOURNAL Follow the journal title with the volume number, a period, the issue number (if given), and the year (in parentheses).

> Gigante, Denise. "The Monster in the Rainbow: Keats and the Science of Life." *PMLA* 117.3 (2002): 433-48. Print.

26. ARTICLE IN A MAGAZINE Provide the date from the magazine cover instead of volume or issue numbers.

> Surowiecki, James. "The Stimulus Strategy." *New Yorker* 25 Feb. 2008: 29. Print.

> Taubin, Amy. "All Talk?" *Film Comment* Nov.-Dec. 2007: 45-47. Print.

MLA SOURCE MAP: Articles in print periodicals

(1) **Author.** List the last name first. End with a period. For variations, see models 2–5.

(2) **Article title.** Put the title and any subtitle in quotation marks; capitalize all major words. Place a period inside the closing quotation mark.

(3) **Periodical title.** Italicize the title; capitalize all major words. Omit any initial *A*, *An*, or *The*.

(4) **Volume and issue / Date of publication.** For journals, give the volume number and issue number (if any), separated by a period; then list the year in parentheses and follow it with a colon. For magazines, list the day (if given), month, and year.

(5) **Page numbers.** List inclusive page numbers. If the article skips pages, put the first page number and a plus sign. End with a period.

(6) **Medium.** Give the medium (*Print*). End with a period.

A citation for the journal article on p. 383 would look like this:

>   1   2   3   4
>
> Marcoplos, Lucas. "Drafting Away from It All." *Southern Cultures* 12.1 (2006):
>
>   5   6
>
> 33-41. Print.

A citation for the magazine article on p. 384 would look like this:

>   1   2
>
> Quart, Alissa. "Lost Media, Found Media: Snapshots from the Future of Writing."
>
>   3   4   5   6
>
> *Columbia Journalism Review* May/June 2008: 30-34. Print.

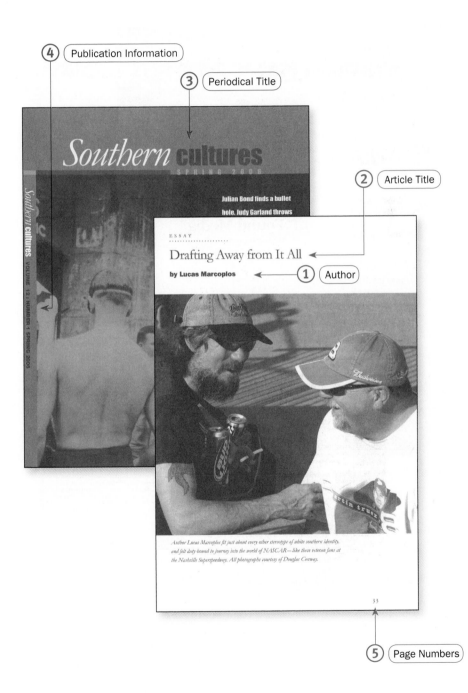

4 Publication Information

3 Periodical Title

Southern **cultures**

SPRING 2006

Julian Bond finds a bullet hole, Judy Garland throws

Southern **cultures** VOLUME 12, NUMBER 1 SPRING 2006

2 Article Title

ESSAY

Drafting Away from It All

by Lucas Marcoplos ◄ **1** Author

Author Lucas Marcoplos fit just about every other stereotype of white southern identity, and felt duty-bound to journey into the world of NASCAR—like these veteran fans at the Nashville Superspeedway. All photographs courtesy of Douglas Conway.

33

5 Page Numbers

(4) Date of Publication

COLUMBIA JOURNALISM REVIEW

May / June 2008 • cjr.org

(3) Periodical Title

The Futur...

Writin...

Nonfiction's disqui...
ALISSA QUART

Kindle isn't it, but...
EZRA KLEIN

UNDER THE SHI...

A reporter recalls...
that got him throu...
CAMERON MCWHIRT...

LOVE THY NEIG...

The religion beat i...
TIM TOWNSEND

(2) Article Title

Lost Media, Found Media

Snapshots from the future of writing

BY ALISSA QUART

(1) Author

If there were an ashram for people who worship contemplative long-form journalism, it would be the Nieman Conference on Narrative Journalism. This March, at the Sheraton Boston Hotel, hundreds of journalists, authors, students, and aspirants came for the weekend event. Seated on metal chairs in large conference rooms, we learned about muscular storytelling (the Q-shaped narrative structure—who knew?). We sipped cups of coffee and ate bagels and heard about reporting history through letters and public documents and how to evoke empathy for our subjects, particularly our most marginal ones. As we listened to reporters discussing great feats—exposing Walter Reed's fetid living quarters for wounded soldiers, for instance—we also renewed our pride in our profession. In short, the conference exemplified the best of the older media models, the ones that have so recently fallen into economic turmoil.

Yet even at the weekend's strongest lectures on interview techniques or the long-form profile, we couldn't ignore the digital elephant in the room. We all knew as writers that the kinds of pieces we were discussing require months of work to be both deep and refined, and that we were all hard-pressed for the time and the money to do that. It was always hard for nonfiction writers, but something seems to have changed. For those of us who believed in the value of the journalism and literary nonfiction of the past, we had

become like the people at the ashram after the guru has died.

Right now, journalism is more or less divided into two camps, which I will call Lost Media and Found Media. I went to the Nieman conference partially because I wanted to see how the forces creating this new division are affecting and afflicting the Lost Media world that I love best, not on the institutional level, but for reporters and writers themselves. This world includes people who write for all the newspapers and magazines that are currently struggling with layoffs, speedups, hiring freezes, buyouts, the death or shrinkage of film- and book-review sections, limits on expensive investigative work, the erasure of foreign bureaus, and the general narrowing of institutional ambition. It includes freelance writers competing with hordes of ever-younger competitors willing to write and publish online for free, the fade-out of established journalistic career paths, and, perhaps most crucially, a muddled sense of the meritorious, as blogs level and scramble the value and status of print publications, and of professional writers. The glamour and influence once associated with a magazine elite seem to have faded, becoming a sort of pastiche of winsome articles about yearning and boxers and dinners at Elaine's.

Found Media-ites, meanwhile, are the bloggers, the contributors to Huffington Post-type sites that aggregate blogs, as well as other work that somebody else paid for, and the new non-profits and pay-per-article schemes that aim to save journalism from 20 percent profit-margin demands. Although these elements are often disparate, together they compose the new media landscape. In economic terms, I mean all the outlets for nonfiction writing that seem to be thriving in the new era or striving to fill niches that Lost Media is giving up in a new order. Stylistically, Found Media tends to feel spontaneous, almost accidental. It's a domain dominated by the young, where writers get points not for following traditions or burnishing them but for amateur and hybrid vigor, for creating their own venues and their own genres. It is about public expression and community—not quite John Dewey's Great Community, which the critic Eric Alterman alluded to in a recent *New Yorker* article on newspapers, but rather a fractured form of Dewey's ideal: call it Great Communities.

To be a Found Media journalist or pundit, one need not be elite, expert, or trained; one must simply produce punchy intellectual property that is in conversation with groups of

Illustration by Tomer Hanuka

(5) Page Numbers

27. ARTICLE IN A NEWSPAPER Include the edition (if listed) and the section number or letter (if listed).

> Bernstein, Nina. "On Lucille Avenue, the Immigration Debate." *New York Times* 26 June 2006, late ed.: A1+. Print.

Add the city in brackets if it is not part of the name: *Globe and Mail [Toronto]*.

28. ARTICLE THAT SKIPS PAGES When an article skips pages, give only the first page number and a plus sign.

> Tyrnauer, Matthew. "Empire by Martha." *Vanity Fair* Sept. 2002: 364+. Print.

29. EDITORIAL OR LETTER TO THE EDITOR Include the writer's name, if given, and the title, if any, followed by a label for the work.

> "California Dreaming" Editorial. *Nation* 25 Feb. 2008: 4. Print.

> Galbraith, James K. "JFK's Plans to Withdraw." Letter. *New York Review of Books* 6 Dec. 2007: 77-78. Print.

30. REVIEW

> Franklin, Nancy. "Teen Spirit." Rev. of *Glee*, by Ryan Murphy, Brad Falchuk, and Ian Brennan. *New Yorker* 10 May 2010: 72-73. Print.

> Schwarz, Benjamin. Rev. of *The Second World War: A Short History*, by R. A. C. Parker. *Atlantic Monthly* May 2002: 110-11. Print.

31. UNSIGNED ARTICLE

> "Performance of the Week." *Time* 6 Oct. 2003: 18. Print.

ELECTRONIC SOURCES

Electronic sources such as Web sites differ from print sources in the ease — and frequency — with which they are changed. In addition, the various electronic media do not organize their works the same way. The most commonly cited electronic sources are documents from Web sites and databases.

32. WORK FROM A DATABASE The basic format for citing a work from a database appears in the source map on pp. 386–87.

For a periodical article that you access in an online database, including a work you find in a library subscription service such as Academic Search Premier, use the model for a print periodical (see models 25–31). Include the page numbers from the print version; if no page numbers are available, use *n. pag.* Then give the name of the online database, italicized; the medium (*Web*); and your most recent date of access.

> Collins, Ross F. "Cattle Barons and Ink Slingers: How Cow Country Journalists Created a Great American Myth." *American Journalism* 24.3 (2007): 7-29. *Communication and Mass Media Complete*. Web. 7 Feb. 2010.

MLA SOURCE MAP: Articles from databases

Library subscriptions—such as EBSCOhost and Academic Search Premier—provide access to huge databases of articles.

(1) **Author.** List the last name first. End with a period. For variations, see models 2–5.

(2) **Article title.** Enclose the title and any subtitle in quotation marks.

(3) **Periodical title.** Italicize it. Exclude any initial *A*, *An*, or *The*.

(4) **Print publication information.** List the volume and issue number, if any; the date of publication, including the day (if given), month, and year, in that order; and the inclusive page numbers. If an article has no page numbers, write *n. pag.*

(5) **Database name.** Italicize the name of the database.

(6) **Medium.** For an online database, use *Web*.

(7) **Date of access.** Give the day, month, and year, then a period.

A citation for the work on p. 387 would look like this:

      1   *2*

Arnett, Robert P. "*Casino Royale* and Franchise Remix: James Bond as

                    3   *4*   *5*

Superhero." *Film Criticism* 33.3 (2009): 1-16. *Academic Search Premier*.

      6   *7*

Web. 16 May 2010.

Title:	**Casino Royale and Franchise Remix: James Bond as Superhero.**
Authors:	Arnett, Robert P.1
Source:	Film Criticism; Spring2009, Vol. 33 Issue 3, p1-16, 16p
Document Type:	Article
Subject Terms:	*JAMES Bond films *FILM genres *BOND, James (Fictitious character) *SUPERHERO films
Reviews & Products:	CASINO Royale (Film)
People:	CRAIG, Daniel
Abstract:	The article discusses the role of the film "Casino Royale" in remixing the James Bond franchise. The author believes that the remixed Bond franchise has shifted its genre to a superhero franchise. When Sony acquired MGM in 2004, part of its plans is to transform the 007 franchise at par with "Spiderman." The remixed franchise re-aligns its franchise criteria with those established by superhero films. The author cites "Casino Royale's" narrative structure as an example of the success of the film as franchise remixed for the future. The portrayal of Bond as a superhero by actor Daniel Craig is discussed.
Author Affiliations:	1Associate professor, Department of Communication and Theatre Arts, Old Dominion University
ISSN:	01635069
Accession Number:	47966995
Database:	Academic Search Premier

Callouts:
- ③ Periodical Title
- ② Article Title
- ① Author
- ④ Print Publication Information
- ⑤ Database Name

387

33. ARTICLE IN AN ONLINE JOURNAL Cite an online journal article as you would a print journal article (see model 25). If an online article does not have page numbers, use *n. pag.* End with the medium consulted (*Web*) and the date of access.

> Gallagher, Brian. "Greta Garbo Is Sad: Some Historical Reflections on the
>   Paradoxes of Stardom in the American Film Industry, 1910-1960."
>   *Images: A Journal of Film and Popular Culture* 3 (1997): n. pag. Web.
>   7 Aug. 2009.

34. ARTICLE IN AN ONLINE MAGAZINE See model 26 for print publication information if the article also appears in print. After the name of the magazine, give the sponsor of the Web site, followed by a comma and the date of publication. Then give the medium (*Web*) and the date of access.

> Shapiro, Walter. "The Quest for Universal Healthcare." *Salon.* Salon Media
>   Group, 21 Feb. 2008. Web. 2 Mar. 2008.

35. ARTICLE IN AN ONLINE NEWSPAPER After the name of the newspaper, give the publisher, publication date, medium (*Web*), and access date.

> Bustillo, Miguel, and Carol J. Williams. "Old Guard in Cuba Keeps Reins." *Los
>   Angeles Times.* Los Angeles Times, 25 Feb. 2008. Web. 26 Feb. 2010.

36. ONLINE BOOK Provide information as for a print book (see models 6–24); then give the electronic publication information, the medium, and the date of access.

> Euripides. *The Trojan Women.* Trans. Gilbert Murray. New York: Oxford UP,
>   1915. *Internet Sacred Text Archive.* Web. 12 Oct. 2010.

Note: Cite a part of an online book as you would a part of a print book (see models 10 and 18). Give the print (if any) and electronic publication information, the medium (*Web*), and the date of access.

> Riis, Jacob. "The Genesis of the Gang." *The Battle with the Slum.* New York:
>   Macmillan, 1902. *Bartleby.com: Great Books Online.* 2000. Web. 31 Mar.
>   2010.

37. ONLINE POEM Include the poet's name, the title of the poem, and the print publication information (if any). End with electronic publication information, the medium (*Web*), and the date of access.

> Dickinson, Emily. "The Grass." *Poems: Emily Dickinson.* Boston, 1891.
>   *University of Michigan Humanities Text Initiative: American Verse
>   Project.* Web. 6 Jan. 2010.

38. ONLINE EDITORIAL OR LETTER Include the word *Editorial* or *Letter* after the author (if given) and title (if any). End with the periodical name, the sponsor of the Web site, the date of electronic publication, the medium, and the access date.

> "The Funding Gap." Editorial. *Washington Post.* Washington Post, 5 Nov. 2003. Web. 19 Oct. 2009.

> Moore, Paula. "Go Vegetarian." Letter. *New York Times.* New York Times, 25 Feb. 2008. Web. 25 Feb. 2010.

39. ONLINE REVIEW Cite an online review as you would a print review (see model 30). End with the name of the Web site, the sponsor, the date of electronic publication, the medium, and the date of access.

> O'Hehir, Andrew. "Parody or Party?" Rev. of *Iron Man 2,* dir. Jon Favreau. *Salon.* Salon Media Group, 7 May 2010. Web. 24 May 2010.

40. ENTRY IN AN ONLINE REFERENCE WORK Cite the entry as you would an entry from a print reference work (see model 19). Follow with the name of the Web site, the sponsor, date of publication, medium, and date of access.

> "Tour de France." *Encyclopaedia Britannica Online.* Encyclopaedia Britannica, 2006. Web. 21 May 2006.

41. WORK FROM A WEB SITE For basic information on citing a work from a Web site, see the source map on pp. 390–91. Include all the following elements that are available: the author; the title of the document, in quotation marks; the name of the Web site, italicized; the name of the publisher or sponsor (if none is available, use *N.p.*); the date of publication (if not available, use *n.d.*); the medium consulted (*Web*); and the date of access.

> "America: A Center-Left Nation." *Media Matters for America.* Media Matters for America, 27 May 2009. Web. 31 May 2009.

> Stauder, Ellen Keck. "Darkness Audible: Negative Capability and Mark Doty's 'Nocturne in Black and Gold.'" *Romantic Circles Praxis Series.* U of Maryland, 2003. Web. 28 Sept. 2003.

42. ENTIRE WEB SITE Follow the guidelines for a specific work from the Web, beginning with the name of the author, editor, compiler, or director (if any), followed by the title of the Web site, italicized; the name of the sponsor or publisher (if none, use *N.p.*); the date of publication or last update; the medium of publication (*Web*); and the date of access.

> Bernstein, Charles, Kenneth Goldsmith, Martin Spinelli, and Patrick Durgin, eds. *Electronic Poetry Corner.* SUNY Buffalo, 2003. Web. 26 Sept. 2006.

> *Weather.com.* Weather Channel Interactive, 2010. Web. 13 Mar. 2010.

MLA SOURCE MAP: Works from Web sites

You may need to browse other parts of a site to find some of the following elements, and some sites may omit elements. Uncover as much information as you can.

(1) **Author.** List the last name first. End with a period. For variations, see models 2–5. If no author is given, begin with the title.

(2) **Title of work.** Enclose the title and any subtitle of the work in quotation marks.

(3) **Title of Web site.** Give the title of the entire Web site, italicized.

(4) **Publisher or sponsor.** Look for the sponsor's name at the bottom of the homepage. If no information is available, write *N.p.* Follow it with a comma.

(5) **Date of publication or latest update.** Give the most recent date, followed by a period. If no date is available, use *n.d.*

(6) **Medium.** Use *Web* and follow it with a period.

(7) **Date of access.** Give the date you accessed the work. End with a period.

A citation for the work on p. 391 would look like this:

```
           1                        2                              3
Tdnnesson, Øyvind.  "Mahatma Gandhi, the Missing Laureate."  Nobelprize.org.

        4              5       6       7
Nobel Foundation,  1 Dec. 1999.  Web.  4 May 2005.
```

1 Author

2 Title of Work

3 Title of Web Site

5 Date of Publication

4 Publisher/Sponsor

Nobelprize.org

NOBEL PRIZES   ALFRED NOBEL   PRIZE AWARDERS   NOMINATION   PRIZE ANNOUNCEMENTS   AWARD CEREMONIES   EDUCATIONAL GAMES

By Year   Nobel Prize in Physics   Nobel Prize in Chemistry   Nobel Prize in Medicine   Nobel Prize in Literature   Nobel Peace Prize   Prize in Economics

Mahatma Gandhi, the Missing Laureate

by Øyvind Tønnesson
Nobelprize.org Peace Editor, 1998–2000
1 December 1999

Mohandas Gandhi (1869–1948) has become the strongest symbol of non-violence in the 20th century. It is widely held – in retrospect – that the Indian national leader should have been the very man to be selected for the Nobel Peace Prize. He was nominated several times, but was never awarded the prize. Why?

These questions have been asked frequently: Was the horizon of the Norwegian Nobel Committee too narrow? Were the committee members unable to appreciate the struggle for freedom among non-European peoples?" Or were the Norwegian committee members perhaps afraid to make a prize award which might be detrimental to the relationship between their own country and Great Britain?

1/6 Gandhi Centenary Year 1969

When still alive, Mohandas Gandhi had many admirers, both in India and abroad. But his martyrdom in 1948 made him an even greater symbol of peace. Twenty-one years later, he was commemorated on this double-sized United Kingdom postage stamp.
Photo: Copyright © Scanpix

Gandhi was nominated in 1937, 1938, 1939, 1947 and, finally, a few days before he was murdered in January 1948. The omission has been publicly regretted by later members of the Nobel Committee; when the Dalai Lama was awarded the Peace Prize in 1989, the chairman of the committee said that this was "in part a tribute to the memory of

Printer Friendly
Comments & Questions
Tell a Friend

The Nobel Peace Prize

All Nobel Peace Prize Laureates

Articles

Nobel Peace Prize Awarded Organizations

Nobel Prize Medal

Nobel Prize Amount

Video Interviews

Video Nobel Lectures

Media Player

Documentary about Muhammad Yunus

All Nobel Peace Prize Laureates

Listen to Peace Prize Laureates

Find Nobel Laureates by year

Try the Nobel Prize Quiz!

Sign up for News from Nobelprize.org

The Peace Doves

Why Was Gandhi Never Awarded the Nobel Peace Prize?

Up to 1960, the Nobel Peace Prize was awarded almost exclusively to Europeans and Americans. In retrospect, the horizon of the Norwegian Nobel Committee may seem too narrow. Gandhi was very different from earlier Laureates. He was no real politician or proponent of international law, not primarily a humanitarian relief worker and not an organiser of international peace congresses. He would have belonged to a new breed of Laureates.

There is no hint in the archives that the Norwegian Nobel Committee ever took into consideration the possibility of an adverse British reaction to an award to Gandhi. Thus it seems that the hypothesis that the Committee's omission of Gandhi was due to its members' not wanting to provoke British authorities, may be rejected.

In 1947 the conflict between India and Pakistan and Gandhi's prayer-meeting statement, which made people wonder whether he was about to abandon his consistent pacifism, seem to have been the primary reasons why he was not selected by the committee's majority. Unlike the situation today, there was no tradition for the Norwegian Nobel Committee to try to use the Peace Prize as a stimulus for peaceful settlement of regional conflicts.

During the last months of his life, Gandhi worked hard to end the violence between Hindus and Muslims which followed the partition of India. We know little about the Norwegian Nobel Committee's discussions on Gandhi's candidature in 1948 – other than the above quoted entry of November 18 in Gunnar Jahn's diary – but it seems clear that they seriously considered a posthumous award. When the committee, for formal reasons, ended up not making such an award, they decided to reserve the prize, and then, one year later, not to spend the prize money for 1948 at all. What many thought should have been Mahatma Gandhi's place on the list of Laureates was silently but respectfully left open.

About Nobelprize.org   Privacy Policy   Terms of Use   Technical Support   RSS   The Official Web Site of the Nobel Foundation   Copyright ©

For a personal Web site, include the name of the person who created the site; the title, in quotation marks if it is part of a larger work or italicized if it is not, or (if there is no title) a description such as *Homepage*, not italicized; the name of the larger site, if different from the personal site's title; the publisher or sponsor of the site (if none, use *N.p.*); the date of the last update; the medium of publication (*Web*); and the date of access.

> Ede, Lisa. Homepage. *Oregon State*. Oregon State U, 2010. Web. 17 May 2010.

43. ACADEMIC COURSE WEB SITE For a course site, include the name of the instructor, the title of the course in quotation marks, the title of the site in italics, the department (if relevant) and institution sponsoring the site, the medium consulted (*Web*), and the access information.

> Creekmur, Corey K., and Philip Lutgendorf. "Topics in Asian Cinema: Popular Hindi Cinema." *University of Iowa*. Depts. of English, Cinema, and Comparative Literature, U of Iowa. Web. 13 Mar. 2007.

For a department Web site, give the department name, the description *Dept. homepage*, the institution (in italics), the site sponsor, the date of publication (if not available, use *n.d.*), the medium (*Web*), and the access information.

> English Dept. homepage. *Amherst College*. Amherst Coll., n.d. Web. 5 Apr. 2010.

44. BLOG (WEB LOG) For an entire blog, give the author's name; the title of the blog, italicized; the sponsor or publisher of the blog (if there is none, use *N.p.*); the date of the most recent update; the medium (*Web*); and the date of access.

> *Little Green Footballs*. Little Green Footballs. 5 Mar. 2010. Web. 5 Mar. 2010.

Note: To cite a blogger who writes under a pseudonym, begin with the pseudonym and then put the writer's real name (if you know it) in square brackets.

> Atrios [Duncan Black]. *Eschaton*. N.p., 27 June 2010. Web. 27 June 2010.

45. POST OR COMMENT ON A BLOG Give the author's name; the title of the post or comment, in quotation marks (if there is no title, use the description *Web log post* or *Web log comment*, not italicized); the title of the blog, italicized; the sponsor of the blog (if there is none, use *N.p.*); the date of the most recent update; the medium (*Web*); and the date of access.

> Marcotte, Amanda. "Rights without Perfection." *Pandagon*. N.p., 16 May 2010. Web. 16 May 2010.

46. ENTRY IN A WIKI Because wiki content is collectively edited, do not include an author. Treat a wiki as you would a work from a Web site (see model 41). Include the title of the entry; the name of the wiki, italicized; the sponsor or publisher of the wiki (use *N.p.* if there is no sponsor); the date of the latest update; the medium (*Web*); and the date of access. Check with your instructor before using a wiki as a source.

"Fédération Internationale de Football Association." *Wikimedia.* Wikimedia
Foundation, 27 June 2010. Web. 27 June 2010.

47. POSTING TO A DISCUSSION GROUP OR NEWSGROUP Begin with the author's name and the title of the posting in quotation marks (or the words *Online posting*). Follow with the name of the Web site, the sponsor or publisher of the site (use *N.p.* if there is no sponsor), the date of publication, the medium (*Web*), and the date of access.

Daly, Catherine. "Poetry Slams." *Poetics Discussion List.* SUNY Buffalo,
29 Aug. 2003. Web. 1 Oct. 2003.

48. POSTING OR MESSAGE ON A SOCIAL-NETWORKING SITE To cite a message or posting on Facebook or another social-networking site, include the writer's name, a description of the posting that mentions the recipient, the date it was written, and the medium of delivery. (The MLA does not provide guidelines for citing postings or messages on such sites; this model is based on the MLA's guidelines for citing email.)

Ferguson, Sarah. Message to the author. 6 Mar. 2008. Facebook message.

49. EMAIL Include the writer's name; the subject line, in quotation marks; *Message to* (not italicized or in quotation marks) followed by the recipient's name; the date of the message; and the medium of delivery (*E-mail*). (MLA style hyphenates *e-mail*.)

Harris, Jay. "Thoughts on Impromptu Stage Productions." Message to the
author. 16 July 2006. E-mail.

50. COMPUTER SOFTWARE OR ONLINE GAME Include the author name (if given); the title, italicized; the version number (if given); the publisher or sponsor; and the publication date (or *n.d.* if no date is given). End with the medium and the date of access.

Web Cache Illuminator. Vers. 4.02. NorthStar Solutions, n.d. Web. 12 Nov.
2003.

51. CD-ROM OR DVD-ROM Include the medium.

Cambridge Advanced Learner's Dictionary. 3rd ed. Cambridge: Cambridge UP,
2008. CD-ROM.

Grand Theft Auto: San Andreas. New York: Rockstar Games, 2004. DVD-ROM.

52. FILM OR DVD If you cite a particular person's work, start with that name. If not, start with the title; then name the director, distributor, and year of release. Other contributors, such as writers or performers, may follow the director. If you cite a DVD instead of a theatrical release, include the original film release date and the label *DVD*. For material found on a Web site, give the name of the site or database, the medium (*Web*), and the access date.

> *Spirited Away*. Dir. Hayao Miyazaki. 2001. Walt Disney Video, 2003. DVD.

> *Inception*. Dir. Christopher Nolan. Perf. Leonardo DiCaprio. Warner
> Brothers, 2010. Film.

53. ONLINE VIDEO CLIP Cite an online video as you would a work from a Web site (see model 41).

> Weber, Jan. "As We Sow, Part 1: Where Are the Farmers?" *YouTube*.
> YouTube, 15 Mar. 2008. Web. 27 Sept. 2010.

54. TELEVISION OR RADIO PROGRAM In general, begin with the title of the program, italicized. Then list important contributors (narrator, writer, director, actors); the network; the local station and city, if any; the broadcast date; and the medium. To cite a particular person's work, begin with that name. To cite a particular episode from a series, begin with the episode title, in quotation marks.

> *The American Experience: Buffalo Bill*. Writ., dir., prod. Rob Rapley. PBS.
> WNET, New York, 25 Feb. 2008. Television.

> "The Fleshy Part of the Thigh." *The Sopranos*. Writ. Diane Frolov and Andrew
> Schneider. Dir. Alan Taylor. HBO, 2 Apr. 2006. Television.

Note: For a streaming version online, give the name of the Web site, italicized. Then give the publisher or sponsor, a comma, and the date posted. End with the medium (*Web*) and the access date. (For downloaded versions, see models 61–62.)

> Komando, Kim. "E-mail Hacking and the Law." *CBSRadio.com*. CBS Radio,
> Inc., 28 Oct. 2003. Web. 11 Nov. 2003.

55. BROADCAST INTERVIEW List the person interviewed and then the title, if any. If the interview has no title, use the label *Interview* and name the interviewer, if relevant. Then identify the source. To cite a broadcast interview, end with information about the program, the date(s) the interview took place, and the medium.

> Revkin, Andrew. Interview by Terry Gross. *Fresh Air*. Natl. Public Radio.
> WNYC, New York, 14 June 2006. Radio.

Note: If you found an archived version online, provide the site's sponsor (if known), the date of the interview, the medium (*Web*), and the access date. For a podcast interview, see model 61.

> Revkin, Andrew. Interview by Terry Gross. *Fresh Air. NPR.org*. NPR, 14 June 2006. Web. 12 Jan. 2009.

56. UNPUBLISHED OR PERSONAL INTERVIEW List the person interviewed; the label *Telephone interview, Personal interview,* or *E-mail interview*; and the date the interview took place.

> Freedman, Sasha. Personal interview. 10 Nov. 2010.

57. SOUND RECORDING List the name of the person or group you wish to emphasize (such as the composer, conductor, or band); the title of the recording or composition; the artist, if appropriate; the manufacturer; and the year of issue. Give the medium (such as *CD, MP3 file*, or *LP*). If you are citing a particular song or selection, include its title, in quotation marks, before the title of the recording.

> Bach, Johann Sebastian. *Bach: Violin Concertos.* Perf. Itzhak Perlman and Pinchas Zukerman. English Chamber Orchestra. EMI, 2002. CD.

> Sonic Youth. "Incinerate." *Rather Ripped*. Geffen, 2006. MP3 file.

Note: If you are citing instrumental music that is identified only by form, number, and key, do not underline, italicize, or enclose it in quotation marks.

> Grieg, Edvard. Concerto in A minor, op. 16. Cond. Eugene Ormandy. Philadelphia Orch. RCA, 1989. LP.

58. MUSICAL COMPOSITION When you are not citing a specific published version, first give the composer's name, followed by the title.

> Mozart, Wolfgang Amadeus. *Don Giovanni,* K527.

> Mozart, Wolfgang Amadeus. Symphony no. 41 in C major, K551.

Note: Cite a published score as you would a book. If you include the date the composition was written, do so immediately after the title.

> Schoenberg, Arnold. *Chamber Symphony No. 1 for 15 Solo Instruments, Op. 9.* 1906. New York: Dover, 2002. Print.

59. LECTURE OR SPEECH List the speaker; title, in quotation marks; sponsoring institution or group; place; and date. If the speech is untitled, use a label such as *Lecture*.

> Colbert, Stephen. Speech. White House Correspondents' Association Dinner. *YouTube*. YouTube, 29 Apr. 2006. Web. 20 May 2010.

Eugenides, Jeffrey. Portland Arts and Lectures. Arlene Schnitzer Concert Hall, Portland, OR. 30 Sept. 2003. Lecture.

60. LIVE PERFORMANCE List the title, appropriate names (such as writer or performer), the place, and the date. To cite a particular person's work, begin the entry with that name.

Anything Goes. By Cole Porter. Perf. Klea Blackhurst. Shubert Theater, New Haven. 7 Oct. 2003. Performance.

61. PODCAST For a podcast you view or listen to online, include all the following that are available: the speaker, the title of the podcast, the title of the program, the host or performers, the title of the site, the site's sponsor, the date of posting, the medium (*Web*), and the access date. (This model is based on MLA guidelines for a short work from a Web site. For a downloaded podcast, see model 62.)

"Seven Arrested in U.S. Terror Raid." *Morning Report.* Host Krishnan Guru-Murthy. *4 Radio.* Channel 4 News, 23 June 2006. Web. 27 June 2006.

62. DIGITAL FILE A citation for a file that you can download — one that exists independently, not only on a Web site — begins with citation information required for the type of source (a photograph or sound recording, for example). For the medium, indicate the type of file (*MP3 file, JPEG file*).

Officers' Winter Quarters, Army of Potomac, Brandy Station. Mar. 1864. Prints and Photographs Div., Lib. of Cong. TIFF file.

"Return to the Giant Pool of Money." *This American Life.* Narr. Ira Glass. NPR, 25 Sept. 2009. MP3 file.

63. WORK OF ART OR PHOTOGRAPH List the artist or photographer; the work's title, italicized; the date of composition (if unknown, use *n.d.*); and the medium of composition (*Oil on canvas, Bronze*). Then cite the name of the museum or other location and the city. To cite a reproduction in a book, add the publication information. To cite artwork found online, omit the medium of composition, and after the location, add the title of the database or Web site, italicized; the medium consulted (*Web*); and the date of access.

Chagall, Marc. *The Poet with the Birds.* 1911. Minneapolis Inst. of Arts. *artsmia.org.* Web. 6 Oct. 2010.

General William Palmer in Old Age. 1810. Oil on canvas. National Army Museum, London. *White Mughals: Love and Betrayal in Eighteenth-Century India.* William Dalrymple. New York: Penguin, 2002. 270. Print.

Kahlo, Frida. *Self-Portrait with Cropped Hair.* 1940. Oil on canvas. Museum of Mod. Art, New York.

64. MAP OR CHART Cite a map or chart as you would a book or a short work within a longer work, and include the word *Map* or *Chart* after the title. Add the medium of publication. For an online source, end with the date of access.

> "Australia." Map. *Perry-Castañeda Library Map Collection.* U of Texas, 1999.
> Web. 4 Nov. 2003.

> *California.* Map. Chicago: Rand, 2002. Print.

65. CARTOON OR COMIC STRIP List the artist's name; the title (if any) of the cartoon or comic strip, in quotation marks; the label *Cartoon* or *Comic strip*; and the usual publication information for a print periodical (see models 25–28) or a work from a Web site (model 41).

> Johnston, Lynn. "For Better or Worse." Comic strip. *FBorFW.com.* Lynn
> Johnston Publications, 30 June 2006. Web. 20 July 2006.

> Lewis, Eric. "The Unpublished Freud." Cartoon. *New Yorker* 11 Mar. 2002: 80.
> Print.

66. ADVERTISEMENT Include the label *Advertisement* after the name of the item or organization being advertised.

> Microsoft. Advertisement. *Harper's* Oct. 2003: 2-3. Print.

> Microsoft. Advertisement. *New York Times.* New York Times, 11 Nov. 2003.
> Web. 11 Nov. 2003.

OTHER SOURCES (INCLUDING ONLINE VERSIONS)

If an online version is not shown here, use the appropriate model for the source and then end with the medium and date of access.

67. REPORT OR PAMPHLET Follow the guidelines for a print book (models 6–24) or an online book (model 36).

> Allen, Katherine, and Lee Rainie. *Parents Online.* Washington: Pew Internet
> and Amer. Life Project, 2002. Print.

> Environmental Working Group. *Dead in the Water.* Washington:
> Environmental Working Group, 2006. Web. 24 Apr. 2010.

68. GOVERNMENT PUBLICATION Begin with the author, if identified. Otherwise, start with the name of the government, followed by the agency. For congressional documents, cite the number, session, and house of Congress (*S* for Senate, *H* for House of Representatives); the type (*Report, Resolution, Document*) in abbreviated form; and the number. End with the publication information. The print publisher is often the Government Printing Office (GPO). For online versions, follow the models for a work from a Web site (model 41) or an entire Web site (model 42).

Gregg, Judd. *Report to Accompany the Genetic Information Act of 2003*. US 108th Cong., 1st sess. S. Rept. 108-22. Washington: GPO, 2003. Print.

Kinsella, Kevin, and Victoria Velkoff. *An Aging World: 2001*. US Bureau of the Census. Washington: GPO, 2001. Print.

United States. Environmental Protection Agency. Office of Emergency and Remedial Response. *This Is Superfund*. Jan. 2000. *Environmental Protection Agency*. Web. 16 Aug. 2002.

69. PUBLISHED PROCEEDINGS OF A CONFERENCE Cite proceedings as you would a book.

Cleary, John, and Gary Gurtler, eds. *Proceedings of the Boston Area Colloquium in Ancient Philosophy 2002*. Boston: Brill Academic, 2003. Print.

70. DISSERTATION Enclose the title in quotation marks. Add the label *Diss.*, the school, and the year the work was accepted.

Paris, Django. "Our Culture: Difference, Division, and Unity in Multicultural Youth Space." Diss. Stanford U, 2008. Print.

Note: Cite a published dissertation as a book, adding the identification *Diss.* and the university after the title.

71. DISSERTATION ABSTRACT Cite as you would an unpublished dissertation (see model 70). For the abstract of a dissertation using *Dissertation Abstracts International (DAI)*, include the *DAI* volume, year, and page number.

Huang-Tiller, Gillian C. "The Power of the Meta-Genre: Cultural, Sexual, and Racial Politics of the American Modernist Sonnet." Diss. U of Notre Dame, 2000. *DAI* 61 (2000): 1401. Print.

72. PUBLISHED INTERVIEW List the person interviewed; the title of the interview (if any) or the label *Interview* and the interviewer's name, if relevant. Then provide information about the source, following the appropriate model.

Paretsky, Sarah. Interview. *Progressive*. Progressive Magazine, 14 Jan. 2008. Web. 12 Feb. 2010.

Taylor, Max. "Max Taylor on Winning." *Time* 13 Nov. 2000: 66. Print.

73. UNPUBLISHED LETTER Cite a published letter as a work in an anthology (see model 10). If the letter is unpublished, follow this form:

Anzaldúa, Gloria. Letter to the author. 10 Sept. 2002. MS.

74. MANUSCRIPT OR OTHER UNPUBLISHED WORK List the author's name; the title (if any) or a description of the material; the form of the material (such as *MS* for manuscript or *TS* for typescript) and any identifying numbers; and the name and location of the library or research institution housing the material, if applicable.

> Woolf, Virginia. "The Searchlight." N.d. TS. Ser. III, Box 4, Item 184. Papers of Virginia Woolf, 1902-1956. Smith Coll., Northampton.

75. LEGAL SOURCE To cite a court case, give the names of the first plaintiff and defendant, the case number, the name of the court, and the date of the decision. To cite an act, give the name of the act followed by its Public Law (*Pub. L.*) number, the date the act was enacted, and its Statutes at Large (*Stat.*) cataloging number.

> Eldred v. Ashcroft. No. 01-618. Supreme Ct. of the US. 15 Jan. 2003. Print.

> Museum and Library Services Act of 2003. Pub. L. 108-81. 25 Sept. 2003. Stat. 117.991. Print.

APA Documentation Guidelines

The following formatting guidelines are adapted from the American Psychological Association (APA) recommendations for preparing manuscripts for publication in journals. However, check with your instructor before preparing your final draft.

For detailed guidelines on formatting a list of references, see pp. 406–22. For a sample student essay in APA style, see pp. 248–56.

- *Title page.* Center the title, and include your name, the course name and number, the instructor's name, and the date. In the top left corner, type the words *Running head:* and a short version of the title, using all capital letters (fifty characters or fewer, including spaces). In the top right corner, type the number *1.*

- *Margins and spacing.* Leave margins of at least one inch at the top and bottom and on both sides of the page. Do not justify the right margin. Double-space the entire text, including headings, set-off quotations, content notes, and the list of references. Indent the first line of each paragraph one-half inch (or five to seven spaces) from the left margin.

- *Short title and page numbers.* Type the short title flush left and the page number flush right at the top of each page, in the same position as on the title page.

- *Long quotations.* For a long, set-off quotation (one having more than forty words), indent it one-half inch (or five to seven spaces) from the left margin and do not use quotation marks. Place the page reference in parentheses one space after the final punctuation.

- *Abstract.* If your instructor asks for an abstract with your paper — a one-paragraph summary of your major thesis and supporting points — it should go on a separate page immediately after the title page. Center the word *Abstract* (not boldface) about an inch from the top of the page. Double-space the text of the abstract, and begin the first line flush with the left margin. APA recommends that an abstract not exceed 120 words.

- *Headings*. Headings (set in boldface) are used within the text of many APA-style papers. In papers with only one or two levels of headings, center the main headings; position the subheadings flush with the left margin. Capitalize all major words; however, do not capitalize articles, short prepositions, or coordinating conjunctions unless they are the first word or follow a colon.

- *Visuals*. Tables should be labeled *Table*, numbered, and captioned. All other visuals (charts, graphs, photographs, and drawings) should be labeled *Figure*, numbered, and captioned with a description and the source information. Remember to refer to each visual in your text, stating how it contributes to the point(s) you are making. Tables and figures should generally appear near the relevant text; check with your instructor for guidelines on placement of visuals.

Directory to APA style for in-text citations

In-Text Citations

APA style requires parenthetical references in the text to document quotations, paraphrases, summaries, and other material from a source. These citations correspond to full bibliographic entries in a list of references at the end of the text.

Note that APA style generally calls for using the past tense or present perfect tense for signal verbs: *Baker (2003) showed* or *Baker (2003) has shown*. Use the present tense only to discuss results (*the experiment demonstrates*) or widely accepted information (*researchers agree*).

An in-text citation in APA style always indicates *which source* on the references page the writer is referring to, and it explains *in what year* the material was published; for quoted material, the in-text citation also indicates *where* in the source the quotation can be found.

1. BASIC FORMAT FOR A QUOTATION Generally, use the author's name in a signal phrase to introduce the cited material, and place the date, in parentheses, immediately after the author's name. The page number, preceded by *p.*, appears in parentheses after the quotation.

> Gitlin (2001) pointed out that "political critics, convinced that the media are rigged against them, are often blind to other substantial reasons why their causes are unpersuasive" (p. 141).

If the author is not named in a signal phrase, place the author's name, the year, and the page number in parentheses after the quotation: (Gitlin, 2001, p. 141). For a long, set-off quotation (more than forty words), place the page reference in parentheses one space after the final quotation.

For electronic texts or other works without page numbers, you may use paragraph numbers, if the source includes them, preceded by the abbreviation *para.*

> Driver (2007) has noticed "an increasing focus on the role of land" in policy debates over the past decade (para. 1).

2. BASIC FORMAT FOR A PARAPHRASE OR SUMMARY Include the author's last name and the year as in model 1, but omit the page or paragraph number unless the reader will need it to find the material in a long work.

> Gitlin (2001) has argued that critics sometimes overestimate the influence of the media on modern life.

3. TWO AUTHORS Use both names in all citations. Use *and* in a signal phrase, but use an ampersand (&) in parentheses.

> Babcock and Laschever (2003) have suggested that many women do not negotiate their salaries and pay raises as vigorously as their male counterparts do.

> A recent study has suggested that many women do not negotiate their salaries and pay raises as vigorously as their male counterparts do (Babcock & Laschever, 2003).

4. THREE TO FIVE AUTHORS List all the authors' names for the first reference.

> Safer, Voccola, Hurd, and Goodwin (2003) reached somewhat different conclusions by designing a study that was less dependent on subjective judgment than were previous studies.

In subsequent references, use just the first author's name plus *et al.*

> Based on the results, Safer et al. (2003) determined that the apes took significant steps toward self-expression.

5. SIX OR MORE AUTHORS Use only the first author's name and *et al.* in every citation.

> As Soleim et al. (2002) demonstrated, advertising holds the potential for manipulating "free-willed" consumers.

6. CORPORATE OR GROUP AUTHOR If the name of the organization or corporation is long, spell it out the first time you use it, followed by an abbreviation in brackets. In later references, use the abbreviation only.

FIRST CITATION   (Centers for Disease Control and Prevention [CDC], 2006)

LATER CITATIONS   (CDC, 2006)

7. UNKNOWN AUTHOR Use the title or its first few words in a signal phrase or in parentheses. A book's title is italicized, as in the following example; an article's title is placed in quotation marks.

> The employment profiles for this time period substantiated this trend (*Federal Employment,* 2001).

8. TWO OR MORE AUTHORS WITH THE SAME LAST NAME If your list of references includes works by different authors with the same last name, include the authors' initials in each citation.

> S. Bartolomeo (2000) conducted the groundbreaking study on teenage childbearing.

9. TWO OR MORE WORKS BY AN AUTHOR IN A SINGLE YEAR Assign lowercase letters (*a, b,* and so on) alphabetically by title, and include the letters after the year.

> Gordon (2004b) examined this trend in more detail.

10. TWO OR MORE SOURCES IN ONE PARENTHETICAL REFERENCE List sources by different authors in alphabetical order by authors' last names, separated by semicolons: (Cardone, 1998; Lai, 2002). List works by the same author in chronological order, separated by commas: (Lai, 2000, 2002).

11. INDIRECT SOURCE Use the phrase *as cited in* to indicate that you are reporting information from a secondary source. Name the original source in a signal phrase, but list the secondary source in your list of references.

> Amartya Sen developed the influential concept that land reform was necessary for "promoting opportunity" among the poor (as cited in Driver, 2007, para. 2).

12. PERSONAL COMMUNICATION Cite any personal letters, email messages, electronic postings, telephone conversations, or interviews as shown. Do not include personal communications in the reference list.

R. Tobin (personal communication, November 4, 2006) supported his claims about music therapy with new evidence.

13. ELECTRONIC DOCUMENT Cite a Web or electronic document as you would a print source, using the author's name and date.

Link and Phelan (2005) argued for broader interventions in public health that would be accessible to anyone, regardless of individual wealth.

The APA recommends the following for electronic sources without names, dates, or page numbers:

AUTHOR UNKNOWN. Use a shortened form of the title in a signal phrase or in parentheses (see model 7). If an organization is the author, see model 6.

DATE UNKNOWN. Use the abbreviation *n.d.* (for "no date") in place of the year: (*Hopkins, n.d.*).

NO PAGE NUMBERS. Many works found online or in electronic databases lack stable page numbers. (Use the page numbers for an electronic work in a format, such as PDF, that has stable pagination.) If paragraph numbers are included in such a source, use the abbreviation *para.*: (*Giambetti, 2006, para. 7*). If no paragraph numbers are included but the source includes headings, give the heading and identify the paragraph in the section:

Jacobs and Johnson (2007) have argued that "the South African media is still highly concentrated and not very diverse in terms of race and class" (South African Media after Apartheid, para. 3).

Content Notes

APA style allows you to use content notes, either at the bottom of the page or on a separate page at the end of the text, to expand or supplement your text. Indicate such notes in the text by superscript numerals ([1]). Double-space all entries. Indent the first line of each note five spaces, but begin subsequent lines at the left margin.

SUPERSCRIPT NUMBER IN TEXT

The age of the children involved in the study was an important factor in the selection of items for the questionnaire.[1]

FOOTNOTE

[1]Marjorie Youngston Forman and William Cole of the Child Study Team provided great assistance in identifying appropriate items for the questionnaire.

Directory to APA style for references

List of References

The alphabetical list of the sources cited in your document is called *References*. If your instructor asks that you list everything you have read—not just the sources you cite—call the list *Bibliography*. Here are guidelines for preparing a list of references:

- Start your list on a separate page after the text of your document but before appendices or notes. Continue consecutive page numbers.

- Center the heading *References* one inch from the top of the page.

- Begin each entry flush with the left margin, but indent subsequent lines one-half inch or five spaces. Double-space the entire list.

- List sources alphabetically by authors' (or editors') last names. If no author is given, alphabetize the source by the first word of the title other than *A*, *An*, or *The*. If the list includes two or more works by the same author, list them in chronological order. (For two or more works by the same author published in the same year, see model 5.)

- Italicize titles and subtitles of books and periodicals. Do not italicize titles of articles, and do not enclose them in quotation marks.

- For titles of books and articles, capitalize only the first word of the title and the subtitle and any proper nouns or proper adjectives.

- For titles of periodicals, capitalize all major words.

GUIDELINES FOR AUTHOR LISTINGS

List authors' last names first, and use only initials for first and middle names. The in-text citations in your text point readers toward particular sources in your list of references (see pp. 401–4).

NAME CITED IN SIGNAL PHRASE IN TEXT

Driver (2007) has noted . . .

NAME IN PARENTHETICAL CITATION IN TEXT

. . . (Driver, 2007).

BEGINNING OF ENTRY IN LIST OF REFERENCES

Driver, T. (2007).

1. ONE AUTHOR Give the last name, a comma, the initial(s), and the date in parentheses.

Zimbardo, P. G. (2009).

2. MULTIPLE AUTHORS List up to seven authors, last name first, with commas separating authors' names and an ampersand (&) before the last author's name.

> Walsh, M. E., & Murphy, J. A. (2003).

Note: For a work with more than seven authors, list the first six, then an ellipsis (. . .), and then the final author's name.

3. CORPORATE OR GROUP AUTHOR

> Resources for Rehabilitation. (2003).

4. UNKNOWN AUTHOR Begin with the work's title. Italicize book titles, but do not italicize article titles or enclose them in quotation marks. Capitalize only the first word of the title and subtitle (if any) and proper nouns and proper adjectives.

> *Safe youth, safe schools.* (2009).

5. TWO OR MORE WORKS BY THE SAME AUTHOR List two or more works by the same author in chronological order. Repeat the author's name in each entry.

> Goodall, J. (1999).

> Goodall, J. (2002).

If the works appeared in the same year, list them alphabetically by title, and assign lowercase letters (a, b, etc.) after the dates.

> Shermer, M. (2002a). On estimating the lifetime of civilizations. *Scientific American, 287*(2), 33.

> Shermer, M. (2002b). Readers who question evolution. *Scientific American, 287*(1), 37.

BOOKS

6. BASIC FORMAT FOR A BOOK Begin with the author name(s). (See models 1–5.) Then include the publication year, title and subtitle, city of publication, country or state abbreviation, and publisher. The source map on pp. 408–9 shows where to find this information in a typical book.

> Levick, S. E. (2003). *Clone being: Exploring the psychological and social dimensions.* Lanham, MD: Rowman & Littlefield.

7. EDITOR For a book with an editor but no author, list the source under the editor's name.

> Dickens, J. (Ed.). (1995). *Family outing: A guide for parents of gays, lesbians and bisexuals.* London, England: Peter Owen.

APA SOURCE MAP: Books

Take information from the book's title page and copyright page (on the reverse side of the title page), not from the book's cover or a library catalog.

(1) Author. List all authors' last names first, and use only initials for first and middle names. For more about citing authors, see models 1–5.

(2) Publication year. Enclose the year of publication in parentheses.

(3) Title. Italicize the title and any subtitle. Capitalize only the first word of the title and the subtitle and any proper nouns or proper adjectives.

(4) City and state of publication. List the city of publication and the country or state abbreviation followed by a colon.

(5) Publisher. Give the publisher's name, dropping any *Inc.*, *Co.*, or *Publishers*.

A citation for the book on p. 409 would look like this:

          1   2   3

Tsutsui, W. (2004). *Godzilla on my mind: Fifty years of the king of monsters.*

                4   5

New York, NY: Palgrave Macmillan.

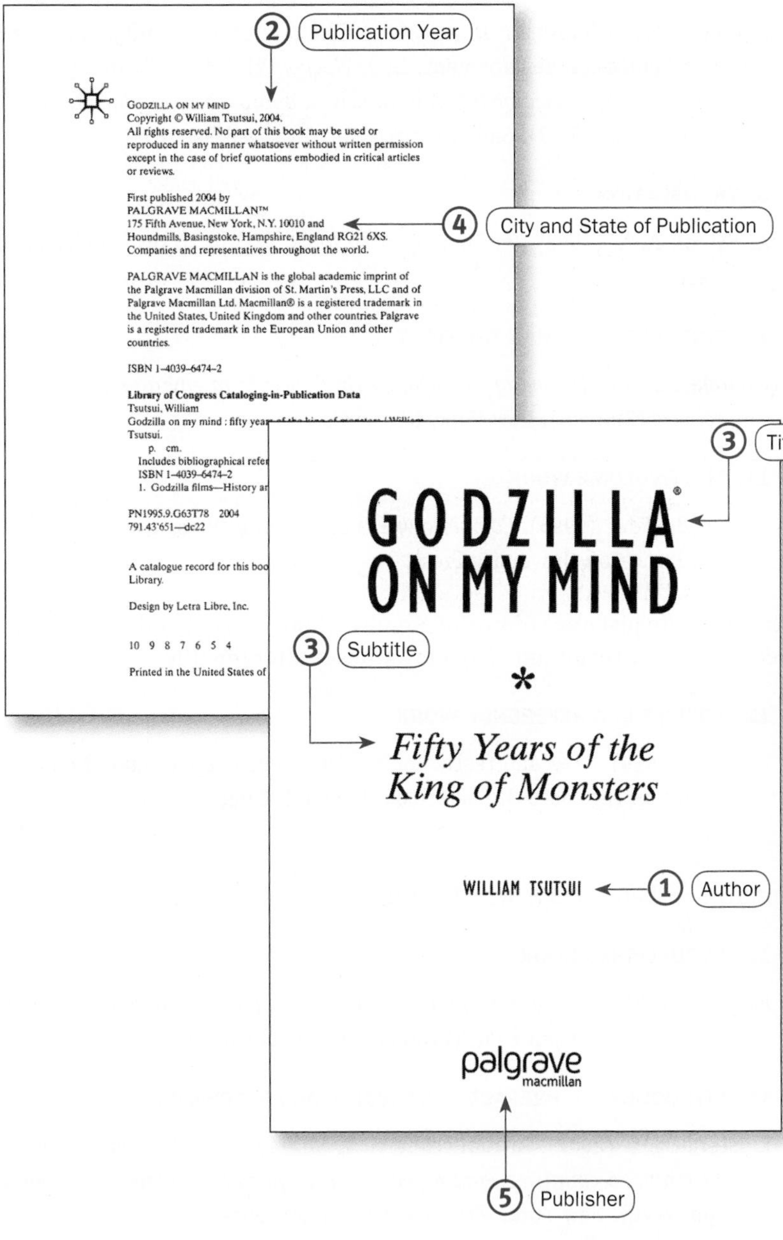

GODZILLA ON MY MIND
Copyright © William Tsutsui, 2004.
All rights reserved. No part of this book may be used or reproduced in any manner whatsoever without written permission except in the case of brief quotations embodied in critical articles or reviews.

First published 2004 by
PALGRAVE MACMILLAN™
175 Fifth Avenue, New York, N.Y. 10010 and
Houndmills, Basingstoke, Hampshire, England RG21 6XS.
Companies and representatives throughout the world.

PALGRAVE MACMILLAN is the global academic imprint of the Palgrave Macmillan division of St. Martin's Press, LLC and of Palgrave Macmillan Ltd. Macmillan® is a registered trademark in the United States, United Kingdom and other countries. Palgrave is a registered trademark in the European Union and other countries.

ISBN 1-4039-6474-2

Library of Congress Cataloging-in-Publication Data
Tsutsui, William
Godzilla on my mind : fifty yea
Tsutsui.
p. cm.
Includes bibliographical refe
ISBN 1-4039-6474-2
1. Godzilla films—History a

PN1995.9.G63T78 2004
791.43'651—dc22

A catalogue record for this boo
Library.

Design by Letra Libre, Inc.

10 9 8 7 6 5 4

Printed in the United States of

GODZILLA®
ON MY MIND

*

Fifty Years of the King of Monsters

WILLIAM TSUTSUI

palgrave
macmillan

2 Publication Year
4 City and State of Publication
3 Title
3 Subtitle
1 Author
5 Publisher

To cite a book with an author and an editor, place the editor's name, with a comma and the abbreviation *Ed.*, in parentheses after the title.

> Austin, J. (1995). *The province of jurisprudence determined.* (W. E. Rumble, Ed.). Cambridge, England: Cambridge University Press.

8. SELECTION IN A BOOK WITH AN EDITOR

> Burke, W. W., & Nourmair, D. A. (2001). The role of personality assessment in organization development. In J. Waclawski & A. H. Church (Eds.), *Organization development: A data-driven approach to organizational change* (pp. 55-77). San Francisco, CA: Jossey-Bass.

9. TRANSLATION

> Al-Farabi, A. N. (1998). *On the perfect state* (R. Walzer, Trans.). Chicago, IL: Kazi.

10. EDITION OTHER THAN THE FIRST

> Moore, G. S. (2002). *Living with the earth: Concepts in environmental health science* (2nd ed.). New York, NY: Lewis.

11. MULTIVOLUME WORK

> Barnes, J. (Ed.). (1995). *Complete works of Aristotle* (Vols. 1-2). Princeton, NJ: Princeton University Press.

Note: If you cite just one volume of a multivolume work, list that volume, not the complete span of volumes, in parentheses after the title.

12. ARTICLE IN A REFERENCE WORK

> Dean, C. (1994). Jaws and teeth. In *The Cambridge encyclopedia of human evolution* (pp. 56-59). Cambridge, England: Cambridge University Press.

If no author is listed, begin with the title.

13. REPUBLISHED BOOK

> Piaget, J. (1952). *The language and thought of the child.* London, England: Routledge & Kegan Paul. (Original work published 1932)

14. INTRODUCTION, PREFACE, FOREWORD, OR AFTERWORD

> Klosterman, C. (2007). Introduction. In P. Shirley, *Can I keep my jersey?: 11 teams, 5 countries, and 4 years in my life as a basketball vagabond* (pp. v-vii). New York, NY: Villard-Random House.

15. BOOK WITH A TITLE WITHIN THE TITLE Do not italicize or enclose in quotation marks a title within a book title.

> Klarman, M. J. (2007). Brown v. Board of Education *and the civil rights movement*. New York, NY: Oxford University Press.

PRINT PERIODICALS

Begin with the author name(s). (See models 1–5.) Then include the publication date (year only for journals, and year, month, and day for other periodicals); the article title; the periodical title; the volume and issue numbers, if any; and the page numbers. The source map on pp. 412–13 shows where to find this information in a sample periodical.

16. ARTICLE IN A JOURNAL PAGINATED BY VOLUME

> O'Connell, D. C., & Kowal, S. (2003). Psycholinguistics: A half century of monologism. *The American Journal of Psychology, 116,* 191-212.

17. ARTICLE IN A JOURNAL PAGINATED BY ISSUE If each issue begins with page 1, include the issue number after the volume number.

> Hall, R. E. (2000). Marriage as vehicle of racism among women of color. *Psychology: A Journal of Human Behavior, 37*(2), 29-40.

18. ARTICLE IN A MAGAZINE

> Ricciardi, S. (2003, August 5). Enabling the mobile work force. *PC Magazine, 22,* 46.

19. ARTICLE IN A NEWSPAPER

> Faler, B. (2003, August 29). Primary colors: Race and fundraising. *The Washington Post*, p. A5.

20. EDITORIAL OR LETTER TO THE EDITOR

> Zelneck, B. (2003, July 18). Serving the public at public universities [Letter to the editor]. *The Chronicle Review*, p. B18.

21. UNSIGNED ARTICLE

> Annual meeting announcement. (2003, March). *Cognitive Psychology, 46,* 227.

22. REVIEW

> Ringel, S. (2003). [Review of the book *Multiculturalism and the therapeutic process*]. *Clinical Social Work Journal, 31,* 212-213.

APA SOURCE MAP: Articles from periodicals

(1) Author. List all authors' last names first, and use only initials for first and middle names. For more about citing authors, see models 1–5.

(2) Publication date. Enclose the date in parentheses. For journals, use only the year. For magazines and newspapers, use the year, a comma, the month (spelled out), and the day, if given.

(3) Article title. Do not italicize or enclose article titles in quotation marks. Capitalize only the first word of the article title and subtitle and any proper nouns or proper adjectives.

(4) Periodical title. Italicize the periodical title (and subtitle, if any), and capitalize all major words.

(5) Volume and issue numbers. Follow the periodical title with a comma, and then give the volume number (italicized) and, without a space in between, the issue number (if given) in parentheses.

(6) Page numbers. Give the inclusive page numbers of the article. For newspapers only, include the abbreviation *p.* ("page") or *pp.* ("pages") before the page numbers. End the citation with a period.

A citation for the periodical article on p. 413 would look like this:

    1   *2*   *3*

Etzioni, A. (2006). Leaving race behind: Our growing Hispanic population creates

                              4   *5*   *6*

a golden opportunity. *The American Scholar,* *75*(2), 20-30.

The AMERICAN
SCHOLAR

④ Periodical Title

⑤ Volume and Issue Numbers

Spring 2006 | Vol. 75, No. 2

② Publication Date

The AMERICAN
SCHOLAR

③ Article Title

Leaving Race Behind

Our growing Hispanic population creates a golden opportunity

AMITAI ETZIONI ◄ ① Author

Some years ago the United States government asked me what my race was. I was reluctant to respond because my 50 years of practicing sociology—and some powerful personal experiences—have under-scored for me what we all know to one degree or another, that racial divisions bedevil America, just as they do many other societies across the world. Not wanting to encourage these divisions, I refused to check off one of the specific racial options on the U.S. Census form and instead marked a box labeled "Other." I later found out that the federal government did not accept such an attempt to de-emphasize race, by me or by some 6.75 million other Americans who tried it. Instead the government assigned me to a racial category, one it chose for me. Learning this made me conjure up what I admit is a far-fetched association. I was in this place once before. When I was a Jewish child in Nazi Germany in the early 1930s, many Jews who saw themselves as good Germans wanted to "pass" as Aryans. But the Nazi regime would have none of it. Never mind, they told these Jews, *we determine* who is Jewish and who is not. A similar practice prevailed in the Old South, where if you had one drop of African blood you were a Negro, disregarding all other facts and considerations, including how you saw yourself.

You might suppose that in the years since my little Census-form protest

Amitai Etzioni is University Professor at George Washington University and the author of *The Monochrome Society*.

20 ◄ ⑥ Page Numbers

23. PUBLISHED INTERVIEW

Smith, H. (2002, October). [Interview with A. Thompson]. *The Sun*, pp. 4-7.

ELECTRONIC SOURCES

When citing sources accessed online or from an electronic database, include as many of the following elements as you can find:

- *Author.* Give the author's name, if available.

- *Publication date.* Include the date of electronic publication or of the latest update, if available. When no publication date is available, use *n.d.* ("no date").

- *Title.* List the document title, neither italicized nor in quotation marks.

- *Print publication information.* For articles from online journals, magazines, or reference databases, give the publication title and other publishing information as you would for a print periodical (see models 16–23).

- *Retrieval information.* For a work from a database, do the following: If the article has a DOI (digital object identifier), include that number after the publication information; do not include the name of the database. If there is no DOI, write *Retrieved from* followed by the URL for the journal's homepage (not the database URL). For a work found on a Web site, write *Retrieved from* and include the URL. If the work seems likely to be updated, include the retrieval date. If the URL is longer than one line, break it only before a punctuation mark; do not break *http://*.

Updated guidelines for citing electronic resources are maintained at the APA's Web site (www.apa.org).

24. ARTICLE FROM AN ONLINE PERIODICAL Give the author, date, title, and publication information as you would for a print document. Include both the volume and issue numbers for all journal articles. If the article has a digital object identifier (DOI), include it. If there is no DOI, include the URL for the periodical's homepage or for the article (if the article is difficult to find from the homepage). For newspaper articles accessible from a searchable Web site, give the site URL only.

Barringer, F. (2008, February 7). In many communities, it's not easy going green. *The New York Times*. Retrieved from http://www.nytimes.com

Cleary, J. M., & Crafti, N. (2007). Basic need satisfaction, emotional eating, and dietary restraint as risk factors for recurrent overeating in a community sample. *E-Journal of Applied Psychology 2*(3), 27-39. Retrieved from http://ojs.lib.swin.edu.au/index.php/ejap/article /view/90/116

25. ARTICLE FROM A DATABASE Give the author, date, title, and publication information as you would for a print document. Include both the volume and issue numbers for all journal articles. If the article has a DOI, include it. If there is no DOI, write *Retrieved from* and the URL of the journal's homepage (not the URL of the database). The source map on pp. 416–17 shows where to find this information for a typical article from a database.

> Hazleden, R. (2003, December). Love yourself: The relationship of the self with itself in popular self-help texts. *Journal of Sociology, 39*(4), 413-428. Retrieved from http://jos.sagepub.com

> Morley, N. J., Ball, L. J., & Ormerod, T. C. (2006). How the detection of insurance fraud succeeds and fails. *Psychology, Crime, & Law, 12*(2), 163-180. doi:10.1080/10683160512331316325

26. ABSTRACT FOR AN ONLINE ARTICLE

> Gudjonsson, G. H., & Young, S. (2010). Does confabulation in memory predict suggestibility beyond IQ and memory? [Abstract]. *Personality & Individual Differences, 49*(1), 65-67. doi: 10.1016/j.paid.2010.03.014

27. DOCUMENT FROM A WEB SITE The APA refers to works that are not peer reviewed, such as reports, press releases, and presentation slides, as "gray literature." Include all the following information you can find: the author's name; the publication date (or *n.d.* if no date is available); the title of the document; the title of the site or larger work, if any; any publication information available in addition to the date; *Retrieved from* and the URL. Provide your date of access only if an update seems likely. The source map on pp. 418–19 shows where to find this information for an article from a Web site.

> Behnke, P. C. (2006, February 22). The homeless are everyone's problem. *Authors' Den*. Retrieved from http://www.authorsden.com/visit /viewArticle.asp?id=21017

> Hacker, J. S. (2006). The privatization of risk and the growing economic insecurity of Americans. *Items and Issues, 5*(4), 16–23. Retrieved from http://publications.ssrc.org/items/items5.4/Hacker.pdf

> What parents should know about treatment of behavioral and emotional disorders in preschool children. (2006). *APA Online*. Retrieved from http://www.apa.org/releases/kidsmed.html

28. CHAPTER OR SECTION OF A WEB DOCUMENT Follow model 27. After the chapter or section title, type *In* and give the document title, with identifying information, if any, in parentheses.

> Salamon, A. (n.d.). War in Europe. In *Childhood in times of war* (chap. 2). Retrieved April 11, 2008, from http://remember.org/jean

APA SOURCE MAP: Articles from databases

① Author. Include the author's name as you would for a print source. List all authors' last names first, and use initials for first and middle names. For more about citing authors, see models 1–5.

② Publication date. Enclose the date in parentheses. For journals, use only the year. For magazines and newspapers, use the year, a comma, the month, and the day if given.

③ Article title. Capitalize only the first word of the article title and the subtitle and any proper nouns or proper adjectives.

④ Periodical title. Italicize the periodical title. Capitalize all major words.

⑤ Print publication information. For journals and magazines, give the volume number (italicized) and the issue number (in parentheses). For journals only, give the inclusive page numbers.

⑥ Retrieval information. If the article has a DOI (digital object identifier), include that number after the publication information; do not include the name of the database. If there is no DOI, write *Retrieved from* followed by the URL of the journal's homepage (not the database URL).

A citation for the article on p. 417 would look like this:

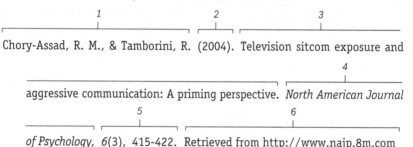

① Author

③ Article Title

⑤ Print Publication Information

Title:	**Television Sitcom Exposure and Aggressive Communication: A Priming Perspective.**
Authors:	Chory-Assad, Rebecca M.1 Tamborini, Ron2
Source:	North American Journal of Psychology; 2004, Vol. 6 Issue 3, p415-422, 8p
Document Type:	Article
Subject Terms:	*TELEVISION comedies *AGGRESSIVENESS *ATTITUDE (Psychology) *TELEVISION programs
Abstract:	This study examined the relationship between exposure to verbally aggressive television sitcoms and aggressive communication, from a priming and cognitive neo-associationistic perspective. Participants reported their trait verbal aggressiveness and exposure to sitcoms approximately one month prior to their participation in the lab portion of the study. Once in the lab, participants evaluated four sitcoms and engaged in a question-response session that was observed and coded for aggression. Results indicated that increased exposure to television sitcoms was associated with lower levels of aggressive communication. Implications of these results for theory and research concerning the effects of exposure to aggression in a humorous context are discussed. [ABSTRACT FROM AUTHOR]
	*Copyright of **North American Journal of Psychology** is the property of **North American Journal of Psychology** and its content may not be copied or emailed to multiple sites or posted to a listserv without the copyright holder's express written permission. However, users may print, download, or email articles for individual use. This abstract may be abridged. No warranty is given about the accuracy of the copy. Users should refer to the original published version of the material for the full abstract. (Copyright applies to all Abstracts.)*
Author Affiliations:	1West Virginia University 2Michigan State University
Full Text Word Count:	2880
ISSN:	15277143
Accession Number:	15630823
Database:	Academic Search Premier

② Publication Date

④ Periodical Title

APA SOURCE MAP: Works from Web sites

(1) Author. If one is given, include the author's name (see models 1–5). List last names first, and use only initials for first names. The site's sponsor may be the author. If no author is identified, begin the citation with the title of the document.

(2) Publication date. Enclose the date of publication or latest update in parentheses. Use *n.d.* ("no date") when no publication date is available.

(3) Title of work. Capitalize only the first word of the title and subtitle and any proper nouns or proper adjectives.

(4) Title of Web site. Italicize the title. Capitalize all major words.

(5) Retrieval information. Write *Retrieved from* and include the URL. If the work seems likely to be updated, include the retrieval date.

A citation for the Web document on p. 419 would look like this:

```
        1              2                    3
  ┌──────┴──────┐ ┌────┴────────┐ ┌─────────┴──────────┐
```

Alexander, M. (2001, August 22). Thirty years later, Stanford Prison

```
                               4                5
  ┌──────────────────┐ ┌───────┴──────┐ ┌───────┴──────────┐
```

Experiment lives on. *Stanford Report.* Retrieved from http://news

```
  ┌──────────────────────────────────────────────────────┐
```

-service.stanford.edu/news/2001/august22/prison2-822.html

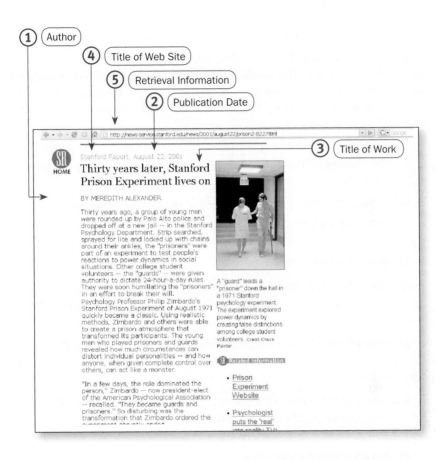

① Author

④ Title of Web Site

⑤ Retrieval Information

② Publication Date

③ Title of Work

Stanford Report, August 22, 2001

Thirty years later, Stanford Prison Experiment lives on

BY MEREDITH ALEXANDER

Thirty years ago, a group of young men were rounded up by Palo Alto police and dropped off at a new jail -- in the Stanford Psychology Department. Strip searched, sprayed for lice and locked up with chains around their ankles, the "prisoners" were part of an experiment to test people's reactions to power dynamics in social situations. Other college student volunteers -- the "guards" -- were given authority to dictate 24-hour-a-day rules. They were soon humiliating the "prisoners" in an effort to break their will.

Psychology Professor Philip Zimbardo's Stanford Prison Experiment of August 1971 quickly became a classic. Using realistic methods, Zimbardo and others were able to create a prison atmosphere that transformed its participants. The young men who played prisoners and guards revealed how much circumstances can distort individual personalities -- and how anyone, when given complete control over others, can act like a monster.

"In a few days, the role dominated the person," Zimbardo -- now president-elect of the American Psychological Association -- recalled. "They *became* guards and prisoners." So disturbing was the transformation that Zimbardo ordered the experiment abruptly ended.

A "guard" leads a "prisoner" down the hall in a 1971 Stanford psychology experiment. The experiment explored power dynamics by creating false distinctions among college student volunteers. Credit: Chuck Painter

Related Information

- Prison Experiment Website

- Psychologist puts the 'real' into reality TV:

29. EMAIL MESSAGE OR REAL-TIME COMMUNICATION Because the APA stresses that any sources cited in your list of references be retrievable by your readers, you should not include entries for email messages, real-time communications (such as IMs), or any other postings that are not archived. Instead, cite these sources in your text as forms of personal communication (see p. 403).

30. ONLINE POSTING List an online posting in the references list only if you are able to retrieve the message from an archive. Provide the author's name, the date of posting, and the subject line. Include other identifying information in square brackets. End with the retrieval statement and the URL of the archived message.

Troike, R. C. (2001, June 21). Buttercups and primroses [Electronic mailing list message]. Retrieved from http://listserv.linguistlist.org/archives/ads-l.html

Wittenberg, E. (2001, July 11). Gender and the Internet [Newsgroup message]. Retrieved from news://comp.edu.composition

31. BLOG (WEB LOG) POST

Spaulding, P. (2010, April 27). Who believes in a real America? [Web log post]. Retrieved from http://pandagon.net/index.php/site/2010/04

32. WIKI ENTRY Use the date of posting, if there is one or *n.d.*, for "no date," if there is none. Include the retrieval date because wiki content can change frequently.

Happiness. (2007, June 14). Retrieved March 24, 2008, from PsychWiki: http://www.psychwiki.com/wiki/Happiness

33. ONLINE AUDIO OR VIDEO FILE

Klusman, P. (2008, February 13). An engineer's guide to cats [Video file]. Retrieved from http://www.youtube.com/watch?v=mHXBL6bzAR4

O'Brien, K. (2008, January 31). Developing countries [Audio file]. *KUSP's life in the fast lane*. Retrieved from http://kusp.org/shows/fast.html

34. DATA SET

U.S. Department of Education, Institute of Education Sciences. (2009). *NAEP state comparisons* [Data set]. Retrieved from http://nces.ed.gov/nationsreportcard/statecomparisons/

35. COMPUTER SOFTWARE

PsychMate [Computer software]. (2003). Available from Psychology Software
Tools: http://pstnet.com/products/psychmate

OTHER SOURCES (INCLUDING ONLINE VERSIONS)

36. GOVERNMENT PUBLICATION

Office of the Federal Register. (2003). *The United States government manual
2003/2004*. Washington, DC: U.S. Government Printing Office.

Cite an online government document as you would a printed government
work, adding the URL. If there is no date, use *n.d.*

U.S. Public Health Service. (1999). *The surgeon general's call to action
to prevent suicide*. Retrieved from http://www.mentalhealth.org
/suicideprevention/calltoaction.asp

37. DISSERTATION If you retrieved the dissertation from a database, give
the database name and the accession number, if one is assigned.

Lengel, L. L. (1968). *The righteous cause: Some religious aspects of Kansas
populism*. Retrieved from ProQuest Digital Dissertations. (6900033)

If you retrieve a dissertation from a Web site, give the type of dissertation,
the institution, and year after the title, and provide a retrieval statement.

Meeks, M. G. (2006). *Between abolition and reform: First-year writing
programs, e-literacies, and institutional change* (Doctoral dissertation,
University of North Carolina). Retrieved from http://dc.lib.unc.edu
/etd/

38. TECHNICAL OR RESEARCH REPORT Give the report number, if avail-
able, in parentheses after the title.

McCool, R., Fikes, R., & McGuinness, D. (2003). *Semantic Web tools for
enhanced authoring* (Report No. KSL-03-07). Stanford, CA: Knowledge
Systems Laboratory

39. CONFERENCE PROCEEDINGS

Robertson, S. P., Vatrapu, R. K., & Medina, R. (2009). YouTube and
Facebook: Online video "friends" social networking. In *Conference
proceedings: YouTube and the 2008 election cycle* (pp. 159-76).
Amherst, MA: University of Massachusetts. Retrieved from http://
scholarworks.umass.edu/jitpc2009

40. PAPER PRESENTED AT A MEETING OR SYMPOSIUM, UNPUBLISHED Cite the month of the meeting if it is available.

Jones, J. G. (1999, February). *Mental health intervention in mass casualty disasters*. Paper presented at the Rocky Mountain Region Disaster Mental Health Conference, Laramie, WY.

41. POSTER SESSION

Barnes Young, L. L. (2003, August). *Cognition, aging, and dementia*. Poster session presented at the 2003 Division 40 APA Convention, Toronto, Ontario, Canada.

42. FILM, VIDEO, OR DVD

Nolan, C. (Director). (2010). *Inception* [Motion picture]. United States: Warner Bros.

43. TELEVISION PROGRAM, SINGLE EPISODE

Imperioli, M. (Writer), & Buscemi, S. (Director). (2002). Everybody hurts [Television series episode]. In D. Chase (Executive Producer), *The Sopranos*. New York, NY: Home Box Office.

44. TELEVISION SERIES

Abrams, J. J., Lieber, J., & Lindelof, D. (2004). *Lost*. [Television series]. New York, NY: WABC.

45. AUDIO PODCAST (DOWNLOADED AUDIO FILE)

Noguchi, Yugi. (2010, 24 May). BP hard to pin down on oil spill claims. [Audio podcast]. *NPR morning edition*. Retrieved from http://www.npr .org

46. RECORDING

The Avalanches. (2001). Frontier psychiatrist. On *Since I left you* [CD]. Los Angeles, CA: Elektra/Asylum Records.

Acknowledgments

Amitai Etzioni, from *The Limits of Privacy*. Copyright © 2000 by Basic Books, a division of the Perseus Book Group. Used by permission of the Perseus Books Group.

Jean M. Twenge, Introduction from *Generation Me*. Copyright © 2006 Free Press, a division of Simon & Schuster. Used by permission of Simon & Schuster, Inc. Excerpt from *Generation Me*. Essay first published in *The Chronicle of Education*, January 23, 1998. Reprinted by permission of the author. "Generational differences in young adults: life goals, concern for others, and civic orientation." From *The Journal of Personality and Social Psychology*, November 2012. Reprinted by permission of the American Psychological Association.

Picture Credits

Chapter 1: 2, Heartland Lab Rescue; **3,** (top) Edward Hausner/The New York Times/Redux; **3,** (bottom) Michael Kamber/The New York Times/Redux; **9,** Used with permission of Inter IKEA Systems B. V.; **11,** © 2007 Steven Meyer-Rassow; **15,** Richard Levine/Alamy; **16,** © Bill Aron/PhotoEdit, Inc. **Chapter 2:** 22, © British Library Board/Robana/Art Resource, NY; **24,** AP Photo/Eric Risberg. **Chapter 3:** 36, Miranda Neuneker; **40,** WhiteHouse.gov; **Chapter 4:** 81, Cover design reproduced with the permission of Simon & Schuster Publishing Group from the Free Press edition of *Generation Me: Why Today's Young Americans Are More Confident, Assertive, Entitled—And More Miserable Than Ever Before* by Jean Twenge, PhD. Cover design, copyright © 2006 by Simon & Schuster, Inc. All rights reserved. Cover photo: UC-San Diego/Zuma Press; **86,** Courtesy of loveisrespect; **87,** Iraq and Afghanistan Veterans of America and the Ad Council; **88,** The Shelter Pet Project; **89,** Earthjustice. **Chapter 5:** 102, Amitai Etzioni. **Chapter 6:** 150, University of Washington Libraries, Special Collections, UW21422; **154,** National Center for Family Literacy; **166,** National Center for Family Literacy. **Chapter 7:** 172, © 2006 Association for Computing Machinery, Inc. Reprinted by permission. Machionini, Gary (2006). "Exploratory Search, from Finding to Understanding" Communications of the ACM 49:4; http://doi.acm.org/10.1145/; **181,** (right) Reprinted with permission of EBSCO Information Services; (left) The content showing search refinement options from ProQuest products is published with permissions of ProQuest LLC. Further reproduction is prohibited without permission. www.proquest.com; **183,** Reprinted with permission of EBSCO Information Services; **186,** University of Pennsylvania Libraries; **188,** Example of a Link-Resolver Button in an Article Database. The content showing search refinement options from ProQuest products is published with permission of ProQuest LLC. Further reproduction is prohibited without permission. www.proquest.com; **200,** Copyright © 2013 ProQuest LLC. All

Index

List of Easy-Reference Guidelines and Questions